DEVELOPMENT WITHOUT FREEDOM

For Father Norbert A. Pacheco, M.M., a true man of God

Development Without Freedom
The Politics of Asian Globalization

SONGOK HAN THORNTON AND WILLIAM H. THORNTON
National Cheng Kung University, Taiwan

LONDON AND NEW YORK

First published 2008 by Ashgate Publishing

Published 2016 by Routledge
2 Park Square, Milton Park, Abingdon, Oxfordshire OX14 4RN
711 Third Avenue, New York, NY 10017, USA

First issued in paperback 2016

Routledge is an imprint of the Taylor & Francis Group, an informa business

British Library Cataloguing in Publication Data
Thornton, Songok Han
    Development without freedom : the politics of Asian
    globalization
    1. Globalization - Political aspects - Asia 2. Asia -
    Foreign relations 3. Asia - Economic policy 4. Asia -
    Politics and government - 21st century 5. Asia - Economic
    conditions - 21st century
    I. Title II. Thornton, William H., 1950-
    327.5'0090511

Library of Congress Cataloging-in-Publication Data
Thornton, Songok Han.
Development without freedom : the politics of Asian globalization / by Songok Han Thornton and William H. Thornton.
        p. cm.
    Includes index.
    ISBN 978-0-7546-7227-2
    1. Asia--Foreign economic relations. 2. Asia--Economic conditions--1945- 3. Financial crises--Asia. 4. Asia--Politics and government--1945- 5. Globalization--Economic aspects. I. Thornton, William H., 1950- II. Title.

 HF1583.T45 2008
 337.5--dc22

                                                                                        2007046440
ISBN 13: 978-1-138-27638-3 (pbk)
ISBN 13: 978-0-7546-7227-2 (hbk)

Contents

Acknowledgements

The authors wish to thank the following journals for using parts of previously published materials: *Development and Society, New Political Science: A Journal of Politics and Culture*, the *Journal of Developing Societie*s, *World Affairs: The Journal of International Issues*, *Radical Society*, and *Znet*.

Introduction

Senism and the Invisible Asia

Strange Bedfellows

A dark secret of the Cold War is that it had two losers, or at least one and a half. While its sudden eclipse marked the beginning of US unipolarity, it also spelled the end of America's geopolitical free ride.[1] No longer would the Soviets be there to enforce "free world" cohesion under US auspices. That inadvertent and unacknowledged gift had given the West, and America in particular, an insurmountable advantage over the "Rest."[2] Had this been more appreciated, Washington might have done less to end the bipolar game.[3] But in the euphoria of the moment, triumphalists took unipolarity at face value—i.e., as the unqualified victory that Francis Fukuyama celebrated with his "end of history" thesis, giving no quarter to cultural or political alternatives. A society could still be different, but henceforth it could not be both different and developed.

That, at least, was the world according to neoliberalism—the emerging Washington Consensus. The problem with this universal decree was that neoliberalism was not the only capitalist system left standing after the Soviet fall. America may have "won the Cold War," but in terms of economic dynamism the Asian tigers were in good position to win the post-Cold War. They now posed a far more threatful ideological challenge than the Soviet "Evil Empire" had in its final years. The bottom line was that the tigers' phenomenal growth owed much to the very statism that neoliberalism proscribed.

The Soviet fall had let this tiger out of its cage, leaving the question of how to get it back in without doing irreparable damage to the capitalist world system. That was the ideological subtext of the actions taken by the International Monetary Fund (IMF) in response to the Asian Crash of 1997. The ensuing Asian Crisis seemed to validate the incontrovertible superiority of American neoliberalism, which was

---

1 What America lost, in Emmanuel Todd's opinion, was its historical raison d'être. From this vantage Madeleine Albright's insistence that the United States was the "indispensable nation" reveals precisely what it tries to hide: the functional obsolescence of the world's sole superpower. See Emmanuel Todd, *After the Empire: The Breakdown of the American Order*, translated by C. Jon Delogu (New York: Columbia University Press, 2003), pp. 11–12.

2 Stalin, as John Lewis Gaddis observes in *The Cold War: A New History*, had expected capitalist fratricidal tensions to dissolve "free world" solidarity. What prevented this from happening, ironically, was the Soviet factor itself. China has so far avoided a similar geopolitical bonding effect by courting the major capitalist power brokers bilaterally.

3 America had done much the same in World War II, when keeping the Soviets afloat was deemed vital to the war effort. See John Lewis Gaddis, *The United States and the Origins of the Cold War, 1941–47* (New York: Columbia University Press, 1972 and 2000), p. 5.

the only system standing tall by the late 1990s. Only then could Washington-based globalization claim to be as preponderant economically as America was militarily.[4] The Asian exception that for years had hectored US leadership appeared to have been subdued,[5] while the 1990s came across as an American victory parade.[6] There was every indication that 21st century capitalism would have its de facto capital in Washington.

That triumphalism hardly made it into the new century. Already in April 2000 William Greider was predicting that America—with a trade deficit in 1999 nearly triple that of 1995—was riding for a fall. This was bad news for the global economy, since by 1998 the world, and Asia in particular, depended more than ever on American demand.[7] With the collapse of the US New Economy and the spate of corporate scandals that followed, neoliberalism lost much of its allure. Asian "crony capitalism" seemed less defective now that it had plenty of American company. The Rim seemed primed for a full rebound.

That was not to be. If the Crash had put the tigers temporarily out of the "miracle" business, it was a more highly charged Asian economy that threatened to keep them out. By 2000 China was already stealing the show, drawing away capital that would have rushed back into Crash-stricken economies. Southeast Asia was especially vulnerable since its comparative advantage was cheap labor rather than high tech.[8] The region's attempt to tap into the China boom—redirecting its industries toward

---

4 Japan, trapped in what appeared to be an endless economic malaise (which in fact was only a relative slump), was conveniently declared out of the running. See Robert Locke, "Japan, Refutation of Neoliberalism" *Post-Autistic Economic Review*, Issue No. 30 (March 21, 2005), http://www.paecon.net/PAEReview/issue23/Locke23.htm. The irony is that without Japan's financing of the burgeoning US debt, America's presumed global supremacy would immediately be exposed as a hoax. See R. Taggart Murphy, "East Asia's Dollars," *New Left Review*, 40 (July/August 2006), http://www.newleftreview.net/?page=article&view=2625.

5 On the initial coexistence but ultimate clash of these two economisms, "Asian values" and neoliberalism, see William H. Thornton, *Fire on the Rim: The Cultural Dynamics of East/West Power Politics* (Lanham, MD: Rowman & Littlefield, 2002), *passim*.

6 A rare voice in the wilderness was Paul Krugman. Even at the peak of the New Economy he recognized that in large part the '90s boom was a product of sluggish wages and worker benefits. See Paul Krugman, "America, the Boastful," *Foreign Affairs*, Vol. 77, No. 3 (May/June 1998), p. 39 (pp. 32–45). A *New York Times* study, covering the New York region and California, showed that the decade left the poor poorer, the middle classes slightly worse off, and only the rich much better off. See Janny Scott, "In '90s Economy, Middle Class Stayed put, Analysis Suggests," *The New York Times* (August 31, 2001), http://www.nytimes.com/2001/08/31/nyregion/31CENS.html.

7 William Greider, "Shopping Till We Drop," *The Nation* (April 10, 2000), http://www.thenation.com/issue/000410/0410greider.shtml.

8 Southeast Asia was also smashed by another big investment change: before the Crash, South Korea had been all but closed to foreign investment, but its FDI inflows rose from $2.3 billion in 1996 to $8.8 billion in 1999. The biggest impact, however, was from China, which in past years had attracted FDI mainly for light manufacturing, real estate, and consumer goods. With China set to join the WTO, TNCs were now equally bullish on Chinese high tech. See G. Pierre Goad, "Anaemic Asean," *The Far Eastern Economic Review* (September 7, 2000), http://www.feer.com./_0009_07/p65money.html.

the supply of parts for Chinese export production—effectively robbed Peter to pay Paul. Once again, as after the Asian Crash, the transnational corporations (TNCs) were calling the shots on what counts as development.[9]

The vast rhetoric that had been vented on Asian cronyism was all but forgotten. Few seemed to care that the Chinese art of *guanxi* (connections) made Southeast Asian cronies look like rank amateurs. We are given to believe that there is no need for concern, since the China that is rising is increasingly integrated into a globalist order that still marches to Washington's music. Kishore Mahbubani (Dean of the Lee Kuan Yew School of Public Policy in Singapore) assures us, moreover, that China is now run by a much reformed Chinese Communist Party (CCP), which is "the best governing class in generations."[10]

Note his choice of words: not the "best government," but the "best governing class." Inadvertently Mahbubani has tipped us off to the key point: The CCP elite is fast joining the ranks of the transnational capitalist class (TCC) that in Leslie Sklair's view forges global bonds without dictating the terms of local governance, so long as these do not impede profitability.[11] For those with the right *guanxi*, the CCP can be a guarantor of profitability in an almost mercantile sense.[12] The fact that it is also an instrument of monumental oppression is not just incidental to this arrangement. The specifically anti-democratic nature of CCP authority is in fact its strongest recommendation, since this power is on loan to TNCs for the right price. Not only has the CCP made the "trains run on time," but, more to the point, it has given the TNCs an inside track.

One of the CCP's most credulous celebrants, Joshua Ramo (an affiliate of Goldman Sachs, former foreign editor of *Time*, and now a professor of what amounts to PRC sycophancy at Tsinghua University), likens his own insights to the paradigm-breaking empiricism of Tycho Brahe. Just as Brahe escaped the confines of medieval astronomy, Ramo sees himself as being ahead of the common lot of Beijing's Western cheerleaders. They view the post-Tiananmen CCP as an unfortunate but inescapable rite of passage—a kind of protracted political adolescence—whereas for Ramo it is the prime mover of China's economic and *moral* (!) development over the last two

---

9 See Martin Hart-Landsberg, "Neoliberalism: Myth and Reality," *Monthly Review*, Vol. 57, No.11 (April 2006), http://www.monthlyreview.org/0406hart-landsberg.htm.

10 Kishore Mahbubani, "Understanding China," *Foreign Affairs*, Vol. 84, No. 5 (September/October 2005), p. 52 (pp. 49–60). Lee Kuan Yew himself, in the same vein, holds that Deng Xiaoping was right to order the Tiananmen massacre: "You have to remember that this is China. When you attack the emperor, that's it." See "Tiananmen Square Uprising: A Perspective," *Sinomania.com*, http://www.sinomania.com/CHINANEWS/Tiananmen_perspective.htm.

11 Leslie Sklair, *The Transnational Capitalist Class* (Oxford, UK: Blackwell, 2001), p. 256.

12 Tapping this resource is what divides the haves and have-nots in *guanxi* terms. Few foreign businessman can even identify the right party personnel to contact for specific needs. See Susan V. Lawrence and David Murphy, "Appearances Can Deceive," *The Far Eastern Economic Review* (December 13, 2001), http://www.feer.com/articles/2001/0112_13/p032china.html.

decades. This is the basis of the new "Beijing Consensus" that Ramo recommends as a prototype for the whole developing world.[13]

A Clash of Rival Capitalisms

It is commonly assumed that Beijing has its chief ideological rival in Washington. Today's CCP/TNC symbiosis does its best to suspend that contest of values, such that fundamental opposition to Sino-globalization is more likely to arise out of local rather than global forces. Beijing is well aware of this fact, and accordingly has been giving greater press freedom to Western reporters even as it cracks down on its own press and domestic non-governmental organizations (NGOs). Likewise, it opens the floodgates for foreign direct investment (FDI) while intensifying its surveillance of domestic entrepreneurs. Though it is wary of the "black hand" of foreign supported NGOs such as the Empowerment and Rights Institute, which has close ties to America's National Endowment for Democracy,[14] it has full faith and confidence in the willingness of capitalism in general to sell out democracy for the right price. What it fears, rather, are the traditional Asian values that suffuse organizations like the Falun Gong.

A similar anti-traditionalism has attended the Asian takeoff in general throughout the "miracle" years. East Asia has been so tightly identified with economic dynamism that in most other respects its very self-identity has been effaced. The paradox is that while the "miracle" has commonly been explained in terms of "Asian values," these in turn have been reduced to market values that were held in low esteem by traditional Asian societies.[15] That commercial paramountcy was clearly imported from the West.[16] To put it bluntly, the line of "Asian values" that has been capsulated in the "Lee thesis" (propounded by the former Singapore prime minister Lee Kuan Yew) is not the least bit Asian.[17]

This emphasis on quasi-Asian economism has obscured one of the darkest secrets of the "miracle": the huge economic boost that Asian "tigers" got from the

---

13   Joshua Cooper Ramo, *Beijing Consensus: Notes on the New Physics of Chinese Power* (London: Foreign Policy Center, 2004), pp. 6 and 13.

14   Yongding, "China's Color-Coded Crackdown," *Yale Global Online*, originally from *Foreign Policy* (October 18, 2005), http://yaleglobal.yale.edu/article.print?id=6376._

15   Lucian W. Pye, "'Asian Values': from Dynamos to Dominoes?," in Lawrence Harrison and Samuel P. Huntington (eds), *Culture Matters: How Values Shape Human Progress* (New York: Basic Books, 2000), pp. 248–9 (pp. 244–55).

16   This cultural import is hardly the best the West has to offer. Rim countries took Western economism without its liberal baggage. Today neoliberalism also drops much of that baggage, even in the West. John Gray contrasts the altruistic liberalism of John Stuart Mill with the rank narcissism that pervades today's consumer culture. Mark Garnett sees this latter-day liberalism as unsustainable—hence the title of his book: *The Snake that Swallowed its Tail: Some Contradictions in Modern Liberalism* (Exeter, UK: Imprint Academic, 2004).

17   Amartya Sen's conception of "development as freedom" refutes both major tenets of the Lee thesis: a) that political liberty and civil rights are uniquely Western values, and b) that withholding these rights helps to stimulate and stabilize the Asian growth economy. See Amartya Sen, *Development as Freedom* (New York: Alfred A. Knopf, 1999), p. 15.

Cold War. That geopolitical leverage did more than distinguish the Pacific Rim from other developing regions. It also allowed Rim economism to profitably coexist with American capitalism. So long as the Cold War lasted, it was in the interest of both systems to downplay this clash of rival capitalisms. Their artificial conflation gave the impression of a single capitalist phalanx on the march. Much as Soviet and Chinese communisms were once equated in Cold War domino theory, capitalism was now treated as a monolith—indeed, as modernity itself. To be part of this global process was to be legitimate. That was the gift of Western capitalism to Rim regimes. They in turn bestowed an image of vitality on enervated Western economies.

More insidiously, and with no mention of Cold War privileges, the success of Rim economies was used to discredit dependency theory or any other apologetic for Third World underdevelopment. Thus the Asian miracle contributed much to the "undevelopment" of the development concept itself. If the idea of Asian exceptionalism set a logical limit on the Rim system as a global model, the post-1997 Asian Crisis did the very opposite: by puncturing the "miraculous" image of Rim economics it produced a global leveling effect. That alone was enough to put globalization on trial, for the Rim had long been cast as the flagship of capitalist development.

This demotion of Rim economism paves the way for new perspectives on underdevelopment. An implicit contribution of the dependency paradigm was its rejection of the "one-size-fits-all" growth formula that was equated in modernist thought with development per se. Unfortunately, dependency theory posited its own one-size excuse for the failure of Third World development. In this respect Rimism and dependency are twin fallacies, like two sides of a counterfeit coin.

This study departs from both, and from the standard antiglobalist polemic as well, by assigning greater importance to the domestic decisions of individual developing countries. In opposition to the neo-modernist singularity of globalist "TINA" (the notion that "There Is No Alternative" to market fundamentalism), we argue that developing nations—and especially those that possess at least the procedural rudiments of democracy—do have real choices. While the Crash put an end to the myth of Asian exceptionalism, the subsequent Crisis (though neoliberal globalists are still in denial)[18] marked the end of one-size-fits-all globalization. The almost exclusively economic focus of IMFism may still obtain,[19] but the developing world is now awake to its agenda.

In this context we turn to the developmental revisionism of Amartya Sen, who offers a path "beyond Right and Left," and beyond the polemics of both globalism and dependency. It is necessary to proceed cautiously here, since the Senian

18 One of the most obtuse cases in point is that of Deepak Lal, who agrees that the Asian model is dead, but insists that its demise proves that "the Anglo-Saxon model of capitalism is the only viable one in the long run." See Deepak Lal, *In Praise of Empires: Globalization and Order* (New York: Palgrave Macmillan, 2004), p. 132.

19 President Hugo Chávez of Venezuela charges that Latin American nations are now so tightly under the grip of the IMF, the World Bank and multinational corporations that they have lost whatever autonomy they once had. In his opinion, therefore, these countries can no longer be considered democracies. See "President Hugo Chavez Frias Says There are No Real Democracies in Latin America," *VHeadline.com* (December 6, 2004), http://www.vheadline.com/printer_news.asp?id=23865.

model we adopt carries us into unexplored territory. Not even Sen himself can be trusted as our unqualified guide. Recently he shocked his antiglobalist followers by underscoring his own place in pro-globalization ranks;[20] yet his model, we contend, has a life of its own. It affords ample space for every democratic country to craft its own developmental objectives. In casting off the constraints of Cold War geopolitics, developing nations do not have to indenture themselves to the post-Cold War dictates of globalization. This study, accordingly, makes no case for a particular developmental politics or policy. Rather it takes an anti-TINA stance for choice itself against globalist co-optation.[21]

That choice was all but impossible during the Cold War, which promoted an almost Faustian political bargain: in return for economic advantages, Rim nations delivered political stagnation in the name of stability. Prior to the Asian Crash the vital role of Cold War geopolitics in the making of the "Asian miracle" had been invisible to most observers. Only when the "miracle" itself became problematic were its political underpinnings exposed. The phenomenal economic growth of the region could no longer be explained by simple reference to cultural norms such as "Asian values." In retrospect we can see how the geopolitical advantage the area enjoyed for several decades went into partial eclipse as the Cold War waned, and into almost full eclipse by the 1990s.

To the degree that the Rim's newly industrialized countries lost their Cold War leverage, they came under intense pressure to revamp their economies in accord with IMF and World Bank visions of globalization. Since this neoliberal agenda would expose these nations to forces beyond their control, they understandably resisted. Weaker economies such as the Philippines capitulated sooner, while the bigger "tigers" held out until the 1997 Crash forced them to relinquish statist independence in return for emergency aid.

We now know that the demands set forth by the IMF as the condition for its assistance contributed in no small part to the trauma of the Asian Crisis. Many critical studies—ranging from those of establishment insiders such as Joseph Stiglitz, Jeffrey Sachs, and George Soros to the growing body of antiglobalist discourse—have charged the "Washington Consensus" with responsibility for turning the Crash into a full-blown socioeconomic Crisis. This study builds on those critiques while treating the Crisis itself as a window on the emerging politics of globalization. Our major theoretical premise is Sen's axiom of "development as freedom," from which it follows that just and sustainable development is best achieved where economic

---

20 See Amartya Sen, "Freedom as Progress," interviewed by Laura Wallace, *Finance and Development* (September 2004), p. 7 (pp. 4–7). In all fairness, however, it should be noted that Sen has never been a *neoliberal* globalist. In a 1982 review of P.T. Bauer's assault on economic equality, Sen ardently defended egalitarianism on both ethical and instrumental grounds. That review reflects his position to this day. See Sen, "Just Desserts," a review of P.T. Bauer, *Equality, the Third World, and Economic Delusion* (1982), http://www.finance.commerce.ubc.ca/~bhatta/BookReview/sen_on_bauer.html.

21 The term "globalist" is here used with reference to an ideological apotheosis of the market. The term does not apply to any and all advocates of globalization. Sen strongly favors globalization, yet stresses that "the market is just one institution among many. It needs to be accompanied by democracy, a free press, and social opportunities ... " *Ibid.*

and political priorities are balanced and hence (to use our term) "concurrent." This is the foundation for the "concurrence model" that we apply throughout the book.

By contrast, the development model advanced by most "Asian values" proponents stresses the priority of economic goals.[22] Too often such economism becomes an obstacle to political development, as growth is taken as a validation of the political status quo. Thus material growth becomes a source of blanket legitimacy. By removing that political stamp of approval, the Asian Crisis had the effect of opening the door for other developmental options. Authoritarian regimes such as Suharto's found themselves de-legitimized. The question was what would fill the resulting void.

Unfortunately this political opening was coupled with economic depression. Sen's development model makes a case for political and economic concurrence, not for less economic concern. From this perspective the post-Crisis condition of Southeast Asia is hardly more conducive to political development than the pre-Crisis situation was, for poverty is as much a developmental obstacle as authoritarianism is. While there is no definitive roadmap for sustainable development, Stiglitz has cogently argued that IMF-directed globalization is definitely the *wrong* map. But the rising current of Washington-directed militarization is even worse.[23] As John Gray stresses, each country needs to draw its own developmental map.

The problem is that such radical diversity could void the very point of a "map," which is directional assistance. The Millennium Challenge Account (MCA), enacted by the US Congress in 2004, recognizes the need for democratic progress as a criterion for development aid.[24] This is a positive step, but it could also provide a coercive device for advancing US interests. Here we try to avoid two methodological imbalances: the Cold War trap of political amoralism (which led Bretton Woods institutions to fund a long list of authoritarian regimes) and the "postmodern" trap of uncritical

---

22 The "Asian values" model works on the official assumption that political advances will follow naturally from economic ones, but also on the unofficial assumption that authoritarianism holds a signal advantage for development. At most this is a short-term advantage, and there is much evidence that even that benefit is largely a myth. Historical data suggest that democracies grow just as fast, and are far better at avoiding catastrophes and promoting a broad range of well-being. The Soviet Union, for example, did at one point achieve a high rate of growth, but not the kind of general well-being that Senism fosters. See Joseph T. Siegle, Michael M. Weinstein, and Morton H. Halperin, "Why Democracies Excel," *Foreign Affairs*, Vol. 83, No. 5 (September/October 2004), p. 58 (pp. 57–71); and Charles Kenny, "Do We Know How to Develop?," *The Globalist* (January 25, 2005), http://www.theglobalist.com/DBWeb/printStoryId.aspx? StoryId=4331.

23 This helps to explain the decline in mass protest against global financial institutions. The global justice movement has shifted attention to US military interventions in support of armed globalization. See James H. Mittelman, "Where Have All the Protesters Gone?," *Yale Global* (October 4, 2004), http://yaleglobal.yale.edu/article-print?id=4637. This has turned out to be a dead-end street. Even as American support for the Iraq war plummeted from 70 percent for to 58 percent against, public protests subsided. See Drake Bennett, "Where's the Protest?," *Boston.com* (November 5, 2006), http://www.boston.com/news/globe/ideas/articles/2006/11/05/wheres_the_protest/.

24 Siegle, Weinstein, and Halperin, *op. cit.*, p. 67.

relativism (which has ensnared many postdevelopment theorists). A modified Senian model can provide, we suggest, a post-Cold War sense of direction.

Sen and the Crash

Initial reactions to the Asian Crash of 1997 included a strong dose of moral repugnance, with indigenous "crony capitalism" taking most of the blame. Gradually, however, it began to dawn on all but the most doctrinaire free marketeers that the problem had a global reach. There was something disingenuous about blaming the Crash on the same "Asian values" that shortly before had been credited with a major role in fueling the "Asian miracle." For the first time, outside radical circles, the prevailing development paradigm was under investigation for the most heinous of capitalist crimes: econocide.[25]

The timing of Amartya Sen's 1998 Nobel Prize in economics was itself a revisionist statement. It acknowledged that the Asian Crisis ran deep, and the solution likewise would have to address deficiencies in the whole modernist concept of development. This paradigm shift had been building for years, but the Crash and the ensuing Crisis provided the critical mass to take Sen's iconoclasm from the revisionist fringe to the inner sanctums of policy analysis, where more strident antiglobalists and postdevelopment critics could not enter. Arguing that simple measures of GNP were inadequate to assess standards of living, Sen integrated economic, political and social criteria of well-being—a method that has since been adopted by the United Nation's Human Development Index.[26]

What did most to prime this reconception was the Asian Crash. The Crash made the work of Robert Merton and Myron Scholes seem dated just one year after they won the 1997 Nobel Prize in economics. They had applied their theories on derivatives to the hedge fund they established in 1994, Long Term Capital Management (LTCM). This paragon of neoliberal theory and practice turned out to be an accident waiting to happen. And it did not require a long wait. The LTCM fiasco was all the more portentous in that it came on the heels of the Asian Crisis. When the Crisis broke that summer, neoliberal globalists tried to shore up its theoretical implications by blaming the countries that were hardest hit: Thailand, Indonesia, Malaysia, South Korea, and the Philippines. This defensive reflex reaffirmed their faith in the solvency and indeed the moral supremacy of Western capitalism.

Then came the September 1998 collapse of LTCM. When it became obvious that the company's capital could not possibly cover its hulking debt,[27] Washington's financial brokers scrambled to garner $4 billion for the emergency purchase of 90

---

25 It is arguable that the "Asian values" school of Rim economism is not Asian in any traditional sense, and indeed is imported from the West. Our case for a postmaterial Asian model is adumbrated in Songok Han Thornton, "Postmaterial Development: The Search for a New Asian Model," *Development and Society*, Vol. 33, No. 1 (June 2004), pp. 25–38.

26 "Food for Thought," *The Guardian* (March 31, 2001), http://www.guardian.co.uk/saturday_review/story/0,3605,465796,00.html.

27 Robert Skidelsky, "The World on a String," *The New York Review of Books*, Vol. 48, No. 4 (March 8, 2001), p. 10 (pp. 10–14).

percent of its besieged equity.[28] The moral hazard of this salvage operation was disregarded. After preaching at length about *Asian* crony capitalism, neoliberals were oddly silent when the US Federal Reserve Board assembled one of the largest flotillas of cronies the world had ever seen,[29] drawn from 15 transnational banks and brokerage firms such as UBS, Goldman Sachs and Merrill Lynch. Not only did the managers of LTCM keep their jobs, but the rescuers even paid them management fees for services rendered in the course of the bailout.[30]

The admonitory value of the LTCM calamity was thus lost, and the chance to implement corrective measures was missed. Three years later the energy giant Enron collapsed, having failed in its attempt to camouflage its mammoth debt. At least it can be said for the Nobel Prize committee that it tacitly admitted its own part in perpetuating a seriously flawed model of economic achievement. The Washington Consensus, unfortunately, has not been willing to draw a similar lesson from the Asian Crisis or its Western counterparts.

In Sen's view, the Asian Crisis exposed the high cost of undemocratic governance. The preventive role that he assigns to democracy translates directly into one of his basic tenets regarding the instrumental freedom of "protective security": "Democratic governance, including multi-party elections and open media, makes it very likely that some arrangements for basic protective security will be instituted. In fact, the ... positive role of political and civil rights applies to the prevention of economic and social disasters in general."[31] In the name of "Asian values" the miracle economies of the Pacific Rim concentrated on economic growth at the expense of political development. Under cover of dynamic and seemingly infallible economies, Western-trained technocrats (hardly the exemplars of indigenous Asian values) dismissed the need for broader goals such as political transparency and social security.

Sen is not denying that "crony capitalism" contributed to the Asian Crash. Rather he differs in his understanding of the political structure that permits cronyism and an associated lack of transparency to prevail. He finds the root cause of this failing in "the absence of an effective democratic forum."[32] Part of the problem is that booming economies make the protective role of democracy less apparent than is the case under conditions of slower growth. In a high-growth country such as pre-Crash Indonesia, that protective role is "strongly missed when it is most needed."[33] Only when things go dreadfully wrong does the advantage of a welfare model such as Europe's become apparent. Asian leaders insisted that such safeguards were

---

28 Ibrahim Warde, "Crony Capitalism: LTCM, a Hedge Fund above Suspicion," *Le Monde diplomatique* (November 5, 1998), http://mondepilo.com/1998/11/05warde2.

29 As Joseph Stiglitz and Paul Krugman point out, this double standard persists in the Bush administration's habit of lecturing Asians on the evils of cronyism while taking the art of corporate politics further than any Western administration, especially in the area of foreign policy. See Jane Hardy, "The State of the Union," *International Socialism Journal*, Issue 102 (Spring 2004), http://pubs.socialistreviewindex.org.uk/isj102/hardy.htm.

30 Kevin Dowd, "Too Big to Fail?: Long-Term Capital Management and the Federal Reserve," *Cato Institute Briefing Papers*, No. 52 (September 23, 1999), p. 11 (pp. 1–12).

31 Sen, *Development, op. cit.*, p. 184.

32 *Ibid.*, p. 185.

33 *Ibid.*, p. 186.

unnecessary—first because "Asian values" included communal means of caring for people in a crisis;[34] and second because it was inconceivable that a deep and prolonged crisis could occur in an era that clearly belonged to the Pacific Rim. Asian exceptionalists held that Western liberalism was not needed in this high-growth sphere, and indeed would be a hindrance.

By contrast, Sen argued on instrumental as well as intrinsic grounds that the expansion of freedom was crucial at all stages of development. Freedom is thus a primary *means* of development as well as one of its foremost *ends*.[35] This takes Sen beyond the purported neutrality of modernist development theory.[36] As he sees it, development requires the removal of tyranny and social deprivation as well as poverty per se. The freedom this entails has profound instrumental value.[37] Against those who consider political development an obstacle to economic success, Sen cites the case of Botswana, Africa's fastest growing country.[38] Democracy has clearly buttressed Botswana's governmental transparency and public accountability, thereby laying a foundation for sustainable economic development. And against those who believe poor voters would always choose the shortcut of welfarism over rights, Sen points out that this assumption has been put to the test only once, when Indian voters categorically rejected Indira Gandhi's suspension of civil and political rights under emergency rule.[39]

A Senian balance between economic and political priorities encourages practical reforms such as social safety nets, but also affords a market-resistant buffer for local cultures.[40] Sen's *Development as Freedom* treats liberty as a key to long-term well-being, as opposed to boom and bust economism.[41] For him freedom is more a social good than an individual right. He stresses that globalization is conducive

---

34 Akash Kapur, "Humane Development: An Interview with Amartya Sen," *The Atlantic Monthly* (December 15, 1999), http://theatlantic.com/unbound/interviews/ba991215.html.

35 Amartya Sen, *Development, op. cit.*, p. 10.

36 Likewise he is at odds with the relativity that attends poststructural strains of postmodernism. This has saturated most postdevelopment theory, which is therefore so politically inert as to pose no threat whatsoever to extant power structures. Senism is potentially much more oppositional. Regarding postdevelopmentalism and its critics, see Arturo Escobar, "'Past,' 'Post,' and 'Future,'" *Development*, Vol. 43, No. 4 (2000), pp. 11–14.

37 Amartya Sen, *Development, op. cit.*, pp. xii, 3 and 11.

38 Sen, *Development, op. cit.*, pp. 149–50. The opposite case is Zimbabwe, which lost its ability to avoid disasters such as famines when it ceased to be a functioning democracy. See Amartya Sen, "Why Half the Planet is Hungry," *The Observer* (June 16, 2002), http://www. observer.co.uk/Print/0,3858,4434647,00. html.

39 *Ibid.*, p. 151.

40 Akash Kapur, "A Third Way for the Third World," *The Atlantic Monthly* (December 1999), http://theatlantic.com/issues/99dec/9912kapur.html.

41 *Ibid.* Harvard's Dani Rodrik contends that the economic growth record of authoritarian regimes tends to be either very good or very bad, whereas that of democracies usually occupies the middle ground. But from a Senian vantage it is arguable that in the longer run almost all authoritarian governments are low achievers, especially where broader developmental objectives are considered. On Rodrik's position see Jeff Madrick, "Democracy Has the Edge When It Comes to Advancing Growth," *The New York Times* (April 13, 2000), http://www. nytimes.com/library/financial/columns/041300econ-scene.html.

to sustainable development only when backed by adequate national policies for social betterment. A country will pay a huge price if it pursues economic growth while forfeiting health care, literacy and general social opportunities. It is "not a question of more or less government but what kind of government."[42] Even well-functioning markets cannot solve the problems that attend a general eclipse of human capabilities,[43] defined as positive freedom rather than the standard legalistic canon of negatively defined human rights. Capabilities, that is, entail the real choices and opportunities available to people—a maximization of welfare that reaches far beyond a mere calculation of GNP per capita.[44]

Sen's revolutionary perspective on social well-being—which since 1993 has been reflected in the capabilities orientation of UNDP (United Nations Development Program) Human Development Reports—is rooted in his equally iconoclastic view of Asian values. Instead of the now standard neoliberal formula for rapid economic growth, Sen proposes an "Eastern strategy" of development that draws on more humane but often overlooked dimensions of growth in a wide variety of countries: first Japan and then the other East and Southeast Asian tigers and dragons. This strategy lays stress on education, basic economic entitlements, land reform, and a delicate balance of free market forces and state intervention. The modern history of Japan discredits the conventional belief that human development is a luxury that a country can afford only *after* it has gained affluence. Even at the time of the Meiji restoration, before the advent of Japanese industrialization, Japan achieved a higher level of literacy than Europe possessed.[45]

That, however, is not the basis of the exceptionalism that the term "Asian values" has come to signify. Proponents of this development model—most notably Singapore's former Prime Minister Lee Kuan Yew—define the term negatively, holding that political liberalism is a Western export unsuited to Asia. Sen, by contrast, stresses that "the championing of democracy and political freedom in the modern sense cannot be found in the pre-enlightenment tradition in any part of the world, west or east."[46] Given Asia's tremendous cultural diversity, Sen denies that any single set of values can speak for the whole region.[47] Only a universal value such as freedom can claim such ubiquity. If freedom is essential to any full life,[48]

42 Amartya Sen, "Globalization Sans Social Welfare is Counter-Productive: Amartya Sen," *Times of India* (October 16, 1998), available online at http://www.nd.edu/~kmukhopa/cal300/sen/art/1015a.htm.

43 "Amartya Sen: First Asian to Win Nobel Prize in Economics for 1998," *Defense Journal* (February/March 1999), http://www.defencejournal.com/global/feb-mar99/amartyasen.htm.

44 John M. Alexander, "Capabilities, Human Rights and Moral Pluralism," originally presented at the International Seminar Development, Law and Social Justice at the Institute of Social Studies, the Hague, the Netherlands, June 2002, and later published in *The International Journal of Human Rights*, Vol. 8, No. 3 (2004).

45 Amartya Sen, "A Plan for Asia's Growth: Build on Much That is Good in the 'Eastern strategy,'" *Asiaweek* (October 8, 1999), p. 62 (pp. 62–63).

46 Amartya Sen quoted in "Food for Thought," *op. cit.*

47 Richard N. Cooper, "The Road From Serfdom. Amartya Sen Argues that Growth Is Not Enough," *Foreign Affairs*, Vol. 79, No.1 (January/February 2000), p. 167 (pp. 163–67).

48 Madrick, *op. cit.*

democracy in turn is essential to the cultivation of freedom. To the criticism that some countries are not "fit for democracy," Sen rebuts that a country "has to become fit *through* democracy."[49]

Development as Resistance

Once the concept of development is freed from raw economism,[50] consensus is exploded on a wide range of policy issues. The resulting pluralism affords options that narrow GNPism would never permit.[51] Consider, for example, the case of the Indian state of Kerala, which is poor even by Indian standards, yet has a remarkable record of achievement in political freedom, health care, education and gender equality. Through land reform and grassroots organization,[52] Kerala achieved political freedom as well as an average life expectancy of 72 years, not far behind the American average of 76, and far higher than the Indian average of 61.[53] Its infant-mortality rate is lower than that of any developing country, and 90 percent of Keralites are literate.[54]

49 Amartya Sen, "Democracy as a Universal Value," *Journal of Democracy*, Vol. 10, No. 3 (1999), http://muse.jhu.edu/demo/jod/10.3sen.thml.

50 To accomplish this it was only necessary for Sen to point out that people in poorer countries often enjoy better life quality than those in richer ones. See Amitai Etzioni, "The Post Affluent Society," *Review of Social Economy,* Vol. LXII, No. 3 (September 2004), p. 413 (pp. 407–20).

51 Sen's capabilities approach can be described as "distributive sensitive," as opposed to the "distributive insensitive" slant of standard GNPism. See Bertil Tungodden, "A Balanced View of Development as Freedom," *CMI Working Papers*, from Chr. Michelsen Institute, Bergen, Norway, No. 14 (2001), p. 5 (pp. 1–22).

52 Arjun Makhijani, *From Global Capitalism to Economic Justice: An Inquiry into the Elimination of Systemic Poverty, Violence and Environmental Destruction in the World Economy* (New York: The Apex Press, 1992), p. 132.

53 China's similar average of 71 masks profound differences in more subtle health matters, such as women's access to medical care. China's ratio of women to men is only .94, just above the Indian average of .93; but Kerala's ratio is 1.06, reflecting women's survival advantages in this poor but highly progressive state. See Amartya Sen, "Passage to China," *The New York Review of Books*, Vol. 51, No. 19 (December 2, 2004), http://www.nybooks. com/articles/17608. It should also be noted that in 1979, when Deng launched his economic reforms, China had a vast lead on India in longevity. While the Chinese government paired economic reform with a reduction in public health services, democratic pressure compelled India to increase its services. Accordingly, the longevity gap between the two countries dropped to seven years. The state of Kerala, however, surpassed China in the same two decades. See Amartya Sen, "Why Democratization is not the Same as Westernization: Democracy and its Global Roots," *TNROnline* (October 6, 2003), http://cscs.umich.edu/~crshalizi/sloth/2003–09-29a.html.

54 Akash Kapur, "Poor but Prosperous," *The Atlantic Monthly* (September 1998), http://thealtantic.com/issues/98sep/kerala.htm.

Perhaps that explains why Kerala has been remarkably free of the xenophobia that plagues other regions. It has a long tradition of welcoming foreign missionaries,[55] and its Hindu majority has harmoniously coexisted with Muslim and Christian minorities. Meanwhile Kerala remains resolutely socialist, in the tradition of its communist electoral victory of 1957. In this spirit it offers a developmental alternative that combines a mandate for economic growth and an equitable distribution of resources. Even Sen's worst critics, such as Joseph Tharmangalam, admit that state intervention (which does not preclude capitalism)[56] has been effective in reducing poverty here since the mid-1970s.[57]

However, the full-throttle globalization of the 1990s put Kerala under ideological siege. Industries have tended to stay away for fear of union activism, pro-union courts and high minimum wages. This has pushed the unemployment rate to 25 percent, the highest in India.[58] Also, by lowering tariffs on agricultural imports, India's economic liberalization has torpedoed Kerala's main sector of production. Tharmangalam takes this as proof of an inherent fallacy in Sen's model.[59] But Kerala's plight actually proves Sen's point that politics and economics are mutually dependent. India's current restructuration stacks the deck against the socialist alternative,[60] and against Sen's model, by ignoring qualitative measures of long-term well-being. Kerala was bound to lose in the quantitative terms of pure economism, but those are precisely the priorities that made for the Asian Crisis.

The Keralan dilemma is typical of the global South under the throes of neoliberal globalization. The collapse of Third World nonalignment strategies in the early 1980s—and especially the decline of the New International Economic Order (NIEO)—left developing countries at the mercy of First World institutions such as the World Bank, the IMF and eventually the World Trade Organization (WTO). Presently, however, the South is organizing a new trade bloc under the "G-20+" label. Its major priority, as reflected at Cancún, is to rectify trade contradictions whereby First World countries pump in $365 billion a year to agricultural subsidies that crush the rural sectors of developing countries, all in the name of "free trade."[61] These subsidies drive down commodity prices by dumping wheat, rice, corn, cotton and other staple products on global markets. Even the World Bank estimates that the

---

55 Binu Mathew, "In memory of Kerala," *Open Democracy* (February 4, 2003), http://www.open democracy.net/articles/ViewPopUpArticle=jsp?id=2&articleId=945.

56 See Govindan Parayil and T.T. Sreekumar, "Kerala's Experience of Development and Change," *Journal of Contemporary Asia*, Vol. 33, No. 4 (2003), p. 470 (pp. 465–92).

57 Joseph Tharmangalam, "The Perils of Social Development with Economic Growth: The Development Debacle of Kerala, India," *Bulletin of Concerned Asian Scholars*, Vol. 30, No. 1 (1998), http://csf.olorado. edu/bcas/kerala/kerther1.htm.

58 Kapur, "Poor but Prosperous," *op. cit.*

59 Tharmangalam, *op. cit.*

60 Due to India's trade liberalization and declining prices in international markets in 2000–1, 5.5 million farmers lost $1.5 billion. See Govindan Parayil and T.T. Sreekumar, *op. cit.*, p. 479.

61 Daniel W. Drezner, "Seventies Chic," *The New Republic* (December 10, 2003), http://www.tnr.com/doc.mhtml?I=scholar&s=drezner121003.

elimination of agricultural subsidies and tariffs could "lift 150 million people out of poverty by 2015."[62]

The North/South income gap is so wide, however, that nothing short of a complete globalist overhaul could offer much promise. That is the sales pitch used by the Washington Consensus to hawk neoliberal restructuration as the only real Third World option. The counter-example of Kerala—where equality coexists with high unemployment and low foreign investment—could never appeal to technocrats steeped in US economic assumptions. A more congenial alternative is available, however, in the "Stockholm Consensus." Neoliberals have devoted great energy to reframing this "Swedish model" as the "Swedish disease," but the fact remains that despite its relatively low per capita GDP, Sweden scores near the top of global ratings that consider actual standards of living.[63]

Thanks largely to its unflinching redistribution program, Sweden ranks second only to Denmark in egalitarian terms.[64] Nonetheless it has capitalized on the high tech surge of the late 1990s and proved itself one of the most competitive "new economies" in the world.[65] Thus it represents something of a cross between Kerala and Silicon Valley.[66] Could Kerala also make that global crossing? With a literacy rate of 91 percent, close to that of the United States,[67] it is in fact the perfect locus for knowledge-based growth as well as "development as freedom." Its commitment to general education has produced remarkable benefits, especially for women. Despite China's one-child policy, Kerala has reduced its fertility rate more than China. It arguably has what it takes to become a veritable Sweden for South Asia.

The Senian model could bring this black sheep in from the cold. But given the fact that Kerala is already on the globalist blacklist, the question is whether Senism can mount an effective antiglobalist resistance. Sen's own politics is not up to this task, but much as classical economics quickly transcended the writings of Adam Smith, and Marxism soon outdistanced Marx, the Senian paradigm already reaches beyond Sen's personal ideology. In *Development* he confronted glaring global inequalities,

---

62 "The Unkept Promise of 2003," *The International Herald Tribune* (December 31, 2003), http://www. iht.com/cgi-bin/generic.cgi?template=articleprint.temph&ArticleId=123242.

63 Daniel Brook, "How Sweden Tweaked the Washington Consensus," *Dissent* (Fall 2004), http://www.dissentmagazine.org/menutest/articles/fa04/brook.htm.

64 The "Danish lesson" has been that an effective growth economy does not require that the welfare state be dismantled. See Jacob Kirkegaard, "A Danish Lesson for Germany," *The Globalist: For Global Citizens, By Global Citizens* (January 26, 2005), http://www. theglobalist.com/DBWeb/printStoryId.aspx?StoryId=4347.

65 Brook, *op. cit.*

66 As such it is the embodiment of what has been called the post-Keynesian approach to post-industrial development. On the contrast between post-Keynesianism and neoliberalism see Thomas I. Palley, "Economic Theories Change But Still Fail to Recognize Natural Resources," *The Progress Report*, originally from *Foreign Policy in Focus* (May 2004), http://www.progress.org/2004/fpif49.htm.

67 Nachammai Raman, "How almost Everyone in Kerala Learned to Read," *The Christian Science Monitor* (May 17, 2005), http://www.csmonitor.com/2005/0517/p12s01-legn.htm.

but paid insufficient attention to TNCs that dominate today's global economy.[68] Likewise he has tended to neglect crucial postmaterial issues such as environmental sustainability,[69] which is far more adequately treated by the postdevelopmentalist Arturo Escobar.

The blackest mark on Sen's project, however, is his insistence that hunger in the Third World is best combated through further trade liberalization and export priority. As Vandana Shiva notes, it is precisely this kind of neoliberal regime that has robbed the rural poor of their land, their water, and their hope. At the WTO's Doha Conference in 2001 more than 100,000 workers and peasants rallied in protest. Again in Hong Kong thousands literally went to the barricades in outrage against the WTO as they know it: World Trade Oppression. This democratic scream in the night is oddly ignored by Sen,[70] whose call for democracy is much stronger in theory than in oppositional practice. His politics depends very largely on the party-mediated mechanisms of the ballot box, and today's parties are under such tight corporate control that the poor are left with no choice but to cast their votes in the streets.

Having brilliantly adumbrated a project for the reintegration of ethics and economics[71]—whose divorce over the last two centuries would have been unthinkable for Adam Smith himself[72]—Sen fails to cross the bridge he has constructed. His institutional commitments prevent him from aborting an international order that he recognizes as ethically decrepit.[73] Like his protégé, the liberal feminist Martha

---

68 James North, "Sen's Sensibility," *The Nation* (December 6, 1999), http://www. thenation.com/issue/991206/1206north.shtml.

69 Kapur, "A Third Way," *op. cit.* By 2004 Sen was trying to salvage his reputation in the environmental sphere by allying himself with the Millennium Ecosystem Assessment report of 2003, *Ecosystem and Human Wellbeing.* See Amartya Sen, "Why We Should Preserve the Spotted Owl," *The London Review of Books*, Vol. 26, No. 3 (February 5, 2004), http://www. lrb.co.uk/v26/n03/print/sen_01_html.

70 Vandana Shiva, "The Real Reasons for Hunger," *The Observer* (June 23, 2002), http:// www.observer.co.uk/Print/0,3858,4446511,00.html.

71 Ben Fine points out that the nexus between ethics and economics, especially in the sphere of development, "has been dominated by Amartya Sen, almost to the extent of being a one-man show with supporting acts." See Ben Fine, "Economics and Ethics: Amartya Sen as Point of Departure," *The New School Economic Review*, Vol. 1, No. 1 (Fall 2004), p. 153 (pp. 151–62).

72 In this sense, as Gertrude Himmelfarb argues, Smith epitomized the British Enlightenment's union of virtue and reason, or in his case moral philosophy and political economy. See her revisionist study of three enlightenments: *The Roads to Modernity: The British, French, and American Enlightenments* (New York: Alfred A. Knopf, 2004).

73 Sen frames this ethical inadequacy in terms of a critique of Rawlsian justice as it relates to transnational issues. He lays out this global dilemma as a no-man's-land between the national particularism of Rawls' (initial) original position and a more Kantian universalism which has no teeth. But Sen's attempt to posit a Third Way beyond those failed paradigms is too mellow and institutionally accommodating to pack much punch. Escobar is right in this regard: before one can construct, one must deconstruct. See Escobar, "'Past,'" *op. cit.*; and Amartya Sen, "Global Justice Beyond International Equity," in Inge Kaul, Isabelle Grunberg, and Marc A. Stern (eds), *Global Public Goods: International Cooperation in the 21st Century* (Oxford, UK: Oxford University Press, 1999), pp. 118–19 (pp. 116–25).

Nussbaum, Sen lays so much stress on the capabilities aspect of positive freedom that he leaves himself open for harsh and sometimes ad hominem criticism from a more pedestrian, "food and shelter" school of activism.[74]

There is no question as to Sen's personal concern over the material trauma of poverty. His effort to humanize economics should not be taken as a retreat from "food-first" imperatives, though he might do more to make this clear to readers who do not happen to know his life story. Our criticism is directed only at his politics, which falls short of the larger project he has launched. To put it bluntly, Sen is not fully Senian. The social capabilities that concern him so much are rooted in a politics of incapability that he has scarcely addressed—viz., the literal "incorporation" of today's public sphere.[75] His failure to confront the domestic and global inroads of neoliberalism was graphically illustrated in 2002 when he "debated" the arch-neoliberal Lawrence H. Summers (former Treasury Secretary and later Harvard University president) on the implications of globalization. The two economists were in so much agreement that debate was nearly impossible.[76]

The key issue, as Ben Fine notes, is how to get the Senian project beyond Sen himself.[77] While Escobar calls for a general strike against the whole discourse of development, the root of the problem is the modernist discourse of economics, which Escobar sees as culturally inscribed.[78] Neglecting cultural variability has been a grievous mistake on the part of developmental modernists as well as neoliberal market ideologists.[79] For them the stability of a market society is a simple matter of enforcing reasonable laws. What this ignores is the cultural and political fragility of the rule of law itself.[80] The assumption is that the market alone can deliver uninterrupted and equitable economic growth. This utopian view, grounded in Enlightenment precepts, not only declares less market-oriented cultures dysfunctional, but proceeds *to make* them so through a remorseless program of structural adjustments. Marginalized cultures lose the power to resist the economic imperialism that goes by the name of globalization. The Keralas of the world are dragged down, and then declared ideologically moribund.

---

74 Gerald Cohen, for example, charges both Sen and Rawls with peddling the freedom mantra at the expense of the food-first imperative. See Christine M. Korsgarrd, "G.A. Cohen: Equality of What? On Welfare, Goods and Capabilites," in Martha Nussbaum and Amartya Sen (eds), *The Quality of Life* (Oxford: The United Nations University and Clarendon Press, 1993), p. 60 (pp. 54–61).

75 See Carl Boggs, *The End of Politics: Corporate Power and the Decline of the Public Sphere* (New York: The Guilford Press, 2000), especially Chapter 3.

76 See Nathan J. Heller, "Sen Sets Sights on World Poverty," *The Harvard Crimson* (June 9, 2004), http://www.thecrimson.com/printerfriendly.aspx?ref=502794.

77 Fine, *op. cit.*, p. 153.

78 See Arturo Escobar, *Encountering Development: The Making and Unmaking of the Third World* (Princeton, NJ: Princeton University Press, 1995), pp. 54 and 62.

79 Escobar, "'Past,'" *op. cit.*; and John Gray, *Enlightenment's Wake: Politics and Culture at the Close of the Modern Age* (London: Routledge, 1995), p. 101.

80 Gray, *op. cit.*, p. 102.

Globalization on Trial

Resistance to the inroads of globalization requires more than the slightly modified economism that has appropriated the "Third Way" label.[81] It requires what we term the *"concurrence" model*, with reference to Sen's focus on concurrent economic and political development. This applies no less to the "developed" West than to Asia. Western democracy is also under threat from the erosion of civil society and media pluralism by globalization. For Sen it is the informational element that is pivotal,[82] since in his view democracy is not so much rooted in elections and ballots as in the social complex of public reasoning.[83] William Tabb likewise measures democracy in terms of public participation in decision making, the availability of information, and ancillary issues such as media control and campaign funding.[84]

American democracy is especially at risk in all these areas. When President Bush abandoned the Kyoto Protocol in 2001, knowing from polls that a large majority of Americans took the opposite view, he was hardly acting democratically.[85] Nor did he have a mandate for his rejection of arms limitation treaties and the International Criminal Court. Clearly the administration's stridently unilateral foreign policy is rooted in an equally unilateral domestic agenda.[86] On both fronts, Bush has rammed through unpopular policies by way of the vastly expanded powers that a "wartime" president enjoys. The trick, Kenneth Roth notes, is to normalize the president's wartime special privileges by way of a perpetual "war on terrorism."[87]

This storm cloud has a silver lining, however. While Bush has expanded the range and definition of "war," his opponents have reciprocated by expanding the range and definition of democracy. Tabb observes how the antiwar and antiglobalization movements now defy national boundaries and evade the constraints of centrist media.[88] Like Sen, they demand more than minimal, *pro forma* democracy. This explains why many antiglobalists have assumed Sen was on their side.[89] Their people-centered development concept has a Rawlsian cast in that it foregrounds

---

81 See James Petras, "The Third Way: Myth and Reality," *Monthly Review*, Vol. 51, No. 10 (March 2000), http://www.monthlyreview.org/300petras.htm.

82 Sen, "Why We Should Preserve the Spotted Owl," *op. cit.*

83 Concerning the democratic limits of election procedures, see Amartya Sen, "Why Democratization is not the Same as Westernization: Democracy and Its Global Roots," *The New Republic* (October 6, 2003), http://cscs.umich.edu/~crshalizi/sloth/2003-09-29a.html.

84 William K. Tabb, "After Neoliberalism?," *Monthly Review* (June 2003), http://www.findarticles.com/cf_o/m1132/2_55/103383506/print.jhtml. Likewise Robert Dahl lays stress on the process of collective decision-making. See Robert A. Dahl, *Democracy and Its Critics* (New Haven: Yale University Press, 1989).

85 Sen, "Why We Should Preserve the Spotted Owl," *op. cit.*

86 See Jed Rubenfeld, "The Two World Orders," *The Wilson Quarterly* (Autumn 2003), http://wwics.si.edu/index.cfm?fuseaction=wq.essay&essay_id=56056.

87 Kenneth Roth, "The Law of War in the War on Terror," *Foreign Affairs*, Vol. 83, No. 1 (January/February 2004), p. 2 (pp. 2–7).

88 See Tabb, *op. cit.*

89 This broader concept of development was harbingered by the International Covenant on Economic, Social and Cultural Rights (ICESCR) of 1976, where the focus was on material needs such as food, shelter and health care as well as education and other non-material rights.

the welfare of the poorest segments of the population.[90] Here Sen's approach falls short. Useful as his informational strategies are for averting social disasters such as famine, or contagious diseases such as SARS and Avian Flu, they are necessary but insufficient elements of participatory democracy in an age of corporate hegemony. "People Power," in the developed West as well as the Rest, requires an added activistic element.

Even where such activism is originally present in People Power, it can easily be lost. In the case of Korea's post-authoritarian development, formal gains in procedural democracy and a free press (Sen's operational forte) actually worked against substantive democracy by projecting an aura of successful reform. This sense of "mission accomplished" functioned as a social "pressure release," undermining the progressive thrust that structural change would require.[91] Thus we end up with the paradox of Philippine People Power, absent an economic dynamic for reform, and Korean economic dynamism, absent the political will for reform.

In the hands of the IMF the word "reform" is collapsed into global economism. It is simply taken for granted that democratization will follow economic growth. Neoliberal reformism places great stock in "transparency" and the so-called "rule of law," but there is little chance that such legal mechanisms, in and of themselves, will redound to genuine democratic development. Globalist legalism is more likely to co-opt and perpetuate extant power structures.

Nowhere is this more obvious than in today's Indonesia. After Suharto's departure the country's free press again came under siege, this time by a court system that professes to defend individuals against libel, but in fact defends crony capitalists and other power brokers. The court has ordered one of the most important progressive newspapers in the country, *Koran Tempo*, to pay $1 million in damages to the arch-crony Tony Winata,[92] thus pushing the paper to the brink of bankruptcy, and sending a strong message to other media that post-Suharto reformism is an idea whose time has passed.

This is not to suggest that Sen's informational strategy is defective. It is simply inadequate. In the absence of an oppositional reform dynamic it could actually work against the democracy it seeks. Giving current power structures a democratic veneer renders them all the more efficient in their social and ecological ravages. A paper like the *Koran Tempo* could survive under Suharto but face extinction under the pseudo-

---

See Frances Stewart, *North-South and South-South: Essays on International Economics* (Basingstoke, UK: Macmillan, 1992), p. 37.

90 European Commission, *The Future of North-South Relations: Towards Sustainable Economic and Social Development* (London: Kogan Page, 1998), p. 38.

91 Democratic proceduralism is the prime ingredient of what the conservative libertarian Justin Raimondo calls (with reference to Susan Sontag's view of the former Soviet system as "fascism with a human face") "fascism with a democratic face." See "Today's Conservatives Are Fascists: Torture, Dictatorship, Phony 'Elections,' and Endless War—It's Fascism with a 'Democratic' Face," *ANTIWAR.com* (January 3, 2005), http://antiwar.printthis.clickabilty. com/pt/cpt?action=cpt&title=Today%27s+Conservatives...

92 Raymond Bonner, "Battle Against Indonesian Press Moves Into the Country's Courts," *The New York Times* (February 1, 2004), http://www.nytimes.com/2004/02/01/international/ asia/01INDO.html.

reformist "rule of law" that has replaced him. In Korea, likewise, ostensive gains in democratic machinery have at best served as a diversion from the anti-democratic processes of crony corporatism.

The setbacks we have noted in the Philippines, Indonesia, and Korea suggest that democratization is a much more complex and culturally embedded process than early globalization theory imagined. There is no global democratic determinism (Huntington's "third wave") or liberal democratic finality (Fukuyama's "end of history") to rely upon. Nor is there any definitive or "consolidated" democracy which, once achieved, can be put on automatic pilot. Democratization is a Sisyphean process which comes in only two flavors: activistic or ersatz.

Sen, more than anyone, has integrated the democratic axiom into practical economic thought. But there is a snag: for one who lays so much stress on freedom, he has surprisingly little to say about resistance to repression, and in his recent writings he takes pains to set globalists at ease about his project. He refuses to be the Marcuse of the new youth politics of antiglobalism. Though he laments the glaring inequalities of global capitalism, he pays scant attention to the TNCs that dominate today's global economy and wreak havoc on his celebrated "development as freedom." Useful as his informational strategies can be for averting catastrophes such as plague or famine, they do little to promote activistic organization in support of People Power. To tap the full oppositional force of concurrence theory, one must liberate Sen's model from Sen himself.

Nonetheless there is much to be said for his "Asian strategy," which gets us past the East/West schism that marked the Asian Crisis. Nothing could be less Senian than those rival, pre-Crash TINAisms: made-in-Singapore "Asian values" and made-in-America globalization. Thanks to post-Crash IMFism and now the post-9/11 "war on terror," America has lost much of its democratic credibility, along with most of the soft power it enjoyed on the Rim in the early 1990s. The winners, by default, could be some of the most undemocratic development models ever conceived, such as Sino-globalization. "Asian values" took a hard blow from the Crash, but returned in this even more virulent form, which is now being packaged for global export. And there are plenty of developing nations waiting in the import line.

This resurgent authoritarianism, however, is still challenged by other Asian values. Sen has done more than anyone to rekindle the democratic development debate on Asian turf. This time the West is left sitting on the sidelines in a distinctly Asian contest of development with or without freedom.[93] The outcome of this trial-by-development will define the political contours of globalization for decades to come.

While the new Asian balance of power is increasingly divided along Sino-Indian lines, nuclear parity between these budding superpowers shifts competition to the

---

93 See, for example, Sen's essay, "Human Rights and Asian Values: What Lee Kuan Yew and Le Peng Don't Understand about Asia," *The New Republic*, Vol. 217, No. 2–3 (July 14, 1997), archived online at http://www.brainsnchips.org/hr/sen.thm.; and http://www.sintercom. org/polinfo/polessays/sen.html. See also Kim Dae-jung, "A Response to Lee Kuan Yew: Is Culture Destiny? The Myth of Asia's Anti-Democratic Values," *Foreign Affairs*, Vol. 73, No. 6 (November/December 1994), http://www.idep.org/conference/program/participants/Kim_ Dae-jung/culture.htm.

economic sphere. The question is whether this will foster another GDP "race to the bottom," marked by an even greater spread between haves and have-nots. Or will democracy give Indo-globalization a Senian ("development as freedom") advantage over Sino-globalization? To tap that advantage India will have to rediscover its Gandhian heritage of the common good. As the following chapters will show, that basic democratic hope has flickered out in country after country. India's success or failure to keep this flame alive will profoundly impact the global prospect for democracy in the 21st century.

Chapter 1

Globalization on Trial: Rethinking Asian Exceptionalism vis-à-vis the Third World

The Making of Third Worldism

The end of the Cold War put America in the curiously unenviable position of having no major geopolitical rival. Triumphalism and growing economic hubris trumped geo-realist common sense about the dangers lurking behind US "unipolarity." Now, instead of having one preeminent enemy, America finds itself at odds with much of the entire world. It is telling that Secretary of Defense Robert M. Gates—who for years served in the CIA tête-à-tête a KGB agent named Vladimir V. Putin—expresses nostalgia toward the "less complex" days of the Cold War.[1]

The last glimmers of appreciation for America's global primacy were seen in the Gulf War coalition and the vanguard role that America was invited to play in Kosovo, after European countries proved incapable of handling this relatively small crisis in their own backyard. However, even as Secretary of State Madeleine Albright toasted America for being the "indispensable nation," the global drift was toward a very dispensable view of US hegemony. In the face of what has justly been called the criminalization of American foreign policy,[2] the only surprising thing is that many nations taking this view—let us call them the contras—are not programmatically anti-American. They are simply non-aligned.

This, to be sure, is a new kind of non-alignment. Whereas the old Non-Aligned Movement had been a distinctly Third World phenomenon, today's version has expanded to include a broad range of both developed and newly industrialized countries (NICs). One of their few common denominators is an intense aversion to US unilateralism. Rarely is this pushed so far as Chávez's anti-American rants or Putin's blasts at the "hyper-force" of US militarism. After throwing down the gauntlet at a February 2007 Security Conference in Munich,[3] Putin rushed over to the Middle East to elaborate his "New Course" for a multilateral world order. Even

1 Quoted in Paul Kennedy, "The Good Old Days of the Cold War," *LA Times.com* (February 18, 2007), http://www.latimes.com/news/opinion/la-op-kennedy18feb18,0,56916 02,print.story?coll=1.

2 Michel Chossudovsky, "The Criminalization of American Foreign Policy," *Global Research* (February 5, 2007), http://www.globalresearch.ca/PrintArticle.php?articleId=4659.

3 Ian Traynor, "Putin Hits at US for Triggering Arms Race," *Observer* (February 11, 2007), http://observer.guardian.co.uk/print/0,,329712412-119093,00.html.

so, he draped himself in the borrowed imagery of US soft power by having his chief propagandist, Vladislav Sourkov, describe him as a new Franklin D. Roosevelt.[4] The point is that Washington has so completely lost its way as to appear, from a Third World perspective, more fundamentally "un-American" than Putin is. What Russia claims to offer, ironically, is nothing less than a global New Deal.

That would be a fine contribution, if only it were true. Unfortunately, as the Chechen holocaust amply proves, this progressive image is a hoax. Putin's patent objective, understood through his actions rather than his words, is a reconfigured Second World. The more likely locus for a real New Deal is Latin America, which naturally takes the contra route after the grievous failure of its Washington-directed restructuration of the 1980s and early 1990s. At that time the Pacific Rim was still relatively content with its US affiliation, and might have remained so as long as its "miracle" era lasted. That all changed with the Asian Crisis, which was intensified and prolonged by IMF-dictated "reforms." It was no secret that these strictures were a product of collusion between the IMF and the US Treasury Department. Asia in general took a hard lesson from this dubious "rescue" operation, and Bush era unilateralism widened the East/West gap still farther.

The Bush agenda not only ignored the core tenets of geopolitical realism but also the dismal outcome of past American flirtations with imperialism. Though neoconservatives often trace their ideas to Teddy Roosevelt, they forget that T.R. tacitly dropped his imperialist stance during his presidency, just as Woodrow Wilson would more openly renounce his.[5] Having pressured Congress to grant citizenship to Puerto Ricans and independence to Filipinos, Wilson worked to put an end to all colonialism after World War I. He was convinced that America faced a stark choice between the ideals of democracy and those of unfettered national interest, which is to say imperialism.[6] Having come to see the latter as both unjust and unstable, his Fourteen Points and his proposal for a League of Nations sought a mediating system of international law to promote global democracy by strictly democratic means. Granted, he hoped other countries would model themselves on his Calvinist vision of America,[7] but he opposed any unilateral imposition of the US model.[8]

---

4 Marie Jego, "Vladimir Putin Wants to Offer an Alternative to Washington's 'Unilateral Policy,'" *Le Monde* (February 14, 2007), http://www.lemonde.fr/web/article/0,1-0@2-3214,36-867230@51-866850,0.html.

5 John B. Judis, "What Woodrow Wilson Can Teach Today's Imperialists," *The New Republic* (June 9, 2003), http://www.tnr.com/doc.mhtml?pt=9aNIN97FJx83cfpk2gpKAZA%3D%3D. Explosive nationalist reactions forced Roosevelt's withdrawal from the Philippines and Wilson's from Mexico. Anticipating the rise of Japanese power in the Pacific following Japan's defeat of Russia in 1905, Roosevelt came to advocate Philippine independence so as to reduce American vulnerability in Asia. See Stanley Karnow, *In Our Image: America's Empire in the Philippines* (New York: Ballantine Books, 1989), pp. 80 and 263.

6 Judis, *op. cit.*

7 William Pfaff, "Manifest Destiny: A New Direction for America," *The New York Review of Books*, Vol. 54, No. 2 (February 15, 2005), http://www.nybooks.com/articles/19879.

8 Rather he advocated a "mandate system" whereby non-imperial nations such as Sweden would guide developing countries toward democracy. In that respect he still stopped short of a full reversal, for he thought it necessary to keep developing countries under the parental wing

This Wilsonian sense of restraint—keeping one's means in tune with one's ends, and foreign policy in tune with democracy—was still an operative principle at the end of World War II. It made its mark, for example, on postwar Bretton Woods organizations: the International Monetary Fund (IMF) and World Bank in 1944, and the General Agreement on Tariffs and Trade (GATT) in 1947. Unfortunately these institutions would soon be absorbed into a Cold War security system that was subject to US fiat and given to callous disregard for Third World interests. This shift was already manifest in the 1947 Truman Doctrine, which stood Wilson's philosophy on its head by casting America as the military and economic policeman of the world. Although Pax Americana worked rather well until the early 1970s,[9] for America at least, it rested on a dubious conflation of capitalist and democratic values.[10] It hardly needs to be said which of these concerns took priority in American foreign policy.

This bracketing of democratic values meant that foreign affairs were cut loose from any serious ethical evaluation or restraint.[11] When friendly persuasion failed, America was more than willing to intervene forcefully, as it did in Korea, Greece, Vietnam, the Dominican Republic, Grenada and Lebanon. Likewise it was behind the destabilization of regimes such as Iran, Turkey, Guatemala, Laos, Cambodia, Cuba, El Salvador, Chile, Ghana, Zaire and Mali.[12] Military adventurism was matched by environmental destruction, such that the US Department of Defense became the world's largest polluter.[13] First World domination and contamination were two sides of the same coin, just as they came together in the Soviet Union's Second World dominion over Eurasia.

Hope for a progressive world order lay with the developing world. Having fought long and hard to rid themselves of colonialism, some Third World countries understandably resisted First World neocolonialism by seeking their own path to

---

of the Western model, albeit not a colonial model. Even this compromise is seen as too much by today's new imperialists, such as Deepak Lal, who blames Wilson for deconstructing the imperialist system which in Lal's view was the only safeguard against the global disorder and economic disintegration that culminated in World War II. See Deepak Lal, *In Praise of Empires: Globalization and Order* (Basingstoke, UK: Palgrave Macmillan, 2004), p. xxiv.

9 Ankie Hoogvelt, *Globalisation and the Postcolonial World: The New Political Economy of Development* (London: Macmillan Press Ltd., 1997), pp. 34 and 33. The Truman Doctrine established a counter-revolutionary policy to crush any leftist movement in the Third World. See David Louis Cingranell, *Ethics, American Foreign Policy, and the Third World* (New York: St. Martin's Press, 1993), pp. 126–27. But the deeper roots of today's imperialistic agenda can be traced to President Benjamin Harrison's "new diplomacy" (1889–1908). His Secretary of State, James Blaine, believed the US should annex Hawaii, Cuba, Puerto Rico, and even Canada. For Blaine and other expansionists, Pan-Americanism was a logical extension of the Monroe Doctrine. See Fareed Zakaria, *From Wealth to Power: The Unusual Origins of America's World Role* (Princeton, NJ: Princeton University Press, 1998), pp. 137–39.

10 Mark Rupert, *Ideologies of Globalization: Contending Visions of a New World Order* (London: Routledge, 2000), p. 27.

11 See Arturo Escobar, *Encountering Development: The Making and Unmaking of the Third World* (Princeton, NJ: Princeton University Press, 1995), p. 15.

12 Hoogvelt, *op. cit.*, p. 34.

13 Bob Feldman, "War on the Earth," *Dollars and Sense* (March/April 2003), p. 24 (pp. 24–27).

development.[14] Thus Third World nationalism of the 1950s and 1960s grew hand-in-hand with a distinctly non-aligned internationalism. At first this Third Way, like early pan-Arabism,[15] was simply anti-colonial; but increasingly its goal shifted to escaping co-optation by the superpowers. That common cause helped Third Worldism bridge the ethnic, religious and linguistic gaps that divided it,[16] thus making it the undeclared second front of the Cold War. Washington found it necessary to depict this thorn in its side as a Soviet pawn. Otherwise there could be no hiding the fact that America's primary goal was hegemony, not global security or democratization.

Rise and Fall of the Old Non-Alignment

One of the first to recognize the threat of capitalist recolonization in the postwar era was India's first prime minister Jawaharlal Nehru. By the late 1940s his government was already forging a non-aligned blend of socialist economic development and secular democracy.[17] Like Gandhi, Nehru rejected both communism and capitalism, but supplemented Gandhi's eco-social austerity with his own pro-tech utopianism. This was most unfortunate, for Nehru's second declaration of Indian independence—liberation from the Cold War system[18]—was coupled with a gigantism that effectively declared war on nature. Thus it duplicated rather than supplanted the eco-imperialism of First and Second World modernisms.

This destructive legacy has yet to be overcome. Its bigger-is-better mindset is so deeply ingrained that more eco-friendly approaches to development have rarely been embraced by ruling elites outside the US and Western Europe.[19] Purging the Third Worldism of Gandhi's values meant that none of the "three worlds" would offer an alternative to the ecosocial pillage that has appropriated the name "development."

---

14 For our purpose "Third World" has special relevance to states which joined the Non-Alignment Movement (NAM) and played a significant role in the decolonization and independence process. That sense of unity has been lost today. See Tony Barnett, "States of the State and Third Worlds," in Peter Golding and Phil Harris (eds), *Beyond Cultural Imperialism: Globalization, Communication & the New International Order* (London: Sage Publications, 1997), pp. 27, 45 and 47 (pp. 25–48).

15 Abdul-Monem Al-Mashat, "Stress and Disintegration in the Arab World," in Tawfic E. Farah (ed.), *Pan-Arabism and Arab Nationalism, the Continuing Debate* (Boulder, CO: Westview, 1987), p. 166 (pp. 165–76).

16 Akira Iriye, *Cultural Internationalism and World Order* (Baltimore, MD: The Johns Hopkins University Press, 1997), p. 161.

17 Meghnad Desai, "Communalism, Secularism and the Dilemma of Indian Nationhood," in Michael Leifer (ed.), *Asian Nationalism* (London: Routledge, 2000), pp. 113–4 (pp. 91–125).

18 "Deconsecrating Gandhi," *The Economist*, Vol. 348, No. 8083 (August 29–September 4, 1998), pp. 79–80.

19 James Petras, "The Third Way: Myth and Reality," *Monthly Review*, Vol. 51, No. 10 (March 2000), http://www.monthlyreview.org/300petra.htm. There are now some notable exceptions, however, such as Kenya's Green Belt Movement, founded by the winner of the 2004 Nobel Peace Prize, Wangari Muta Maathai.

In other respects Nehru's vision was more progressive. His idea of nationalism drew upon his sense of Asia's relatively harmonious past, as compared to Europe's. Using secularism and federalism to bridge the gap between Hindus and Muslims, Nehru urged the new nation-state to seek unity in diversity rather than uniformity.[20] Meanwhile he continued his struggle against imperialism by refusing to enter the Cold War or the US-directed world system. When the World Bank retaliated by refusing to fund two badly needed oil refineries, Soviet funding came to the rescue. That of course threw Washington into a state of apoplexy. The rift with Washington was widened further by India's Foreign Exchange Regulation Act (FERA) of 1973, which set limits on Western equity holdings. Corporations that refused to comply were forced to leave the country. So it was that Indians were deprived of Coca Cola.[21]

African non-alignment followed a similar pattern. In the 1950s Africans had been optimistic about their postcolonial future. The aims of African nationalism reached far beyond the raw economism that would mark Pacific Rim development in coming decades. Stress was laid on freedom as well as the dignity and equality of African peoples.[22] Rather than pure Marxist materialism, African socialism was rooted in tradition and culture. This capacious sense of Third Worldism infused the 1955 Bandung Conference in Indonesia, where Asian and African countries jointly framed a non-aligned development strategy.[23]

Likewise, the 1958 Conference of Independent African States in Accra, attended by all independent African governments, tried to assert a distinctive African voice. Despite America's charge that African non-alignment was a mere front for Soviet vassalage,[24] Accra refused co-optation by either superpower.[25] Its initiatives were echoed in later Third World demands for a reformed world system, e.g., the New International Economic Order (NIEO), launched at the 1973 non-aligned summit in Algiers. The NIEO attempted to stabilize the prices of raw materials and to regulate the capital flows of TNCs.[26]

Naturally this strategy met strong resistance from US corporations, and hence from the US government. The Tunis non-aligned meeting of 1976 took anti-

---

20 Desai, *op. cit.*, p. 111.

21 Deepa Ollapally, "Third World Nationalism and the United States after the Cold War," *Political Science Quarterly*, Vol. 110, No. 3 (Autumn, 1995), pp. 425–6 (pp. 417–34).

22 Klaas van Walraven, *Dreams of Power: The Role of the Organization of African Unity in the Politics of Africa, 1963–1993* (Hants, UK: Ashgate, 1999), p. 80.

23 Attended by India's Nehru, China's Zhou Enlai, and Egypt's Gamal Abdual Nasser, Bandung put Sukarno's Indonesia and Nehru's India in the Third World driver's seat. See Michael R.J. Vatikiotis, *Political Change in Southeast Asia: Trimming the Banyan Tree* (London: Routledge, 1996), p. 174.

24 Frank Füredi, *The New Ideology of Imperialism: Renewing the Moral Imperative* (London: Pluto Press, 1994), p. 75.

25 Van Walraven, *op. cit.*, pp. 93 and 94.

26 Kees van der Pijl, "The Sovereignty of Capital Impaired: Social Forces and Codes of Conduct for Multinational Corporations," in Henk Overbeek (ed.), *Restructuring Hegemony and the Global Political Economy: The Rise of Transnational Neoliberalism in the 1980s* (London: Routledge, 1993), p. 38 (pp. 28–57).

imperialism as its theme,[27] with special stress given to cultural hegemony.[28] That same year UNESCO presciently called for the decolonization of information technology (IT).[29] By the early 1980s, however, the growing internationalization of capital was undermining Third World autonomy.[30] Foreign aid likewise came with more strings attached. The top four African recipients of US aid in the 1980s—Somalia, Sudan, Zaire (now Congo) and Liberia—were grandly rewarded for their Cold War services,[31] such that Zaire's infamous President Mobutu Sese Seko received nine World Bank loans.[32]

It is hardly surprising, therefore, that India would pay dearly for its non-alignment in terms of American aid. By contrast, many Rim nations enjoyed lavish US funding and export advantages. Official aid figures do not begin to reflect the scope of this difference, for America's tolerance of trade imbalances with countries on the Cold War frontline was a disguised form of aid. This pattern laid the foundation for the so-called "miracle" economics that would be used to discredit other development models and non-development explanations, such as dependency theory.

Meanwhile the democratic erosion of postcolonial nationalism bled into Third World internationalism, sapping its ideals to the point that co-optation by the dominant world system was bound to follow when the price was right.[33] As a truly autonomous Third Way, rather than a simple negotiating strategy for playing one superpower off against the other, non-alignment was ebbing fast by the 1980s. It was the end of the Cold War, however, that dealt it the final death blow.

Globalization and the Making of the 'South'

This outcome calls to mind Rosa Luxemburg's suspicion of nationalism as a vehicle for progressive change. On the one hand she appreciated, as few on the Left did, the vital importance of noncapitalistic cultures as a bulwark against capitalist pillage.[34] On the other hand, as Joan Cocks puts it, she refused "to be swept away by the glamour of struggles for national self-determination or to conflate those struggles

---

27 Collen Roach, "The Western World and the NWICO [New World Information and Communication Order]: United they Stand?," in Peter Golding and Phil Harris (eds), *Beyond Cultural Imperialism: Globalization, Communication & the New International Order* (London: Sage Publications, 1997), pp. 94–5 (pp. 94–116).

28 Mohammed Musa, "From Optimism to Reality: An Overview of Third World News Agencies," in Peter Golding and Phil Harris (eds), *Beyond Cultural Imperialism: Globalization, Communication & the New International Order* (London: Sage Publications, 1997), p. 121 (pp. 117–46).

29 Roach, *op. cit.*, p. 95.

30 Van der Pijl, *op. cit.*, p. 46.

31 David Francis, "For Rich, Foreign Aid is a Tool for Persuasion," *The Christian Science Monitor* (June 26, 2003), http://www.csmonitor.com/2003/0626/p14s02-wogi.htm.

32 *Ibid.*

33 Iriye, *op. cit.*, pp. 186 and 169.

34 See Joan Cocks, *Passion and Paradox: Intellectuals Confront the National Question* (Princeton and Oxford: Princeton University Press, 2002), p. 57.

with the struggle for social and political democracy."[35] Under cover of national sovereignty, postcolonial regimes duplicated the injustice of former colonialism and turned Third World internationalism into a body of local potentates. These neo-authoritarians extracted what they could from the great powers while squeezing their citizens to the limit.

Foreign aid could compensate for shortages of capital and technology,[36] but it also helped to militarize the Third World at the expense of civil society.[37] This of course happened on the Pacific Rim as well, but here national leaders were in a better position to leverage Cold War geopolitics to their advantage. That difference helped propel the "miracle" growth that left other developing regions far behind. Unfortunately Asian intellectuals tended to attribute this dynamism not to geopolitics but to the growth-first authoritarianism that they dubbed "Asian values."

Although these claims of unique dynamism and distinct Asianness were fraudulent, they won wide acceptance, and on this basis dependency theory was discredited. It was forgotten that rates of economic growth among Latin American, African and Asian "tiger" economies were not so divergent between 1960 and 1982: 5 percent, 4 percent, and 7 percent, respectively.[38] The 2 percent difference between Latin American and Asian tiger growth during those years hardly deserved a "miracle" label.

The Cold War version of "globalization" conjured the "Asian miracle" through a reverse dependency that worked in favor of the Pacific Rim while relegating the Third World to peripheral status. Exactly as dependency theory charged, alternative modes of development were stunted by a process that can fairly be labeled the development of underdevelopment. So long as Third World alternatives were forced to compete on this unlevel playing field, any country that wanted rapid economic growth would have to choose its development model according to its relationship to the superpowers.[39] The invisibility of the geopolitical factor buttressed the Cold War system by keeping it beyond criticism.

The final nail in the underdevelopment coffin was the massive expansion of Third World debt. The General Assembly of the UN sounded a warning call with its *Declaration on the Establishment of a New International Order* in 1974 and the *Charter of Economic Rights and Duties of States* in 1976,[40] but the admonition came too late. Two geoeconomic factors had changed everything: the dollar had been disconnected from the gold standard as of August 1971, and new oil money had flooded into the Atlantic financial system after the OPEC (Organization of Petroleum

35 *Ibid.*, p. 56.

36 Keith Griffin, *Studies in Globalization and Economic Transitions* (Basingstoke, UK: Macmillan Press, 1996), p. 38.

37 *Ibid.*, p. 57.

38 Walden Bello, Shea Cunningham and Bill Rau, *Dark Victory: The United States and Global Poverty* (London: Pluto Press, new edition, 1999), pp. 13 and 30.

39 Mohamed Ariff and Ahmend M. Khalid, *Liberalization, Growth and the Asian Financial Crisis: Lessons for Developing and Transitional Economies in Asia* (Cheltenham, UK: Edward Elgar, 2000), p. 7.

40 Manuel Castells, *The Rise of the Network Society* (Massachusetts and Oxford: Blackwell Publishers, 1996), p. 163.

Exporting Countries) oil hike of 1973. Commercial banks thus became financiers not only for Western countries but also for Arab, Latin American and East Asian ones.[41] The result was a truly global capitalism that ripped the developmental leverage away from struggling national economies. Petrodollars from the oil hikes fueled both financial globalization and reactionary nationalism, which in turn joined hands in the development of underdevelopment. This dual effect tends to be forgotten, because globalism associates the rise of globalization with the demise of regressive nationalism. In fact, as Edward Herman well argues, globalization has supported regressive statism by weakening the government's ability to pursue progressive ends.[42]

In this mid-Cold War financial circuit, northern nations tapped into OPEC profits by serving as banking conduits for petrodollars in route to the Third World.[43] In 1974 alone the current-account surplus of OPEC jumped from $9 billion to $65 billion, reaching $104 billion by 1980.[44] While Third World debt had been contracted at fixed and low interest rates in the mid-1970s, the early 1980s witnessed the advent of floating loan terms, exposing the Third World to financial peril when the US raised its prime interest rate to combat domestic inflation and strengthen the dollar. For the developing world this meant soaring debt and capital flight.[45]

Well over $250 billion exited these countries between 1981 and 1986, an amount far exceeding the $13 billion supplied by America's Marshall aid for Europe's postwar recovery.[46] The total Third World debt of $500 billion in 1982 jumped to $1.2 trillion by 1989,[47] and tended to strike harder in places that were less important geopolitically. Meanwhile the emergence of full-fledged financial globalization—marked by a rising tide of capital flows relative to production and trade[48]—greatly increased Third World vulnerability. At first this seemed to give Rim nations an even greater edge, but the days of their Cold War advantage were numbered.

---

41 See F. William Engdahl, "A New American Century?: Iraq and the Hidden Euro-Dollar War," *Current Concerns* (April 2003), http://www.currentconcerns.ch/config_03/print.php?source=../archive/2003/04/source/200; and Henk Overbeek and Kees van der Pijl, "Restructuring Capital and Restructuring Hegemony," in Henk Overbeek (ed.), *Restructuring Hegemony and the Global Political Economy: The Rise of Transnational Neoliberalism in the 1980s* (London: Routledge, 1993), p. 18 (pp. 1–27).

42 Edward S. Herman, "The Threat of Globalization," *New Politics*, Vol. 7, No. 2, Whole No. 26 (Winter 1999), http://www.wpunj.edu/~newpol/issue26/herman26.htm.

43 Riccardo Petrella, "Globalization and Internationalization: The Dynamics of the Emerging World Order," in Robert Boyer and Daniel Drache (eds), *States Against Markets: The Limits of Globalization* (London: Routledge, 1996), p. 69 (pp. 62–83).

44 Robert Solomon, *The Transformation of the World Economy* (Basingstoke, UK: Macmillan Press, second edition, 1999), p. 154.

45 Arjun Makhijani, *From Global Capitalism to Economic Justice: An Inquiry into the Elimination of Systemic Poverty, Violence and Environmental Destruction in the World Economy* (New York: The Apex Press, 1992), p. 37.

46 Castells, *op. cit.*, p. 166.

47 Makhijani, *op. cit.*, pp. 39–40.

48 Peter Drucker, *The New Realities* (London: Heinemann, 1989), p. 120.

No longer would there be a "peace dividend" on the Rim. The Middle East had been the major recipient of arms from the United States and the Soviet Union during the Cold War, but afterwards this dubious honor would go to East Asia, where tripwire tensions only intensified. The Middle East and North Africa (MENA) still imported a quarter of the world's conventional arms, but over a third now went to East Asia.[49] It is estimated that between 1992 and 1996, Thailand, Indonesia, Malaysia, Singapore and Myanmar spent more than $8 billion on weapons, and in 1996 East Asia as a whole imported more than the total international arms purchases of NATO and Western Europe.[50] This financial incubus has been ignored in most accounts of Asian "crony capitalism," perhaps because the spotlight could easily turn on the West's complicity in the region's crony militarism.

So long as the Cold War lasted, Rim nations enjoyed the "inside track" development that accompanied geopolitical exigency. Globalization theory has painted a rosy, "win-win" picture that ignores the very existence of this "inside track," for to grant it would be to acknowledge the central role of politics in the neoliberal World Order. The actual relationship of Rim development and Third World undevelopment fits the "zero-sum" pattern of global capital-dependency.[51]

Notwithstanding Rim exceptionalism, which became far less "exceptional" after the Cold War, the global center still held. By the 1980s about four-fifths of global capital flows were between the "triad" countries of Europe, North America and Japan.[52] And by the mid-1990s, just prior to the Asian Crash, about 85 percent of global FDI was within this same "triad."[53] The Crash should have buried the myth that globalization is an unambiguous leveling process, but of course it has been interpreted by neoliberals as proof that their policies need to be applied all the more stringently. This was the end of the late Cold War truce between neoliberal universalism and Asian exceptionalism.

Currently the gap is widening between the global center (comprising most nations of the Organization for Economic Cooperation and Development, or OECD) and the periphery.[54] Efforts to bridge this North/South divide—e.g., the North American Free Trade Agreement (NAFTA) and the Free Trade Area for the Americas (FTAA)—have conspicuously failed.[55] The percentages speak for themselves: the richest 20 percent of the world's population rakes in 82.7 percent of global income; the second

---

49 Clement M. Henry and Robert Springborg, *Globalization and the Politics of Development in the Middle East* (Cambridge: Cambridge University Press, 2001), p. 33.

50 Victor Mallet, *The Trouble with Tigers: The Rise and Fall of South-East Asia* (London: HarperCollins, 1999), p. 212.

51 See Hoogvelt, *op. cit.*, pp. 89 and 162.

52 Petrella, *op. cit.*, p. 77.

53 Robert Boyer and Daniel Drache, "Introduction," in Robert Boyer and Daniel Drache (eds), *States Against Markets: The Limits of Globalization* (London: Routledge, 1996), p. 2 (pp. 1–27).

54 Castells, *op. cit.*, p. 108.

55 Dorval Brunelle, "Toward a 'Free Trade Area of the Americas': Chasing the Holy Grail of Free Trade," *Le Monde diplomatique* (April 5, 2001), http://www.en.monde-diplomatique. fr/2001/04/05americas summit.

20 percent claims 11.7 percent; the third 20 percent gets only 2.3 percent; while the fourth and fifth brackets are left with a mere 1.9 and 1.4 percent, respectively.[56]

What is most astonishing about these figures is that they have not inspired more revolutionary reaction. In the case of Latin America, this mystery is compounded by the fact that earlier high growth years did see widespread resistance. Most Latin American nations grew rapidly in the 1960s and 1970s, with 6 percent per year growth in the entire Latin sphere. But in the 1980s the regional GDP grew at a meager 1 percent per year, while per capita GDP fell by more than 10 percent.[57] Heavy borrowing during the 1970s, when interest rates were low, set the stage for this "lost decade." The total long-term debt (with a maturity of more than one year) of the region increased from $27.6 billion in 1970 to $238.5 billion in 1982. During these years the ratio of long-term debt to the region's GNP rose from 18.3 percent to nearly 34 percent,[58] laying the foundation for unprecedented economic dependency. Mexico, for example, saw its current-account deficit grow from $5.8 billion in 1989 to $29.7 billion in 1994.[59]

In the early 1990s this problem was offset by the neoliberalization of cross-border trade and investment. Nine out of ten Latin American countries enjoyed huge capital inflows in the 1992–93 period,[60] with more than $30 billion pouring into Mexico alone in 1993.[61] However, this ostensive remedy would be short-lived. When Mexico's exports declined in the early 1990s due to a strong peso, the government tried to restore competitiveness with a devaluation, but dollar debts soared as the value of the peso fell. The "Mexican miracle" turned out to be a mirage. By the end of 1994 the country was thrown into the financial maelstrom that came to be called the "tequila crisis."[62]

Global capitalism was spared serious examination, however, by the ongoing "Asian miracle." By now the myth of Asian exceptionalism was so deeply ingrained that the lessons from the "tequila crisis" were all but ignored by Pacific Rim nations, despite their similar pattern of risk exposure through heavy foreign borrowing. Net flows of private capital to Thailand, Indonesia, Malaysia, South Korea and the Philippines jumped from $48 billion in 1994 to $93 billion in 1996, setting the region up for the 1997 Crash.[63] The fact that this "Asian flu" was a global malady could not be

---

56 Robert Hunter Wade, "Inequality of World Incomes: What Should Be Done," *Open Democracy* (November 14, 2001), http://www.opendemocracy.net/themes/article-7-257.jsp.

57 Robert Solomon, *The Transformation of the World Economy* (Basingstoke, UK: Macmillan Press, second edition, 1999), p. 165.

58 *Ibid.*, p. 166.

59 *Ibid.*, pp. 176 and 169.

60 Michael P. Dooley, "Are Capital Inflows to Developing Countries a Vote For or Against Economic Policy Reforms?," in Pierre-Richard Agénor, Marcus Miller, David Vines and Axel Weber (eds), *The Asian Financial Crisis: Causes, Contagion and Consequences* (Cambridge: Cambridge University Press, 1999), p. 115 (pp. 112–26).

61 Paul Krugman, *The Return of Depression Economics* (New York: W.W. Norton, 1999), p. 45.

62 *Ibid.*, p. 39.

63 Victor Mallet, *The Trouble with Tigers: The Rise and Fall of South-East Asia* (London: HarperCollins, 1999), p. 167.

mentioned without putting globalization itself on trial. Every effort would be made, therefore, to portray the problem as distinctly Asian. Thus Asian exceptionalism was turned on its head: instead of explaining the miracle, it now was used to explain the Crash. What it really represented was the perennial irresponsibility of Washington-directed globalization, which first washed its hands of Latin America's plight, and then of the Asia Pacific's.

From Miracle to Mirage

Following the 1982 debt crisis in the Western Hemisphere, eight out of ten developing nations in the region experienced crippling capital outflows during the "lost decade" of the 1980s.[64] The stark contrast between the Latin American malaise and the Asian "miracle" seemed to invalidate dependency theory. In fact the Rim was joining Latin America in a more subtle, delayed-action dependency. NICs such as Indonesia, Malaysia, Thailand, Singapore and China attracted $70 billion of the world's $300 billion FDI between 1987 and 1996.[65] This massive capital influx resulted in currency appreciation, a rapid increase in borrowing, and still more investment. Of course, this process could easily be thrown into reverse through capital exit, currency depreciation, a lending hiatus, and investment collapse.[66]

Even neoliberal gurus such as Jeffrey Sachs and Lance Taylor admit that Washington Consensus globalism was not an innocent bystander in the Asian Crash and its aftermath. Globalist institutions had a habit of stimulating growth at a terrible cost. Debt burdens grew markedly after 1970, as lending to the Third World jumped from $2.7 billion in 1970 to $8.7 billion in 1978, finally peaking at $12 billion in 1981. Between 1983 and 1989 global FDI grew at nearly three times the rate of exports and almost four times the rate of world GDP.[67] Instability was compounded as foreign exchange reached nearly $1 trillion daily by the early 1990s, or 40 times the daily volume of international trade.[68]

After the Cold War, American banks drastically cut their loan exposure to the Third World. For international creditors the debt crisis of the 1980s was over, but there would be no exit door for the debtor countries themselves. The South was crippled by the rise of external Third World debt from $785 billion in 1982 to

---

64 Dooley, *op. cit.*, p. 115.

65 Ariff and Khalid, *op. cit.*, p. 29.

66 Philippe Aghion, Philippe Bacchetta and Abhijit Banerjee, "Capital Markets and the Instability of Open Economies," in Pierre-Richard Agénor, Marcus Miller, David Vines and Axel Weber (eds), *The Asian Financial Crisis: Causes, Contagion and Consequences* (Cambridge: Cambridge University Press, 1999), p. 167 (pp. 167–94).

67 Paul Bowles and Brian MacLean, "Regional Blocs: Can Japan be the Leader?," in Robert Boyer and Daniel Drache (eds), *States Against Markets: The Limits to Globalization* (London: Routledge, 1996), p. 158 (pp. 155–69).

68 Eric Helleiner, "Post-Globalization: Is the Financial Liberalization Trend Likely to be Reversed?," in Robert Boyer and Daniel Drache (eds), *States Against Markets: The Limits of Globalization* (London: Routledge, 1996), p. 193 (pp. 193–210).

$1.3 trillion by 1992.[69] For many years the Rim managed to escape this lethal undertow, but the globalization of financial markets finally foreclosed on Asian exceptionalism. In Walden Bello's view, the Crash was a product of the liberation of speculative capital from national and international regulation.[70] Thus the Asian Crisis was a subset of the globalization process.[71]

As Paul Krugman argues, the major lesson of the Crash has more to do with politics than economics.[72] A big part of the problem is that the current global system has no stake in the welfare of a particular people or their environment, and certainly it has no stake in their political development. For Amartya Sen that political factor is central to development as such. To curtail freedom in the name of "Asian values" is not only an insult to Asian political culture—as if to say that Asians are morally or intellectually unfit for democracy. It also puts the public at risk in a material sense, as the Crash amply proved.

Prior to the Crash, however, there was an even greater danger: the risk that the Asian "miracle" would act like a global beacon, causing highly illiberal "Asian values" to break free from their quarantine in "Asian exceptionalism." They could even become the developmental norm for the coming century. This is already starting to happen under the auspices of a capitalist but programmatically anti-democratic China.[73] That dread possibility is what Amartya Sen has been trying to forestall. He can succeed only if most Asians recognize that the "miracles" they long nurtured at the expense of political development were a mirage. So long as the Cold War lasted, Rim NICs were exempted from the inexorable logic of boom and bust globalization. Their exceptionalism had always been more geopolitical than geoeconomic, and in 1997 that fact came home to roost.

"Altering" Globalization

It has been a quarter of a century since Margaret Thatcher rendered her *ex cathedra* verdict that "There Is No Alternative" ("TINA") to the global processes of deregulation, privatization, and government downsizing that go by the name of globalization.[74] The point was to preclude any serious consideration of alternatives

---

69 Bello, *Dark, op. cit.*, p. 69.

70 Walden Bello, *The Future in the Balance: Essays on Globalization and Resistance* (Oakland, CA: Food First Books, 2001), p. xiii.

71 See Bello, *Dark, op. cit.*, p. 118.

72 Paul Krugman, "What Ever Happened to the Asian Miracle?," originally in *Fortune* (August 18, 1997), archived http://web.mit.edu/krugman/www/perspire.htm. See also Gerald Epstein, "International Capital Mobility and the Scope for National Economic Management," in Robert Boyer and Daniel Drache (eds), *States Against Markets: The Limits of Globalization* (London: Routledge, 1996), p. 215 (pp. 211–24).

73 See Naazneen Barma and Ely Ratner, "China's Illiberal Challenge," *Democracy: A Journal of Ideas*, Issue 2 (Fall 2006), http://www.democracyjournal.org/printfriendly. php?ID=6485.

74 Myron J. Frankman, "Global Economy and Civil Society," in Ted Schrecker (ed.), *Surviving Globalism: The Social and Environmental Challenges* (Basingstoke, UK: Macmillan Press, 1997), p. 97 (pp. 95–107); and also see John McMurtry, "The Global Market Ideology,"

to the market ideology that came to be known as neoliberalism. The Pacific Rim had bucked the system by way of power politics, but finally it too succumbed to TINA.

At the 1993 APEC summit, Washington demanded that the Asian tigers open up their financial markets to free capital flows. Once those controls were lifted, Korea and the other tigers were swept away by a flood of foreign dollars. Hedge funds like George Soros's Quantum Fund and Julian Robertson's Tiger Fund closed in for the kill, raking in billions.[75] One by one the tigers fell, leaving their governments no choice but to seek IMF assistance. What they got, in the name of a bailout, was a fire sale.

Grassroots aversion to TINA mounted over the years, but only recently was nongovernmental resistance joined by a phalanx of developing nations. This coalition of the unwilling made its full debut with the breakdown of the September 2003 WTO meeting at Cancún, Mexico. Whereas the Seattle anti-WTO protests of November 1999 brought a "chorus of others" to the cause of "global antiglobalism,"[76] Cancún replaced that "anti" with a more realistic "alter."[77] The idea was not to combat globalization as such, but only to contest the monolithic corporatism that took shape after the Cold War under the banner of the New World Order. The economic wing of that Order—advanced by the WTO, the IMF and the World Bank[78]—is now joined by the armed globalization that Washington unleashed after 9/11.[79] Alterglobalism defies both, but does not simply define itself negatively. Its "alter" imperative weds globalization with values such as democracy, human rights, economic justice, and

---

in Ted Schrecker (ed.), *Surviving Globalism: The Social and Environmental Challenges* (Basingstoke, UK: Macmillan Press, 1997), p. 194 (pp. 177–98).

75 William Engdahl, *A Century of War: Anglo-American Oil Politics and the New World Order* (Ann Arbor, MI: Pluto Press, 1992, revised edition), p. 230.

76 William H. Thornton, *Fire on the Rim: The Cultural Dynamics of East/West Power Politics* (Lanham, MD: Rowman & Littlefield, 2002), pp. 196–7.

77 One of the driving forces behind alterglobalism is the emergence of the G-20 as a major player in trade negotiations. Since Cancún, the US has attempted to undermine G-20 solidarity by shifting to a strategy of "divide-and-rule": selectively including a few developing countries such as Brazil and India at the global bargaining table. See Walden Bello and Aileen Kwa, "G-20 Leaders Succumb to Divide-and-Rule Tactics: The Story behind Washington's Triumph in Geneva," *TNI (Transnational Institute: Beyond the WTO) Publications*, originally from *Focus on the Global South* (August 10, 2004), http://www.tni.org/archives/bello/geneva.htm.

78 Barbara Epstein, "Anarchism and the Anti-Globalization Movement," *Monthly Review* (September 2001), http://www.findarticles.com/cf_dls/m1132/4_53/784131381print.jhtml. Concerning the alter-globalist distinction between the neoliberal ideology of globalism and the historical process of globalization, see Benjamin Ardin, "From Globalism to Globalization: The Politics of Resistance," *New Political Science*, Vol. 26, No. 1 (March 2004), p. 10 (pp. 5–22).

79 Mark Engler, a commentator for *Foreign Policy in Focus*, holds that there is a complete disjunction between Clinton's neoliberal corporatism and Bush's corporate imperialism. Our position, by contrast, is that these disparate globalisms have effectively merged in a post-9/11 "neoglobalism." See Mark Engler, "Are the War and Globalization Really Connected?," *Foreign Policy in Focus* (October 18, 2004), http://www.fpif.org/papers/0410warglob.html; and William H. Thornton, *New World Empire: Civil Islam, Terrorism and the Making of Neoglobalism* (Lanham, MD: Rowman & Littlefield, 2005).

environmental protection.[80] Most especially it combats TINA with TAMA: the recognition that "there are *many* alternatives." This gets us beyond the orthodox Left as well as the globalist Right.[81]

One prototype for this new direction was the UN's Brundtland Report (*Our Common Future*, 1987), which challenged the prevailing economic paradigm by stressing that developmental and environmental issues are inseparable: It is "futile to attempt to deal with environmental problems without a broader perspective that encompasses the factors underlying world poverty and international inequality."[82] Sustainable development is here defined as meeting the needs of the present without hampering the ability of future generations to meet their needs.[83] By its very nature this focus on intergenerational equity is "global" in scope,[84] demanding fair exchange between nations as well as sustainable ecosystems.[85]

Alterglobalization likewise invites an "alter" Third Way. The better known Third Way of Blair and Giddens fame acknowledges many problems of current globalization yet never breaks out of the neoliberal orbit. Operating in the shadow of TINA, such dubious reformism at best rises to the level of what Robert Cox has called "problem solving" as opposed to more robust "critique."[86] Ultimately, though, it serves as an ideological prop, perpetuating the economic and political order it purports to criticize.

The task of genuine critique must be taken up by less "centered" groups such as the World Development Movement (WDM), a British organization with affiliates around the world. Athough WDM does not demand the abolition of major globalist organizations, it urges the WTO to promote trade policies that are fair, transparent and democratic.[87] This would mean revamping policies that intensify global inequality and consistently favor TNCs. The TNC agenda has long since moved beyond tariff reduction to a far more ambitious program of political control. Under

---

80 "Alter-globalization," *Wikipedia: The Free Encyclopedia* (downloaded on August 13, 2004), http://en2. wikipedia.org/wiki/Alterglobalization.

81 Massimo De Angelis, "'There Are Many Alternatives!' versus 'There Is No Alternative!,'" *The Commoner*, No. 8 (Autumn/Winter 2004), http://www.commoner.org. uk/tinavstama.htm.

82 See W.M. Adams, *Green Development: environment and sustainability in the third world* (London: Routledge, 1990), p. 58.

83 Matthew A. Cole, *Trade Liberalization, Economic Growth and the Environment* (Cheltenham, UK: Edward Elgar, 2000), pp. 51–52.

84 See Tables 3.3 and 3.4 of the Brundtland Report for the concepts and requirements of sustainable development in Adams, *op. cit.*, pp. 60 and 62.

85 Adams, *op. cit.*, p. 61.

86 See Stephen Hodben and Richard Wyn Jones, "Marxist Theories of International Relations," in John Baylis and Steve Smith (eds), *The Globalization of World Politics: An Introduction to International Relations* (Oxford: Oxford University Press, second edition, 2001), p. 212 (pp. 200–23).

87 "The WTO in Cancun," *The World Development Movement*, http://www.wdm.org. uk/campaign/cancun03/cancunfacts.htm.

this regimen poor nations are shorn of the autonomous policy choices that constitute their economic sovereignty.[88]

As TNCs vastly extend their size and global reach, corporations such as IBM, Microsoft, Dow Chemical, Nestlé, Toyota, and Coca-Cola easily earn more than half their revenues outside their home countries.[89] That makes their power greater than many poor countries. By the late 1990s global communications corporations such as Disney/ABC, Microsoft, IBM, Apple, AOL-Time Warner, Bell Atlantic and AT&T controlled more than $5 trillion in assets,[90] while the world's three richest men commanded more wealth than the 48 poorest countries combined.[91] These economic behemoths operate at the expense of democratic development, and ultimately at the expense of material development as well, insofar as bad government hampers growth as well as freedom.

As this becomes common knowledge, the Washington Consensus suffers a stupendous crisis of legitimacy. The result is a "soft power" vacuum that cannot be repaired by the token Third Way that globalists have applied like a band-aid to a patient needing intensive care. Cancún and its ideological affiliates, such as the World Social Forum, have at best provided an accurate diagnosis of the malady.[92] What is sorely needed is the new Third Way that is rising out of the ashes of Third World non-alignment. Unfortunately there is also a new Second World and a concomitant "Second Way," which is the very antithesis of Amartya Sen's "development as freedom." The most flagrant case in point is Russia's Putinism, which is worse than Sino-globalization in that it subverts democracy from within. It won popularity by challenging IMF-directed neoliberalism while at the same time turning the pro forma apparatus of democracy against democratic values.

By comparison, the Chinese Communist Party (CCP) can be seen as brutally honest, in that it makes no pretense about its anti-democratic animus. Only its Western corporate sponsors still insist that it is marching towards democracy. This has been a long march, as Mao himself claimed to be a proto-democrat prior to his full seizure of power, and a host of Western analysts followed Edgar Snow in taking the bait.[93] The China model's major attraction for the world's autocratic regimes is precisely that it promises economic growth with no democratic strings attached. This perverse form of

---

88 See William Greider, "Why the WTO Is Going Nowhere," *The Nation* (September 22, 2003), http://www.thenation.com/docprint.mhtml?I=20030922&s=greider.

89 Leslie Sklair, *Globalization: Capitalism and Its Alternatives* (Oxford: Oxford University Press, third edition, 2002), p. 36.

90 Songok Han Thornton, "Let Them Eat IT: The Myth of the Global Village as an Interactive Utopia," *CTheory* (January 17, 2002), A103, http://www.ctheory.net/text_file. asp?pick=327.

91 "About WDM," *The World Development Movement* (downloaded on August 13, 2004), http://www. wdm.org.uk/about/index.htm.

92 Anthony Barnett wryly notes that even the World Economic Forum (WEF) is better than the WSF when it comes to policy questions on vital issues such as global warming. See Anthony Barnett, "The Three Faces of the World Social Forum," *Red Pepper* (February 2007), http://www.redpepper.org.uk/x-feb-07-barnett.htm

93 In his last book, *The Long Revolution*, Snow recognized the danger of his long delusion that Chinese communism was marching toward agrarian democracy.

alterglobalism is all the more streamlined for not being encumbered by the quasi-liberal baggage that neighboring Asian tigers must carry. Likewise, terrorist organizations such as Al Qaeda can be described as alterglobalist rather than antiglobalist insofar as their funding and tactics have a global reach.[94] What is fast emerging is a new "war of the worlds" whereby First World neoglobalism (the newly militarized Washington Consensus)[95] confronts not only global NGOs such as Al Qaeda but a rising host of Second World globalisms such as Putinism and the Beijing Consensus. These reactionary alterglobalisms are abetted by the stigma Bush II has given democratic development. His unilateralist innovations—pre-emptive warfare, "extraordinary renditions" (i.e., kidnappings), imprisonment without trial, and barely disguised torture—are neoconservative gifts to the cause of Second World resurgence.

Clearly democratic values are under siege in the First World as well as the Second. The best hope for reform was raised on the Pacific Rim after the Asian Crash. Given the fact that this region was the unchallenged lead goose of the developing world, the global stakes were high, and the cost of failure would be all the more lamentable. Even before the Crash, Kim Dae Jung saw democratic reform as a pan-Asian trend.[96] That was before he traded in Korean social democratization for IMF restructuration. Thailand and other Rim nations did the same, leaving no doubt that most Asian leaders were perfectly willing to sacrifice freedom for GDP gains.

The Beijing Consensus, accordingly, has met little ideological resistance from ASEAN ranks. It must be asked if this tilt toward reactionary globalization on the part of Asian elites is representative of Asians in general. If so, Anwar Ibraham's hopes for an "Asian Renaissance" are entirely misplaced, and Amartya Sen's "Eastern Strategy" is utterly utopian. After post-Crash idealism in Thailand gave way to Thaksinocracy, and that in turn gave way to an even more overt autocracy, it must be asked if this is the harbinger of a new set of pan-Asian values. The coup that ousted Thaksin only extended the authoritarian power he had amassed with very little censure from the West. Even India, the home base of Senism, seems to be sliding in this same direction, whereby global capitalism strikes a deal with militant nationalism.

The question is what went wrong with Asian political development, and can the problem be rectified? Ten years after the Asian Crash, commercial prosperity has returned to much of the Rim, but the "miracle" has not, because a miracle by definition

---

94 It enjoys at least tacit support from many non-Muslims on the grounds that the enemy of my enemy is my friend. Christopher Hitchens deplores such pro-Islamism in his former colleagues on the Left. But the same globalizing impulse can be seen in Western anti-Islamism. Olivier Roy faults Bush's global war on terror (WOT) for conflating disparate issues such as the Palestinian crisis and the Iraq quagmire, which have little intrinsic connection and should be dealt with separately and locally. See Christopher Hitchens, "A Man with a Score to Settle," a review of *What's Left? How the Liberals Lost Their Way* by Nick Cohen, *Times Online* (January 21, 2007), http://www.timesonline.co.uk/printFriendly/0,,1-534-2550492-534,00. html.; and Olivier Roy, "De-Globalize the Jihad," *New Perspectives Quarterly (NPQ)*, Vol. 23, No. 4 (Fall 2006), http://www.digitalnpq.org/archieve/2006_fall/02_roy.html.

95 Thornton, *New World Empire, op. cit.*, p. 49.

96 Kim Dae-jung, "A Response to Lee Kuan Yew: Is Culture Destiny? The Myth of Asia's Anti-Democratic Values," *Foreign Affairs*, Vol. 73, No. 6 (November/December 1994), http://www. idep.org/conference/program/participants/Kim_Dae-jung/culture.htm.

must be exceptional. For better or worse, the Asian development experience is now subject to the same global forces that hold Latin America and Africa in thrall. This will be for the better if Senian "development as freedom" finds a base camp here, but for the worse if Sino-globalization becomes the regional norm. Either way, Asian exceptionalism is defunct. For that very reason what happens here matters more than ever, since it signals the likely future of the whole Third World.

Chapter 2

Korean Social Democratization: A Good Idea While it Lasted

The "Miracle" Revisited

Our search for an alternative Asian globalization must begin with the question of what went wrong with the development model that for two decades passed itself off as the "Asian miracle." Our answer is that it followed too closely in Japan's footsteps, such that political development was strictly subordinated to economic growth. After the Pacific War, when Japan showed signs of once again taking democracy seriously, America hit the brakes. A truly popular vote was too risky a proposition in a country where the Left stood a chance of winning political ground.

The resulting "reverse course" of 1947 and the Yoshida plan of 1953 set a precedent for American anti-democratization the world over. As will be covered in Chapter 9, the clipped-wing democracy that survived these machinations was basically a deal struck between the American hegemon and Japan's power elite. The latter would surrender not only real democracy but genuine national sovereignty in return for America's security blanket. In the bargain, Japan got an economic free ride, including a vast export outlet and freedom from the burden of full-scale military expenses. Though its neighbors would not get such a munificent deal on the military side, they reaped many of the same economic benefits. Thus was born the growth formula, premised on putative "Asian values," that would set the pace for the whole developing world. Meaningful democracy would be its first casualty. This was the grand opening of today's "development without freedom."

Among the new Asian tigers, the fastest growing cub was the military-industrial state of South Korea. What will concern us in this chapter, from a Senian vantage, is Korea's second miracle: its democratic revolution of the late 1980s. It had not been the least bit obvious in the early 1980s that such an event was imminent. Even Korea's capitalist elite had not gained much freedom as a result of its astounding achievement. Korea, Inc. was promoted insofar as it served the state, and was never allowed to forget that it was the junior partner in the government/corporate symbiosis.

Throughout the "miracle" years all Korean companies, including the giant chaebols, remained subject to policy direction and financial discipline by the presidential Blue House.[1] When Korean officials planned new projects, they forcefully extracted donations from corporations. Chung Ju Yong, Hyundai's founder, admitted

---

1 Walden Bello and Stephanie Rosenfeld, *Dragons in Distress: Asia's Miracle Economies in Crisis* (San Francisco, CA: Food First Book, 1990), p. 47; and Stephan Haggard, *The*

that he personally handed political bribes to the Park, Chun and Roh regimes in the amounts of 1 billion, 5 billion and 10 billion *won*, respectively.[2] For their very survival business executives had to master the arts of political entrepreneurship. That meant placating the military elites who had dominated Korea's social hierarchy since the military coup of May 1961. This military paramountcy, comparable in many ways to Indonesia's, made Japan, Inc. look almost democratic by comparison. No one in South Korea dared to question Park Chung Hee, the man at the top of the military-industrial pyramid.

Favoring economic growth at all costs, Park had adopted an outward-looking strategy for export-oriented industrialization.[3] What made this possible was Korea's geopolitical indispensability. The resulting neo-mercantilist development model was primed not only by massive US grants-in-aid in the 1950s, but by America's continued willingness to open its market to a flood of Korean imports.[4] Thus the Korean "miracle" was anything but, and it must be asked if the Korean pattern of development has been too dependent on outside factors, or on the unique circumstances of its time and place, to have much value as a general development model.[5]

After all, copious US aid and loans funded 70 percent of Korea's imports and 80 percent of its domestic capital between 1952–62.[6] When US military aid and spending in support of US troops is included, total US outlays were up to $1 billion annually by the late 1950s, with tens of millions more provided by NGOs such as the Ford Foundation.[7] Even in the mid-sixties this capital influx covered more than 50 percent of Korea's total capital. From the early 1960s to 1979 aid accounted for more than 30 percent of the annual GDCF.[8] The geopolitical motive behind this infusion needs far greater attention than it has received. Gains from Korea's involvement in Vietnam between 1965 and 1969 brought in an estimated $546 million, and that figure is no doubt understated.[9] This input was crucial in molding the second Five-Year Plan

---

Political Economy of the Asian Financial Crisis (Washington, DC: Institute for International Economics, 2000), p. 20.

2 David C. Kang, *Crony Capitalism: Corruption and Development in South Korea and the Philippines* (Cambridge: Cambridge University Press, 2002), p. 163.

3 Gerald Caiden and Yong-Duck Jung, "The Political Economy of Korean Development under the Park Government," in Changsoo Lee (ed.), *Modernization of Korea and the Impact of the West* (Los Angeles: East Asian Studies, University of Southern California, 1981), pp. 303–4 (pp. 285–310).

4 See Lee Chan-Keun, "Korean Economy in Era of Globalization," *Korea Focus*, Vol. 7, No. 2 (March/April, 1999), p. 92 (pp. 86–98).

5 See Dilip K. Das, *Korean Economic Dynamism* (London: Macmillan, 1992), p. 185.

6 Peter F. Bell, "Development or Maldevelopment?: The Contradictions of Thailand's Economic Growth," in Michael J.G. Parnwell (ed.), *Uneven Development in Thailand* (Aldershot, UK: Avebury, 1996), p. 57 (pp. 49–62).

7 David Ekbladh, "How to Build a Nation," *The Wilson Quarterly* (Winter 2004), http://wwics.si.edu/index.cfm?fuseaction=wq.print&essay_id=87163&stoplayout=true.

8 Hyun-Chin Lim, *Dependent Development in Korea, 1963–1979* (Seoul: Seoul National University Press, 1985), pp. 92–3.

9 Kang, *op. cit.*, pp. 38–39. During the Vietnam War, Korea exported 94 percent of its steel, machinery and chemicals through US contracts. See Ekbladh, *op. cit.*

of 1967–71. Such highly dependent development resulted in a triple alliance of the Korean state, local business and foreign (especially US) capital.[10]

That exogenous factor did not, however, "internationalize" the Korean economy in any neoliberal sense of the word. On the contrary, within a year of his rise to power Park had nationalized five major banks. Not until the Asian Crash of 1997–8 would this financial absolutism—the very heart of the Korean growth model—be seriously questioned. Nor did Park's iron grip on the private sector deter foreign banks from funneling billions of dollars into Korean enterprises. Blue House priorities supplied the economic stability these lenders sought.

Many have concluded that this nationalist structure was the key factor in the Korean "miracle," as if Cold War geopolitics had nothing to do with it. The World Bank, for example, endorsed this statist perspective in its adulatory 1993 report, *East Asian Miracle*. Manuel Castells sets the record straight. While avoiding the Leftist term "puppets," he calls Korean and the other Asian tigers "vassal states," in recognition of their distinctive statist autonomy within the context of geopolitical dependency.[11]

It is ironic that Park's regime, with its pronounced socialist structure, was widely regarded as a bastion against communism. His social and political model was drawn in large part from a Japanese Marxist, Takahashi Kamekici, who had been influential in the 1920s and 1930s. Despite the West's endless criticism of crony capitalism after the Asian Crash, the Korean "miracle" was built on more of a crony socialism: an illiberal bond between government, business, and banks.[12] Mark Clifford exaggerates the difference between Korea and Japan where the politicization of business is concerned,[13] but is correct in his crucial observation concerning Korea's social militarization. The postcolonial Korean state was born without a distinct capitalist class, or even a developed business class. Consequently the Korean government looked to the military—which grew from 100,000 in 1950 to 600,000 in 1961—for its managerial needs.[14] In the postwar years this highly illiberal

---

10 Suk Joon Kim, "Crisis, Regime Change, and Development: A Quantitative Analysis of South Korean Political Transformation, 1945–1987," in Gerald E. Caiden and Bun Woong Kim (eds), *A Dragon's Progress: Development Administration in Korea* (West Hartford, Connecticut: Kumarian Press, 1999), pp. 59–60 (pp. 58–66).

11 Manuel Castells, *End of Millennium* (Oxford, UK: Blackwell, 1998), p. 283.

12 Regarding the selective and highly preferential allocation of government funds and materials, see Yeon-ho Lee, *The State, Society and Big Business in Korea* (London, Routledge, 1997), p. 23.

13 See Mark L. Clifford, *Troubled Tiger: Businessmen, Bureaucrats, and Generals in South Korea* (Armonk, NY: An East Gate Book/M.E. Sharpe, revised edition, 1998), p. 63; and in support of our position see T.W. Kang, who notes the similarity between Japan and Korea with regard to economic planning, export-oriented developmental strategies, and conglomerate-dominated industries. He contrasts this approach with Taiwan's emphasis on SMEs (small and medium size enterprises). See his *Is Korea the Next Japan?: Understanding the Structure, Strategy, and Tactics of America's Next competitor* (New York: The Free Press, 1989), pp. 23 and 26–38.

14 Clifford, *op. cit.*, p. 64; and Carter J. Eckert, "The South Korean Bourgeoisie: A Class in Search of Hegemony," in Hagen Koo (ed.), *State and Society in Contemporary Korea*

system was buttressed by massive foreign aid and military support,[15] and during the 1970s and 1980s by foreign loans.[16] In effect the US ended up supporting the Blue House,[17] thereby entrenching the military power structure of this rising tiger.

In an effort to secure some measure of self-sufficiency, Park made energy and steel the core of his modernization drive.[18] He established the Korea Electric Power Company (KEPCO), and in a radical departure from economic common knowledge he decided to build a world class steel mill, the Pohang Iron and Steel Corporation (POSCO) in the early 1970s. Such compressed modernization—with development centered around a few big businesses[19]—was a product of the nation's military-economic organization rather than any accepted economic logic. South Korean technocrats and international experts agreed that Korea had no comparative advantage in iron and steel production. The World Bank was therefore reluctant to fund the project. One technocrat, Park Tae Joon, turned to Japan for funds and got approval for $500 million in grants and loans. So it was that the little fishing village of Pohang became the world's largest production site by the mid-1980s.[20]

Taking an "in it but not of it" approach to the international market, the government aimed at a measure of domestic "self-reliance"—a milder version, one could argue, of North Korea's *ju-che* philosophy. Rising dependence on Heavy and Chemical Industries (HCI) entrenched the dominance of the chaebols in the Korean economy, but also laid the foundation for periodic crises.[21] So too it distinguished Korea from other Asian tigers such as Hong Kong, Singapore, and Taiwan. This plan, which was implemented directly from the Blue House in 1973,[22] had the double effect of consolidating domestic power even as it subordinated that power to foreign capital. The HCI drive was accelerated after the Carter administration announced a never

---

(Ithaca: Cornell University Press, 1993), pp. 108 and 129 (pp. 95–130).

15 Castells, *op. cit.*, p. 255.

16 Meredith Woo-Cumings, "The State, Democracy, and the Reform of the Corporate Sector in Korea," in T.J. Pempel (ed.), *The Politics of Asian Economic Crisis* (Ithaca: Cornell University Press, 1999), p. 120 (pp. 116–42).

17 See Hong Nack Kim, "The 1987 Political Crisis and its Implication for U.S.-Korean Relations," in Ilpyong J. Kim and Young Whan Kihl (eds), *Political Change in South Korea* (New York: The Korean PWPA, Inc. 1988), p. 222 (pp. 221–41).

18 Donald Stone Macdonald, *The Koreans: Contemporary Politics and Society*, third edition, edited and revised by Donald N. Clark (Boulder, CO: Westview Press, 1996), pp. 208–9. Both KEPCO and POSCO were listed in the 1995 Fortune 500.

19 See Kim Cul-Kyoo, "Impact of Korea's Economic Development on Social Conditions," *Korea Focus*, Vol. 12, No. 3 (May/June 2004), p. 115 (pp. 114–31).

20 Walden Bello, Shea Cunningham and Bill Rau, *Dark Victory: The United States and Global Poverty* (London: Pluto Press, new edition, 1999), p. 73.

21 Gregory W. Noble and John Ravenhill, "The Good, the Bad and the Ugly? Korea, Taiwan and the Asian Financial Crisis," in Gregory W. Noble and John Ravenhill (eds), *The Asian Financial Crisis and the Architecture of Global Finance* (Cambridge: Cambridge University Press, 2000), p. 84 (pp. 80–107).

22 As outlined in the *Declaration of Heavy and Chemical Industrialization*, see Joseph J. Stern, Ji-hong Kim, Dwight H. Perkins, and Jung-ho Yoo, *Industrialization and the State: The Korean Heavy and Chemical Industry Drive* (Cambridge, MA: Harvard Institute for International Development, 1995), p. 17; also see Bello and Rosenfeld, *op. cit.*, pp. 56–57.

implemented plan to completely withdraw American troops from Korea.[23] Between 1977 and 1979 some 80 percent of manufacturing investment went to heavy industry, stoked by massive foreign loans. This inflated foreign debt from $2.2 billion in 1970 to $27.1 billion in 1980.[24]

Undeniably the HCI plan and the Yushin ("revitalizing") Constitution molded Korea's economic takeoff. One should recognize, however, that political development was obstructed by the Yushin Constitution's prohibition against any kind of criticism. This blueprint for militaristic economism was drawn up in the 1970s by a small circle of technocrats such as Park's economic advisor, Kim Chong Yom, and his military-political advisor, Lee Hu Rak. Mark Clifford believes this system well served Korea throughout the 1970s. But the high growth of that decade resulted mainly from an influx of new capital and labor, and a high price was paid for that infusion. In the late 1970s investment was increasingly funneled into five industries: electronics, capital goods, transport equipment, textiles and clothing, and basic chemicals.[25] Korea's development of heavy industry in the 1970s was largely based on external borrowing that by 1982 had put Korea on the IMF's list of the 20 most heavily-indebted countries.[26]

Enter the Technocrats

Those growth-at-all-costs priorities were set by the Blue House, whose relationship with the technocrats had been rocky since the 1960s. Park despised these made-in-America experts, who advocated a textbook approach to comparative advantage through cheap labor and labor-intensive industry. In turn, most technocrats viewed Park's HCI plan as foolish. Park trumped all criticism by using the North Korean threat as an excuse for his economic gigantism. By the end of the 1970s the country was paying the price in terms of overinvestment and chaebol overcapacity.[27] The technocrats, however, were powerless to implement their own ideas.

That changed after Park's assassination in 1979. President Chun Doo Hwan was in such desperate need of legitimacy, especially after the May 1980 Kwangju massacre,[28] that he gave the technocrats almost full control over economic affairs.

---

23 Joon-Kyung Kim, Sang Dal Shim and Jun-Il Kim, "The Role of the Government in Promoting Industrialization and Human Capital Accumulation in Korea," in Takatoshi Ito and Anne O. Krueger (eds), *Growth Theories in Light of the East Asian Experience* (Chicago: The University of Chicago Press, 1995), p. 186 (pp. 181–96).

24 Bello and Rosenfeld, *op. cit.*, p. 58.

25 Wolfgang Hillebrand, *Shaping Competitive Advantages: Conceptual Framework and the Korean Approach* (London: Frank Cass, 1996), pp. 155 and 157–59.

26 Robert Solomon, *The Transformation of the World Economy* (Basingstoke, UK: Macmillan Press, second edition, 1999), p. 142.

27 Jong-Chan Rhee, *The State and Industry in South Korea: The Limits of the Authoritarian State* (London: Routlege, 1994), pp. 60 and 81.

28 For details of the May 1980 Kwangju incident, see James Fenton, "The Heroes of Kwangju," *The New York Review of Books* (February 22, 2001), http://www.nybooks.com/nyrev/wwwarchdisplay.cgi? 20010222026R.

They wasted no time in consolidating their leadership.[29] In the early 1980s, Kim Jae Ik's Economic Planning Board (EPB)[30] set the tone for economic development by reducing government deficits, limiting monetary growth, and slowing wage increases. These policies would lead to government budget surpluses by the late 1980s. But they also led to a triangular power struggle between the Blue House, the chaebols and the technocrats. In the early and mid-1980s, the chaebols saw the possibility of acquiring influence over the financial system through local and regional commercial banks that were undergoing IMF-directed structural adjustment. But the technocrats also tried to seize power in their own right, as the government-chaebol alliance was weakened. By no means were these proto-globalists simple puppets of the IMF. They used it as surely as it used them. All the while, as an ardent advocate of free market restructuration, Kim Jae Ik earned enemies among the chaebols. His neoliberal agenda was cut short when he was killed by North Korean saboteurs in the Rangoon bombing of 1983.

Unlike Park's "bonapartist" vision of Korea, Inc., the government took on more of a "regulator" function under Chun. Lacking the power to tame the chaebols through personal fiat, Chun resorted to the device of credit control under the rubric of free market competition.[31] Part of the 1980s reform agenda was massive corporate restructuring to eliminate noncompetitive and overlapping businesses. This brought the era of full employment to an end, and reversed the trend toward urbanization. Masan, an industrial city created under Park, experienced a population drop of 26,000 as workers returned to the countryside.[32] GNP was down 5.2 percent by the end of 1980.[33]

---

29 Late in 1979 and early in 1980 the technocrats raised bank interest rates from 19 percent to 25 percent, putting great strain on businesses that depended on cheap loans. So too they devalued the *won* by 20 percent—the first devaluation since 1975. Then Deputy Prime Minister Lee Hahn Been and his economic advisors decided to let the *won* float. This mixture of floating exchange rates and increased interest rates was a hard blow to borrowers, who could no longer count on inflation to assist them with their loan repayments. Obviously this was a risky departure. Recession might have followed, given the second oil crisis and the political instability attending Park's assassination. 1980 brought a negative real growth rate of 3.7 percent, but devaluation helped to keep the export economy afloat, and Hyundai's exports doubled that year. See Clifford, *op. cit.*, p. 174; and Jong-Chan Rhee, *op. cit.*, p. 134.; and Chong-Hyun Nam, "The Role of Trade and Exchange Rate Policy in Korea's Growth," in Takatoshi Ito and Anne O. Krueger (eds), *Growth Theories in Light of the East Asian Experience* (Chicago: The University of Chicago Press, 1995), p. 158 (pp. 153–77).

30 Under President Kim Young Sam, the EPB was merged with the Finance Ministry in 1994 to establish a new Board of Finance and Economics (BFE). See Macdonald, *op. cit.*, p. 205.

31 Yeon-ho Lee, *The State, Society, and Big Business in South Korea* (London: Routledge, 1997), pp. 1 and 202.

32 Clifford, *op. cit.*, p. 189.

33 More positively, inflation fell from 29 percent in 1980 to 7 percent in 1982 and finally to 3 percent in 1983. The government announced an import liberalization plan for the 1983 to 1988 period, forcing chaebols into a more competitive environment. Increasingly they were compelled to justify their existence. The Kukje Group, Korea's sixth largest, was entirely dismantled in 1985, which sent a strong message to the business community that no chaebol was exempt from reform. Only aggressive lobbying by Daewoo's chairman, Kim

Three economic issues of the 1980s profoundly affected policy-making: income inequality, the chaebol problem, and external public debt.[34] Foreign debt had doubled between 1980 and 1984, making South Korea the fourth largest foreign borrower after Argentina, Brazil, and Mexico. Korea's solution was more of the same, leaving the problem unresolved. A combination of low corporate profits and high capital investment required huge external financing, which drove corporate leverage (total debt over equity) to far higher levels than any country in the world from 1988 to 1996, the peak of the so-called miracle years. As interest rates shot up in late 1997, 40 percent of Korean firms found themselves not only illiquid, but insolvent.[35] Heavy dependence on short-term foreign debt left Korea vulnerable to currency fluctuations, dollar interest rate changes, export slowdowns, and other shifts in the global market. All these factors would surface volcanically in the Crash of 1997.[36]

Although the debt crisis was temporarily alleviated after the 1985 economic recovery, this simply camouflaged the underlying defects of technocratic development. The ensuing economic boom kept those defects out of view for years to come. Between 1986 and 1988, the economy grew at an unprecedented 12 percent a year for three consecutive years.[37] It is telling that in 1989 the Korean stock exchange raised more equity than the New York stock exchange, making for a capital reserves bonanza.

This only aggravated the structural flaws of a chaebol-dominated financial system. Debt-led expansion and a "bigger is better" mentality are nothing new, but this time the state was unable to constrain the business sector. Later charges of crony capitalism papered over the fact that critics had long kept their silence on this and other unsavory aspects of the "miracle" economy. They had been perfectly aware of

---

Woo Choong, saved Daewoo from the same fate. Meanwhile Chun launched a policy to revive SMEs, which had been systematically starved of credit under Park. See Clifford, *op. cit.*, pp. 206 and 224; C.H. Nam, *op. cit.*, p. 158; and Bello and Rosenfeld, *op. cit.*, p. 72.

34 Hang Yul Rhee, "The Economic Problems of the Korean Political Economy," in Ilpyong J. Kim and Young Whan Kihl (eds), *Political Change in South Korea* (New York: The Korean PWPA, Inc., 1988), pp. 191–216 (pp. 189–220).

35 Woo-Cumings, *op. cit.*, p. 123.

36 The problem of short-term debt reached a crisis stage when foreign banks refused to roll over their short-term loans. See Joseph E. Stiglitz, *Globalization and Its Discontents* (New York: W.W. Norton, 2002), p. 110.

37 This was due in part to the 1985 Plaza Accord, which devalued the dollar against the yen. Being loosely pegged with the dollar, Korea became more competitive in the global market. Exports to the US doubled between 1985 and 1988, rising from $10.8 billion in 1985 to $21.4 billion in 1988. With a current account surplus reaching nearly 8 percent of GDP in 1988, the government was forced to remove the controls on capital flows which had kept a brake on foreign debts. Meanwhile low dollar interest rates encouraged the chaebols to borrow heavily from foreign banks, laying the foundation for the debt crisis that would trigger the Crash of 1997. As an alternative to heavy borrowing, the government turned to stock market investment, which contributed to soaring stock prices between 1986 and 1988. See Clifford, *op. cit.*, pp. 236 and 239–40; and Dongchul Cho, "Coping with Capital Flows and Monetary Policy Framework: The Case of Korea," in C.H. Kwan, Donna Vandenbrink and Chia Siow Yue (eds), *Coping with Capital Flow in East* Asia (Tokyo and Singapore: Nomura Research Institute and Institute of Southeast Asian Studies, 1998), p. 82 (pp. 79–110).

Korea's excessive dependence on foreign capital, and it was well known that just as chaebols were dominated by foreign capital, local SMEs (small and medium size enterprises) were exploited by the chaebols. By the late 1980s wage accretion and other cost factors compelled the chaebols to look for an alternative to the export-oriented system of the takeoff years. Increasingly they sought greener pastures in the cheap labor of Southeast Asia and the Caribbean, leaving Korean workers and SMEs behind.

Political Undevelopment

Frozen in its Parkian mode, the structure of the Korean economy underwent little basic reform in the 1980s. The economy grew quantitatively, but did not become more equitable. By no means was economic development the necessary and sufficient force behind Korea's political development, as myth has it. On the contrary, economism worked against social and political modernization.[38] This "growth first" excuse for political undevelopment could work only so long as the "miracle" lasted. The oil crisis of 1979 led to recession coupled with inflation, and an unprecedented spate of bankruptcies and strikes threw the Park regime off balance.

The Carter administration had quietly engineered a large release of dissidents, and now Kim Young Sam, leader of the opposition New Democratic Party, felt the time was right to openly blast the government. Predictably this brought out the worst in Park, whose actions inflamed the public even more. By the time of Park's assassination, his popularity had plummeted even within his own camp. American officials at his funeral noticed a conspicuous lack of grief among his former supporters.[39]

The military coup that brought Chun Doo Hwan to power gave the country a leader who was even less attuned to the need for political development than Park had been. Korea's new affluence stoked dissatisfaction in a growing middle class that was allowed little voice. This inclined it to favor the student and proletarian resistance that was mounting in the streets. To forestall this cross-class alliance, Chun belatedly expanded civilian participation in the government while reducing that of the military.[40] So too he promised more local autonomy.[41] Even then, however, Chun seriously underestimated the public's thirst for reform. The key to the June 1987

---

38 Harold Hakwon Sunoo, *America's Dilemma in Asia: The Case of South Korea* (Chicago: Nelson-Hall, 1979), pp. 131–2. Suk Joon Kim, likewise, emphasizes how economism contributed to Korea's political underdevelopment. See S.J. Kim, *op. cit.*, p. 58.

39 Don Oberdorfer, *The Two Koreas: A Contemporary History* (Reading, MA: Addison-Wesley, 1997), pp. 111–13.

40 C.I. Eugene Kim, "The South Korean Military and its Political Role," in Ilpyong J. Kim and Young Whan Kihl (eds), *Political Change in South Korea* (New York: The Korean PWPA, Inc., 1988), pp. 105–6 (pp. 91–112).

41 Yong Duck Jung, "The Territorial Dimension of the Developing Capitalist State: Measuring and Explaining Centralization in Korea," in Gerald E. Caiden and Bun Woong Kim (eds), *A Dragon's Progress: Development Administration in Korea* (West Hartford, Connecticut: Kumarian Press, 1991), p. 147 (pp. 147–60).

democratic revolution was the success of student and proletarian activists in gaining the backing of the disfranchised middle class.[42]

As Korea's first direct popular vote, the 1987 presidential election was an undeniable democratic milestone, while new constitutional revisions expanded the power of the legislature.[43] Given their close political relationship,[44] President Roh Tae Woo inherited Chun's legitimacy problem, as well as his dependence on military and intelligence bureaucracies.[45] By 1991 the Blue House was losing its grip on Korea, Inc. Roh found it necessary to relax popular pressure by giving more autonomy to local governments to elect their city and county representatives, and by liberalizing some national security laws.[46] This, however, was a case of too little, too late.

With growth falling behind expectations and unemployment rising, economic reform became the major issue in the 1992 presidential election. President Kim Young Sam promised to cure the "Korean disease" and create a "New Korea" of "clean politics" and "anti-corruption."[47] Nor did he entirely renege on his pledge. He struck a hard blow against high-level corruption by censuring, firing, or arresting more than a thousand officials in business and government.[48] He also called for full disclosure of the personal assets of politicians and high ranking civil servants,[49] backed with a "real name" rule for all financial transactions. Tax evasion would henceforth require some legal talent. And for added measure, former Presidents Roh and Chun were convicted and jailed for corruption.[50]

Unfortunately this political housecleaning left most of the furniture in place. Kim Young Sam's "reform" agenda turned out to be little more than a pressure-release mechanism. By leaving state-chaebol collusion untouched, Kim's administration

---

42 Wonmo Dong, "Student Activism and the Presidential Politics of 1987 in South Korea," in Ilpyong J. Kim and Young Whan Kihl (eds), *Political Change in South Korea* (New York: The Korean PWPA, Inc., 1988), pp. 176 and 178 (pp. 169–88).

43 Young Whan Kihl, "South Korea's Search for a New Order: An Overview," in Ilpyong J. Kim and Young Whan Kihl (eds), *Political Change in South Korea* (New York: the Korean PWPA, Inc., 1988), p. 7 (pp. 3–21).

44 Robert E. Bedeski, *The Transformation of South Korea: Reform and Reconstruction in the Sixth Republic under Roh Tae Woo, 1987–1992* (London: Routledge, 1992), pp. 27 and 39.

45 Young Whan Kihl and Ilpyong J. Kim, "The Sixth Republic: Problems, Prospects, and the 1988 Olympiad," in Ilpyong J. Kim and Young Whan Kihl (eds), *Political Change in South Korea* (New York: the Korean PWPA, Inc., 1988), p. 247 (pp. 243–51).

46 Macdonald, *op. cit.*, p. 124; and Bedeski, *op. cit.*, p. 41.

47 James Cotton, "Introduction," in James Cotton (ed.), *Politics and Policy in the New Korean State: from Roh Tae-Woo to Kim Young-Sam* (New York: St. Martin's Press, 1995), pp. 1–2 (pp. 1–5).

48 William H. Thornton, *Fire on the Rim: The Cultural Dynamics of East/West Power Politics* (Lanham, MD: Rowman & Littlefield, 2002), p. 105.

49 Bae Sun-Kwang, "Continuity or Change: The Voter's Choice in the 1992 Presidential Election," in James Cotton (ed.), *Politics and Policy in the New Korean State: from Roh Tae-Woo to Kim Young-Sam* (New York: St. Martin's Press, 1995), p. 78 (pp. 66–82).

50 Geir Helgesen, *Democracy and Authority in Korea: The Cultural Dimension in Korean Politics* (Surrey, UK: Curzon Press, 1998), p. 247.

preserved the corporate status quo.[51] Moreover, by merging the Economic Planning Board with the Ministry of Finance in 1993, the government forfeited its coordinating role, thereby setting the stage for corporate overinvestment. Though the chaebols were pressed to designate core businesses and eliminate non-performing ones, this was anything but a constraint on corporatism. On the contrary, credit controls and regulations were dangerously curtailed, and in his last year Kim pushed through new labor laws to make mass layoffs possible.[52] This was in early 1997, long before the IMF would mandate such measures in response to the Crash. The IMF would simply be used as an excuse to complete the corporate takeover that was already in progress.

More in the way of progressive reform was expected from Kim Dae Jung. His activist past lent credibility to his pledge to dissolve the triad of government, big business, and banking. The Crash he inherited certainly limited the scope of his fiscal opportunity, but it also weakened the corporate power base he would have to contend with to effect egalitarian reforms. He appeared to be challenging this power structure when Korean Airlines (KAL) chairman Cho Yang Ho was arrested on charges of tax evasion and embezzlement. The cardinal fact, however, was that Cho had not supported Kim. It happened that Asiana Airlines, the rival of KAL, had its origin in the Cholla region, Kim's home turf.[53] As with the former Kim, the thrust of Kim Dae Jung's so-called "reform" policy would move in the opposite direction: toward a *stronger* bond between government and post-Crash business.[54] Kim was in fact a consummate politician from the old school, with no qualms about cutting deals with the extant power structure.[55] Even without the financial crisis this would have disabled any reformism worthy of the name.

The underlying corporatism of the two Kims formed a seamless continuity. The Crash and subsequent IMFism provided perfect cover for unpopular measures such as downsizing. Corporatism was being streamlined, not buffered. The illiberal alliance that was President Park's legacy reached its apogee of corruption and corporate largess in the mid-1990s, as total external debt increased from $43.8 billion in 1993 to nearly $162 billion by late 1997.[56] Park's statist capitalism was a Cold

---

51 Barry K. Gills and Dong-Sook S. Gills, "South Korea and Globalization: the Rise to Globalism?," in Samuel S. Kim (ed.), *East Asia and Globalization* (Lanham, MD: Rowman & Littlefield, 2000), pp. 81–2 (pp. 81–103).

52 David McNally, "Globalization on Trial: Crisis and Struggle in East Asia," *Monthly Review* (September 1998), http://www.findarticles.com/cf_dls/m1132/n4_v50/21186772/print.jhtml.

53 Frank Ching, "Law of the Jungle," *The Far Eastern Economic Review* (March 30, 2000), p. 24 (pp. 24–25).

54 "Declaration of Present Situation in Korea," *Civil Society*, 35/45 (October – December 2001), provided by CCEJ News (Citizen's Coalition for Economic Justice), http://www.domos.or.kr/eng/ngos.html.

55 Sang-Hun Choe, "South Korean President to Quit Governing Party," *International Herald Tribune* (February 22, 2007), http://www.iht.com/bin/print.php?id=4690150.

56 Stephan Haggard and Andrew MacIntyre, "The Political Economy of the Asian Financial Crisis: Korea and Thailand Compared," in Gregory W. Noble and John Ravenhill (eds), *The Asian Financial Crisis and the Architecture of Global Finance* (Cambridge: Cambridge University Press, 2000), p. 26 (pp. 57–79); and also Gills and Gills, *op. cit.*, p. 86.

War vestige that could no longer be sustained. Its transformation by way of rapid financial liberalization set the stage for the Korean Crash, which only intensified corporate power under the name of "reform." In two decades the country had moved from Park's crony socialism to globalist crony capitalism.

The Crash was harbingered by the January 1997 bankruptcy of Hanbo, a chaebol specializing in steel and construction. Yet the speed and scope of the Crash took the nation by surprise. By September 1997, bankruptcies and loan defaults amounted to almost 8 percent of the nation's GDP,[57] and by October major chaebols were collapsing. Under these straits South Korea accepted a $60 billion IMF rescue package and began massive corporate restructuration, especially in the financial sector. In short, a problem that had been triggered by inordinate liberalization was to be cured by still more intensive liberalization. For instance, a new Foreign Investment Promotion Act was passed in November 1998, offering unprecedented incentives to foreign investors. Acting on the newly liberalized labor laws that he inherited from Kim Young Sam, Kim Dae Jung implemented massive layoffs that would have a lasting impact on the social and economic fabric of the country. This is how Kim repaid his debt to the working classes for their steadfast support in the streets and at the ballot box.

Efforts to raise profitability by rapidly downsizing and restructuring precipitated a social crisis.[58] It is remarkable that the government's indifference to the common worker did not provoke serious political instability, as was the case in Indonesia. Under cover of IMFism, Kim managed to implement radical trade and investment liberalization at little political cost. The resulting "fire sale"—which corporate buyers commonly referred to as their "Korea discount"[59]—left Korea's best known companies, such as Samsung and Posco, with over 50 percent of their stock owned abroad, while around 40 percent of the country's stock market capitalization was non-domestic. Such full-thrust liberalization had proved impossible when Korea first joined the OECD in 1996. It took the Crash and subsequent IMFism to fulfill this globalist dream.[60]

"Sunshine" Tactics

To divert public attention from volatile issues such as the economic fire sale and a near-bankrupt health care system, Kim turned increasingly to his "sunshine" policy with North Korea. On April 10, 2000—just days before the National Assembly election on April 13—Kim dropped the bombshell of his upcoming June 2000 summit with Kim

---

57 Castells, *op. cit.*, p. 289.

58 Ho Keun Song, "The Birth of a Welfare State in Korea: The Unfinished Symphony of Democratization and Globalization," *Journal of East Asian Studies*, No. 3 (2003), p. 405 (pp. 405–43).

59 Hasung Jang, "Significance of the 'Korean Discount,'" *Korea Focus*, Vol. 12, No. 6 (November/December 2004), p. 32 (pp. 32–34).

60 Philip Bowring, "Who Owns South Korea?," *The International Herald Tribune* (July 19, 2004), http://www.iht.com/bin/print.php?file=530020.html.

Jong Il of North Korea.[61] Clearly this revelation was designed to tip popularity ratings in his party's favor. Meanwhile the People's Solidarity for Participatory Democracy (PSPD), one of the most influential NGOs, joined other grassroots groups in expressing disappointment at the ruling party's neglect of real reform.[62] Eventually it became known that just before the historic summit, the government had slipped $186 million through Hyundai to the North.[63] What this purchased, at tax payers' expense, was a photo-session with Kim Jong Il and a Nobel Prize for Kim Dae Jung. The Summit briefly renewed Kim's popularity, but soon that began to wear off. By early 2001 his approval ratings had fallen below 30 percent.[64]

Kim's successor, Roh Moo Hyun, promised to continue the "sunshine" policy,[65] but its popular appeal had waned. To win the election he had to play his anti-American card.[66] Conversely, Roh's rival Lee Hoi Chang favored traditional containment and an end to financial aid to the North,[67] objectives that were associated with US priorities. It is fair to say that anti-Americanism won the election.[68]

---

61 Charles S. Lee, "Point of No Return," *The Far Eastern Economic Review* (April 20, 2000), p. 40 (pp. 40–41).

62 Michael Vatikiotis and Shim Jae Hoon, "People's Advocate," *The Far Eastern Economic Review* (March 23, 2000), p. 28.

63 Joseph Coleman, "S. Korean Leader Apologizes for Summit Scandal," *The Washington Post* (February 14, 2003), http://www.washingtonpost.com/ac2/wp-dyn/A6007-2003Feb14?language=primter.

64 John Larkin, "Kim Dae Jung Comes Up Short," *The Far Eastern Economic Review* (May 24, 2001), http://www.feer.com/_0105_24/p018region.html.

65 Howard W. French, "Liberal Wins South Korea's Presidential Election," *The New York Times* (December 19, 2002), http://www.nytimes.com/2002/12/19/international/19CND-KORE.html? pagewanted=print.

66 "The North and the Vote," *The Economist* (December 12, 2002), http://economist.com/world/asia/PrinterFriendly.cfm?Story_ID-1494971.

67 Caroline Gluck, "Korean Vote Swayed by Anti-US Mood," *BBC News* (December 11, 2002), http://news.bbc.co.uk/1/hi/world/asia-pacific/2562297.stm.; and also see "Anti-US Protests Grow in Seoul," *BBC News* (December 8, 2002), http://news.bbc.co.uk/1/low/world/asia-pacific/2552875.stm. Anti-Americanism and economic turmoil also brought Park Geun Hye, the daughter of Park Chung Hee, into politics. Like Indonesia's Megawati Sukarnoputri, Park's popularity was based purely on the nostalgia-effect of her father's name. See John Larkin, "Following in Father's Footsteps," *The Far Eastern Economic Review* (May 24, 2001), http://www.feer.com/_0105_24/p024region.htm. Older voters (over 40) tend to support the conservatism of her Grand National Party (GNP), whereas younger voters tend to be more liberal. This generational divide was a prominent factor in the public reaction to the impeachment of President Roh in March 2004. See James Brooke, "South Korean Conservatives Try to Regain Voter Confidence," *The New York Times* (April 4, 2004), http://www.nytimes.com/2004/04/04/international/asia/04KORE.html.

68 This sentiment, which had been building since the 1997 Crash, peaked when South Koreans found out that the Yongsan US military base had been dumping toxic chemicals into a river that was a main source of drinking water for 12 million Seoulites. Many were equally angry at the rising subsidies for US troops: from $314 million in 1998 to $444 million in 2001, with indirect subsidies reaching more than $700 million. See "South Korea, U.S., Sign Swap Deal," *Newmax Wires* (March 29, 2003), http://www. newmax.com/cgi-bin/print_friendly.pl?page=http://www.newsmax.com/arc...

Earlier disclosure of Kim's dealings might have put Lee in office. This would have terminated the sunshine policy, which violated the 1994 Agreed Framework and the 1991 inter-Korean Joint Declaration on the Denuclearization of the Korean Peninsula.[69] Six months after the election, Park Jie Won, Kim's closest advisor and a key player in setting up the 2000 Inter-Korean Summit, was arrested for bribery and the abuse of power. There would be allegations that Kim's government transferred much more to the North than was originally thought—perhaps as much as $500 million.[70] Suspicions were raised even further when the government refused to investigate the incident.[71]

Roh would be no improvement over Kim. This former labor lawyer and human rights activist soon forgot that his close victory in December 2002 owed much to the working classes and their unions. When his government announced its intention to privatize the railroad system, prompting strikes in four cities, Roh found himself at the same crossroads Kim had faced: the choice of serving faithful supporters or foreign investors. His real agenda was clarified when he declared the rail walkout illegal and threatened to fire striking workers.[72]

The one good thing that can be said about Roh's administrative style is that he failed to master the art of the imperial presidency. Unfortunately he put nothing of substance in its place. This dearth of leadership tainted what little was left of the social democratic ideals that had propelled liberal progressivism in its more insurgent phase. Ironically Roh's administration got a second wind after the conservative opposition failed miserably in its effort to impeach him. A sympathetic public tossed his nascent Uri Party a majority in the legislature as of April 2004, putting him in full parliamentary control. Not since the end of military rule in 1987 had any president had such a reform opportunity.[73]

Roh had no clue as to how to use this mandate. What he provided was more empty rhetoric than even his supporters could endure. The bluster that had added spice to his oppositional speeches now came across as unpresidential, such that his own minister of commerce, Chung Sye Kyan—who would take over as head of the Uri Party after Roh's forced resignation early in 2007—complained that the president had provided the government with no compass for setting meaningful policy.[74] At least Kim had had the excuse of a global recession for his political apostasy. After

---

69 Brendan Conway, "Letter from Seoul: Sunset Approaches," *The National Interest*, Vol. 1, No. 7 (October 23, 2002), http://www.inthenationalinterest.com/Articles/Vol1/Issue7/Vol1Issue7/Conway PFV.html.

70 Don Kirk, "Key Figure in Korean Summit is Arrested," *The International Herald Tribune* (June 19, 2003), http://www.iht.com/cgi-bin/generic.cgi?template=articleprint.tmplh&ArticleId=100093.

71 Conway, *op. cit.*

72 Kim Jung Min, "Labour Pains," *The Far Eastern Economic Review* (July 10, 2003), p. 19.

73 "Off the Hook," *The Economist* (May 14, 2004), http://economist.com/agenda/PrintFriendly.cfm? Story_ID=2682431; and "Commentary: Korea's Roh has a Second Chance. Now He has to Use it," *Business Week* (May 3, 2004), http://www.businessweek.com/print/magazine/content/04_18/b3881076.htm?chan=mz.

74 Choe, *op cit.*

years of administrative drift, it was little wonder that the public lost interest in the Left and looked mainly to a field of conservative candidates in the closing months before the December 2007 elections. Lee Myung Bak's landslide victory marked the triumph of corporatism. Given his business ties, his campaign motto might as well have been chaebol power. The reform spirit of 1987 was now as remote and irrelevant as the military dictatorship that inspired it.

Rise and Fall of the Civil Dynamic

As in so many cases of IMF "rescue," Korea's post-Crash "reform" created a host of new problems. Financial "liberalization" turned out to be a recipe for what Rene Dumont calls "misdevelopment."[75] Walden Bello likewise sees the deregulation of speculative capital as the main source of Asia's fall,[76] while Joseph Stiglitz blames the IMF and the US Treasury for promoting the capital market liberalization that led to destabilizing speculation and bad lending practices.[77] The Crash resulted when the massive influx of capital of the early 1990s was reversed in 1997. Bello traces this problem to the global debt crisis of 1982, when the IMF and World Bank offered assistance to derelict countries in return for sweeping structural adjustments.[78]

The Bank and the Fund were determined to eliminate the protectionism of state-assisted capitalism—the very system that had nurtured the "Asian miracle"—in favor of privatization. Giving its own spin to events, the Bank spotlighted the "miracle" as the ultimate capitalist showcase, as did the business press and the media in general.[79] That fiction drew still more capital into the region, leading to grotesque overinvestment—a balloon waiting for the right pen. The real "miracle" was that the Crash did not come sooner.

Foreign affairs issues of the 1990s would be closely linked to trade and economic objectives. In this respect South Korea mimicked Japan's approach to comprehensive security. This was the essence of the "New Diplomacy" that Foreign Minister Han Sung Joo fostered within the Kim Young Sam government. While the Crash revived Han's emphasis on economic globalism and regionalism, it also invited postmaterial action on the part of NGOs.[80] These groups issue from the deep structure of Korean civil society, a site of change that has been largely neglected by political and

---

75 In Raff Carmen, *Autonomous Development—Humanizing the Landscape: An Excursion into Radical Thinking and Practice* (London: Zed Books, 1996), p. 196.

76 Walden Bello, *The Future in the Balance: Essays on Globalization and Resistance* (Oakland, CA: Food First Books, 2001), pp. xiii and 69.

77 Stiglitz, *op. cit.*, p. 212.

78 Bello, *Future, op. cit.*, pp. 10 and 13.

79 Bello, *Future, op. cit.*, pp. 75 and 71.

80 Hyuk-Rae Kim, "The State and Civil Society in Transition: The Role of Non-Governmental Organizations in South Korea," *The Pacific Review*, Vol. 13, No. 4 (2000), p. 608 (pp. 595–613). The most notable NGOs are the Citizen's Coalition for Economic Justice (CCEJ), the Korean Federation of Environmental Movements (KFEM), and the People's Solidarity for Participatory Democracy (PSPD).

economic scholarship.[81] The less told side of Korean history is a continuous story of social struggle against state power. That bottom-up force of change was contained but never extinguished by the centrist engine of Korean modernization. This was a potent element in the *minjung* movement of the 1970s and 1980s, which in turn helped to cement the alliance of peasants, workers and progressive segments of the middle class.[82]

This rare and fleeting civil union developed by way of reaction to state repression.[83] Gregory Henderson's famous "politics of the vortex" is accurate so far as it goes, but misses the volcanic forces building beneath the country's social surface. The political ferment of the 1980s did not arise *ex nihilo* from a docile Confucian ethos.[84] It was in fact a time bomb waiting to explode, given the right social and political environment. The Park regime, favoring the upper bourgeoisie,[85] did everything within its power to de-activate this bomb. But its suppression of opposition parties, civil rights and civil society only delayed the explosion. The military autocrats of the 1980s tried in vain to fill the vacuum left by Park's assassination. Although martial law was declared in 1980, workers launched massive strikes such as those at the Sabuk coal mine in Kangwon province, the Tongguk Steel Mill in Pusan and Hyundai's Steel Mill at Inchon.[86]

The upper bourgeoisie and petty bourgeoisie had forged a tacit alliance whereby, through their very passivity, they endorsed the existing power structure. But a split formed along regional lines. In Pusan, Kwangju and other cities, far more than in Seoul, the lower middle class tended to support student activism,[87] which became more militant after the Kwangju massacre of 1980. By 1987 the whole middle class was losing patience with the government. To avoid an even worse outcome,

---

81 Hagen Koo argues that the standard description of "Korea, Inc." as a typical "post-Confucian state" overlooks the input of Korean civil society, which is "far from weak, submissive, and quiescent." See Hagen Koo, "Introduction: Beyond State-Market Relations," in Hagen Koo, ed, *State and Society in Contemporary Korea* (Ithaca: Cornell University Press, 1993), p. 2 (pp. 1–11).

82 Hagen Koo, "The State, *Minjung*, and the Working Class in South Korea," in Hagen Koo (ed.), *State and Society in Contemporary Korea* (Ithaca: Cornell University Press, 1993), pp. 143 and 146 (pp. 131–62); and Sallie Yea, "Maps of Resistance and Geographies of Dissent in Cholla Region," *Asian Studies Institute Publications*, http://www.vuw.ac.nz/asianstudies/publications/working/maps.html.

83 Hagen Koo, "Strong State and Contentious Society," in Hagen Koo (ed.), *State and Society in Contemporary Korea* (Ithaca: Cornell University Press, 1993), p. 248 (pp. 241–49).

84 Thornton, *op. cit.*, p. 125.

85 Jang Jip Choi, "Political Cleavages in South Korea," in Hagen Koo (ed.), *State and Society in Contemporary Korea* (Ithaca: Cornell University Press, 1993), p. 26 (pp. 13 50).

86 *Ibid.*, p. 29.

87 *Ibid.*, p. 32.

President Roh Tae Woo issued his fateful proclamation of June 29, 1987,[88] effectively surrendering to the demand for political reform.[89]

A decisive factor in this proto-democratic revolution was the flood of labor unrest that swept over industrial cities between July and September 1987. Around 3,500 labor risings broke out, more than the total number of active conflicts during the Park and Chun era.[90] This strife soon shifted from the SMEs to the large chaebols. In response, the upper bourgeoisie renewed its unity with the state,[91] but on their terms. At this point almost everyone wanted some form of "democracy." In the wake of the 1987–8 worker's movement, the business class pushed its agenda on the state, and had the financial resources to gain the upper hand in the new electoral politics.[92] Even though labor union membership doubled between 1986 and 1990,[93] capital was already winning the war which labor had fought.

New entrepreneurial players entered the field, changing the rules of the game. Like Ross Perot in the US, Chung Ju Yong, chairman of the Hyundai Group, formed a distinctly bourgeois party: the Unification National Party (UNP).[94] This was a statement in itself, sending a clarion message that the chaebols would no longer be subordinate to the state. Unfortunately the shift from military to civilian politics[95]— President Chun's accidental legacy—was less a democratic transformation than a corporate one.[96]

Meanwhile the solidarity of civil resistance was fast dissolving. As a political force, the *minjung* movement reached its critical mass in the 1980s. One way to trace its rise and fall is through its artistic expression. Challenging the apolitical abstraction and elitist aestheticism of Korean modernism, *minjung* art focused on working class suffering. By the early 1990s, however, its influence was already on the wane, and its virtual demise as a political force can be dated, ironically, with the

---

88 Sung Chul Yang, "An Analysis of South Korea's Political Process and Party Politics," in James Cotton (ed.), *Politics and Policy in the New Korean State: from Roh Tae-Woo to Kim Young-Sam* (New York: St. Martin's Press, 1995), p. 8 (pp. 6–34).

89 Manwoo Lee, "South Korea's Politics of Succession and the December 1992 Presidential Election," in James Cotton (ed.), *Politics and Policy in the New Korean State: from Roh Tae-Woo to Kim Young-Sam* (New York: St. Martin's Press, 1995), p. 39 (pp. 35–65).

90 Hagen Koo, "The State, *Minjung*, and the Working Class in South Korea," *op. cit.*, p. 156.

91 Jang Jip Choi, *op. cit.*, p. 39.

92 Carter J. Eckert, "The South Korean Bourgeoisie: A Class in Search of Hegemony," in Hagen Koo (ed.), *State and Society in Contemporary Korea* (Ithaca: Cornell University Press, 1993), pp. 108 and 129 (pp. 95–130).

93 McNally, "Globalization on Trial," *op. cit.*

94 Yang Gil-Hyun, "Liberalization and the Political Role of the *Chaebôl* in Korea: The Rise and Fall of the Unification National Party (UNP)," in James Cotton (ed.), *Politics and Policy in the New Korean State: from Roh Tae-Woo to Kim Young-Sam* (New York: St. Martin's Press, 1995), pp. 84 and 86–7 (pp. 83–108).

95 Chung-In Moon and Kang Mun-Gu, "Democratic Opening and Military Intervention in South Korea: Comparative Assessment and Implications," in James Cotton (ed.), *Politics and Policy in the New Korean State: From Roh Tae-Woo to Kim Young-Sam* (New York: St. Martin's Press, 1995), pp. 175–6 (pp. 170–91).

96 Yang Gil-Hyun, *op. cit.*, p. 89.

exhibition that the Kim Young Sam government staged for it at the National Museum for Contemporary Art in 1994. By then a new generation of students, caught up in the burgeoning ethos of consumerism, had lost touch with the peasant and working class issues that fueled the *minjung* ethos. At this point, the best *minjung* art could be afforded only by members of the very social elite which had been the target of *minjung* politics.[97]

After the democratic revolt of 1987, the middle class distanced itself from student and worker activism, even as morally aloof student radicalism left the workers behind. The general public's de-radicalization continued until 1997, when the Korean Crash re-opened the question of whose democracy this was. Ironically it was the veteran dissident-turned-president Kim Dae Jung who effectively answered that question: it belonged to the highest bidder.

---

97 See Frank Hoffmann, "Images of Dissent: Transformation in Korean Minjung art," *Asia Pacific Review*, Vol. 1, No. 2 (Summer 1997), http://koreaweb.ws/minjungart.

Chapter 3

Booty Globalism:
The Neocolonization of the Philippines

Dependency in a Democratic Key

The year 1946 was very ironic in US-Philippine relations. Long before World War II, Washington had lost faith in the strategic importance of the Philippines.[1] But in 1946, just as the US relinquished its Philippine colony, that faith bounced back with a vengeance. The presumed threat of global communism turned this geopolitical backwater into a vital forward base, profoundly affecting American attitudes toward Philippine domestic affairs. To control those affairs in the absence of formal colonial oversight would require a new form of intervention: the neocolonial puppet state. This has been Washington's strategy of choice for guilt-free political subversion ever since.[2]

For all its democratic trappings, this model is a postwar time capsule where dissent is concerned. Many Filipinos who had fought alongside the Americans against the Japanese would now be blacklisted. These included not only members of the Communist Party of the Philippines (*Partido Komunista ng Pilipinas*, or PKP) but nearly all veterans of the Huk (*Hukbalahap*) guerrilla army, whose call for land reform and other egalitarian measures would signal socialism in the minds of McCarthy-era Americans.[3] Throughout the war the Huks had defended peasants against oppressive landlords, which was not a separate cause, since the landlords consistently sided with the Japanese. So too, prior to his exit to the US in 1941, President Manuel Luis Quezon had ordered government officials to cooperate with the Japanese. But the vast majority of Philippine elites needed no presidential encouragement. They collaborated with gusto, even as a million Filipinos died at Japanese hands.[4]

Then America stepped in to stabilize the "liberated" country by handing it over to these very same elites. This action had a déjà vu quality, as half a century before America had "stabilized" the democratic uprising against Spain in much the same

---

1 Stanley Karnow, *In Our Image: America's Empire in the Philippines* (New York: Ballantine Books, 1989), p. 324.

2 See Stephen Shalom, "The Philippine Model," *Znet* (October 21, 2003), http://zmag. org/sustainers/content/2003-10/21shalom.cfm.

3 William Blum, *Killing Hope: U.S. Military and CIA Interventions Since World War II* (Monroe, Maine: Common Courage Press, 1995), pp. 39 and 40.

4 "Philippines History," *Windows on Asia* (downloaded April 30, 2006), http:// asianstudies.msu.edu. wbwoa/seasia/Philippines/History/hist_Jap_occupation.html.

way. In the late 1950s, following General MacArthur's august precedent,[5] the entire Central Committee of the PKP was arrested and imprisoned. That same year the legendary Lt. Col. Edward Lansdale arrived to vanquish the new Huk Army (renamed *Hukbong Mapagpalaya ng Bayan*, or the People's Liberation Army). The PKP's General Secretary Jose Lava would remain in prison for the next two decades.

The newly formed Central Intelligence Agency (CIA) cut its teeth on this project. Like MacArthur, the CIA trusted the Philippine Old Guard over its democratic challengers: the 500,000 strong National Peasant Union (PKN) and other members of the emerging Democratic Alliance.[6] An appropriate puppet, Ramon Magsaysay, was implanted as president in 1953. This virtual CIA agent would lead the anti-communist crusade that set the pattern for most of Southeast Asia for the next two decades.[7] Thus the new postcolonial instrument of imperialism was born, giving a democratic veneer to made-in-America policies. This neocolonialism, which Benedict Anderson dubbed "cacique democracy,"[8] cut ordinary Filipinos out of the political loop. The Philippines missed the early postwar land reform that even Taiwan and South Korea (reactionary as they were in other respects) laid as a foundation for a budding middle class.[9] That would limit domestic demand and foster the economic dependency that would distinguish Philippine development from the far more statist economies of the leading "Asian tigers."

The prime beneficiary of this neocolonization would be the Armed Forces of the Philippines (AFP), which would hold sway both politically and economically.[10] By 1970 Ferdinand Marcos had retooled the military for martial law, with 59,000 men in uniform and a $572 million budget.[11] But even as he closed his grip on the AFP,[12]

---

5 In 1945 MacArthur had ordered the disbanding of the Huks and had jailed the Huk leaders Taruc and Casto Alejandrino. See "The Huk Rebellion," *U.S. Library of Congress Country Studies* (downloaded May 2, 2006), http://countrystudies.us/philippines/25.htm.

6 "The Huk Rebellion," *Los-Indios-Bravos.com—The Filipino Solidarity Project* (2001), http://www.los-indios-bravos.com/english/eng_hist_26.html.

7 Blum, *op. cit.*, p. 43. The CIA found its next puppet in Diosdado Macapagal (the father of the future President Gloria Macapagal Arroyo), who would become the Philippine president in 1961. See Karnow, *op. cit.*, pp. 15 and 363.

8 Benedict Anderson, *The Spectre of Comparision: Nationalism, Southeast Asia and the World* (London: Verso, 1998), p. 225.

9 Pepe Escobar, "Poverty, Corruption: The Ties that Bind," *Asia Times Online* (October 5, 2004), http://www.atimes.com/atimes/printN.html.

10 Carl H. Landé, "Introduction: Retrospect and Prospect," in Carl H. Landé (ed.), *Building a Nation: Philippine Challenges and American Policy* (Washington, DC: The Washington Institute Press, 1987), p. 12 (pp. 7–44).

11 Gretchen Casper, *Fragile Democracies: The Legacies of Authoritarian Rule* (Pittsburgh and London: University of Pittsburgh Press, 1995), p. 88.

12 Richard J. Kessler, *Rebellion and Repression in the Philippines* (New Haven: Yale University Press, 1989), p. 116.

the US closed its grip on him. "Stability" would be a prime objective for both,[13] and political development would be its main victim.[14]

The postwar history of the Philippines unhinges the modernist myth that political progress flows naturally from economic advantage. Thanks to its geopolitical centrality, plus a massive infusion of foreign capital,[15] the Philippines emerged in the 1950s as the most economically vibrant nation in Southeast Asia.[16] Under Marcos, however, that frontrunner status was forfeited in favor of "booty capitalism," whereby the nation's economic elite bled the state in much the same way that a Mafia takeover bleeds a healthy company.[17] US support allowed Marcos to fend off reform and maintain the booty system through the 1970s, but at the cost of economic dynamism. During his twenty years of rule, seven out of ten Filipinos would remain below the poverty line,[18] earning the country its reputation as "the sick man of Asia."[19]

The 1980s became the country's "lost decade," as per capita income actually fell by 7.2 percent between 1980 and 1992.[20] A banking crisis in 1981 compelled the government to liberalize financial policies, rendering it even more vulnerable to the global recession that struck in 1982. The Philippines had been on the IMF's loan strings since 1962, and underwent a major IMF Structural Adjustment Program (SAP) in 1979.[21] Marcos now had little choice but to "SAP" the nation still more,[22] contributing greatly to the balance-of-payments crisis of 1984–85.[23] The

---

13 Emmanuel M. Pelaez, "The Philippines and the United States," in Carl H. Landé (ed.), *Building a Nation: Philippine Challenges and American Policy* (Washington, DC: The Washington Institute Press, 1987), pp. 51 and 52 (pp. 45–55).

14 Eero Palmujoki, *Regionalism and Globalization in Southeast Asia* (Basingstoke, UK: Palgrave, 2001), p. 13.

15 Alasdair Bowie and Danny Unger, *The Politics of Open Economies: Indonesia, Malaysia, the Philippines and Thailand* (Cambridge: Cambridge University Press, 1997), p. 105.

16 Anderson, *op. cit.*, pp. 208–9.

17 Bowie and Unger, *op. cit.*, p. 100. The regime's hegemonic success is suggested by the fact that as of July 1973 90 percent of Filipinos supported the extension of Marcos's presidential term. See Samuel Charng Yeong Ku, *Southeast Asian Governments and Politics* (Taipei, Taiwan: Wu Nan, second edition, 2000), p. 208.

18 Gregg R. Jones, *Red Revolution: Inside the Philippine Guerrilla Movement* (Boulder, CO: Westview, 1989), p. 155.

19 See Pepe Escobar, "The Sick Man of Asia," *Asia Times Online* (October 1, 2004), http://www.atimes. com/atimes/printN.html.

20 Paul D. Hutchcroft, "Sustaining Economic and Political Reform: The Challenges Ahead," in David G. Timberman (ed.), *The Philippines: New Directions in Domestic Policy and Foreign Relations* (Hong Kong and Singapore: Asia Society and Institute of Southeast Asian Studies, 1998), pp. 23–24 (pp. 23–47).

21 "The IMF and WB are Killing the Filipino People," *Statement of the BAYAN, Bagong Alyansan Makabayan*, or *New Patriotic Alliance* (April 16, 2006), http://www.hartford-hwp. com/archives/54a/113.html.

22 See Walden Bello, "Pacific Panopticon," *The New Left Review*, No. 16 (July/August 2002), p. 72 (pp. 68–85).

23 Manuel F. Montes, "The Philippines as an Unwitting Participant in the Asian Economic Crisis," in Karl D. Jackson (ed.), *Asian Contagion: The Causes and Consequences of a Financial Crisis* (Boulder, CO: Westview Press, 1999), p. 244 (pp. 241–68).

domestic business sector was growing wary of such international exposure,[24] and was beginning to question the nepotistic regime that had squandered the country's regional supremacy. Political storm clouds were building among the marginalized rich as well as the poor.

Fearing opposition from Corazon Aquino, Marcos called for snap elections in February 1986 and unconvincingly declared himself the winner. This sparked the "People Power" upsurge that exposed the pillars of the establishment—cronies, technocrats and military brass—as fickle allies.[25] The regime was doomed when civilian protest was joined by a military mutiny. Defense Minister Juan-Ponce Enrile and some 300 members of the Reform the Armed Forces Movement initiated the EDSA revolution, an acronym for the highway running between two military camps where the uprising began.[26]

The People Power movement took the Philippines to a fateful developmental crossroads. In April 1986 President Aquino sought a cease-fire with insurgents, and planned to negotiate directly with the communists.[27] But by October this effort had met strong resistance from the AFP as well as Washington. At this critical juncture Aquino yielded to the military and toughened her rhetoric toward the rebels.[28] Some would argue that she had little choice. The economy had been drained by a nearly $28 billion foreign debt contracted by Marcos,[29] who had also funneled billions into Swiss banks.[30] She desperately needed US assistance to revive the sinking economy. Though she obtained $350 million in extra aid after her speech to the US Congress on September 18, 1986,[31] this was still not enough. Her attempt to further placate the US would have serious domestic consequences. Already her administration was being called the "US-Quezon puppet show."[32] What it accomplished was the conversion of People Power, and hence democracy, into a hegemonic device.

This putative people's President had reached much the same crossroads that South Korea's Kim Dae Jung would face ten years later when he filed for IMF assistance.

---

24 David C. Kang, *Crony Capitalism: Corruption and Development in South Korea and the Philippines* (Cambridge: Cambridge University Press, 2002), p. 173.

25 Temario C. Rivera, *State of the Nation: Philippines* (Singapore: Institute of Southeast Asian Studies, 1996), p. 15.

26 David G. Timberman, *A Changeless Land: Continuity and Changes in the Philippine Politics* (New York and Singapore: M.E. Sharpe and Institute of Southeast Asian Studies, 1991), p. 149.

27 Leonard Davis, *Revolutionary Struggle in the Philippines* (Basingstoke, UK: The Macmillan Press, 1989), p. 3.

28 *Ibid.*, p. 168.

29 Karnow, *op. cit.*, p. 425.

30 As one Philippine journalist put it, "The $15 billion to $20 billion that Marcos creamed off has had a big effect. There's a kind of corruption that just recycles the money, but all this was taken out." See Teodoro C. Benigno, "Culture: The Culprit," *Philippine Star* (March 11, 2002), http://www.geocities.com/benignO/aboutus6.html?200720.

31 Landé, *op. cit.*, p. 27.

32 Theodore Friend, "The 'Yellow Revolution': Its Mixed Historical Legacy," in Carl H. Landé (ed.), *Building a Nation: Philippine Challenges and American Policy* (Washington, DC: The Washington Institute Press, 1987), p. 76 (pp. 69–86).

Though Aquino's name had become synonymous with People Power, it was now necessary for her to choose between fidelity to the reform movement that brought her to power and surrender to the dictates of international capitalism. From the moment of her inauguration, her international drift had been challenged by her reformist defense minister, Enrile, who was consequently ostracized by inner circle advisors such as Joker Arroyo.[33] Enrile would be implicated in an aborted coup and forced to resign;[34] and already Aquino had fired her activist labor secretary, Augusto "Bobbit" Sanchez. Tellingly he was replaced with a corporate lawyer, Franklin Drilon,[35] while the government was packed with technocrats with strong US ties.

Repeated coup attempts prompted Father Bernas, a distinguished constitutional lawyer, to declare the country a "nation in crisis."[36] Aquino's inherently indecisive coalition government was rendered even more inert by policy differences over how to deal with communist resistance.[37] There was a similar split in the military between the traditional Old Guard and reformists, resulting in the military coup of 1987. The reformists were far from defeated, and might have triumphed in a purely domestic arena. Once again, however, Washington tipped the scales against substantive democratization. More and more America was insinuating itself at all levels of Philippine policy making. It even provided air support to save the Aquino government in the Great Coup of 1989.[38]

Not surprisingly the administration balked at its promised land reform. The issue was thrown to the still unelected Congress, dominated by landlords.[39] This incited the "Mendiola" incident of January 1987, a demand for action involving 15,000 peasant protesters led by the Movement of Filipino Farmers (*Kilusang Magbukid ng Pilipinas*, or KMP). Aquino refused to meet the KMP when it submitted a proposal detailing how to achieve land reform within five years[40] Nineteen farmers were killed in associated police gunfire.[41]

Progressive hopes were fast evaporating. As the tactical command center of People Power, NGOs had entered a brief alliance with the government after the fall of Marcos, but the "Mendiola" incident and the May 11, 1987 Congressional elections (which restored the "caciques," or traditional agrarian elites as legislative

---

33 Timberman, *op. cit.*, p. 179.

34 W. Scott Thompson, *The Philippines in Crisis: Development and Security in the Aquino Era, 1986–92* (New York: St. Martin's Press, 1992), pp. 25 and 60.

35 *Ibid.*, p. 25.

36 *Ibid.*, p. 26.

37 Rivera, *op. cit.*, p. 18.

38 *Ibid.*, p. 135.

39 Jose Maria Sison, with Rainer Werning, *The Philippine Revolution: The Leader's View* (New York: Crane Russak/Taylor & Francis Group, 1989), p. 113.

40 Davis, *op. cit.*, p. 7.

41 Thompson, *op. cit.*, pp. 52–53.

representatives)[42] weakened the foundation for state-NGO collaboration.[43] The growing role of the AFP further undermined such ties. After 1988, when the administration failed to reach a peace agreement with the National Democratic Front (NDF), mounting insurgency pushed Aquino toward greater military dependence.[44] The AFP was now targeting NGO workers and human rights activists with impunity. Although the number of NGOs grew significantly in the late 1980s and 1990s, their influence on the government waned. This was symptomatic of People Power in general. The Philippines had escaped overt authoritarianism only to fall prey to the more covert and therefore sustainable repression that scholars would euphemistically label "polyarchy," or "low intensity" democracy.[45]

Booty Globalism

Thus democratic reformism was pushed to the social margins at the very moment of its declared victory. The same would happen in Korea, except that in the Philippines the movement retained greater potency outside the halls of power. Perhaps this was because it was less seduced by the false promises of raw economism. The very absence of an economic "miracle" invited political dynamism by way of resistance. But this opposition proved so ineffective in achieving even its minimal goals that the Philippines failed on both sides, in political as well as economic terms.

Aquino made her orientation clear as she turned her attention from domestic reform to the repayment of the nation's $28 billion foreign debt. This shift came at the expense of economic recovery and natural resource sustainability,[46] not to mention broken promises regarding equitable income distribution. By 1991 People Power was effectively orphaned.[47] This invited a revival of communist and Muslim insurgencies,[48] which in turn invited still more militarization and US dependency.

---

42 Out of two hundred members of the House of Representatives, 130 belonged to traditional political families, while another 39 were relatives of those families. See Anderson, *op. cit.*, p. 221.

43 Along with the growth of the military, the number of NGOs burgeoned in the late 1970s. During the 1950s and 1960s the Philippines was not a major recipient of Official Development Assistance (ODA)—a crucial stimulant to NGO growth in Southeast Asia at the time. But with increasing poverty, caused by domestic economic problems and the second global oil hike, the Marcos regime increasingly depended on ODA, and on NGOs to manage it. See Gerald Clark, *The Politics of NGOs in South-East Asia: Participation and Protest in the Philippines* (London: Routledge, 1998), pp. 62, 63 and 74.

44 *Ibid.*, p. 82.

45 Herbert Docena, "Philippines: Power, not Gloria," *Asia Times* (March 3, 2006), http://www.atimes.com/atimes/Southeast_Asia/HC03Ae03.html.

46 Walden Bello, *The Future in the Balance: Essays on Globalization and Resistance* (Oakland, CA: Food First, 2001), p. 52.

47 See Solita Collas-Monsod, "The War Against Poverty: A Status Report," in David G. Timberman (ed.), *The Philippines: New Directions in Domestic Policy and Foreign Relations* (Hong Kong and Singapore: Asia Society and Institute of Southeast Asian Studies, 1998), p. 100 (pp. 85–110).

48 Kang, *op. cit.*, p. 155.

Pushed into this corner, Aquino now placed all her bets on economic liberalization. Foreign investment began to pour in, but was stalled in the early 1990s in the face of political instability and other setbacks, such as the earthquake of July 1990.[49] With debt consuming 40 percent of the nation's budget, labor protests were sparked when oil prices rose 32 percent in September 1990.[50] Aquino settled for a smaller increase, which may have spared her the fate awaiting Suharto, who would be toppled after he raised oil prices and public transportation fees. Aquino's remedy was booty globalization, a precocious mix of global and local cronyism. In 1991 she pushed through an unprecedented law to liberalize foreign investments,[51] and later that year she signed the pseudo-reformist Local Government Code. In the name of democratic localism this law transferred political power and financial resources from the national government to local oligarchs.[52]

Aquino's attempt to placate the Old Guard hit a snag, however, where trade liberalization was concerned. Ultimately she had to choose between domestic and global cronies, the pivotal issue being American bases on Philippine soil. Here the Old Guard and the masses came together against her. Without a domestic power base, she ended up more a US puppet than even Marcos had been. In September 1991, under public pressure to end the lease for the Subic Bay and Clark bases,[53] the Philippine Senate voted to cancel the Military Bases Agreement (MBA). Aquino nonetheless bowed to US counter-pressure by accepting a $481 million a year rental agreement for these bases.[54] This was far less than the $1.2 billion proposed in the MBA review of 1988,[55] but the US threw in an additional $160 million a year in "multilateral assistance," making these combined funds more than the total foreign direct investment (FDI) of $544 million.[56]

---

49 Emilio T. Antonio, Jr., Emilio S. Neri, Jr. and Teresa V. Taningco, "Capital Inflows and the Philippine Economy: Issues and Policy Options," in C.H. Kwan, Donna Vandenbrink and Chia Siow Yue (eds), *Coping with Capital Flow in East Asia* (Tokyo and Singapore: Nomura Research Institute and Institute of Southeast Asian Studies, 1998), p. 273 (pp. 272–92).

50 Bowie and Unger, *op. cit.*, p. 125.

51 Emmanuel S. de Dios, "Philippine Economic Growth: Can it Last?," in David G. Timberman (ed.), *The Philippines: New Directions in Domestic Policy and Foreign Relations* (Hong Kong and Singapore: Asia Society and Institute of Southeast Asian Studies, 1998), p. 62 (pp. 49–84).

52 Steven Rood, "Decentralization, Democracy and Development," in David G. Timberman (ed.), *The Philippines: New Directions in Domestic Policy and Foreign Relations* (Hong Kong and Singapore: Asia Society and Institute of Southeast Asian Studies, 1998), pp. 116, 117 and 126 (pp. 111–35).

53 See James Putzel, "Social Capital and the Imagined Community: Democracy and Nationalism in the Philippines," in Michael Leifer (ed.), *Asian Nationalism* (London: Routledge, 2000), p. 179 (pp. 170–86).

54 Karnow, *op. cit.*, p. 433.

55 William E. Berry, Jr., *U.S. Bases in the Philippines: The Revolution of the Special Relationship* (Boulder, CO. Westview Press, 1989), p. 295.

56 Jonathan Napack, "Stuck at Base," *The Far Eastern Economic Review* (October 19, 2000), http://www. feer.com/_0010_19/p88current.html.

Public outrage at her puppetry spilled over into the 1992 elections. Despite the usual cheating and violence,[57] hopes were raised for a truly independent Philippines. Some thought these would be the first elections where American influence was transcended.[58] It seemed auspicious that Fidel Ramos won with less than 24 percent of the vote,[59] meaning he would have to work hard to gain public support. He sought this by way of his Security Advisor, Jose Almonte, a vocal critic of cartels and oligarchic privileges. Ramos gave the impression of attacking the vested interests and family monopolies that the Americans had sustained since their colonial period.[60]

As president, however, Ramos soon pushed for further trade liberalization. Then Senator and now President Gloria Macapagal Arroyo led the same push in the Senate, promising that WTO membership would create half a million industrial jobs and another half a million agricultural ones.[61] Filipinos largely took the bait, accepting the argument that their cheap labor would compensate for competitive defects such as low technology and poor transportation. Trickle down economics would take care of distribution.

In fact, the Philippines lost hundreds of thousands of farming jobs after joining the WTO in 1995.[62] This should have been no surprise, for the US, Europe and Japan funneled nearly $1 billion *per day* in tax subsides to their agro-industries,[63] all the while insisting upon "free" international trade with developing countries. There was moderate growth in 1994 and 1995 (5.1 and 5.7 percent, respectively),[64] but foreign exchange shortages forced a cut in government spending.[65] The number of Filipinos living in dire poverty reached 17 million in 1995, as compared to 15 million in 1975.[66]

---

57 Carl H. Landé, *Post-Marcos Politics: A Geographical and Statistical Analysis of the 1992 Presidential Election* (New York and Singapore: St. Martin's Press and Institute of Southeast Asian Studies, 1996), p. 108.

58 David G. Timberman, "Introduction: The Philippines' New Normalcy," in David G. Timberman (ed.), *The Philippines: New Directions in Domestic Policy and Foreign Relations* (Hong Kong and Singapore: Asia Society and Institute of Southeast Asian Studies, 1998), p. 15 (pp. 15–22).

59 Greg Bankoff and Kathleen Weekley, *Post-Colonial National Identity in the Philippines: Celebrating the Centennial Independence* (Aldershot, UK: Ashgate, 2002), p. 22.

60 Hutchcroft, *op. cit.*, pp. 25 and 30.

61 Renato Redentor Costantino, "Progress and Regression in the Philippines," *Znet* from *Business Mirror*, Philippines (February 24, 2006), http://www.zmag.org/content/print_article. cfm?itemID=9794&section ID=1.

62 "Trade Rigged against the Poor," *The International Herald Tribune* (July 21, 2003), http://www.iht.com/generic.cig?template=articleprint.tmplh&ArticleId=103448.

63 "The Rigged Trade Game," *The New York Times* (July 20, 2003), http://www. nytimes.com/2003/07/20/opinion/20SUN1.html.; and "Trade Rigged Against the Poor," *The International Herald Tribune* (July 21, 2003), http://www.iht.com/cgi-bin/generic.cgi?templa te=articleprimt.tmplh&ArticleId=103448.

64 Hutchcroft, *op. cit.*, p. 26.

65 De Dios, *op. cit.*, p. 50.

66 By contrast, Thailand managed to cut those numbers from 3.4 million to less than 500,000 during the same period. See Deidre Sheehan, "Rural Poor are the Real Key," *The Far Eastern Economic Review* (May 24, 2001), http://www.feer.com/_0105_24/p26region.html.

The plight of farmers fueled communist and Islamic resistance, especially on the island of Mindanao, home to more than two-thirds of the nation's corn production.[67] Only in retrospect would Ramos blame globalist trade practices for their devastating impact on rural society.[68] Nor did the nation as a whole have much to show for its liberalization. Philippine technocrats looked on in dismay as foreign debt mushroomed from $28 billion in 1986 to $31 billion in 1992 and finally to $45 billion in 1997.[69] This was not what they had been taught to expect in their economics indoctrination at US universities.

Although Ramos had implemented some banking reforms by 1997,[70] he packed top government positions with retired generals who were sure to suppress People Power. During his visit to Manila, Lee Kuan Yew told Ramos that the Philippines needed "discipline more than democracy,"[71] but what Ramos provided, along with the usual democratic promises, was simply more of Ramos: he decided to go for a second term, which meant amending the Constitution and wasting his last two years in office in battles over this issue.[72] By mid-1997 the country simply wanted less of Ramos.

Politics of the Crash

The world business press gave the impression that the economic trauma of 1997 was greater in other Southeast Asian countries than in the Philippines. That delusion was based purely on the relative losses of foreign investors, not the suffering of the working classes. The country's poor were *already* on the edge of bare subsistence, and could scarcely afford further distress. If other Rim nations seemed harder hit, this was simply because the Philippines had never risen so high. It could not be expelled from a "miracle" club it had never joined. Its average growth between 1960 and 1996 was 3.8 percent, as compared to South Korea's 8.2.[73] As of the early 1970s it was still a richer country than its Southeast Asian neighbors, but in years to come, as they began to forge the second Asian miracle, the Philippines limped along with a 2 percent growth rate.[74]

That contrast was definitely not due to a better "free market" record on the part of the miracle makers. Quite the contrary, the Philippine government had played a less intrusive role in the economy. That, against neoliberal preachments, may help

---

67 Subsidies continue unabated, amounting to nearly $35 billion between 1995 and 2003. *Ibid.*

68 "Trade Rigged Against the Poor," *The International Herald Tribune* (July 21, 2003), http://www.iht.com/cgi-bin/generic.cgi?template=articleprint.tmplh&ArticleId=103448.

69 Bankoff and Weekley, *op. cit.*, p. 24.

70 Putzel, *op. cit.*, p. 181.

71 Jon Liden, "The Ramos Model for Asian Leadership," *The Asian Wall Street Journal* (October 27, 1998), p. 10.

72 *Ibid.*

73 Kang, *op. cit.*, p. 54.

74 "The Jeepney Economy Revs up," *The Economist* (August 16, 2007), http://economist.com/world/asia/PrintFriendly.cfm?story_id=9657147.

to explain why both local and international investment remained weak. In any case, as one Filipino businessman put it, "We got to the party late, so we didn't get as drunk."[75] Capital account liberalization so seriously backfired that much capital exit had occurred long before the Crash.[76] Even during the final quarter of 1997, when other Rim countries were smashed by capital outflows (South Korea, Singapore and Thailand losing $17 billion, $13.3 billion and $8.4 billion, respectively), the Philippines attracted $204 million.[77] In short, its economy had been on a recovery path when the Crisis struck.

Thus the financial side of the Asian Crisis was more an "intruder" here than elsewhere. The trauma of 1997 is better reflected in the nation's political upheaval than in its economic condition. It is no accident that tension between the military and the Moro Islamic Liberation Front (MILF) intensified during 1997. The conflict escalated when the AFP launched an attack on one of the MILF's base camps in Central Mindanao.[78] This confrontation continued into the next two administrations, but was eclipsed by more mainstream political unrest.

The landslide victory of Joseph Estrada, a former C-grade movie star, would have been unthinkable without the turmoil that followed in the wake of the Crash. Here again the Philippines was in a different cycle from most Rim nations. Having come to the democratic reform party early, it also met disillusionment early. Hopes were plummeting here just when Indonesia and Thailand were riding a wave of democratic optimism. Even in Korea, where democratization lost much of its reformist zeal in the 1990s,[79] the fall from grace was not so great as in the Philippines, which failed its people economically as well as politically.

Drawing on his acting experience, Estrada cast himself as a defender of the poor, but like Aquino he quickly sold his loyalty to globalist interests that sought only "stability" on their terms. He not only stood opposed to strikes,[80] but soon began rehabilitating old Marcos cronies. This killed any hope for an end to communist insurgency.[81] The general public soon caught on to Estrada's duplicity, and after 15 months in office he found himself facing more than 150,000 protesters in Manila. Their main complaint was that he was trying to remove constitutional restrictions that prohibited foreigners from owning land or holding more than 40 percent ownership of local companies.[82]

---

75 Kang, *op. cit.*, p. 151.

76 Montes, *op. cit.*, p. 266.

77 *Ibid.*, p. 157.

78 Cristina V. Rodriguez, "Reporting on an Inexplicable War," *Philippine International Review* (winter 1997–98), http://www.philso.nl/pri/Evacuation-97p.htm.

79 See Songok Han Thornton, The 'Miracle' Revisited: The De-Radicalization of Korean Political Culture, *New Political Science*, Vol. 27, No. 2 (June 2005), pp. 161–76.

80 Joseph Ejercito Estrada, "The Philippine Advantage," *The Asian Wall Street Journal* (December 16, 1998), p. 6.

81 "Estrada Support of Marcos Cronies Threatens Peace Talks," *The Hong Kong Standard* (June 28, 1998), http://www.hartford-hwp.com/archieves/54a/117.html.

82 "Constitution Changes Protested," *The New York Times* from *The Associated Press* (August 20, 1999), http://www.nytimes.com/aponline/i/AP-Philippines-Protest.html.

Estrada's graft and playboy antics set the stage for People Power II, born of broad-spectrum opposition to the government's neoliberal agenda. Among the protesters, ironically, was former President Aquino, along with small business owners and Catholic leaders such as Cardinal Jaime Sin, who had initiated People Power I in 1986.[83] As tens of thousands of people gathered at the Malacanang presidential palace, Estrada found himself abandoned by his army, the police and even his cabinet.[84] The economy had slid into recession, while swelling deficits prompted the World Bank and the IMF to hold back scheduled loans of over $500 million.[85] Estrada, moreover, was accused of stealing $80 million,[86] which led to impeachment proceedings.[87] The night before his fall, more than one million demonstrators took to the streets, with much of the protest centered around the shrine of the 1986 People Power uprising.[88]

The final blow came in January 2001, when the military switched its support to Vice President Arroyo.[89] This was in fact a preemptive strike against a fledgling People Power II. Solid backing from the military allowed Arroyo to crack down on counter-protesters who realized that as bad as Estrada was, Arroyo would almost certainly be worse.[90] On the surface she won, but her hard-line tactics proved a boon to the Philippine Left. This polarity was further aggravated after September 11, 2001, when she emerged as the chief Asian cheerleader for the US-led war on terrorism.

Arroyo's master plan since 9/11 has been to brand her enemies as terrorists: the CPP (Communist Party of the Philippines), the NPA (New People's Army) and even Professor Jose Maria Sison, in exile in the Netherlands.[91] Under cover of this threat she conveniently renewed military ties with Washington, once again offering the

---

83 "Travails of a Philippine President," *The New York Times* (November 8, 2000), http://www.nytimes. com/2000/11/08/opinion/08WED3.html; and Seth Mydans, "Philippine House Impeaches President Estrada," *The New York Times* (November 13, 2000), http://www. nytimes.com/2000/11/13/world/13CND-FILIP.html.

84 Mark Landler, "Manila Moves Incite Talk of 'Dark Side of People Power,'" *The New York Times* (May 3, 2001), http://www.nytimes.com/2001/05/03/world/03FILI.html.

85 Tom Holland, "Manila's Recession Risk," *The Far Eastern Economic Review* (November 2, 2000), http://www.feer.com/_0011_02/p024region.html.

86 Deidre Sheehan, "Rural Poor are the Real Key," *The Far Eastern Economic Review* (May 24, 2001), http://www.feer.com/_0105_24/p026region.html.

87 Seth Mydans, "Philippine House Impeaches President Estrada," *The New York Times* (November 13, 2000), http://www.nytimes.com/2000/11/13/world/13CND-FILIP.html.

88 Kim Scipes, "Round Two: People's Power in the Philippines Removes Another President," *ZNet Commentary* (February 2, 2000), http://www.hartford-hwp.com/archives/54a/122.html.

89 Seth Mydans, "Brief Mutiny was Pale Shadow of Past Philippine Coups," *The New York Times* (July 28, 2003), http://www.nytimes.ocm/2003/07/28/international/asia/28FILI.html.

90 Deidre Sheehan, "More Power to the Powerful," *The Far Eastern Economic Review* (February 1, 2001), http://www.fcci.com/_0102_01/p016region.html.

91 Pepe Escobar, "All Quiet on the Second Front," *Asia Times Online* (October 7, 2004), http://www.atimes.com/atimes/printN.html.

Philippines as a refueling depot.[92] Worse still, against the Philippine constitution, US troops were brought in to fight on Philippine soil. The result was an unprecedented anti-American alliance: a potpourri of nationalists, moderate reformists, and hard-left groups such as Bayan Muna (or Nation First).[93] 75,000 leftists joined marches under the slogan "resign all," aimed at the president and her entire government.[94]

With her back to the wall domestically, Arroyo focused all the more on the international front, seeking to lure foreign investors. She not only installed a US-trained technocratic cabinet, but even hired an American public relations firm on an $800,000 contract to promote her image abroad.[95] Meanwhile her domestic popularity continued to plummet and in December 2002 she announced that she would not seek reelection, but would devote her remaining time in office to complete her putative "reforms."[96] She changed her mind, however, as her rising geopolitical status energized her administration.

On the pretext of combating global terrorism—which is to say Islamism—Washington poured in more than $90 million in military aid between fall 2001 and January 2003, as compared with less than $2 million per year previously.[97] However, the root of the insurgency is not religion or ethnicity so much as poverty and social injustice. The military well knows this, and therefore considers the New People's Army (NPA), the military wing of the Communist Party, a much bigger threat than all the Islamic resistance groups combined. The numbers speak for themselves: the NPA now has 128 guerrilla fronts in 8,000 villages, or 20 percent of all villages in the country.[98]

Along with its comrades in the National Democratic Front, the NPA has been stigmatized by the US State Department as a "terrorist" group, but in fact it is part of a long struggle for substantive democracy.[99] After 35 years in open rebellion, at a cost of 40,000 lives,[100] the Communists are again gaining strength. Indeed, they function almost like a government in many remote areas, their popular appeal being

---

92 James Hookway, "Just Say 'No' To U.S. Troops," *The Far Eastern Economic Review* (December 6, 2001), http://www.feer.com/articles/2001/0112_06/p024region.html.

93 James Hookway, "In the Clutches of the Eagle," *The Far Eastern Economic Review* (February 7, 2002), http://www.feer.com/articles/2002/0202_07/p16region.html.

94 Mark Mitchell, "Shut out of People Power," *The Far Eastern Economic Review* (February 8, 2001), http://www.feer.com/_0102_08/p022region.html.

95 James Hookway, "All Things to All People," *The Far Eastern Economic Review* (February 7, 2002), http://www.feer.com/articles/2002/0202_07/p014region.html.

96 "Lame Duck Plan to Soar," *The Economist* (January 30, 2003), http://economist.com/world/asia/PrintFriendly.cfm?Story_ID=1560385.

97 Joshua Kurlantzick, "Stop Arming Southeast Asia," *The New Republic* (January 20, 2003), http://www. thenewrepublic.com/doc.mhtml?I=20030120&s=kurlantzick012003.

98 Carlos H. Conde, "In Philippines, a threat revives," *The International Herald Tribune* (December 26, 2003), http://www.iht.com/cgi-bin/generic.cgi?template=articleprint.tmplh&ArticleId=122828.

99 E. San Juan, Jr., "Imperialist War Against Terrorism & Revolution in the Philippines," *Dissident Voice* (September 15, 2004), http://www.dissidentvoice.org/Sept04/SanJuan0915.htm.

100 "Accord on Philippine Human Rights Inquiry," *The New York Times* (February 15, 2004), http://www.nytimes.com/2004/02/15/international/asia/15FILI.html.

the hope of simple justice for people with no other recourse.[101] If a farmer's water buffalo is stolen, it is extremely unlikely that the police will do anything about it. But the NPA will.[102] For the poor and oppressed, that is a winning argument.

The quest for justice also fuels resistance in more mainstream politics, where graft is the salient issue. In 2003 some 300 junior Philippine Army officers mutinied over corruption within the military and administration.[103] Twice in two years Arroyo's husband, Miguel Arroyo, was mired in scandal,[104] and another scandal engulfed Chief Justice Hilario Davide, who previously had a clean reputation. This compromised Davide's effort to maintain the judiciary's independence from political co-optation,[105] including the machinations of Arroyo herself.

Her 2004 reelection campaign came under fire from Senator Panfilo Lacson, a former police chief under Estrada, who was backed by the Kilusang Bagong Lipunan, or KBL Party.[106] Lacson's hard-line reputation compelled Arroyo to adopt similar measures, such as the reinstatement of the death penalty. An increase of kidnapping cases involving business executives made such measures attractive to the business community, which Arroyo could not ignore.[107] At the same time, however, she has all but endorsed a shocking pattern of violence against dissident journalists, lawyers, union organizers and human rights workers. Hundreds have been liquidated in recent years,[108] with very few arrests and scarcely any convictions.[109]

An investigation led by former Philippine Supreme Court Justice Jose Miro held military personnel responsible for most of the 830 murders that had taken place under Arroyo by early 2007. The pace of these assassinations surpassed even the

---

101 Carlos H. Conde, "Communist Revival Worries the Philippines," *The New York Times* (January 4, 2004), http://www.nytimes.com/2004/01/04/international/asia/04FILI.html.

102 Simon Montlake, "In Capitalist Asia, Philippines still Grapples with Communists," *The Christian Science Monitor* (December 7, 2005), http://www.csmonitor.com/2005/1207/p04s01-woap.htm.

103 Simon Montlake, "Mutiny Raises Questions of Philippine Army Corruption," *The Christian Science Monitor* (July 28, 2003), http://www.csmonitor.com/2003/0728/p07s01-woap.htm.

104 Marites Danguilan Vitung, "Wanted: Democratic Institutions," *The International Herald Tribune* (September 19, 2003), http://www.iht.com/articles/110428.html.

105 Philip Bowring, "The Philippines: Democracy in Crisis," *The International Herald Tribune* (November 3, 2003), http://www.iht.com/articles/116036.html.

106 Rodney Tasker, "A Tough Line at the Top," *The Far Eastern Economic Review* (February 20, 2003), p. 20 (pp. 20–21).

107 Carlos H. Conde, "Philippine Reinstates Death Penalty," *The International Herald Tribune* (December 5, 2003), http://www.iht.com/cgi-bin/generic.cgi?template=articleprint.tmplh& ArticleId=120403.

108 E. San Juan, Jr., "We Charge Genocide: A Brief History of US in the Philippines," *Political Affairs.net* (December 2005), http://www.politicalaffairs.net/article/articleview/2274/1/133/

109 Carlos H. Conde, "Philippine Leader Vows to Pursue Culprits in Killings of Journalists," *The New York Times* (December 10, 2004), http://www.nytimes.com/2004/12/10/international/asia/10filip.html; and Herbert Docena, "Killing Season in the Philippines," *Asia Times* (June 2, 2006), http://www.atimes.com/atimes/Southeast_Asia/HF02Ae04.html.

worst periods of Marcos' 20-year tyranny.[110] Whether or not Arroyo directly ordered these crimes,[111] her patent indifference is contemptible, and should be enough, under the provisions of the Leahy Amendment, to end US military or police assistance to the Philippines.

Except for Iraq, there is no place on earth where a reporter's job is so dangerous as here.[112] Meanwhile the government is issuing new restrictive guidelines for journalists, some of whom have already been charged with sedition.[113] Naturally the question is how America will respond. So far Washington has refrained from any substantive reaction, which of course sends a green light for Arroyo to keep up the good work.

Conclusion: End of an Era

Much as Aquino forfeited People Power I, Arroyo's turn to military solutions in her "war on terrorism" is in fact a bulwark against People Power II. Her desperate bid for foreign aid could have been leveraged by Washington as a reform incentive. Instead the Bush administration encouraged raw militarism and blatant anti-Islamism.[114] Arroyo had no trouble playing this 9/11 card. Conveniently timed bombings of Christian targets preceded her state visit to Washington in May 2003. She of course blamed the MILF, but their denials were consistent with the organization's past policy of avoiding civilian targets.[115]

This "anti-terrorist" gambit paid off in the short run: Arroyo got her American aid and won reelection in May 2004 by a margin of a million votes.[116] This left her, however, at the helm of a sinking ship. At 80 percent of GDP,[117] the country's public debt (due in large part to corporate and elite tax evasion)[118] resembles that

---

110 Cher S. Jimenez, "Deadly Dirt Work in the Philippines," *Asia Times* (February 13, 2007), http://www.atimes.com/atimes/Southeast_Asia/IB13Ae01.html.

111 It is clear—in the words of the Asian Human Rights Commission—that these killings could continue only with her direct or indirect approval . . . ." See "The President Fails to Take Decisive Steps to End Extrajudicial Killings," *Asian Human Rights Commission—Statement* (July 25, 2006), http://www.ahrchk.net/statements/mainfile.php/2006statements/656/.

112 Diana Mendoza, "Philippines: Dangers of Journalism," *ZNet* (August 26, 2004), http://www.zmag.org/content/print_article.cfm?itemID=6111&sectionID=1.

113 "Dark Days for Philippine Democracy," *The New York Times* (April 5, 2006), http://www.nytimes.com/2006/04/05/opinion/05wed4.html.

114 Steven Rogers, "Beyond the Abu Sayyaf: The Lessons of Failure in the Philippines," *Foreign Affairs*, Vol. 83, No. 1 (January/February 2004), p. 20 (pp. 15–20).

115 *Ibid.*, p. 18.

116 "Profile: Gloria Arroyo," *BBC News* (June 20, 2004), http://news.bbc.co.uk/go/pr/fr/-/2/hi/asia-pacific/2614607.stm.

117 Simon Montlake, "As Asia booms, the Philippines is awash in red ink," *The Christian Science Monitor* (December 24, 2004), http://www.csmonitor.com/2004/1224/p07s02-woap.htm.

118 Philip Bowring, "Time for Arroyo to get tough," *The International Herald Tribune* (June 1, 2004), http://www.iht.com/bin/print.php?file=522761.html.

of Argentina before its crash.[119] The social turmoil she calls "terrorism" cannot be contained by any amount of military aid.

The thousands of protesters who marched in Manila in September 2003, in unison with anti-WTO protests in Cancún, Mexico, evoked memories of the original People Power. Spearheaded by 30 social movements and NGOs, marchers chanted "Globalization: Betrayal of the People" and "the Philippines is not for sale."[120] But in fact the Filipinos themselves are for sale worldwide in the form of migrant labor.[121] Of a less than 90 million population, 10 million work abroad as contract workers or domestics.[122] Their country neither offers them a living wage at home nor defends their human rights abroad. They are commodities for export, pure and simple.

Why has Arroyo's national sellout, punctuated by obvious election fraud,[123] brought such a tepid public reaction? The answer, Walden Bello suggests, is the cumulative disillusionment of so many dashed reform hopes in the past. Just as demonstrations against Estrada put Arroyo in office, there is great public confidence that demonstrations against Arroyo could result in someone as bad or worse.[124]

Having joined the WTO in 1995, the Philippines was obligated to fully implement its regulations by 2005. That meant terminating the import restrictions that had shielded not only domestic capitalists but also (by pure accident) subsistence farmers, despite massive illegal imports from China. Now Filipino peasants face the global market alone,[125] while the upper bourgeoisie affiliates itself ever more with the transnational capitalist class. It is hardly surprising that lower class incomes have plummeted throughout the country. This trend is epitomized by Smoky Mountain, a 40-year-old garbage heap on the outskirts of Manila. Thirty thousand indigents eke out a living here by rummaging through smoldering trash in search of things to sell, recycle, or eat. Although 80 percent of their children do not attend school, some feel

---

119 Marites Danguilan Vitung, "Star power holds perils for the Philippines," *The International Herald Tribune* (February 20, 2004), http://www.iht.com/cgi-bin/generic.cgi?template=articleprint.tmplh& ArticleId=130353.

120 "Anti-globalization initiatives on the WTO: A country updated—Philippines," *Global Network—Asia: An Alliance of Trade Concerns an Labor NGOs in Asia* (downloaded December 3, 2004), http://www.globalnetwork-asia.org.; and Herbert Docena, "Thousands march in Manila against WTO, corporate globalization, and war," *Nadir.org* (September 14, 2003), http://www.nadir.org/nadir/initiative/agp/free/cancun/action/asia/0914march_manila.htm.

121 Only India and China export more labor than the Philippines, whose overseas workforce leapt from 380,000 in 1986 to about 1 million in 2006. See Constantino, *op. cit.*

122 San Juan, Jr., "We Charge Genocide," *op. cit.*

123 Arroyo's voice on intercepted tapes leaves no doubt that she attempted to influence an electoral commissioner. See Walden Bello, "The Global Crisis of Legitimacy of Liberal Democracy," *Spectrezine* (November 29, 2005), http://www.spectrezine.org/global/Bello3.htm.

124 Bello, "The Global Crisis," *op. cit.* This very disillusionment may explain why Arroyo felt secure enough to lift the state of emergency she had declared after an alleged coup attempt. See Donald Kirk, "People-Powered Out in the Philippines?," *The Christian Science Monitor* (March 15, 2006), http://www.csmonitor.com/2006/0315/p07o02 woap.htm.

125 See Maria Linder-Hess, "Economic globalization," *A Common Place* (November 2003), http://www.mcc. org/us/globalization/viewpoints/Linder_Hess.html.

fortunate to make as much as 300 pesos a day (over 5 dollars).[126] Such are the fruits of global restructuration.

Not all the poor are deluded about the benefits of booty globalization. Those who join resistance movements will be labeled "terrorists," and their numbers are sure to swell. Meanwhile globalism is armor-plating itself with a new security agenda.[127] This is necessary because one of globalization's best local allies is no longer up to the task. For nearly two decades successive waves of People Power have served primarily as an instrument of hegemony: to contain subversive social forces, reducing pressure for structural change from below, as opposed to globalist restructuration from above. Transnational capital could not have gained its present grip on Philippine policies without this populist cover.

For that very reason, despite its awesome financial clout, booty globalization faces an uncertain political future. People Power has lost so much of its popular appeal that the Aquino-style center no longer holds. Right and Left confront each other with no centrist buffer, such that a toughened security apparatus is required to ward off militant resistance. At this juncture, with globalization effectively moving millions of workers from the Third World into the Fourth, booty globalism will either be defeated or will triumph as never before.

In the latter case the country will become a happy hunting ground for global capital, with many more Smoky Mountains on hand to keep the underclasses gainfully employed. The big question in a country with an active and growing Left is how resistance can be stunted. This includes democratic resistance. Capital will flee any country that cannot offer a "stable" investment climate, and in our era the greatest destabilizing force, even greater than Islamic jihad, is unmanaged democracy. In recent years there have been two proven formulas for such management: democratic co-optation and Tiananmen-style repression. Arroyo fails on both sides, having neither the power to crush democracy in the Beijing manner nor the populist credibility to lull reformists into a renewed state of "democratic" inertia.

Whatever the future of booty democracy in the Philippines itself, its application elsewhere in Asia and the developing world is not in doubt. Thailand's Thaksin used this democratic control mechanism to entrench his plutocracy, while his enemies used their variant of it to challenge his political machine. He was in no position to call in American reinforcements, as nearly all Philippine presidents have at some point, for as prime minister he had devoted much of his energy to tilting the globalist balance of power in his favor.[128] Anti-IMFism had been the crowning glory of early Thaksinocracy, with Washington's tacit consent, but later the tycoon-in-chief tipped the balance too far. When he finally sent out an S.O.S. for Washington's help

---

126 Escobar, "Poverty, Corruption," *op. cit.*

127 On neoglobalist securitization see William H. Thornton, *New World Empire: Terrorism, Civil Islam, and the Making of Neoglobalism* (Lanham, MD: Rowman & Littlefield, 2005), pp. 20 and 21; and on securitization in the Philippines see William H. Thornton, "Insecurity Forces: The Asian Costs of the War on Terrorism," *Radical Society: Review of Culture and Politics*, Vol. 28, No. 2 (July 2002), p. 60 (pp. 57–64).

128 William H. Thornton, "Another Thailand was Possible: Thaksin and the Thai Response to Globalization," *Radical Society: Review of Culture and Politics*, Vol. 32, No. 2 (Summer 2006), p. 73 (pp. 71–80).

(effectively surrendering to the Washington Consensus, since any such assistance would certainly come with tight strings attached) he got no more than a polite reply from Bush.[129] The message to future Thaksins was clear regarding the delineation of center and periphery in the global system.[130]

Like Aquino before, Arroyo knows better than to question her status as a kept woman. She limits herself to testing her power on the domestic rather than US side of the globalist equation. The outcome of this experiment in political retrenchment will say much about the future of globalism's "democratic" legitimacy. If the Philippine power elite can get along without the camouflage of ersatz People Power, so can other developing authoritarianisms. In that case the winner may well be Sino-globalism, which makes no democratic claims whatsoever.

The clear loser in this political race to the bottom appears to be democratic development: Amartya Sen's "development as freedom." If there is any ground for optimism here, it issues from the fact that booty globalism—which is to say the Smoky Mountain school of development—no longer has People Power as its "democratic" prop. Instead it seeks legitimacy from the same post-9/11 fear factor that President Bush has made the leitmotif of his foreign as well as domestic policy. However, as Thaksin learned too late, this security imperative has a short shelf life. Tellingly it was the urban bourgeoisie, in league with the military and the King, that toppled Thaksin in September 2006. The irony is that Thaksin himself had become the chief obstacle to the implicit promise of Thaksinocracy, which was to broadly share the spoils of globalization among the affluent classes. Thaksin, however, had behaved more and more like another Marcos or Suharto. The urban Right felt it was not getting its share of the take.

Arroyo, by contrast, has much more to fear from unrest on the Left—a fire that could easily spread out of control. This could have a devastating effect on foreign direct investment. To avoid capital flight, or simply to keep the peace, some form of People Power will have to be reactivated as a pressure release mechanism. This time, however, the general public is going to demand more of the real thing. The resurgence of People Power on these terms could bring an end to six decades of "democratic" neocolonization.

---

129 On Thaksin's urgent call for help from the White House, see Seth Mydans, "Saving Thai Democracy: Will the Cure Kill the Patient?," *New York Times* (August 30, 2006), http://www.nytimes.com/2006/08/30/world/asia/30letter.html.

130 Nonetheless, as Washington was fully aware, Thaksin was still a moderate when it came to tipping the globalist balance. He made a show of paying back IMF loans early—symbolically declaring independence from Washington-based globalization—yet all the while he worked assiduously to link Thai farm production to the global market. This put him at odds with economic nationalists, including King Bhumibol himself, who had worked just as hard to tie the rural sector to self-sufficient domestic markets. See "Of Kings, Coups, and Asian Democracies," *The Christian Science Monitor* (September 21, 2006), http://www.csmonitor.com/2006/0921/p08s02-comv.htm.

Chapter 4

Lesson of the "Broken Hearts": The Rise and Fall of Indonesian *Reformasi*

Fragile Miracle

More than anywhere else on the Rim, the Indonesian "miracle" economy came wrapped in a political straight-jacket. To miss this fact is to minimize the emancipatory potential of the Crash of 1997–98. It is telling that the Crash as a whole is commonly referred to as the Asian *financial* crisis, as if political and other non-economic factors can be bracketed out of consideration. Such erasure long shielded corrupt regimes, and then played a key part in turning the Crash into an ongoing Crisis.

Calls for reform were so rampant after the Crash that it is astonishing how little has changed. There was a changing of the guard, but not of the system or the basic ideology. In Indonesia's 2004 election campaign, no candidate or party questioned the neoliberal agenda of Suharto-era technocrats.[1] Post-Crash "reforms" only intensified this fixation. The very word "reform," in IMF parlance, was so economized that it ended up as little more than a bailout mechanism for foreign and domestic investors. The global institutions that rushed in to repair this "financial crisis" helped to stanch the one positive effect that might have come from the Crash: the escape it promised from developmental authoritarianism.[2]

Throughout the region, but especially in Indonesia, pent-up reform energies held out hope for a developmental sea change. Once again the Trojan Horse of Western technocracy was rolled in to guarantee the stability that a "healthy investment climate" required. The ironic result was instability on an epoch scale. Those who blame the IMF and other international institutions for compounding the crisis are actually optimists. They seem to assume that these blunders were rare exceptions to the rule, rather than cases of deliberate conformity to a global pattern that could not have been missed by policy makers. Even in good times, IMF and World Bank lending policies had stimulated growth at a ghastly political, social and environmental price.[3] And once the crisis struck, as they knew it would, these institutions stood ready to impose counter-Keynesian policies that served market interests at all costs.

---

1 Max Lane, "The Distraction is Over," *Inside Indonesia* (January/March 2005), http://www. insideIndonesia.org/edit81/p19-20_lane.html.

2 William H. Thornton, *Fire on the Rim: The Cultural Dynamics of East/West Power Politics* (Lanham, MD. Rowman & Littlefield, 2002), p. 139.

3 Arturo Escobar, *Encountering Development: The Making and Unmaking of the Third World* (Princeton, NJ: Princeton University Press, 1995), p. 56.

The Asia Pacific region would now be fully exposed to a development regimen that others knew all too well. Consider, for example, the global debt crisis of 1982, which should have been no surprise after lending to the Third World jumped from $2.7 billion in 1970 to $12 billion in 1981.[4] The sweeping restructuration that followed resulted in Latin America's "lost decade," which stood in stark contrast to East Asia's boom of those same years. Asians were pleased to have that growth gap explained in terms of Asian values, which took the wind out of Latin dependency theory. Few noticed that another form of dependency was at work on the Rim, where geopolitical advantages guaranteed a constant capital influx throughout the 1980s.[5] This unlevel playing field also ensured tolerance for massive trade imbalances that were tantamount to economic aid.

With the end of the Cold War that tolerance started to wane, and by the time of the Asian Crash the IMF saw no reason to treat Rim economies with more solicitude than it extended to other developing regions. The Rim was effectively downgraded to the status of Mexico in its Tequila Crisis. Rim nations may later have regretted the IMF loan terms they accepted, but at the time of the Crash they still trusted their erstwhile benefactor. The devastating effect of IMF directives can be measured against the base line of Malaysia, a country that bucked the system, yet weathered the Crisis better than its more compliant neighbors.[6]

Conversely, no country did worse than Indonesia, despite the fact that it yielded almost unconditionally to IMF dictates. This was out of habit. To placate the West in the wake of its bloody 1965 takeover, the Suharto regime implemented liberalization policies as early as 1967, with capital accounts opened to foreign investors in 1970. Jakarta sought foreign capital by way of repeated devaluations of the rupiah: 10 percent in 1971, 50 percent in 1978, 40 percent in 1983, and 32 percent in 1986.[7] Scant attention was given to the fact that what flowed in could just as easily rush out. Oblivious to the danger, technocrats pushed for further liberalization.[8]

Rise and Fall of the Technocrats

By 1988 neo-classical economists such as Professors Widjoyo Nitisastro and Ali Wardhana had taken over Jakarta's economic planning, but these technocrats (known to critics as the "Berkeley Mafia")[9] rarely wielded power in their own right. Their

---

4 Waden Bello, Shea Cummingham, and Bill Rau, *Dark Victory: The United States and Global Poverty* (London: Pluto Press, new edition, 1999), p. 5 and p. 13.

5 *Ibid.*, p. 34.

6 That is not to say that Malaysia was economically independent. Its protectionism was made possible by an ample influx of Japanese investment. See *Ibid.*

7 Mohamed Ariff and Ahmed M. Khalid, *Liberalization, Growth and the Asian Financial Crisis: Lessons for Developing and Transitional Economies in Asia* (Cheltenham, UK: Edward Elgar, 2000), p. 157 and p. 159.

8 Adam Schwarz, *A Nation in Waiting: Indonesia's Search for Stability* (Boulder, CO: Westview, 2000), p. 49.

9 Rizal Sukma, *Indonesia and China: The Politics of a Troubled Relationship* (London: Routledge, 1999), p. 76.

success rested on their alliances. Working closely with the Army, they became a bulwark of Suharto's New Order. The Armed Forces of the Republic of Indonesia (ABRI)—now called the Indonesian National Military (TNI)—needed civilian partners to disguise its double function (*"dwifungsi"*) of politics and security. In this way ABRI increasingly dominated state enterprises such as oil companies.[10]

From the early years of the New Order, the technocrats implemented policies to secure foreign aid, loans and investment, especially from the US and Japan.[11] Thanks to the interpenetration of military and civilian institutions, aid that was not earmarked for the "military" could still promote the militarization of the New Order and the de-pluralization of Indonesian politics. This techno-military merger was strongly anti-communist and pro-development, those being two sides of the same geopolitical coin. Indonesia would be one of the largest recipients of US aid in Asia,[12] while America would be Indonesia's major supplier of arms.[13] The first priority of New Order foreign policy was to clean up Jakarta's international image so as to attract capital. Loaded down with foreign debt, the regime had little choice in the matter. It depended upon a continuous infusion of capital for its very solvency.[14] The military therefore backed the technocrats, who in turn became rubber stamps for ABRI policies.[15]

Two groups competed with the technocrats in this rubber-stamp capacity: economic nationalists, who held that the government should tightly manage the economy, and Suharto's cronies and relatives, who simply wanted their share of the take. Friction with the nationalists can be divided into three phases. In the first, from 1966 to 1974, the technos were at the helm of most economic policymaking. Their international connections were in great demand at this time of acute dependency, but their influence waned with the relative autonomy that Indonesia gained from the global surge in oil prices of the 1970s. Windfall revenues reached $4.2 billion in 1974, while the second surge of 1979–80 pushed that figure to $13.4 billion by 1981. This enabled the nationalists to seize control and press for heavily subsidized

---

10 Syed Farid Alatas, *Democracy and Authoritarianism in Indonesia and Malaysia: The Rise of the Post-Colonial State* (London: Macmillan Press, 1997), p. 137.

11 Dewi Fortuna Anwar, *Indonesia in ASEAN: Foreign Policy and Regionalism* (New York and Singapore: St. Martin's Press and Institute of Southeast Asian Studies, 1994), p. 280 and p. 287.

12 *Ibid.*, p. 281.

13 *Ibid.*, p. 283. Benedict Anderson shows that the US knew about the plan to invade East Timor. Kissinger simply advised Jakarta to "do it quickly." Some 90 percent of the weapons used in the invasion were provided by the US, in clear violation of US treaty agreements. See *The Spectre of Comparision: Nationalism, Southeast Asia and the World* (London: Verso, 1998), p. 133. For more on this US complicity, see Adam Schwarz, *A Nation, op. cit.,* pp. 203–4. Concerning the CIA's false report and the grossly biased coverage of the 1965 coup, see Benedict Anderson and Ruth McVey, "What Happened in Indonesia?," *The New York Review of Books* (June 1, 1978), http://www.nybooks.com/article/8144; and their *A Preliminary Analysis of the October 1, 1965 Coup in Indonesia* (Ithaca, NY: Cornell Modern Indonesia Project, 1971).

14 Anwar, *op. cit.,* pp. 38–39.

15 Sukma, *op. cit.,* p. 77.

new industries. For the moment that put the technocrats out to pasture. They were soon back in vogue, however, as oil prices dropped from $30 a barrel in 1984 to $10 in 1986.[16]

Not surprisingly the technos adopted a more liberal development strategy, reversing the nationalist preference for import substitution. They devalued the rupiah in 1986, so as to boost export competitiveness and attract foreign investment. Their success lent credibility to technocratic logic, but storm clouds were building. Between early 1989 and 1992 Indonesia's money supply increased more than two and a half times, which fueled inflation and prompted the central bank, Bank Indonesia, to tighten its monetary control. The result was a sharp rise in interest rates, higher costs for businesses,[17] and a plethora of bad debts.

Along with other Rim nations, Indonesia covered its surging debts by still more borrowing. Foreign debt stood at around $3.2 billion at the beginning of Suharto's regime, and rose to $130 billion by 1998.[18] Between 1982 and 1991 the debt jumped from 29 to 72 percent of GNP. This was much higher than the debts of Mexico and Brazil at the time of the Latin American crisis of 1981–82: 52 percent and 36 percent of GNP, respectively.[19] But on the Rim this pattern was becoming the norm. Foreign borrowing continued to grow throughout the Asia Pacific region until the time of the Crash.[20]

Nationalist reaction was sure to follow. Even in the 1980's the CSIS group—the research and intelligence wing of the late General Ali Murtopo's political faction—had demanded close state supervision of Indonesia's capital growth, and especially its foreign capital.[21] CSIS arguments gained credibility as the total debt (including private commercial loans) skyrocketed, finally producing a banking crisis in 1993.[22] Clearly it was the liberal camp, not CSIS-style nationalism, which put the economy at risk.

The search for solutions led to complete polarization. Some blamed the technocrats for their precipitous liberalization schemes, while others blamed Suharto for not allowing the technocrats greater sway.[23] Western critics would later put the onus on "crony capitalism," but these very cronies had opened the door to Western neoliberalism. What won them over to the technocrat's way of thinking was their realization that opening up the banking sector would increase the flow of capital to themselves.[24] Laksamana Sukardi, former Minister of investment and state enterprises, condemned these globalist converts as "predators" who "stole billions

---

16 Schwarz, *op. cit.*, pp. 53–56.

17 *Ibid.*, pp. 74–75.

18 Margaret Scott, "Indonesia Reborn?," *The New York Review of Books*, Vol. 45, No. 13 (August 13, 1998), p. 46 (pp. 43–48).

19 Schwarz, *op. cit.*, p. 79.

20 Brian Bremner, Michael Shari, Bruce Einhorn, Moon Ihlwan, Mike McNamee, and Kerry Capell, "Rescuing Asia," *Business Week* (November 17, 1997), http://www.businessweek.com/1997/46/b3553001.htm.

21 Richard Robison, "The Transformation of the State in Indonesia," in John G. Taylor and Andrew Turton (eds), *Sociology of "Developing Societies": Southeast Asia* (New York: Monthly Review Press, 1988), p. 59 (pp. 48–68).

22 Schwarz, *op. cit.*, p. 78.

23 *Ibid.*, p. 74 and p. 342.

24 *Ibid.*, p. 317.

from state coffers."[25] Few in the West showed much concern about this glaring fact prior to the Crash.

The popular notion that Asia's "crony capitalists" were evil nationalists locked in mortal combat with neoliberal saviors was a disastrous error, for this myth guaranteed that the cure for the subsequent Crisis would be sought in still greater neoliberalization. Far more than nationalist protectionism, two main causes of the Crash were wasted foreign investment (especially in real estate) and mounting private debt, which lunged from $23 billion in 1992 to nearly $80 billion in 1997.[26]

Between June 1997 and January 1998 the rupiah lost 80 percent of its value, which pushed interest rates up 60 percent. Millions of Indonesians were plunged into abject poverty, as per capita income dropped from $1,000 to $350.[27] Nonetheless Suharto was unanimously re-elected by the People's Consultative Assembly in March 1998. His new cabinet—including his daughter Tutut and his arch crony Bob Hasan—epitomized the corruption and nepotism that condemned the country to chronic maldevelopment. Student and worker protests finally toppled Suharto on May 21, 1998. *Eighty* political parties had been established by late 1998, twenty of them being Islamic.[28] The New Order seemed to be giving way to a New Disorder.

The Suharto Mire

By the mid-1990s, sensing this gathering storm, Suharto turned to his technocrats for a solution. Unfortunately their specialty was economic acceleration. They had no idea how to apply the brakes, and in any case their economic leverage had eroded. They were no longer the crucial magnets for foreign investment, since foreign investors were now tripping over each other in their rush to win favor with Suharto's better-positioned cronies for projects worth billions,[29] on paper at least. Far from offering advice on braking techniques, international institutions joined the investment frenzy. The World Bank organized donors' conferences to rake in billions more, even knowing that an estimated one third of this money would be lost to Golkar Party corruption.[30]

---

25 Quoted in Mark Landler, "For Indonesia, Solvency is Political," *The New York Times* (April 20, 2001), http://www.nytimes.com/2001/04/20/business/20INDO.html?ex=1075266 000&en=08f9f734d50e5ea5 &ei=5070. Hence economic reformers focused their efforts on the control of financial institutions such as state-owned banks. A case in point was the shady financing of Tommy Suharto's clove monopoly, BPPC. By February 1992, even Tommy admitted that the BPPC was a total failure. See Schwarz, *op. cit.*, p. 151 and pp. 155–6.

26 Schwarz, *op. cit.*, p. 312.

27 David Bourchier and Vedi R. Hadiz, "Introduction," in David Bourchier and Vedi R. Hadiz (eds), *Indonesian Politics and Society: A Reader* (London: RoutledgeCurzon, 2003), p. 19 (pp. 1–24).

28 Jamhari, "Islamic Political Parties: Threats or Prospects?," in Geoff Forrester (ed.), *Post-Suharto Indonesia: Renewal or Chaos?* (The Netherlands and Singapore: KITLV Press and Institute of Southeast Asian Studies, 1999), p. 171 (pp. 170–80).

29 *Ibid.*, p. 316.

30 Abigail Abrash, "Indonesa After Suharto," *Foreign Policy*, Vol. 3, No. 34 (November 1998), http://www. foreignpolicy-infocus.org/briefs/vol13/v3n34ind_body.html (also available

The IMF, likewise, put no pressure on Suharto to stop public subsidies for schemes such as Tommy Suharto's national car project or B.J. Habibie's efforts to manufacture aircraft domestically. As usual the IMF served the interest of international finance, disregarding its nominal function of easing economic trauma. Previously Southeast Asian economies had tended to enjoy low inflation, budget surpluses, and rising foreign exchange revenues, but between 1993 and 1996 investment banks and international money market managers went on a lending binge.[31] Even free-market proponents such as George P. Schultz, William E. Simon, and Walter B. Wriston blamed the IMF for the global financial meltdown that followed.[32] Economist Jeffrey Sachs accused the IMF of worsening the Crash by closing banks and slashing public spending—this at a time when the private sector was already deflated.[33]

To add insult to injury, the World Bank and the IMF wrapped these decisions in a cloak of cultural sensitivity, treating Suharto's corruption, cronyism and nepotism as natural expressions of "Indonesian culture." Meanwhile the Clinton administration carried on business as usual by refusing to suspend Indonesia's tariff advantages under the Generalized System of Preferences, despite Jakarta's crackdown on unions and its failure to ensure decent working conditions. Industries linked to gross human rights abuses and environmental destruction got full US backing.[34] This long-standing indifference to real development needs would be recycled after the Crash, starting with Washington's lethargic response to the Thai crisis of August 1997. As of October 26, Secretary of the Treasury Robert Rubin still ruled out an Asian bailout on the IMF's part. Nor did he want any other institution to do the job. Both he and Larry Summers would vehemently oppose the formation of a Japanese "Asian Monetary Fund," which they saw as a potential competitor of the IMF, and hence a challenge to American hegemony.[35]

Only when Rubin realized that American corporations were in serious jeopardy did he start to shift his position, announcing on October 31 that "Financial security around the world is critical to the national security and economic interest of the United States. These countries are not only key markets for U.S. exports, but are also crucial to our efforts to promote growth, peace and prosperity throughout the

---

at http://www.fpif.org/briefs/vol13/v3n34ind.html); and Schwarz, *op. cit.*, p. 316.

31   John Bresnan, "The United States, the IMF, and the Indonesian Financial Crisis," in Adam Schwarz and Jonathan Paris (eds), *The Politics of Post-Suharto Indonesia* (New York: Council on Foreign Relations Press, 1999), p. 87 (pp. 87–112).

32   *Ibid.*, p. 102.

33   Schwarz, *A Nation, op. cit.*, p. 339 and p. 341. One of the 16 banks that closed belonged to Suharto's son, Bambang Trihatmodjo. A week later he reopened his bank under a new name. See Adam Schwarz, "Introduction: The Politics of Post-Suharto Indonesia," in Adam Schwarz and Jonathan Paris (eds), *The Politics of Post-Suharto* (New York: Council on Foreign Relations Press, 1999), p. 6 (pp. 1–15).

34   See Abrash, *op. cit.*

35   T.J. Pempel, "Conclusion," in T.J. Pempel (ed.), *The Politics of Asian Economic Crisis* (Ithaca, NY: Cornell University Press, 1999), p. 230 (pp. 224–38).

world."[36] A \$40 billion bailout package was finally arranged for Indonesia alone.[37] This action cut the political strings that could have tied the bailout to progressive reform. The White House was content with IMF packages that left Suharto alone. This can be explained in two ways. Not only does Washington accept the "Asian values" myth that dictatorship is natural to Southeast Asia, but it clearly prefers authoritarian regimes that can be controlled better than unruly democracies.

The lesser of these two evils (the notion that democracy is a distinctly Western value) would allow that US policy is not designedly imperialistic, but is simply orientalist. Suharto certainly encouraged the perception that liberal objectives like democracy and human rights are incompatible with Indonesian culture,[38] despite the pluralist implications of the official state ideology of Pancasila. In fact it was the nation's democratic propensity, which even the 1965–66 massacre could not expunge, that necessitated the regime's iron-fist policies.[39]

The New Order had increasing difficulty with the flip side of its seeming success. Tension set in as economic development not only outpaced political development, but in many ways precluded it. Pressures for change were mounting, however. Although the regime's legitimacy depended on rapid economic growth, that very growth could have a destabilizing impact when newly affluent sectors of society began to demand a political voice.[40] Middle-class disaffection was amplified by the centrifugal force of the country's geographic expanse and ethnic diversity. While real per capita GDP trebled between 1965 and 1990,[41] the regime's absolute power ebbed after the mid-1980s.[42]

This alone was not enough to turn the political tide, for the middle-class was too satisfied with the economic status quo. The fate of democratic reform rested, therefore, with another suppressed sector of society: the Muslims who comprised 90 percent of the population.[43] As in many Islamic countries, the mosque became the locus of oppositional politics. Realizing the growing power of Islamism, Suharto shifted his position in the last twelve years of his regime. For twenty years he had obstructed organized Islamic activities, but now he encouraged them, so as to counterbalance

---

36 Quoted in Abrash, *op. cit.*

37 Brian Bremner, Michael Shari, Bruce Einhorn, Moon Ihlwan, Mike McNamee, and Kerry Capell, "Rescuing Asia," *Business Week* (November 17, 1997), http://www.businessweek.com/1997/46/b3553001.htm.

38 Robert W. Hefner, *Civil Islam: Muslims and Democratization in Indonesia* (Princeton: Princeton University Press, 2000), p. xvi and p. 5.

39 Ariel Heryanto, "Indonesian Middle-Class Opposition in the 1990s," in Garry Rodan (ed.), *Political Oppositions in Industrializing Asia* (London: Routledge, 1996), p. 242 (pp. 241–71).

40 Edward Aspinall, "The Broadening Base of Political Opposition in Indonesia," in Garry Rodan (ed.), *Political Oppositions in Industrializing Asia* (London: Routledge, 1996), p. 226 (pp. 215–40).

41 *Ibid.*, p. 225.

42 Heryanto, *op. cit.*, p. 241.

43 Seth Mydans, "In Indonesia, Once Tolerant Islam Grows Rigid," *The New York Times* (December 29, 2001), http://www.nytimes.com/2001/12/29/international/asia/29INDO.htm?pagewanted=print.

powerful military leaders such as General Benny Murdani, who openly confronted Suharto over the issue of his family's corruption.[44]

This contributed to a split between ABRI and Suharto over the choice of Golkar chairman Sudharmono as vice-president.[45] ABRI challenged that choice during the 1988 election, which in turn prompted Suharto to actively court tractable elements of the Muslim community.[46] His creation of the Indonesian Association of Muslim Intellectuals (ICMI) in December 1990 was a blatant attempt to control Islam by exploiting the divide between the Nahdlatul Ulama (NU) traditionalists and the Muhammadiyah modernists.[47] The ICMI co-opted ultraconservative Muslim organizations such as the Indonesian Council for Islamic Predication, or DDII, at the expense of other groups.[48] Many ABRI officers admitted that Suharto's sponsorship of ICMI was a shrewd means of controlling Islamic radicals.[49]

Not surprisingly this had a divisive impact on Muslim politics. While Islamic modernists tended to welcome ICMI, the NU leader and later president Abdurrahman Wahid stood his ground. He proclaimed his loyalty to the Constitution and the official state ideology of Pancasila, yet declared the ICMI a Trojan Horse.[50] He further infuriated Suharto by questioning the motive behind his Islamic turn. Just as Suharto had successfully turned techno-reformists into reactionary modernists,[51] he now tried to turn Islamic reformists into cronies. It was in this divide-and-conquer context that B.J. Habibie, the minister of research and technology, was put in charge of ICMI, so as to marginalize moderate independents like Dawam Rahardjo.

Nonetheless Muslims would play a key role in the reform coalition that finally toppled Suharto. Robert Hefner's civil Islam thesis hinges on his contention that nowhere in the world have Muslim intellectuals been so engaged in the formation of

---

44 Hefner, *Civil Islam, op. cit.*, p. 18.

45 See Schwarz, *A Nation, op. cit.*, p. 37.

46 Douglas E. Ramage, *Politics in Indonesia: Democracy, Islam and the Ideology of Tolerance* (London: Routledge, 1995), p. 85.

47 Schwarz, "Introduction," *op. cit.*, pp. 9–10. On January 20, 2002 the latest division came with the creation of a new party by members of the United Development Party (PPP), the nation's biggest Islamic group. The National Awakening Party (PKB), which draws members from the NU, is also subject to factionalism. See Dini Djalal, "Indonesia: Missed Opportunities," *The Far Eastern Economic Review* (January 31, 2002), http://www.feer.com/articles/2002/0201_31/p021region.html.

48 Robert W. Hefner, "Islam and Nation in the Post-Suharto Era," in Adam Schwarz and Jonathan Paris (eds), *The Politics of Post-Suharto Indonesia* (New York: Council on Foreign Relations Press, 1999), p. 48 (pp. 40–72); and also see Anders Uhlin, *Indonesia and the "Third Wave of Democratization": The Indonesian Pro-Democracy Movement in a Changing World* (Surrey, UK: Curzon Press, 1997), pp. 66–7.

49 Ramage, *op. cit.*, p. 142.

50 *Ibid.*, p. 68.

51 In his autobiography, Suharto describes techno-economists as a necessary evil. See William Liddle, "Indonesia's Unexpected Failure of Leadership," in Adam Schwarz and Jonathan Paris (eds), *The Politics of Post-Suharto Indonesia* (New York: Council on Foreign Relations Press, 1999), p. 23 (pp. 16–39).

democratic civil society as in Indonesia.[52] No one knew this better than Suharto, who devoted his last years in office to undermining civil Islam as a political free agent. By uncritically supporting Suharto, global institutions helped to suppress liberal democratization during the "miracle" years when political development might have been accomplished peacefully and with little material sacrifice.

Nor was globalization's economic impact any less pernicious. Capital export from Western countries stoked the "Indonesian miracle," which in turn did its part to revitalize faith in capitalism as a global development strategy. Again it had to be learned the hard way that foreign capital can be a two-edged sword. The Crash afforded a kind of remedial education. The rapid exodus of capital from Asian NICs, coupled with "rescue" policies that turned a mere recession into a regional depression, signaled a crisis of globalist ideology.

The Post-Suharto Malaise

Except for its political unrest, Indonesia had all the makings of an investors' paradise. It had been blessed with cheap labor and inflated prices for its vast oil reserves, and the ostensive stability of the post-Sukarno years made foreign investment fairly easy to obtain.[53] This changed, however, after the collapse of oil prices in the mid-1980s. At that point the nation had to work hard to attract foreign capital, pushing it into the waiting arms of neoliberal restructuration.

For those who were plugged into this surging current of globalization, Indonesia of the early 1990s once again seemed like a land of boundless opportunity. Yet economic technocrats knew this promise depended on massive foreign investment, which in turn depended on political stability. The question of succession cast doubt on the future of the increasingly dysfunctional New Order.[54] It was whispered that to avoid a political upset Suharto should relinquish power before the 1998 election.[55] Even prior to the Asian Crash, a viable pro-democracy movement was taking shape across a wide spectrum of moderate opposition: NGOs, intellectuals, and campus activists, as well as PDI and NU factions.

---

52 Seth Mydans qualifies this optimism by noting the rise of religious violence in areas such as Sulawesi, Maluk and Aceh. Islamic politicians, especially the Defenders of Islam, also sacrifice broader influence when they call for prohibitions on drinking, gambling, etc. Accordingly, voters in the 1999 election overwhelmingly chose secular nationalist parties over Islamic ones. See Mydans, *op. cit.* Islamic extremists struck back by calling for an Indonesian Islamic State (NII). See Dini Djalal, "Indoneisa: Forced to Serve," *The Far Eastern Economic Review* (April 4, 2002), http://www.feer.com/articles/2002/0204_04/p050current.html.

53 Adam Schwarz, *A Nation in Waiting: Indonesia's Search for Stability* (Boulder, CO: Westview, 2000), p. 41.

54 Michael R.J. Vatikiotis, *Indonesian Politics Under Suharto: Order, Development and Pressure for Change* (London: Routledge, revised edition, 1994), p. 139.

55 Afan Gaffer, "Indonesia 1995: Setting the Tone for Transition towards the Post-Suharto Era," In Colin Barlow and Joan Hardjono (eds), *Indonesia Assessment 1995: Development in Eastern Indonesia* (Canberra: Research School of Pacific and Asian Studies/Australia National University, 1996), pp. 43–4 (pp. 43–57).

The regime had to react, but there was no consensus as to what response was appropriate—retrenchment or accommodation. Even supposedly neutral technocrats were emotionally divided on the issue. After the currency collapse of 1997—as the rupiah plummeted from 2,500 against the dollar in early 1997 to 13,450 in June 2001[56]—three groups jousted for influence within the cabinet: economic technocrats, followers of Habibie, and the entourage of Suharto's daughter Tutut.[57] Habibie still looked to technology as a developmental panacea, with special stress given to electronics, telecommunications, and transport industries,[58] but other technocrats were finally catching on to the fact that economic development barren of political development was a ruse. When they let this be known, Suharto summarily fired them. These outcasts formed a group called the "Front of the Broken Hearts"— belated reformists who dropped their façade of technocratic neutrality and proposed a "new morality" in opposition to Suharto's "state criminality."[59]

The major technocratic split was between moderate reformists like Habibie, who stuck with the geriatric New Order, and more radical factions such as the "Broken Hearts." Early in his career Habibie had gained control of many state-owned strategic industries, including naval shipyards, armaments plants, and an airplane factory. After he joined parliament as a Golkar member in 1982, his family, like Suharto's, began to forge its own business empire, centered around the Timsco Group. These enterprises engaged in everything from chemicals to crocodile farming, and finally came to be worth at least $60 million.[60]

Thus when Habibie talked about technological strategies to enhance competitive advantage,[61] it was not clear if the benefit he had in mind was his country's or his own. Clearly he was no enemy of Suharto's political machine. Though he was forced to make some changes during his seventeen-month administration—e.g., he released hundreds of political prisoners and allowed a free election in 1999[62]—these alterations were hardly satisfactory to *reformasi* activists. Habibie's administration, after all, retained half of Suharto's cabinet.

---

56 Samuel Charng Yeong Ku, *Indonesia: Politics, Economy and Society* (Kaohsiung, Taiwan: Kaohsiung Fu Wen, 2002), p. 65.

57 See "Indonesia's New Dynamic Cabinet," *Inside Indonesia* (March 15, 1998), http://www.inside indonesia.org/digest/dig53.htm.

58 B.J. Habibie, "Industrialisation and the Technological Transformation of a Nation" (1986), in Ian Chalmers and Vedi R. Hadiz (eds), *The Politics of Economic Development in Indonesia: Contending Perspectives* (London: Routledge, 1997), p. 177 and p. 179 (pp. 176–81).

59 Margaret Scott, "Indonesia Reborn?" *The New York Review of Books*, Vol. 45, No. 13 (August 13, 1998), p. 46 (pp. 43–48).

60 See "A Transitional Figure," *South China Morning Post* (March 15, 2000), http://special.scmp.com/wchal/profiles/habibie.

61 See Hal Hill, *The Indonesian Economy Since 1966: Southeast Asia's Emerging Giant* (Cambridge, UK: Cambridge University Press, 1996), p. 248.

62 Anthony L. Smith, "Indonesia: Transforming the Leviathan," in John Funston (ed.), *Government and Politics in Southeast Asia* (Singapore: Institute of Southeast Asian Studies, 2001), p. 80 (pp. 74–119).

As a technocrat, Habibie lacked a broad power base, whereas Wahid was closely linked to the Islamism of rural Java. Megawati Sukarnoputri drew support from the legend of her father's nationalism, while Amien Rais found a following among urban, modernist Muslims.[63] Habibie's only solid support came from the armed forces of General Wiranto and the funding garnered by his minister, Ginandjar Kartasasmita, the technocrat who steered Indonesia's compliance with the IMF restructuration package.

The absence of stable government and robust leadership made the economic crisis even more injurious. Habibie did improve the country's image by ratifying a number of UN conventions on human rights, and he signed the UN's Ocean Charter to use maritime resources in a sustainable way.[64] So too he lifted the restrictive press law that Suharto had imposed between 1994 and 1995, when three of the most respected newsweeklies—*Tempo*, *DeTik* and *Editor*—were summarily shut down.[65] Ironically, it would be these three magazines that vocalized the public's call for real reform and actively investigated Habibie's budget after his purchase of East German navy vessels.[66] *Tempo* even invited Benedict Anderson, who had been banned from entering Indonesia since 1972, for a candid interview.[67] To his credit, Habibie yielded to the public's demand for free and fair elections.[68] Forty-eight parties competed in the general election of June 7, 1999, and on October 20 the MPR (People's Consultative Assembly) chose Wahid as the nation's fourth President.[69]

Habibie's greatest service to his country was to let himself be voted out of office. His successor, however, would be no real improvement. It would be an understatement to say that Wahid's leadership lacked consistency. Having shocked his allies with the rank opportunism of his 1996 détente with Suharto, Wahid again reversed himself by jumping back on the opposition band wagon when the economic crisis worsened in late 1997. Soon he had moved to the center of the reform movement against Suharto, and by July 1998 he was seeking a new alliance with Megawati.[70]

Given these vacillations, it should have come as no surprise that as president Wahid would fail to deliver the main item on the reform agenda: civilian supremacy

---

63 Jose Manuel Tesoro, "Insider-Outsider," *Asiaweek*, Vol. 25, No. 52 (December 31, 1999–January 4, 2000), http://www.asiaweek.com/asiaweek/magazine/99/1231/year.habibie. html.

64 Bilveer Singh, *Succession Politics in Indonesia: The 1998 Presidential Elections and the Fall of Suharto* (London: Macmillan Press, 2000), p. 242.

65 See Margot Cohen, "Unsilenced: Indonesia Discovers Free Speech," *The New Republic* (June 15, 1998), http://www.thenewrepublic.com/archive/0698/061598/cohen061598.html; Bruce Grant, "Crackdown in Indonesia," *The New York Review of Books* (Oct. 20, 1994), http://www.nybooks. com/articles/2111; and Catherine Drucker, "Indonesia's Unfree Press," *The New York Review of Books* (July 13, 1995), http://www.nybooks.com/articles/1837; and Hefner, "Islam and Nation," *op. cit.*, p. 53.

66 Hefner, "Islam and Nation," *op. cit.*, p. 55.

67 Scott Sherman, "A Return to Java," *Lingua Franca*, Vol. 11, No. 7 (October 2001), http://www. linguafranca.com.

68 Liddle, *op. cit.*, p. 36.

69 Abubakar E. Hara, "The Difficult Journey of Democratization in Indonesia," *Contemporary Southeast Asia*, Vol. 23, No. 2 (August 2001), pp. 307–26.

70 Hefner, "Islam and Nation," *op. cit.*, p. 55 and p. 59.

over ABRI. Many analysts believe the retired army general and future president Susilo Bambang Yudhoyono was already in charge of security matters,[71] as he would be under Megawati.[72] Meanwhile Wahid found himself hostage to an emerging alliance between Megawati's Indonesian Democratic Party for Struggle and Suharto's former Golkar Party, led by Akbar Tanjung. Together the two parties held 273 of 500 lower-house seats.[73] Megawati and Tanjung (who would later become embroiled in a \$4 million corruption scandal)[74] shot down Wahid's proposal to appoint a single coordination minister, pressuring him to name two instead.[75] His desire to please everyone was reflected in his motley cabinet.

Clifford Geertz is not alone in his lament that Habibie and Wahid squandered Indonesia's chance to start over after Suharto.[76] It was under them that residual Cold War politics gave way to an equally regressive politics of globalization. The rise of the *reformasi* against Suharto would have had no teeth had it not been joined by the urban and rural poor whose strikes and rioting pushed the government into a corner. This upsurge had its roots in social protests of the 1980s against New Order oppression launched in the name of modernization. Its real name was neoliberalism, and its thrust was only intensified after Suharto's fall.[77]

Losing on Both Fronts

For many years *reformasi* storm clouds had been building within the middle-class public. This idealism, however, would find little expression in the new mass politics. Lacking the leadership qualities of rivals such as Amien Rais,[78] Megawati won the presidency on the strength of her family legacy and her largely symbolic opposition to Suharto's corruption. Unfortunately she had no idea what to do with her victory. To win public trust she was advised to seed her administration with a host of techno-

---

71 Michael Vatikiotis and John McBeth, "Marching Back," *The Far Eastern Economic Review* (October 12, 2000), http://www.feer.com/_0010_12/p4region.html.

72 It did not help that Wahid's reformist ally, Lt. General Agus Wirahadikusumah, was alienated from his fellow military officers. See John McBeth, "Military Maneuvers," *The Far Eastern Economic Review* (November 9, 2000), http://www.feer.com/_0011_09/p032region.html.

73 John McBeth, "Reinventing Democracy," *The Far Eastern Economic Review* (August 24, 2000), http://www.feer.com/cgi-bin/HSE/HSE.cgi?url=http://www.feer.com/2000/0008_...

74 Dini Djalal, "Missed Opportunities," *The Far Eastern Economic Review* (January 31, 2002),http://www.feer.com/articles/2002/0201_31/p021/region.html.

75 John McBeth and Dan Murphy, "Balancing Act," *The Far Eastern Economic Review* (November 4, 1999), http://www.feer.com/cgi-bin/HSE/HSE.cgi?url=http://www.feer.com/1999/9911_...

76 Clifford Geertz, "Indonesia: Starting Over," *The New York Review of Books* Archives (May 11, 2000), http://www.nybooks.com/nyrev/WWWarchdisplay.cgi?20000511022F (also available at http://www.nybooks.com/articles/article-preview?article_id=108).

77 Lane, *op. cit.*

78 Jamie Mackie, "In the Shadow of Sukarno," *The Asian Wall Street Journal* (November 4, 1998), p. 8.

functionaries,[79] devotees of the very policies that the poor had risen against under Suharto. Thus the posts of the Finance Minister and Economic Coordination Minister went to seasoned technocrats such as the ex-Bank Indonesia director, Budiono, and the ambassador to the US, Dorodjatun Kuntjoro-Jakti.[80] Megawati's fusion of technologism and deflected populism slammed the door on more substantive reform.

Even if Megawati had wanted progressive change, her ministers would have had to negotiate the minefield of a parliament where most MPs answered to recalcitrant party bosses.[81] Critics rightly saw her appointments as an attempt to duplicate Suharto's old trick of relegating the economy to technocrats while keeping a tight grip on security matters and the legal system.[82] This time, however, the old order had her firmly in its grip. By no accident she kept in her cabinet Supreme Court Chief Justice Bagir Manan, who had served in Suharto's infamous judiciary throughout his career. The country was fast returning to the authoritarian devil it knew. At least Suharto's regime had been effective in maintaining a semblance of national unity in its economic programs, and of winning investor and donor confidence.[83] Repression under Megawati lost on both fronts: its retreat from reform was matched by a failure "to make the trains run on time."

Clearly technocracy was more the problem than the solution. The economic crisis, as Geertz recognized, provided a unique opportunity for Indonesia to establish the rule of law, governmental transparency and accountability, and basic human rights—all the ingredients that Western critics found wanting after the Crash. Arief Budiman believes this was the time for Indonesian intellectuals to intervene decisively rather than entrust the political process to technocrats who saw reform as a top-down enterprise. At best they regarded democracy as a loan to

---

79 John McBeth and Michael Vatikiotis, "Indonesia: Lady in Waiting," *The Far Eastern Economic Review* (May 17, 2001), http://www.feer.com/cgi-bin/HSE/HSE.cgi?url=http://www.feer.com/2001/0105_...; see also "Analysts Hail Megawati's Economics-Team Appointments," *ASEAN Free Trade Area* (December 4, 2001), http://www.aftaonline.com/frontpageasean.html.; and see John McBeth and Dini Djalal, "The Puppet President," *The Far Eastern Economic Review* (August 2, 2001), http://www.feer.com/cgi-bin/HSE/HSE.cgi?url=http://www.feer.com/2001/0108_...

80 John McBeth, "A Parade of Surprises," *The Far Eastern Economic Review* (August 23, 2001), http://www.feer.com/cgi-bin/HSE/HSE.cgi?url=http://www.feer.com/2001/0108_...

81 Sadanand Dhume, "Economic Recovery Starts Here," *The Far Eastern Economic Review* (August 2, 2001), http://www.feer.com/cgi-bin/HSE/HSE.cgi?url=http://www.feer.com/2001/0108_...; and also Sadanand Dhume, "Debtor Nation," *The Far Eastern Economic Review* (September 6, 2001), http://www. feer.com/cgi-bin/HSE/HSE.cgi?url=http://www.feer.com/2001/0109_...

82 John McBeth, "Rule of Law's Let-Down," *The Far Eastern Economic Review* (September 6, 2001), http://www.feer.com/cgi-bin/HSE/HSE.cgi?url=http://www.feer.com/2001/0109_...

83 See John McBeth on the new economic disunity, "When Jakarta Fails to Act," *The Far Eastern Economic Review* (November 15, 2001), http://www.feer.com/2001/0111_15/p018region.html; and also see Sadanand Dhume on the lack of investor and/or donor confidence, "Donor Fatigue," *The Far Eastern Economic Review* (November 29, 2001), http://www.feer.com/2001/0111_29/p028region.html.

the people by the state,[84] and usually they gave it a lower priority than economic development or national stability.[85]

This attitude, which in good times helped to allay investors' fears of unruly populism, now contributed to the post-Crash inertia that kept those same investors on edge. Real political reform could have done no worse, for the unrest that bred economic disincentives might have been ameliorated by a strong dose of hope. The economy itself was not beyond redemption, before or after Suharto's fall. Indonesia had moderate inflation relative to other hard-hit 'miracle' economies, and it suffered less of a bubble effect than most. What killed confidence was the increasingly unpredictable behavior of Suharto's government. The same iron fist which had made for an image of "stability" now became a huge liability, for it was obvious that no institution or set of political actors could temper Suharto's dictates.[86] Thus the malady behind the Indonesian Crash was more political than economic, and its long-term solution would likewise have to be found in the political domain.

Under Megawati, unfortunately, the country rapidly returned to *dwifungsi*. The threat of terrorism was used to justify an undeclared war on civilian autonomy. Once again, and with patent US complicity, the military was taking charge.[87] In fact, Megawati gave TNI more independence than it had ever enjoyed under Suharto. In the absence of effective domestic or international pressure for reform, civilian rule lost by default. This removed any chance for peaceful negotiation with the Free Aceh Movement (*Gerakan Aceh Merdeka*, or GAM).[88] The Acehnese rebels were anything but the rabid extremists that TNI would have us imagine. By preference most would have been civil Islamists, for they disdained the brutality of Laskar Jihad (Army of Islam) or Jemaah Islamiyah, which allegedly spearheaded the 2002 Bali bombing and the Christmas Eve bombings of 29 Christian churches two years before. GAM leader Teuku Kamaruzzaman (one of two peace negotiators who in October 2003 got 13-year prison sentences on charges of "treason and

---

84 Arief Budiman, "The Lonely Road of the Intellectual: Scholars in Indonesia," inaugural professional lecture on October 9, 1997, at the University of Melbourne in Australia, http://www. icsea.or.id/sea-span/0497/OT1925LL.htm.; and, for the earlier development of nationalism and the role of the intellectuals, see J.D. Legge, *Intellectuals and Nationalism in Indonesia: A Study of the Following Recruited by Sutan Sjahrir in Occupation in Jakarta* (Ithaca, NY: Cornell Modern Indonesia Project, 1988).

85 Alatas, *op. cit.*, p. 159.

86 Andrew MacIntyre, "Political Institutions and the Economic Crisis in Thailand and Indonesia," in T.J. Pemple (ed.), *The Politics of the Asian Financial Crisis* (Ithaca: Cornell University Press, 1999), pp. 154–55 (pp. 143–62).

87 Rizal Sukma, director of the Center for Strategic and International Studies in Jakarta, observes that no political party dares to confront the military. See Alan Sipress, "Indonesian Army's Upper Hand," *The Washington Post* (June 26, 2003), p. A10; and http://www. washingtonpost.com/ac2/wp-dyn/A33811-2003June25?language=printer.

88 *Ibid.*

terrorism")[89] pointed out that "We have Christian churches here and none have been attacked."[90]

As in East Timor before, the Army was responsible for the worst brutality in Aceh.[91] Far from reducing radical violence, government action accomplished the very opposite: smothering the moderate Islamism that could have provided a natural dike against more radical foreign imports.[92] The health of civil Islam is ultimately tied to the economic and political development of the community in general. Hopes for a civil solution collapsed when Megawati declared martial law on May 18, 2003. Some 50,000 troops were sent to combat 3,000 lightly-armed separatists.[93] While senior government officials downplayed the activities of real terrorist organizations such as Jemaah Islamiyah, TNI stoked militancy in Aceh by making a habit of executing unarmed civilians.[94]

In his capacity as Megawati's security minister, later president Susilo Bambang Yudhoyono ("SBY") approved a crackdown that cost more than 2,000 lives. Student protesters and human rights groups well remember SBY from his similar activites under Suharto. He had served as a commander in East Timor at a time of heinous human rights abuses,[95] yet the fact that he was running for the presidency against the even more notorious General Wiranto helped him to pass himself off as a military reformer as well as the essential anti-terrorist. In fact, it was on his watch that thousands of militant Javanese Islamists joined foreign insurgents in an assault on Christians in Maluku Province, while the TNI looked the other way.[96]

---

89 "Two more ex-rebel negotiators sentenced in Indonesia's Aceh province," *Agence France-Presse*, via *ClariNet* (October 22, 2003), http://quickstart.clari.net/qs_se/webnews/wed/dd/Qindonesia-aceh-trial.RQTb_DOM.html.

90 Roger Mitton, "The New Crusade," *Asiaweek*, Vol. 27, No. 8 (March 2, 2001), http://www.asiaweek. Com/asiaweek/magazine/nations/p,8782,100233.99html. This is consistent with NU's policy, launched in 1998, of helping to guard churches. See Tom McCawley, "Muslims guard Jakarta's Christians," *The Christian Science Monitor* (December 23, 2005), http://www.csmonitor.com/2005/1223/p01s03-woap. html.

91 "Brutal mistakes in Indonesia," *The International Herald Tribune* (January 5, 2004), http://www.iht. com/cgi-bin/generic.cgi?template=articleprint.tmplh&ArticleId=123604.

92 William H. Thornton, *New World Empire: Islamism, Terrorism, and the Making of Neoglobalism* (Lanham, MD: Rowman & Littlefield, 2005), Chapter 4.

93 John McBeth, "A Futile Fight," *The Far Eastern Economic Review* (June 5, 2003), p. 16 (pp. 16–17).

94 Raymond Bonner, "Report Cites Emergence of New Islamic Militia in Indonesia," *The New York Times* (February 4, 2004), http://www.nytimes.com/2004/02/04/international/asia/04INDO.html.

95 Of the eighteen Indonesians convicted of abuses, all have had their convictions overturned. See "Indonesian Wins Appeal Against Rights Verdict," *The New York Times* (November 6, 2004), http://www.nytimes.com/2004/11/06/international/asia/06timor.html.

96 Paul Dillon, "Profile: Susilo Bambang Yudhoyono," *Aljazeera.Net* (July 4, 2004), http://english. aljazeera.net.?NR/exeres/554FAF3A-B267-427A-B9FC-54881BDE0A2F.ht...

Full Retreat

Indonesia's political turmoil is rooted in economic oppression. Even the infamous Bali bombings cannot be completely understood as an exogenous product of global terrorism. Here especially, global and local animosities were intertwined. Like multinational oil and mining operations, global tourism brings in badly needed foreign exchange for Jakarta's projects, but scarcely trickles down to local workers and communities. While global firms like McDonalds, KFC and Starbucks push local venders out of business, the bulk of the profit exits Indonesia.[97]

People in many provinces, but especially in Aceh, Irian Jaya and Riau, consider themselves every bit as colonized today as they were under the Dutch. In their view Java simply replaced Holland.[98] Though it has little to show for it, Irian Jaya has been the source of 15 percent of Indonesia's foreign exchange earnings. Renamed Papua, it is the nation's largest province, and the site of the world's largest gold and copper mining operation. Freeport McMoRan Copper and Gold Inc. of New Orleans has monopolized this $50 billion enterprise since 1967, while dumping a billion tons of waste into local rivers.[99] Papua is also the site of the world's largest gas fields, developed by Atlantic Richfield Co., a unit of BP/Amoco. The financial and environmental wreckage of these extractions has sparked a largely Christian reaction in the form of the Free Papua Movement (*the Organisasi Paua Merdeka*, or OPM).[100]

More than ever, Papuans feel they have no peaceful options. The so-called "Act of Free Choice" that delivered them into the Indonesian state in 1969 has now been revealed as a fraud, yet neither their former Dutch overlords nor the world community has any interest in setting history straight. A Special Autonomy Law was passed in 2002, but was sabotaged in 2003 by a presidential decree that divided the

97 Pamela Nowicka, "Invisible in Paradise," *The Guardian* (October 5, 2005), http://www.guardian.co.uk/print/0,3858,5301699-103677,00.html.

98 William Nessen, "Why not Independence?," *Inside Indonesia* (January/March 2003), http://www. insideindonesia.org/edit81/p4-7nessen.html.

99 Jane Perlez and Raymond Bonner, "Below a Mountain of Wealth, a River of Waste," *The New York Times* (December 27, 2005), http://www.nytimes.com/2005/12/27/international/asia/27gold.html.

100 Angel Rabasa and Peter Chalk, *Indonesia's Transformation and the Stability of Southeast Asia* (Santa Monica, CA: Project AIR FORCE/RAND, 2001), p. 27. A similar conflict site is Borneo, divided between Indonesia, Malaysia and Brunei. To increase agricultural productivity in Kalimantan, on the Indonesian side of Borneo, Jakarta converted the forest into commercial rubber and palm oil plantations. Meanwhile it subsidized a massive "transmigration" of labor from Java and Madura, leading to clashes between Madurese settlers and indigenous Dayaks. One such incident, in 1999, resulted in 185 deaths in just a few days. See Michael T. Klare, *Resource Wars: The New Landscape of Global Conflict* (New York: A Metropolitan/Owl Book and Henry Holt and Company, 2001), p. 207. Likewise, in Sarawak, on the Malaysian side, there has been continuing conflict since 1987 between Dayaks and government-backed logging companies. Amendment S90B of the Malaysian Forest Ordinance makes it a major offense for anyone to obstruct logging operations in Sarawak. Even designated parks and biospheres for the Penan indigenous people have been invaded by logging companies, which invoke S90B to have Dayak protesters arrested and sometimes shot. *Ibid.*, p. 206.

province into three more manageable zones, with the military making its presence felt all the more. As its other operations subside, TNI has a vested interest in fanning the flames of Papuan resistance so as to justify its bloated budget.[101] In Papua it is funded directly by Freeport, which openly bribes generals for security services.[102]

Aceh and Riau, likewise, have little to show for providing half of Indonesia's oil output.[103] In 1971 natural gas was discovered in Aceh, where Mobil constructed the world's largest natural gas refinery.[104] GAM took shape in 1976 in response to a grossly unjust distribution of gas revenues. Suharto's regime fired back by declaring Aceh a military operations zone (*Daerah Operasi Militair*, or DOM), a designation that lasted until after the dictator's fall in May 1998.[105] After numerous abortive truce attempts, a much empowered military under (or over) President Megawati decided to destroy the resistance once and for all in 2003. Their failure opened the door in August 2005 for more promising negotiations aimed at Aceh's eventual autonomy.[106] Similar hopes have collapsed before, but this case could be different, thanks to the global spotlight that fell on Aceh after the apocalyptic tsunami of December 2004. The question is what will happen after the Western press loses interest.

Unfortunately that interest has not lent itself to the one thing the Acehnese want even more than peace: independence. The global community flatly dismisses Aceh's claim to legal secession. We are told by the world press that most Acehnese just want peace. They are presented as helpless victims caught in the middle of a war they want no part of.[107] GAM, by contrast, is portrayed as a violent and irresponsible rogue organization with little local support. It is often accused, moreover, of having active Al Qaeda connections, although both GAM and the military itself deny this.[108] Even when it is granted that TNI and its affiliates are terroristic, the suggestion is given that the two forces basically deserve each other, while the Acehnese deserve freedom from both.

This view of GAM grotesquely distorts its membership, its public support, and the historical realities behind it. For several hundred years, and into the 20th Century, Aceh was a sovereign state. The Dutch knew the Acehnese as their most determined anti-colonial foes. If any people deserve their freedom, these do. But after expelling the Dutch, they found themselves under similar occupation by the Javanese, who

101 Feije Duim, "Fixing Papua's history?," *Inside Indonesia* (July/September 2004), http://www.insideindonesia.org/edit79/p23-24_duim.html.

102 "Recklessness in Indonesia," *The New York Times* (January 9, 2006), http://www.nytimes.com/2006/01/09/opinion/09mon2.html.

103 Rabasa and Chalk, *op. cit.*, p. 27.

104 Anthony Ried, "Aceh and Indonesia: A Stormy Marriage," *PROSEA Research Paper*, No. 42 (February 2001), from Program for Southeast Asian Area Studies (Taipei: Academia Sinica), p. 5 (pp. 1–11).

105 "Background on Aceh," *Think Centre: Toward a Vibrant Political Society* (August 25, 2001), http://www.ThinkCentre.org.

106 Simon Montlake, "Aceh's Rebels Give up Guns, Warily" *The Christian Science Monitor* (September 19, 2005), http://www.csmonitor.com/2005/0919/p06s01-woap.htm.

107 Nessen, *op. cit.*

108 Amy Chew, "Aceh Links to al Qaeda Dismissed," *CNN.com* (July 14, 2002), http://cnn.worldnews. printthis.clickability.com/pt/cpt?action=cpt&title=CNN.com.

proceeded to rob their natural resources and to rule them once again as de facto colonial subjects. Non-violent protest was useless, while armed resistance was almost suicidal. The military responded in its usual way: with rape, torture, and murder. Nonetheless international opinion—including the vast majority of policy analysts, NGOs, foreign governments, and international media—fully backed Jakarta. Only the Acehnese saw independence as a just and viable solution.[109]

The standard international view of this issue is that Aceh surrendered its right to independence when it joined Indonesia after the Dutch departure in 1949. This, we are told, is a legal axiom that applies no matter what crimes might later be perpetrated against the population. Never mind that numerous exceptions have been made to this supposedly absolute rule, as in the former Yugoslavia, Bangladesh, Eritrea, and Bougainville, which has been promised progressive autonomy leading to a referendum on independence after 10 years. As William Nessen put it, "Independence was the ultimate solution for people suffering under European colonial domination. Why shouldn't it be available for people, like the Acehnese, experiencing a similar lack of political control, economic exploitation, and intolerable human rights abuses?"[110]

The answer, of course, has less to do with international law than with hard economic reality. The global investment community has reason to appreciate Jakarta's iron grip on the archipelago. That is why it took so long for world opinion to solidify behind East Timor's undeniably lawful claim of independence. The kind of UN support that it eventually gained, following the November 1991 Santa Cruz massacre,[111] will not be extended to Aceh or any other province. Even the partial autonomy that Aceh has been promised is unlikely to be honored once world attention dissipates. That is of little concern to the global financial institutions that Jakarta courts. For them SBY, more than Megawati or Wahid before her, has what it takes to protect their interests. They see hard-line tactics as necessary for stability, especially in a region of "Islamic extremism." The present regime is therefore well-served by the imagery of Islamism as a terrorist powderkeg ready to explode.

In fact, the most influential Muslim organizations, the NU and Muhammadiyah, have joined hands since 9/11 to resist what they see as the twin evils of radical Islamism and government corruption. Along with the Liberal Islam Network, a new youth organization, these groups are working to reignite the country's reform agenda from the bottom up—hence the term "deformalization." So too, in stark contrast to

---

109 *Ibid.* The tsunami of December 26, 2004, however, sapped their will to continue the struggle. Within a month of the disaster GAM was sitting down with the government in serious talks in Helsinki. Jakarta, for its part, needed to divert attention from its heinous conduct, now that international floodlights were aimed on Aceh. It was therefore prepared to offer Aceh a measure of autonomy, and the Acehnese were prepared to accept the deal. That, of course, does not resolve the sovereignty issue, any more than it did when the Dutch packed their guns and left. See Gareth Evans, "Aceh is Building Peace from its Ruins," *The International Herald Tribune* (December 23, 2005), http://www.iht.com/bin/print_ipub. php?file=/articles/2005/12/23/news/edevans.p...

110 Nessen, *op. cit.*

111 Lesley McCulloch, "Building Solidarity: Why is Solidarity for Aceh so Much Weaker than for Timor?," *Inside Indonesia* (January/March 2005), http://www.insideindonesia.org/edit81/p12-13_mcull.html.

most Arab Islamism, they are trying to cut direct, ICMI-style ties between politics and religion.[112] No less they oppose the government's politicization of the media. Vice President Jusuf Kalla, for example, recently blasted the press for reporting on hunger in Papua, and went on to laud the censorship policies of Singapore, Malaysia, Thailand, and China.[113]

Given this shameless reversion to Suharto's ways and means, it is understandable that former president Wahid would condemn the present regime.[114] It is precisely SBY's return to old habits that has rekindled globalist interest in Indonesia. Foreign investment is on the mend, spurred by the World Bank's decision to restore Indonesia's "high case" credit status. Loans of up to $1.2 billion annually have been granted for the 2005 to 2007 period.[115] Meanwhile a new crop of technocrats, having forgotten the lesson of the "Broken Hearts," are there to manage the next round of boom and bust economism.

---

112 Ziauddin Sardar, "Can Islam change?," *New Statesman* (downloaded September 10, 2004), http://www.newstatesman.com/nscoverstory.htm.

113 "Bad Press," *Jakarta Post* (December 16, 2005), from *Asia Media: Media News Daily*, http://www.asiamedia.ucla.edu/article.asp?parentid=35772. Tellingly, Kalla's chief rival in policy matters within the SBY regime is the arch-technocrat Budiono, who is silent concerning Kalla's call for press repression. To Budiono the word "reform" means exactly what it did to Suharto's technocrats, the "Berkeley Mafia": compliance with the neoliberal agenda of the IMF and the World Bank. The egalitarian meaning of reform that flowered following the Crash has long since wilted. On Budiono's in-house contest with Kalla see Bill Guerin, "A Fight for Indonesia's Soul," *Asia Times* (August 4, 2007), http://www. atimes. com/Southeast_Asia/IH4Ae01.html.

114 "Progress Slow in Indonesia's Democratic Transition: Gus Dur," *The Jakarta Post* (July 30, 2007), http://www.thejakartapost.com/yesterdaydetail.asp?fileid=20070730.Ho4.

115 Jane Perlez, "World Bank Again Giving Large Loans to Indonesia," *The New York Times* (December 2, 2003), http://www.nytimes.com/2003/12/02/international/asia/02INDO. html. Likewise, there are increasing calls for a restoration of full military relations between the United States and Indonesia. See "Next Step with Indonesia," *Washington Post* (February 8, 2005), p. A22; And Australia is expected to sign a similar security pact. See Tom McCawley, "Indonesia's Stature Rises," *The Christian Science Monitor* (January 17, 2006), http://www. csmonitor.com/2006/0117/p06s02-woap.htm.

Chapter 5

Another Thailand Was Possible: Thaksin and the Thai Response to Globalization

The New Sheriff

The economics of the Asian Crisis may be fading into history, but the same cannot be said of its politics. Post-Crash Asia finds itself at a fateful crossroads between liberal and authoritarian development. Unfortunately it all comes down to cash value, and the most dynamic Asian economy, on paper at least, has been the P.R.C. China's record of recent years seems to prove what James Fallows was arguing back in the mid-1990s: that political repression can be a boon to economic growth. Nor is China the only Asian proving ground for this verdict. The case of post-Crash Thailand is even more compelling in that here a democratic development model was actually put to the test. This chapter will explore the reasons why Thailand so definitively flunked that test.

One obvious reason was the pernicious genius of Thaksin Shinawatra, the prime minister who would be king. Thaksinocracy turned democratic reform on its head by exploiting the executive privileges that were built into the 1997 constitution. The assumption had been that a weak executive undercut democracy by leaving a power vacuum for the military to fill.[1] Thaksin's conduct, however, gave many urban elites second thoughts as to whether the military was as bad as a democratically empowered tyrant. It can fairly be said that the military coup of September 2006 could not derail Thai democracy, for Thai democracy had already derailed itself.

In many ways Thaksin's TRT (Thai Rak Thai, or Thais Love Thais Party) echoed the "Asian values" mantra of Thailand's authoritarian neighbors. But even Lee Kuan Yew and Mohamad Mahathir—the autocratic godfathers of Singapore and Malaysia, respectively—had serious reservations about their protégé Thaksin, who refused to heed their warnings concerning TRT tactics toward Thai Muslims. Under the guise of anti-terrorism and a shooting war on drugs, Thaksin was prone to apply the Führer principle whenever it suited his need. Granted, he submitted his policies to nominal democratic review, and swore fealty to King Bhuminol Adulyadej, but his "C.E.O." style was as much at odds with standard "Asianism" as with the minimalist model of statehood preached by neoliberals. While his anti-IMF hype earned him a reputation as an antiglobalist, the sad truth is that Thaksin lacked the commitment

---

1 "The Long March Back to the Barracks," *The Economist* (August 23, 2007), http: economist.com/opinion/PrinterFriendly.cfm?story_id=9687376.

to be consistently "anti" anything. He kept those features of globalization (such as privatization) which served his interest, while shedding those (such as due process of law) which got in his way.

This rank opportunism fits a pattern that has been aptly termed "neoliberal populism," in reference to Thaksin's ingenious fusion of business elitism with highly exaggerated aid for the poor.[2] Matt Steinglass noted the same mix in Russia's Putin, Italy's Berlusconi, Ukraine's Tymoshenko, Turkey's Erdogan, and Britain's Blair,[3] and we may add America's Bush. Thaksin, however, had the inside track where developmental politics was concerned. Part of what set him apart was pure happenstance: his location at the juncture of two very contrary Asian futures. Democratic hopes raised during Thailand's "miracle" years were tied so closely to capitalist development that the Crash threatened to take democratization down with the ship. Thaksin saved the ship, but very much on his terms, with democracy kept on board for purely instrumental purposes. This would seem to put him squarely in the "Asian values" camp of Lee and Mahathir, except that these "soft authoritarians" kept a well-lighted place for "good governance" in their one-party operations. Thaksin, in Pasuk Phongpaichit's view, revived the Thai tradition of leaders as "action men" whose virtue is proven by being utterly above the law.[4]

This leadership model applies, of course, to the action man's henchmen as well. A window on its practical effect was provided by the tsunami of December 2004. One of the most devastated Thai communities was the village of Nam Khem,[5] where authorities acted fast, but not on behalf of the victims. Armed goons were rushed in to seal off beachfront property before it could be resettled. Survivors among fifty families were not even allowed to search for their dead, much less to repossess what remained of their homes. For years developers had met a stone wall of local resistance when they tried to appropriate this prime real estate.[6] The tsunami came to their aid, serving hundreds of coastal families their eviction papers, and sweeping whole villages like Nam Khem into the assets column of a newly globalized Thailand.[7]

---

2 Pasuk Phongpaichit, "Thailand under Thaksin: A Regional and International perspective," Core University Project, Center for Southeast Asian Studies, Kyoto University (September 6–8, 2004), p. 5 (pp. 1–8).

3 Matt Steinglass, "Party professionals: What Thailand's Embattled Prime Minister has in Common with Silvio Berlusconi and Tony Blair," Boston.com (March 26, 2006), http://www.boston.com/news/globe/ideas/articles/2006/02/26/party_professionals?mode=PF.

4 Pasuk, "Thailand under Thaksin," *op. cit.*, p. 4.

5 In addition to the 5,000 dead or missing in Nam Khem, another 5,000 illegal immigrants from Myanmar had disappeared. Moreover, the village lost all but half a dozen of its 300 boats. See Seth Mydans, "The Tsunami's Horror Haunts a Thai Fishing Village," *The New York Times* (February 14, 2005), http://www.nytimes.com/2005/02/14/international/asia/14thai.html.

6 Seth Mydans, "Devastated by Tsunami, Villagers Fight Builder for Land," *The New York Times* (March 12, 2005), http://www.nytimes.com/2005/03/12/international/asia/12tsunami.html.

7 See Simon Montlake, "In Thailand, a Land Grab," *The Christian Science Monitor* (April 8, 2005), http://www.csmonitor.com/2005/0408/p07s02-woap.htm. Several hundred thousand Acehnese survivers of the tsunami in Indonesia have similarly been refused permission to resettle, though here the government's motive is clearly more political than commercial. See

This could not have happened without at least tacit approval from Thaksin. His rule has been likened to that of the notorious Field Marshal Sarit Thanarat,[8] but a more apt comparison, in terms of anti-terrorist imagery, might be to Peru's Alberto Fujimori. In any case the buck stopped with Thaksin. The most that can be said in his defense is that he was more the product than the producer of Thai maldevelopment.[9] He was simply its brand name. The hallmark of "Thaksinomics" was its ability to convert natural and human resources, and even natural disasters, into instant capitalist opportunities.

The tsunami, for example, gave a boost to the sex trade industry, as thousands of sex tourists rushed from resort beaches to Bangkok. Luckily there was a buyer's market waiting for them: a severe drought and a failed rice crop in northeast Thailand late in 2004 had forced an unusually large number of village girls to seek gainful employment in the capital.[10] Thus, in a Panglossian twist, the drought and the tsunami served the economy well. Red light tourists got more bang for their buck, and there was even a new commercial attraction born in the rubble: busloads of Thai tourists driving through ruined areas such as Nam Khem to take in the sights and gawk at the survivors.[11]

In terms of GDP growth—the Holy Grail of standard economic calculation— such diversions count as much as health care or educational activities. By this standard Thailand is again on the right track, as it was before the Asian Crash, and before the onslaught of IMFism turned most of Southeast Asia into a developmental disaster zone. At the worst possible time, IMF strictures forced the virtual surrender of Thailand's economic sovereignty.[12] The justifiable outrage this produced set the stage for Thaksin's grand entry into politics. In many ways his appeal mimicked that of Malaysia's Mahathir, whose blasts at the IMF rekindled his flagging popularity.[13]

Simon Montlake, "Squatters aren't Waiting for Jakarta's Post-Tsunami Plan," *The Christian Science Monitor* (March 15, 2005), http://www.csmonitor. com/2005/0315/p07s01-woap.htm.

8 Thirayuth Boonmi of Thammasat University has famously stressed this point, and more recently has called Thaksin a "monster." See Nantiya Tangwisutijit and Subhatra Bhumiprabhas, "Is Thaksin Another Dictator like Field Marshal Sarit Thanarat?," *MGGPillai. com* (February 28, 2005), http://www.mggpillai. com/print.php3?artid=9688. In fact, Sarit never attained the preeminence of a Suharto, Mahathir or Lee Kuan Yew. Clearly Thaksin intended to play in their league, and in pan-Asian terms he might have surpassed them if he had kept his own house in order. On the limitations of previous Thai elites relative to these major players, see William Case, *Politics in Southeast Asia: Democracy or Less* (London: RouledgeCurzon, 2002), pp. 147–48.

9 Thus Michael Conners prefers to speak of "Thailand's Thaksin" rather than "Thaksin's Thailand." See Michael Kelly Conners, "Thaksin's Thailand—to Have and to Hold: Thai Politics in 2003–2004," a paper presented to the Thai Update Conference, Macquarie University (April 20–21, 2004).

10 Alex Renton, "Learning the Thai Sex Trade," *Prospect*, Issue 110 (May 2005), http://www.prospect magazine.co.uk/article_details.php?id=6889.

11 Mydans, "The Tsunami's Horror," *op. cit.*

12 See Pasuk Phongpaichit and Chris Baker, *Thailand's Crisis* (Singapore and Copenhagen: Institute of Southeast Asian Studies and Nordic Institute of Asian Studies, 2000), p. 36.

13 Peter Symonds, "Thai billionaire Capitalizes on Anti-IMF Sentiment to Win National Elections," *World Socialist Web Site* (January 11, 2001), http://www.wsws.org/articles/2001/

But Thaksin's plutocratic populism looked more like the future. If taken up by other Asian countries, it could cast a longer shadow than the Crash itself.

Here, it seemed, was the man to lead Thailand out of the globalist captivity that the Democrat Party had come to represent under Chuan Leekpai. By the time of the October 2003 APEC Summit in Bangkok, Thaksin had consolidated his social base, winning over the rich with the fastest GDP growth in Southeast Asia, the poor with a sprinkling of health care and rural benefits, and the middle classes with the lure of easy credit and a revived sense of national pride. Now Thaksinomics—or Thaksinocrony, as Thirayuth Boonmi dubs it[14]—was ready to do for the region what it had done for Thailand: to show the IMF and Washington-directed globalization the exit door. Indonesia, the Philippines and even China went to APEC as avid observers of Thaksin's mode of development.[15]

This was more than the old Asian statism. Pre-Crash miraclism had gone far toward reducing development to economic growth, which in turn was used to justify political stasis.[16] Yet through it all a rule-of-law veneer had been preserved. The Crash led many to demand more in the way of political reform,[17] but no ASEAN country was willing to forfeit even a fraction of its GDP growth for non-material gains. If Rim governments could not deliver a full and speedy economic recovery, the public would soon give up on the political side of reform. The departure of Suharto and Mahathir left a regional leadership void that any human rights or democratic activist would have to appreciate. Then, however, a prolonged economic slump invited a reversion to old voting habits, or worse.

Thaksin's contrarian miracle formula—economism without the liberal baggage— was not on the surface anti-democratic. Quite the contrary, TRTism found in democracy a useful power tool, not unlike the "democratization" that Bush brought to the Middle East. By no means did Thaksin's resignation of April 2006 spell the end of Thaksinocracy, a development model which ironically might be better off without him. After the Crash, liberal democratization on the Rim hung on a slender economic thread. Democratic reformism was already being blamed for economic dysfunction when Thaksin, the new sheriff, rode into town. Liberalism as such was faulted for the defects of neoliberalism, such that the very word "reform" took on the odor of malaise. This gave Thaksin his license to ditch liberal restraints, as he did in his extra-judicial drug war of 2003, which by some estimates claimed 2500 lives.

---

jan2001/thai-j11.shtml.

14 "Academics Take Aim," *Bangkok Post* (August 3, 2004), http://216.46.170.184/education/site2004/wnau0304.htm.

15 Andrew Perrin, "The Thaksin Effect," *Time Asia* (October 27, 2003), http://www.time.com/time/asia/magazine/article/0,13673,501031027-524520,00.html.

16 Surin Pitsuwan, "The Asian Crisis, Good Governance and the *Tsunami* of Globalization," in Charles Sampford, Suzanne Condlln, Margaret Palmer and Tom Round (eds), *Asia Pacific Governance: from Crisis to Reform* (Aldershot, UK: Ashgate, 2002), p. 26 (pp. 25–30).

17 See Allen Hicken, "The Politics of Economic Reform in Thailand: Crisis and Compromise," *William Davidson Institute Working Paper*, No. 638 from The William Davidson Institute (January 2004), p. 24 (pp. 1–30).

Perhaps it helped to control illegal drugs, but its real point was to serve notice on both domestic rivals and foreign powers that the sheriff was above the law.

Prototype for Re-cronification

In the wake of 9/11, the American response to TRT recalcitrance would be muffled at best. Washington was too pleased to get Thailand's anti-terrorist cooperation, and was too morally compromised by its own anti-terrorist tactics, to voice any serious criticism of an ally's domestic affairs. Even Thaksin's anti-IMFism was swallowed by Washington as the price of preserving robust capitalism in the face of depressed social expectations. Thai radicalism had waned since the end of CPT (Communist Party of Thailand) hostilities in the late 1980s, so there was nothing to compare with the Philippine CPP/NPF. Wanting to keep it that way, Washington went so far as to propose Thaksin as a replacement for Kofi Annan as UN Secretary-General.[18]

Here, as elsewhere in the region, the big question was how to divide the spoils of globalized "development." Thai voters looked to Thaksinomics for economic salvation—their humble sliver of the capitalist pie. As the first Thai politician to fully tap the sound bite power of the mass media, Thaksin got the message across that a vote for him was a vote for one's bank account. Being one of the richest businessmen in Southeast Asia, he could market himself as the ideal CEO for an ailing Thailand, Inc. He added a Peronist touch by expressing contempt for the "Bangkok elite" that plagued ordinary Thais as much as the IMF had. In practice, however, this opprobrium was reserved for those who were not yet enmeshed in the TRT's political net—a more organized and expansive version of the old cronyism. Clearly Thaksin was superbly qualified for the role of crony-in-chief. His fortune, after all, had been secured through concessions granted him by the Telephone Authority of Thailand in 1990. That gave him an exclusive twenty-year monopoly over mobile phone services, which became the cash cow for his roaring computer business.

One of his prime tasks, once in office, was to streamline the re-cronification process that was already in motion. The first general election under the celebrated 1997 constitution had put many familiar faces back in power. Sanoh Thientong, a major power broker from the pre-Crash era, was back in full stride, as was Surakiart Sathirathai, who would end up as the TRT deputy secretary. It was Thaksin, however, who kicked the process into high gear. No sinner would be unwelcome under the TRT revival tent. This unite-and-conquer method would complete Thailand's "junker" synthesis: the drift over the past two decades toward the co-optation of local political networks by a new capitalist class.

Although the resulting hybrid is in many ways less democratic than the system it displaces—in that it is clearly aimed at the creation of a one-party system reminiscent of Mahathir's 22-year junta[19]—the absence of a credible Thai Left permitted the TRT to pass itself off as the party of the people. This Peronist subterfuge effectively

---

18 "Thaksin Blows Chance of UN Top Job," *Aljazeera.com* (October 31, 2004), http://www.aljazeera.com/cgi-bin/review/article_full_story.asp?service_id=5428.

19 See Thitinan Pongsudhirak, "Asia's Age of Thaksin?," *Project Syndicate* (April 2005), http://www. project-syndicate.org/print_commentary/pongsudhirak1/English.

displaced "People Power." While Thaksin struck a nationalist pose in his contest with Democrat globalism, TRT policy was no less committed to the connectivity and privatization that his predecessors embraced. It simply provided local cronies with a better seat at the global bargaining table. This seating arrangement can be compared to India's uncanny alliance of multinational and Hindutva power bases under the BJP. That too involved a global/local coupling of two seemingly opposite worlds. In both cases this turned out to be an unstable alliance—vulnerable to a challenge from either of two sides: from a more focused business party, rather like the American Republican Party, or from real competition on the populist side.[20]

Washington understandably kept its silence concerning the reactionary tilt of both the BJP and TRT, for Right populists were considered more pliable than Left ones such as Venezuela's Hugo Chavez. Thaksin was recognized as a useful instrument of globalist de-radicalization. Rather like President Bush, he subverted the pluralist meaning of democracy while milking its populist potential. Meanwhile he won applause throughout the ASEAN sphere as the man who restored Thailand's pre-Crash dynamism on his terms rather than the IMF's. US-based globalists might grumble, but they much preferred Thaksin's regional leadership to the more noxious antiglobalism that was waiting in the wings. Mahathir, for example, was prone to make caustic comments at the worst of times, such as after 9/11, when Washington was mounting its war on terrorism. By contrast, Thaksin sent troops to Iraq.

The question was how long Thaksin could keep his domestic house in order, and especially his urban house. This depended in part on how long he could maintain the state of emergency that put him in office. At first this was mainly an economic sense of distress, tinged with national insult. While nationalist revulsion against the IMF explained the TRT's success in 2001, that political ticket would give Thaksin a short ride. This, even more than his shady dealings, was the key to his ouster in April 2006. To retain legitimacy he had to get the economy rolling, but doing that removed the exigent atmosphere that was his political raison d'être. He had to sustain the "Grand Coalition" that gave him leverage over the old patronage politics, but this would require a renewable source of emergency.

As surely as it did for Bush, 9/11 came to Thaksin's rescue, and like Bush he used fear tactics to constantly recharge national anxieties. Some thought his days numbered by late 2003 and early 2004, but to the surprise of many critics his heinous actions in the south actually boosted his popularity. Few cared about his friendliness toward the Burmese junta, and even his deadly silence during the bird flu crisis hardly dented his re-electability. His brash refusal to accept tsunami aid, no matter how much the victims needed it, recharged his popularity in the closing weeks before the general elections of February 2005. The TRT won 377 out of 500 seats in parliament, making it the first party in the country's history to have no need of a coalition to form a government. It also got by with less direct vote buying than usual, as it already had the election in the bag.

---

20 See Pasuk Phongpaichit, "Thailand: Wide Angle," Keynote Speech at the 9th International Conference of Thai Studies, University of Northern Illinois, Dekalb (April 4, 2005), p. 9 (pp. 1–10).

Like the CCP/TNC symbiosis in China, Thaksin's TRT fused the new forces of globalization with old guard politics. This worked domestically, allowing Thaksin to become the first prime minister to win a consecutive term. But tactics that succeeded locally met a very different response outside Thailand. The question was how far Thaksin's political sway could extend in Asia, given his baneful treatment of Thai Muslims. After the massacre of 85 peaceful Muslim protesters at Tak Bai on October 25, 2004, with countless more killed that same year, Malaysia and Indonesia issued public criticism, and Thailand's king called Thaksin in for a drubbing. Mahathir went even further, urging Thailand to consider granting autonomy to the south before the crisis became the ASEAN equivalent of the Palestinian quagmire.

With the elections behind, Thaksin set about repairing the regional damage by calling for social justice, as if he bore no responsibility for the injustice that had stained his first term. It says much about the "democratic" values espoused by globalists that they kept their silence about state terrorism in southern Thailand. Like Aceh in Indonesia, this area remained conveniently closed to journalists and aid workers.[21] The government had too much to hide. While it is known that a handful of Thai insurgents had fought in Afghanistan—first against the Soviets and later against the Americans—the scale of the southern conflagration made it obvious that its prime mover was TRT policy. Muslim violence had all but disappeared by 2002, but now returned with a vengeance. Al Qaeda would pray that all Asian governments might behave in this manner.

It at least can be said of Thaksin that he kept a few of his populist promises: paying attention to rural problems, reigniting the economy, and unhinging America's financial hold on the region. In his October 2002 keynote address to the East Asia Economic Summit, Thaksin effectively declared independence from US-directed globalization. His language was veiled, but everyone knew that when he vowed to reap the benefits of globalization in a "sustainable" way he was not talking about saving trees.

The unsustainability of IMFism was common knowledge. Neoliberal mandates had exacerbated the Asian Crisis by stunting social assistance and discouraging counter-cyclical actions that could have halted the deflationary spiral. Thus a recession had been turned into a prolonged depression, and a putative recovery operation into a neoliberal shopping spree. The political rebound this produced came gift wrapped to Thaksin. Even as he continued privatization—a central pillar of IMFism—he promised his own de-liberalized "Third Way," along with a regional alternative to globalist recovery schemes. In 2002, under the flag of a New Asian Realism, he proposed an Asian bond project and an 18 country Asian Cooperation Dialogue reaching from the Middle East to East Asia. Naturally Thailand was to be the locomotive driving this new Asianism, and Thaksin was to be the engineer at its throttle. Its ultimate destination would be a pan-Asian "junker" synthesis: the worst of the old and the new.

---

21 Amir Taher, "Thailand: Origami Politics Won't Do," *Arab News* (December 18, 2004), http://arabnews.com/services/print/print.asp?artid=56210&d=18&m=12&y=2004&hl=Th…

Balancing Act

To tap popular resentment of carpetbagger globalism, Thaksin had to make a show of resistance. In fact he was simply returning to an old Thai tradition of geopolitical tradeoff. Myth has it that Thailand has had little direct experience with colonialism, but Siam, as it was once known, had little choice but to accept an informal colonization of mind and policy in lieu of formal colonization. From the time of Rama IV (King Maha Mongkut, who reigned from 1851 to 1868), the idea was to ride the foreign tsunami rather than stand against it.

So, like Japan after its Meiji Restoration, Thai rulers welcomed many aspects of Westernization. Unlike Japan, however, they found it necessary to surrender much of their autonomy to avoid outright conquest. The 1932 Thai Constitution ended 800 years of absolute monarchy, but in many ways it was a hoax: less a document of popular sovereignty than a manifestation of "deep colonialism," to borrow Thirayuth Boonmi's term.[22] In that same spirit, Thailand yielded without resistance to Japanese occupation during World War II, and served America's needs (including the carnal needs of its troops) during the Vietnam War.

It is hardly surprising in this light that after the Crash Thailand surrendered almost unconditionally to IMF strictures. At first glance Thaksin's recoil from Washington's neoliberal program would seem to be an historical aberration. But the social ramifications of this "resistance" have been vastly exaggerated. What the TRT challenged was not globalization's social and economic injustice but the share of the spoils allotted to Thailand's own capitalist elite. In the name of resistance, local cronies would now demand a much bigger share of the take. The TRT agenda was one of globalist redistribution, not antiglobalist reform.

The question is whether the TRT phenomenon marks a major departure from Thailand's foreign relations record. That tradition is rooted in the country's location, squeezed as it once was between British territory to the West and French to the East. The remarkable thing is that any trace of Thai sovereignty could survive. The deft diplomacy of Mongkut and his son Chulalongkorn (Rama V) made them at once, in Benedict Anderson's words, "the most dependent and the most powerful sovereigns in Thai history."[23] It is telling that Chulalongkorn's choice of a modernization model was not that of European nations but rather European *colonies* such as the Dutch East Indies and British Malaya.[24] He improved on that model by playing colonial powers off against each other, much as Thaksin would in our time.

Taking up where his father left off, Chulalongkorn launched such occidental marvels as a railway, a police force, and the rudiments of a modern navy, with the king's own yacht doubling as a gunboat.[25] None of this prevented the theft of today's

---

22 See his "Not anti-Western, rather Post-Western," *The Nation* (Thailand, April 15, 2003), http://www.wsisasia.org/ml/communication/200304.month/627.html.

23 Benedict Anderson, *The Spectre of Comparisons: Nationalism, Southeast Asia and the World* (London: Verso, 1998), p. 162.

24 Benedict Anderson, *Imagined Communities: Reflections on the Origin and Spread of Nationalism* (London: Verso, 1983), p. 94.

25 He imported from the West the "civilized" principle of royal primogeniture, which in 1910 resulted in the succession of the mentally unstable Rama VI, who would never have

Laos and part of Cambodia by France, and part of today's Malaysia by Britain, but through it all the king stayed on amiable terms with the West. By any definition short of complete conquest these were imperialist terms, yet the official independence of Siam reduced the one fringe benefit that literal colonialism afforded other Southeast Asian countries: a profound anti-colonial impulse. Thailand would lack the kind of nationalist rebound that could have stabilized its political structure. It remains to be seen whether any Thai leader can supply such cohesion in today's globalist context. That would be a world-class achievement, given the reputation of globalization for undermining nationalism.

This is a country that has had sixteen coups, eight of them successful, since the overthrow its absolute monarchy in 1932. Indecisive leadership made Thailand the perfect base camp for America's military operations in the 1960s. Virtual US occupation sowed the seeds for a possible nationalist reflex, but this rebound effect was put on hold by the complacence money could buy. Here as elsewhere, the growth-first development model sponsored by Washington was a time bomb set to explode whenever the economy faltered. Until then, Thailand remained the perfect neocolony, the very archetype of dominated development.[26] Thus America reaped the benefits of imperialism with few of the costly responsibilities. As of 1959 it got an ideal puppet dictator in Sarit Thanarat, who proved his worth by banning strikes, closing down unions, and paying heed to US-trained technocrats. It hardly mattered that his successors, Thanom and Praphat, were clumsy hacks, for they were riding the crest of an unprecedented wartime boom.

By the early 1970s, however, inflation was on the rise, and everyone could see that the US was packing its bags. This voided the regime's social contract, whereby political undevelopment was tolerated in return for fast-track economic growth. Only then could real democracy break out, as it finally did in October 1973. Unfortunately that was the very month that the global oil crisis also broke out, compounding the economic slippage that was sure to follow America's regional retreat. Paradoxically, the government was blamed for both its overdependence on the US and its failure to secure lasting American commitments.[27]

These conditions prompted the rise of the Thai Left, which gained ground even within Buddhist ranks, while the Right embraced the monarchy and struck with unmitigated fury against a reformism that could no longer be taken lightly. The democratic experiment that began in 1973 was crushed by 1976. The October 6 massacre at Thammasat University in Bangkok has been compared to the 1968 massacre in Mexico City and the 1947 "two-twenty-eight" butchery in Taiwan. In all three cases it is the subsequent silence that speaks loudest concerning the continuing plight of democracy. Apart from that remarkable three year interlude, Thai politics

---

made the cut before. See Anderson, *Imagined, op. cit.*, pp. 27–28.

26 On "dominated development" see Daniel Bensaïd, "Theses of Resistance," *International Viewpoint* (December 2004), http://www.3bh.org.uk/IV/Issues/2004/IV362/iv36211.htm.

27 Anderson, *Spectre, op. cit.*, p. 154.

could be aptly described as "an old-fashioned mix of kings, coups, and generals."[28] As Victor Mallet notes, the country has achieved neither a substantive democracy nor an efficient authoritarianism. What it has done extremely well is sell elections. $800 million was spent, for example, buying votes in the 1996 campaign.[29] The leadership this purchased set the stage for the coming Crash.

To "Asian values" hardliners, the Crash proved beyond all doubt that the halfway house of Thai democracy was half too much. In fact there was little in the way of political development to lose. In the last quarter century ties between politicians and criminal gangs had tightened, while vote-buying had become so rampant that in one province, as late as 1996, 29% of the voters polled thought it was a perfectly legal activity.[30] If this is the best that Asian democracy can offer, authoritarianism will win by default. The Crash, in short, brought development theory to a stark crossroads: either democratization would have to be upgraded to a first priority concern, on a par with economic growth, or downgraded in the manner of Singaporean economism. Thai "democracy" had long operated as an instrument of decentralized patronage, with public offices bought and sold like any other commodity. Most Thais simply did not care.

The Crash woke some from their lethargy, and also made it harder for globalists to dodge the reform issue by way of capitalism's presumed democratic teleology. If the liberal democratic road to development was to be taken at all, it would have to be taken more seriously. Neoliberals who claimed to be pro-democratic could no longer rest content with the minimal device of elections and ballots alone. It was in this context that Amartya Sen's "democracy as freedom" thesis won him a Nobel Prize, for mere procedural democracy had failed miserably. Even classic modernists now balked at giving economic growth full developmental priority.

To be sure, Sen's democratic axiom cuts both ways: political development is also unsustainable without a solid economic foundation, and a fairly egalitarian one as well. That clandestine radicalism is the largely ignored side of Sen's development model. As in Indonesia, a lack of developmental concurrence (i.e., balanced political and economic progress) doomed Thailand's post-Crash reformism. The irony is that the Crash did release reform energies in Thailand, but like the Thai democratic experiment of 1973, the same economic downturn that spawned democracy also thwarted it. Hence the Crash at once activated and deactivated the new current of reform.

The problem traces back to the 1950s, when the World Bank set Thailand on the path of rapid industrialization and "free market" capitalism. As in Japan and Korea, Thai corporatism was not at first a political behemoth, but after the Plaza Accord of 1985 the business lobby reaped the benefits of a ten-fold foreign investment

---

28 Pasuk Phongpaichit and Chris Baker, *Thailand's Boom and Bust* (Chiang Mai, Thailand: Silkworm, 1998), p. 1.

29 Victor Mallet, *The Trouble with Tigers: The Rise and Fall of South-East Asia* (London: HarperCollins, 1999), pp. 228–29.

30 James Ockey, "The Rise of Local Power in Thailand: Provincial Crime, Elections and the Bureaucracy," in Ruth McVey (ed.), *Money and Power in Provincial Thailand* (Copenhagen, Denmark: NIAS Publishing, Nordic Institute of Asian Studies and Singapore: Institute of Southeast Asian Studies, 2000), pp. 85–86 (pp. 74–96).

boom. A new wave of cronyism had crested by the time Chuan Leekpai took office in 1992, and subsequent Banharn and Chavalit governments offered more of the same. Under them global corporatism struck up a love affair with the old patronage networks. It was Thaksin, however, who pushed this global/local "engagement" to its matrimonial phase.

By the late 1990s, in the throes of depression, the ruling Democrat Party had deservedly lost public confidence. Its failure was rooted in the economic liberalization of the late 1980s. Prevailing globalist values allowed Thailand's miracle economy to be celebrated even as a third of the country's population subsisted on less than $2 per day. Indeed, one in six people in the agricultural northeast survived on less than $1 per day. Neoliberal deregulation froze these conditions in place, putting local agriculture at the mercy of global forces. Prices plummeted after trade barriers were lifted with China, yet Thai capitalists had good reason to cheer. After its WTO entry China opened itself more broadly to Thai products, such that by 2001 Thailand's largest conglomerate, the CP Group, was the biggest single foreign investor in China.

This put Bangkok in a position to play Beijing off against Washington. By contrast to the latter's terror-focused militarism, China could present itself to all of Asia as an agent of commercial peace and harmony, with Bangkok as one of its key partners. However, even as China set about building roads and railways to secure that partnership, Thaksin—in classic Thai style—redoubled his cooperation with US anti-terrorist programs. This traditional balancing act locked China and the US into regional competition—a clear sign that globalization, on the Rim at least, was entering an abrasive new phase.

Not-so-new Maldevelopment

No longer does America enjoy the hegemony over Thailand that went unquestioned in the Cold War and early post-Cold War eras. The ball is in a different court, and the whole developing world is waiting to see how it will bounce. Thai domestic politics will certainly be affected as the chasm between globalization's winners and losers grows even wider. Some still insist that globalization is fostering Thai democracy, but at best this is the kind of procedural democracy that can be bought and sold. Since the highest bidder is sure to be the most globally connected one, the new "democratic" politics redounds to neocolonialism.

As we have seen, Thailand's economic and even political sovereignty was thrown in doubt after the Crash by its surrender to the IMF. This enabled Thaksin, on the rebound, to pose as both a guardian of democracy and of anti-colonialism. Washington took his January 2001 victory in stride, and doubtless preferred him to a weaker figure who could not have deflected social unrest. His anti-terrorism simply sealed the deal. Solid US approbation allowed him to roll back many of the reforms that had given Thai globalization a progressive aura. He set about solidifying his power base through policies modeled on the infamous Internal Security Acts (ISAs) of Malaysia and Singapore.[31] Reversing the country's drift toward federalism, which in the 1990s had pacified the south by allowing a measure of local autonomy, he also eliminated the "Board" (the Civil Police Military Command) and other safeguards against military abuses.

By 2003, in the midst of his mounting war on drugs, Thaksin had laid the foundation for a virulent new strain of the East Asian security state. The idea was to impose permanent one-party rule, Singapore-style, but with less pretense of legal restraint. Security forces were given a green light to shoot anyone suspected of narcotics violations. No doubt many drug pushers were eliminated, along with a host of political undesirables such as reformists, NGO workers, and lawyers who had the audacity to defend blacklisted clients. That of course was the main point. From Thaksin's vantage the program proved so effective, and so uncostly internationally, that it was revived in 2004. Far from trying to curtail these developments, Washington rewarded Thailand with a free-trade agreement.

Globalization on these terms removed all doubt that democratic reform was expendable. Thaksin openly co-opted provincial magnates who had been the arch-enemies of democratization. Meanwhile he turned his "CEO" tactics on the government itself. Officials became afraid to file reports that might upset the tycoon-in-chief. Thus, in a perfect inversion of Sen's doctrine of informational democracy, problems such as the bird flu epidemic were blacked out as long as possible. A press that had once been known for its boldness and candor was now afraid of its own shadow. Despite its democratic cloak, Thaksinocracy was starting to bear a striking resemblance to the statist capitalism of post-Soviet Russia, if not (as yet) post-Tiananmen China.[32] Clearly Sen has overrated the formal apparatus of democracy as a guarantor of liberal reform. Dictators have less to fear from universal suffrage than from the cultural dimensions of democracy. Thaksin set a sordid precedent for the whole developing world by turning the legitimating device of democracy against real reform.

Having solidified his domestic base, and secured his international flanks, Thaksin could now deal with the south on his own terms. Muslims began disappearing from their homes, sparking violent resistance from a minority once known for moderation. Whether by accident or design, this well served the TRT cause. The growing civil war, which claimed over a thousand lives in 2004 and 2005,[33] recharged the sense of emergency that brought Thaksin to power and licensed his tactics. Apart from these Islamic "terrorists," however, his consistent strategy was to co-opt and conquer competing political factions. The idea was to enlist local patronage networks rather

---

31 Joshua Kurlantzick, "Thai Breakdown: Paradise Lost," *The New Republic* (February 21, 2005), http://www.tnr.com/docprint.mhtml?i=20050221&s=kurlantzick022105.

32 On the former, see Michael McFaul, "Political Charades," *The Moscow Times* (September 30, 2005), http://context.themoscowtimes.com/print.php?aid=156467.

33 Jürgen Kremb, "Attacks Threaten Religious Harmony in Southeast Asia," *Der Spiegel* 47 (November 21, 2005), http://service.spiegel.de/cache.international/spiegel/0,1518.druck-386606.00.html.

than reform them, thus joining the country's two main power structures: old guard politics and new urban capitalism.[34]

Tension between these camps had peaked in the early 1990s, after which the forces of globalization tipped the power balance decisively toward the corporate side. Much as China's booming capitalist class found itself tête-á-tête with the CCP rank and file—such that Jiang Zemin's mediatory role became the linchpin of his success in the post-Tiananmien era[35]—Thaksin played the role of bridge builder in post-Crash Thailand. Those who refused to cross the TRT bridge would be politically banished, and most got the point. Thaksin's major political legacy is this reactionary bonding of old and new power elites.

Writing in 1997, the year of the Crash, Paul Handley astutely recognized that while Thailand's rising economic order might be revolutionary, it was not substantially different from the old ruling order in its quest for power and economic privilege. The new contenders differed from the old civil and military bureaucrats only in terms of their strictly capitalist origins and goals. As a product of the 1987–96 economic boom, their twin objectives were unfettered capital accumulation and maximal privatization of state enterprises.[36] Neither the old nor new elites had any taste for People Power, so globalist support was assured. While Thaksin did not initiate this global/local alliance, he consummated it with ruthless efficiency.

That rearguard drift had not been so obvious when these rival camps had their classic showdown in May 1992. Writing in that same year, Anek Laothamatas compared Thai bourgeois politics with the role assigned the middle class by Marx and Weber. For them modern capitalism was a positive social force when set against a semi-feudal backdrop. Likewise, Laothamatas saw Thai politics as a zero-sum contest between the old military-bureaucratic establishment and the business class that rose to prominence since the early 1980s. It was this bifurcated power structure that distinguished Thai politics as of the early 1990s,[37] but that duality would not last long. The Old Guard lost the competition after the popular uprising of 1992,[38] thus paving the way for almost uncontested globalization.

---

34 Analysts writing in the *Far Eastern Economic Review* had predicted this merger as early as January 2001. See Shawn W. Crispin, "Thailand Incorporated," *The Far Eastern Economic Review* (January 18, 2001), http://www.feer.com/_0101_18/p016region.html.

35 William H. Thornton, *Fire on the Rim: The Cultural Dynamics of East/West Power Politics* (Lanham, MD: Rowman & Littlefield, 2002), p. 141.

36 See Paul Handley, "More of the Same? Politics and Business, 1987–96," in Kevin Hewison (ed.), *Political Change in Thailand: Democracy and Participation* (London: Routledge, 1997), p. 94 (pp. 94–113); and "The Secrets of Thaksin's Success," *ABC.net* (October 9, 2004), http://www.abc.net.au/cgi-bin/common/printfriendly.pl?/asiapacific/focus/ asia/GoAsiaPacifi...

37 Anek Laothamatas, *Business Associations and the New Political Economy of Thailand: From Bureaucratic Polity to Liberal Corporatism* (Boulder, CO and Singapore: Westview and Institute of Southeast Asian Studies, 1992), pp. xi–xii.

38 Ukrist Pathmanand, "Globalization and Democratic Development in Thailand: The New Path of the Military, Private Sector, and Civil Society," *Contemporary Southeast Asia*, Vol. 23, No. 1 (April 2001), p. 27 (pp. 24–42).

When the seasoned activist Chuan Leekpai, leader of the Democrat Party, became prime minister in September 1992, Thailand's democratic prospect seemed bright. Few were bothered by the fact that everything hinged on an endless economic miracle. Although Chuan continued the economic liberalization of the preceding administration, which had specialized in government by and for big business, he seemed to offer a broader slicing of the capitalist pie. This was consistent with neoliberalism's democratic claims, freshly minted in Washington.

Such deference to made-in-America ideology rested on the trustful notion that what was good for Washington was *ipso facto* good for the Pacific Rim. But by 1996, with Thai exports stagnant at a time when Wall Street was booming, doubts should have abounded. Doug Henwood (*After the New Economy*, 2003) makes a cogent argument that there never was an American "New Economy," at least not in the sense that technophiles such as Thomas Friedman saw it. The roaring '90s were not so much stoked by the celebrated Information Revolution as by the de-regulation of capital markets. That fostered a no-holds-barred commercialism which seemed to favor the Asian tigers, or at least their urban elites, as wild speculation pushed foreign investment far beyond productive limits. Countless warning signs were ignored as Thailand fell prey to explosive private debt and balance of payment deficits. The resulting currency crisis, as in 1980–81, forced the government to seek IMF assistance. That of course was inviting the fox to guard the chickens.

The fox was on very familiar ground. Our image of Thailand's historic independence is shattered when we recall the steady infusion of Western capital and advisors that reaches back to 1850. It is even arguable that "there was never a time when Thai society was not globalizing."[39] Only the deluge of American and Japanese capital since the Vietnam War makes the pre-1960s era seem relatively autonomous.[40] Nonetheless the full thrust of international hegemony was averted. Likewise, Thaksin's quite traditional strategy was to dance on both sides of the geopolitical fence: indulging America's fixation on terrorism while reaping the rewards of China's commercial overtures.

Undeniably this dance gave Thailand a better bargaining position than it had in the sputtering 1990s. On Thaksin's watch Bangkok rejected development assistance from global titans such as Japan and challenged the IMF by establishing aid and soft loan packages for Asian neighbors.[41] Thus Thailand moved from the ranks of peripheral, aid-directed development to the top of the regional pyramid. It was mainly Thai capitalists, however, who reaped the rewards. The reactionary tilt of Thaksinocracy was camouflaged by the fact that its primary targets, the IMF and the World Bank, are hardly paragons of progressivism. Rather they have propped up odious regimes and consistently impeded non-commercial reform. No wonder they so easily forgave Thaksin's transgressions against them. They knew it was all a front, as he was a member in good standing of their transnational capitalist club. His

---

39 Quoted from a Thai intellectual by Natasha Hamilton-Hart, "Thailand and Globalization," in Samuel S. Kim (ed.), *East Asia and Globalization* (Lanham, MD: Rowman & Littlefield, 2000), p. 189 (pp. 187–207).

40 Anderson, *Spectre, op. cit.*, p. 143.

41 Pongsudhirak, *op. cit.*

highly publicized anti-IMFism allowed him all the better to defuse the revulsion of the Thai public toward globalization. It took five years for the fact to sink in that his antiglobalist rhetoric was a hoax.

In the name of nationalistic resistance, Thaksin had invited the return of the old dinosaurs, as Thais call the magnates of patronage politics-as-usual. Locally managed maldevelopment may seem preferable to globally managed maldevelopment, but for the people of Nam Khem it comes to the same thing. Their interests could only be served by a development model that reconciles economic dynamism with equalitarian democracy. That is what the Senian model does when it is not hijacked by neoliberals or their "Third Way" equivalents, both of whom are determined to keep equality out of the picture. Senism is at odds with any power elite, be it the old Thai dinosaurs, the new globalists, or a Thaksinian merger of the two.

Conclusion: the Road to Sustainable Cronyism

The real nature of that merger was fully exposed early in 2006 when Thaksin sold controlling interest in his telecommunications firm, Shin Corporation, tax-free for $1.9 billion. Shin's market value had trebled during Thaksin's five years in office. It did not help that the buyer, Temasek, is owned and managed by the Singapore government. Nationalist outrage was thus added to a growing sense of working class betrayal. Student-led protests, reminiscent of 1973, brought tens of thousands into the streets—100,000 on February 4 alone.[42] By then two cabinet members had resigned, and more were doubtless standing by their life boats.

Government coverage of these events on state-run television and radio stations was blocked, much as it had been in 1992, but that only underscored the threat TRTism posed to democratic institutions. To confirm his populist power base, Thaksin felt compelled to call for an April election, three years ahead of schedule. Though his formal victory was hardly in doubt, the solidarity of his "grand coalition" was severely shaken. After all, his 2001 victory had been built on his promise to defend nationalist interests against the globalist inroads of the IMF. Now he had not only executed the biggest corporate sellout in Thai history, but was busy negotiating a free-trade agreement with Washington. The IMF could not have wished for more.

Under siege in Bangkok, Thaksin focused his campaign all the more on his rural constituents, handing out 1,000-baht banknotes from his own wallet in village after village. The April election became a classic brawl between a rural majority that unabashedly sold its votes to Thaksin and an urban minority that demanded the removal of a vile but democratically elected leader. Whichever side prevailed, democracy would be the loser.

Middle-class discontent was ably manipulated by Thaksin's media rival, Sondhi Limthongkul, while craven opposition leaders stood aside.[43] The military coup that finally ousted Thaksin in September 2006, with the full approval of the king, could

---

42 Noknoi Daeng, "Mass Upsurge in Thailand: Students and Workers on the March," *MRZine* (February 14, 2006), http://mrzine.monthlyreview.org/daeng140206.html.

43 Veer Prateepchaikul, "Thaksin's Top Critic could Seek Dignified Exit," *Bangkok Post* (January 23, 2006), http://www.asiamedia.ucla.edu/print.asp?parentid=37611.

not so easily expel the TRT machine. Thaksinocracy had taken on a life of its own apart from Thaksin. Though the TRT was disbanded by court order in May 2007, its more stalwart members soon regrouped under the banner of a new People's Power Party (PPP).

This reincarnation marked a distinct shift to the Right from the TRT's post-coup leadership under Chaturon Chaisaeng. The new PPP leader, Samak Sundaravel, was no enemy of militarism. Having faithfully served military governments during the bloody repressions of 1976 and 1992,[44] he was the perfect political hybrid for the moment: a confessed Thaksin proxy with close Army ties.[45] Thus he stood a chance of winning centrist support away from the military royalism of General Sonthi Boonyaratglin. When the December 2007 election brought the PPP to power, thanks largely to the poor economic showing of the junta, reactionary globalism was back on track. The only good news was that "Dog Mouth" Samak, as the press dubbed him, would not enjoy the political monopoly that his boss had wielded. He would have to rule by way of a six-party coalition.[46]

That ostensive blessing carries a price, however. The PPP victory restores many of the worst features of TRTism without its one positive attribute: its ability to overcome the leadership void that has plagued Thailand through endless regime cycles. The new constitution that was passed by referendum in August 2007 so weakened the power of future prime ministers that good as well as bad executive authority would be stifled. On the zero-sum scales of Thai politics, any diminution of civilian authority will translate into permanent military supervision of the country's political life.[47]

The democratic prospect that seemed so close at hand with the 1997 constitution has suffered the same fate as the hopes once vested in Korean *minjung*, Philippine People Power, and Indonesian *reformasi*. None of these cases bodes well for the Senian model of concurrent development advanced by this study. It must be asked, therefore, if Sen's "Asian strategy" is a complete delusion. Our next four chapters, covering China, India, and Japan, will put the question of democratic efficacy front and center: What is the cash value of freedom or repression in these budding Asian superpowers?

44 Simon Montlake, "The Majority Coalition is Expected to Name a Controversial Prime Minister," *The Christian Science Monitor* (January 25, 2008), http://www.csmonitor. com/2008/0125/p04s01-woap.html.

45 Shawn W. Crispin, "Politics by Proxy in Thailand," Asia Times (August 10, 2007), http://www.atimes.com/atimes/Southeast_Asia/IH10Ae01.html.

46 "Good Riddance," *The Economist* (January 24, 2008), http://www.economist.com/ opinion/PrintFriendly. cfm?story_id=10566710.

47 Seth Mydans, "New Thai Constitution would Strengthen Role of the Military," *International Herald Tribune* (August 17, 2007), http://www.iht.com/articles/2007/08/17/ news/thai.php.

Chapter 6

Sino-Globalization—Part 1:
Politics of the CCP/TNC Symbiosis

Line in the Sand

When Fei Xiaotong died at 95 in 2005, China lost one of its last effective voices for democratic reform from within establishment ranks. Fei's classic, *Peasant Life in China*, reminds us of how rural Chinese paid the price for change in the formative years of Chinese communism.[1] Now, likewise, they are paying for Chinese capitalism. The difference is that the former gave them some actual benefits in return. They not only got minimal health care, but the psychological satisfaction of knowing that however bad things were, the hardship was broadly distributed. Anyone who thinks those are insignificant benefits should consider becoming a World Bank economist.

Having so much to like about current PRC policies, corporate CEOs and their neoliberal scribes have developed a political double vision about this erstwhile backwater of the Second World. Even as they vilify Cuban communism, they refuse to process the grim realities of PRC power politics.[2] This double standard also infects assessments of China's economic performance. CCP policies have generally been considered beneficial for the vast majority of Chinese, which is a portentous myth. Deng's economic restructuration tipped China like a seesaw, with the spotlight aimed at the winning side. Even by the mid-1980s inflation of up to 28 percent was sorely felt on the losing end of the seesaw.[3] Public resentment was natural, but lacked a political outlet. Reformist officials such as Hu Yaobang struck terror in the CCP Old Guard by simply broaching the subject of political reform. That not only killed Hu's chance to be Deng Xiaoping's successor, but probably killed him literally. Many suspect Li Peng of giving the order. In any case Hu conveniently expired on April 15, 1989.

It will be left for historians to debate how close the Hu faction had been to effecting political reform from within CCP ranks. The *Tiananmen Papers* (documents smuggled out of CCP archives and published early in 2001) suggest that China's power elite was divided over the proper course of development, but the bottom line

---

1 See Anne F. Thurston, "An Optimist's Life," *The Wilson Quarterly* (Autumn 2005), http://www. wilsoncenter.org/index.cfm?fuseaction=wq.print&essay_id=146858&...

2 See Michael Parenti, "The Logic of U.S. Intervention," in Carl Boggs (ed.), with a foreword by Ted Rall, *Masters of War: Militarism and Blowback in the Era of American Empire* (New York and London: Routledge, 2003), p. 27 (pp. 19–36).

3 Sophia Yee, "China expert Pye examines Tiananmen massacre," *The Tech.*, Vol. 109, No. 60 (January 24, 1989), http://www-tech.mit.edu/V109/N60/china.60n.html.

was the fact that the Army answered only to Deng.[4] He had never been the budding liberal that neoliberal commentators like to imagine. The one who came closest to fitting that mold was the CCP general secretary Zhao Ziyang. Zhao did his best to cushion the CCP crackdown that was all but inevitable by late 1986 and early 1987, after Fang Lizhi (the dissident physicist known widely as China's Sakharov) lit the fuse on a string of pro-democracy demonstrations across China.

It was encouraging that although Fang was thrown out of the Party (for the third time), he was allowed to continue his academic career and even permitted to travel abroad. The message this sent to his mostly silent intellectual sympathizers, inside and outside the Party, was almost as stunning as the crackdown itself. Even Fang was plainly surprised, during an interview with NBC anchorman Tom Brokaw, when he was shown footage of an interview with Zhao the day before. Here was the general secretary giving assurance that although Fang would be ousted from the Party, his freedom and that of other intellectuals would be respected in their capacity as citizens.[5] The CCP Old Guard was angered by Fang's speeches, but it was even more appalled by Zhao's temperate response. The decision was made to slam the door on such tolerance. Far from a panicked reaction to unforeseen events, the government's action at Tiananmen was part of a carefully scripted CCP plan to abort Zhao's reformism while accelerating GDPism. From this point on the hard-liners took the offensive, or rather the counter-offensive.

A key player in this rearguard shift was the future president, Hu Jintao, who in December 1988 was appointed to the dismal post of Party Secretary of TAR (the Tibet Autonomous Region), replacing the relatively liberal-minded Wu Jinghua. This was the Chinese equivalent of Siberia, and Hu—complaining of altitude sickness and Tibet's "lack of culture"—would avoid physical location in Tibet as much as possible. In retrospect it is obvious that this posting was no demotion. It put Hu in close working contact with the military, which was more active in TAR than in any other Chinese province or region.

This was in fact a warm-up exercise for an ominous new development strategy, fusing international globalism with domestic fascism. The day after Hu's appointment was announced, a large demonstration erupted in Lhasa, Tibet's capital. It was savagely suppressed by the People's Armed Police, which targeted Tibetans carrying their outlawed national flag.[6] The violence so exceeded the threat that its real point was patently not restricted to Tibet. The PLA was practicing for bigger things to come, much as the Japanese Army once practiced in Manchuria, the German Nazis in Spain, and the Bush administration in Afghanistan, prior to its more ambitious Middle East incursion.

The next month, shortly after his belated arrival in Lhasa, Hu attended a meeting in which he sat next to the legendary Panchen Lama, the second highest Tibetan spiritual

---

4 William H. Thornton, *Fire on the Rim: The Cultural Dynamics of East/West Power Politics* (Lanham, MD: Rowman & Littlefield, 2002), p. 31.

5 Orville Schell, "China's Andrei Sakharov," *The Atlantic* (May 1988), http://www. tsquare.tv/film/SchellFLZ.html.

6 "Background Information on Hu JinTao," *International Campaign for Tibet* (October 18, 2005), http://www.savetibet.org/news/positionpapers/hujintao.php?printable=yes.

leader. To everyone's dismay, this deeply spiritual man delivered a riveting speech condemning Chinese oppression. He had just signed his death warrant. A few days later he would die under conspicuously mysterious circumstances, leaving behind a leadership vacuum in Tibet which remains to this day. Massive demonstrations followed, in which the police fired wildly, killing not only dozens of demonstrators but also innocent people in their homes. And that was just the prelude.

In March Hu ordered full martial law, including the arrest of hundreds of Tibetans. The extended sentences they got, and the unspeakable torture they suffered, had Hu's fingerprints all over it, just as his Tibet assignment bore Deng's fingerprints. The Tibetan rising was no surprise to either. It allowed the hard-liners to send a suspiciously well-timed message: that economic reform should not be misconstrued as a road to democracy. "People power" had recently come to fruition in the Philippines, and similar democratic eruptions had shaken the ruling orders of South Korea and Taiwan. Deng's circle was determined to keep China off this reform list. Lhasa became the PLA's model for how to deal with political dissent.[7]

Hu Yaobang's death ignited demands for more and faster reforms, and soon thousands of students were converging on Tiananmen Square. As many as a million camped out at Tiananmen at one point, and by late May another three to five million unemployed workers were roaming the streets of Beijing protesting inflation and corruption.[8] Many workers joined the students in the hunger strikes that began on May 13. On May 17 several of China's top leaders visited Deng's home to get his word on how to proceed. He artfully summed it up for them: "If things continue like this, we could even end up under house arrest."[9] Deng knew he could count on the CCP rank and file to back him, because the demonstrators were demanding not only democracy but an end to corruption. That was hitting too close to home.

Martial law was declared at the end of May, and on June 3 Deng gave the green light for the Army to apply its well-honed Tibetan tactics on the unarmed demonstrators.[10] The tragic events of June 4, 1989 (the day that Polish Solidarity won its first national election) marked the dead end of any serious hope that economic liberalization would foster democratic reform. Hu Yaobang and Zhao had been the last direct links between those Senian twins, development and freedom. For advocating reform, and for opposing the use of military violence, Zhao would spend

---

7 *Ibid.*

8 See "Tiananmen Square Uprising: A Perspective," *Sinomania.com*, http://www. sinomania.com/CHINANEWS/Tiananmen_perspective.htm.

9 Richard Bernstein, "New Window on Tiananmen Square Crackdown," *The New York Times* (January 6, 2001), http://www2.kenyon.edu/Depts/Religion/Fac/Adler/Reln270/TAM1.htm.

10 The *Tiananmen Papers* show that the five-man standing committee was deadlocked over what course to take, so it fell on Deng to make the fateful decision. This supports the claims of Li Peng that Deng, the Paramount Reformer himself, was the prime mover. On these papers see "The U.S. 'Tiananmen Papers': New Documents Reveal U.S. Perceptions of 1989 Chinese Political Crisis," in Michael L. Evans (ed.), *A National Security Archive Electronic Briefing Book* (June 4, 2001), from The National Security Archive, http://www. gwu.edu/~nsarchiv/NSAEBB/NSAEBB47/index2.html.

the rest of his life under house arrest.[11] His top aid, Bao Tong (lambasted by Li Peng for wearing blue jeans inside the Forbidden City), would get six years in prison.[12] Even at the time of Zhao's death in January 2005, extraordinary security measures were taken, lest his political ghost might come back to haunt.[13]

It is important to realize, however, that Deng's seeming reversal of 1980s reformism was entirely in keeping with his lifelong habits. Much as Hu Jintao was sent to Tibet as Deng's personal axe-man, Deng himself had been handpicked by Chairman Mao for the same role in the aftermath of the 1957 "let a hundred flowers bloom" crackdown on reform-minded intellectuals. Only then, with the Party firmly in his grip, would Mao launch his infamous Great Leap Forward.[14] Deng similarly used Tiananmen for ideological housecleaning before launching another great leap: China's bid for geoeconomic supremacy in Asia.

Lhasa and Tiananmen were integral parts of that leap, sending a message as unambiguous as Truman's message at Hiroshima and Nagasaki. Finally the students got the point: Beijing was not going to be Manila or Seoul. Here there would be just one party, and one ruling faction within it. The only question was how the world community would take this seeming reversal. Tiananmen drew a line in the sand, and global capitalism could no longer duck the issue. It either stood for or against democracy.

The CCP/TNC Partnership

It says much about the real priorities of neoliberal globalization that China's mega-growth of the 1990s, fueled largely by Western investors, took place under the long shadow of Tiananmen. The PRC's pogrom on its own best and brightest was a high-stakes gamble that TNCs would put profits over principles. They did exactly that, throwing their enormous political weight behind a policy of forgive-and-forget

---

11 Zhao was never seen in public after May 9, 1989, when he went to Tiananmen Square and made an impassioned plea for students to withdraw. When he died in January 2005, his former secretary, Bao Tong, lashed out at the government, calling their actions a "showcase of shame." Zhao's daughter simply said he was "free at last." In April 2005 Ching Cheong, a Hong Kong reporter, was arrested in China for trying to obtain Zhao's interview transcripts. See Robert Marquand, "China Ratchets up Control on Expression," *The Christian Science Monitor* (January 3, 2006), http://www.csmonitor.com/2006/0103/p06s01-woap. htm.; "Chinese reformer Zhao Ziyang dies," *BBC News*, http://newsvote.bbc.co.uk/mpapps/ pagetools/print news.bbc.co.uk/1/hi/world/asi...; and Ching Cheong, "Hong Kong journalist Ching Cheong accused of spying," *Reporters without Borders*, http://www.rsf.org/article. php3id_article=13973.

12 Allen T. Cheng and Tim Healy, "The Ghosts of Tiananmen," *Asiaweek*, Vol. 27, No. 2 (January 19, 2001), http://www.asiaweek.com/asiaweek/magazine/nations/0,8782,94722,00. html.

13 Isabel Hilton, "Reaching beyond the myth of Mao," *Guardian* (June 4, 2005), http:// www.guardian.co. uk/print/0,3858,5208236-103677,00.html.

14 Bryan Caplan, "Autocratic ghosts and Chinese hunger," *Independent Review* (Winter 2000), in *Britannica.com*, http://www.britannica.com/magazine/print?content_id=167079.

"engagement." Business was roaring by 1992, but for added impetus China tossed further market reforms into the bargain. Capital inflows responded on cue.

There was no ambiguity in the message this sent to the developing world: the unreformed Chinese development model had received a green light. There would be no geoeconomic penalty for the worst police state atrocity of the post-Mao era. Little international pressure would be exerted on China to add political reform to the four modernizations (agriculture, industry, science and technology) set forth by Deng Xiaoping and Zhou Enlai in 1975. By dropping all significant qualifiers to US engagement, the Washington Consensus added its signature to the horrors of Lhasa and Tiananmen.

On the economic side, labor reform would have been perfectly in keeping with Deng's pledge to forge a capitalism with "socialist characteristics," whereas wholesale privatization could benefit only bureaucratic elites and their cronies.[15] Such reform could also have delivered higher aggregate demand for Western products—that being a stated goal of Washington's China agenda, as reaffirmed by Secretary of the Treasury John Snow on his 2005 China tour.[16] This long-term benefit, however, was dwarfed by the instant gratification of cheap labor and quick profits. Deng's economic reform was in fact a device to buy off the local and global forces that might have pressed for matching political development. But with the carrot came the stick: the rights of ordinary workers were drastically curtailed, and peasant farmers were increasingly disenfranchised.

In the early 1980s Deng himself gave the order to limit legal appeals, thereby freeing provincial courts to strip workers of their most basic socialist rights. One especially heinous result has been the rise of an Eichmann-style industry of capital punishment. China issues somewhere between 10,000 and 15,000 death sentences per year. The exact number remains a "state secret," but not because the government fears that a large number would spark unrest. Rather it fears the number might be too small to contain unrest. The magnifying effect of rumor works better, yet even that has not been enough to staunch rural protests.

No longer trusting provincial courts to do Beijing's bidding, the People's Supreme Court reversed Deng's decentralization order as of October, 2005. This, however, only restored the Maoist system of judicial subordination.[17] The fact that Beijing deemed this necessary is suggestive of how desperate matters have become. The problem traces to the grand bargain that Deng brokered with bureaucratic and entrepreneurial classes at the expense of workers and farmers. Lower strata comrades are offered much the same "trickle down" that Ronald Reagan and Margaret Thatcher promised

---

15 Yiching Wu, "Rethinking 'Capitalist Restoration' in China," *Monthly Review*, Vol. 57, No. 6 (November 2005), http://www.monthlyreivew.org/1105wu.htm.

16 Edmund L. Andrews, "U.S. Offers Plan for Open Markets in China," *The New York Times* (October 16, 2005), http://www.nytimes.com/2005/10/16/business/16china.html.

17 Jim Yardley, "In Worker's Death, View of China's Harsh Justice," *The New York Times* (December 31, 2005), http://www.nytimes.com/2005/12/31/international/asia/32china.html.

their workers. In China and America alike the effect of globalization could better be described as "trickle up."[18]

That is just one more reason for the loyalty that TNCs have showered on Beijing. In turn, the Chinese handling of FDI has departed from the miracle-era formula of the East Asian tigers by not building the Chinese economy behind a stiff tariff wall. Although FDI has been largely restricted to Special Economic Zones (SEZs), Chinese capitalism has joined hands with neoliberalism in labor practices that ensure a global "rush to the bottom." Much as Western workers have watched the American dream slipping away from them, Chinese workers lost their grip on their "iron rice bowl." On both sides this has produced the kind of insecurity that was common throughout the Pacific Rim after the Crash.[19] Insecurity is what keeps wages down and profits up, and that is what the CCP/TNC bargain is all about.

It should be noted, however, that while Chinese policies often serve globalist interests—promoting global capitalism better than any democracy could have[20]— they have never followed the neoliberal script. China has been exempted from IMF-style restructuration pressures. It has been welcomed into the global community despite the fact that it rigidly controls capital flows, closely oversees external trade, and sustains a large state-owned system of heavy manufacturing.[21] Meanwhile there has been only modest protest as the PRC trade surplus goes off the charts, tripling in 2005 alone. Most of this surplus is with the United States. In fact, excluding America, the PRC ran a trade deficit of about $12 billion, mainly with Japan and China's oil providers.[22]

There is, of course, full reciprocity, as China supports American consumerism as well as militarism through massive purchases of US debt instruments. The question is how far deficit spending can be pushed before this house of cards collapses. A US recession would spell a Chinese depression, for private consumer spending is too low in China to cushion an economic slump.[23] In the long run both sides would be

---

18 It is no surprise that Chinese workers lack the political leverage to demand a better deal, but it is startling how American labor finds itself a political orphan. Neither the Democrats nor Republicans will take up the working class cause. Labor leaders are telling workers that the issue is no longer how to secure better pay and benefits, but simply how not to be laid off. They are well aware that one in five manufacturing jobs was lost between Bush's first inauguration and September 2005, when his approval ratings finally took a dive. Unions are either unable or unwilling to confront corporate priorities. China's rise serves as a global enforcer of neoliberal downsizing.

19 Martin Hart-Landsberg and Paul Burkett, "Introduction: China and Socialism" *Monthly Review*, Vol. 56, No. 3 (July-August 2004), http://www.monthlyreview.org/0704intro.htm.

20 William H. Thornton, *New World Empire: Civil Islam, Terrorism, and the Making of Neoglobalism*. Lanham, MD: Rowman & Littlefield, 2005, p. 109.

21 Jacob Middleton, "Trading on Poverty," *International Socialism: A Quality of Socialist Theory*, Issue 107 (Summer 2005), http://www.isj.org.uk/index/php4?id=118issue=107.

22 David Barboza, "China's Trade Surplus Tripled in 2005," *The New York Times* (January 11, 2006), http://www.nytimes.com/2006/01/11/business/11cnd-yuan.html.

23 "Fearing Social Unrest, China Tries to Rein in Unbridled Capitalism," *Spiegel Online* (January 18, 2006), http://service.spiegel.de/cache/international/spiegel/0,1518,druck-395833,00.html.

better served by slower-paced trade, which for China would mean less dependence on foreign capital. But there are political as well as economic reasons for the PRC's FDI addiction. Growing inequality—with more than 60 percent of the nation's wealth held by less than one percent of its households[24]—gives the CCP good reason to fear spreading unrest. But most of all it dreads the "perfect storm" of combined working class and bourgeois resistance. That partly explains why Beijing favors soporific SOEs on the one hand and rapacious TNCs on the other.[25]

Beijing regards FDI as a Trojan Horse, yet cannot bring itself to close the globalist gates. It is torn between fear of domestic reformism and suspicion that the US is using foreign investment in a "war without the smoke of gunpowder," as Deng Xiaoping put it.[26] Without a heavy injection of FDI, Chinese industrialists could quickly gain the upper hand. Foreign capital has saved the CCP both politically and economically, but how dependable is this salvation? Foreign investors stand to profit as the Chinese development model is packaged for transfer to other developing nations.

Neoliberals point to China's capital dependency as reason to dismiss the dangers of engagement. Labor is still cheap (though upward wage pressures have been noted in major industrial cities),[27] but resource costs are not, and more resources are needed here than in developed countries. Poor productivity means that to manufacture something of like value in China requires seven times more resources than in Japan, six times more than in the US, and three times more than in India.[28] Globalists reason that so long as Chinese firms remain instruments of CCP privilege, China will require massive doses of foreign investment and expertise, not to mention balance of trade forgiveness, simply to function. This dependency permits neoliberals to imagine that they, not the CCP, are ultimately in charge.

Sino-optimists still insist that engagement is a sure route to political reform as well as mega-profits.[29] They see no need for contingency plans in case engagement collides head-on with Tiananmen-style reality. What evidence is there that FDI will favor liberal democratization and human rights, especially when foreign investors are openly playing on the CCP team? Rupert Murdoch, for example, had no qualms about banning the BBC from his Star TV network after it ran reports about human rights violations in China.[30] Such "see no evil" accommodation is a basic operating principle of the CCP/TNC accord.

---

24 C.T. Kurien, "Giants of the East," *Frontline*, Vol. 23, No. 26 (December 30, 2006 to January 12, 2007), http://www.hinduonnet.com/fline/stories/20070112000507400.htm.

25 George J. Gilboy, "The Myth Behind China's Miracle," *Foreign Affairs*, Vol. 83, No. 4 (July/August 2004), p. 34 (pp. 33–48).

26 Russell Ong, *China's Security Interests in the Post-Cold War Era* (Richmond, Surrey, UK: Curzon, 2002), Chapter 6.

27 Barboza, *op. cit.*

28 *Spiegel* Interview, "The Chinese Miracle Will End Soon," *Der Spiegel* (March 7, 2005), http://service.spiegel.de/cache/international/Spiegel/0,1518,druck-345694,00.html.

29 E.g., Gilboy, *op. cit.*, pp. 34–35.

30 Tina Rosenberg, "Building the Great Firewall of China, With Foreign Help," *The New York Times* (September 18, 2005), http://www.nytimes.com/2005/09/18/opinion/18sun3.html.

"Business is Business"

Some of the worst corporate complicity in the making of Sino-globalization now comes from that celebrated force of liberation, the Internet. In the short run it did show some promise. China's online generation has been quick to convert to Net news sources, which they trust more than state-supported print papers. Just one such online source, *Sina*, has a readership thirty times that of the government-run *People's Daily*,[31] though obviously both are heavily censored. The biggest challenge for the authorities has been personal Internet messages. Reporter's Without Borders, the Paris-based advocacy group, has designated China as the "world champion" of Internet censorship,[32] with an estimated fifty-thousand full-time net detectives.[33]

Without assistance from Western firms these online police would be hunting in the dark. Firms such as Microsoft, Yahoo and Google have trashed any possible claim to a higher purpose beyond profitability by signing contracts with China to actively control Internet content. While Microsoft and Cisco were selling China firewalls and other security tools, Yahoo went the extra mile by helping authorities track down and convict Shi Tao, a journalist who got a ten year prison sentence in April 2005 for exposing what Beijing calls "state secrets," which is to say any information that the government finds embarrassing. First Yahoo claimed that under Chinese law it had no choice but to comply in every way with Beijing's wishes. This turned out to be an utter fabrication, since Yahoo was registered in Hong Kong, where no such legal obligation obtained.[34] Finally the company's chief in China, Jack Ma, shrugged the matter off with three words: *"business is business."*[35] A commentator in

31 Weigui Fang, "Reflection on China's internet boom," *Open Democracy* (July 3, 2003), http://www.opendemocracy.net/debates/article-8-85-1334,jsp.

32 Of the 62 "cyberdissidents" known to be imprisoned around the world, 54 are in China. See Tom Zeller, Jr., "China, Still Winning Against the Web," *The New York Times* (January 15, 2006), http://www.nytimes. com/2006/01/15/weekinreview/15zeller.html.

33 Kathleen E. McLaughlin, "China's model for a censored Internet," *The Christian Science Monitor* (September 22, 2005), http://www.csmonitor.com/2005/0922/p01s02-woap. html; and Becky Hogge, "The Great Firewall of China," *Open Democracy* (May 20, 2005), http://www.opendemocracy.net/articles/ViewPopUpArticle.jsp?id=8&articleId=2524.

34 Rosenberg, *op. cit.*

35 William Falk, "When You Were Sleeping," *The New York Times* (December 30, 2005), http://www.nytimes.com/2005/12/30/opinion/30falk.html. He might have added that business is also geopolitics, and vice versa. Consider the case of the telecom giant, Global Crossing, which fell in January 2002 in the fourth largest bankruptcy in US history. Until that time Global had been the biggest spender of them all on campaign contributions. Its board included William Cohen, the Secretary of State under Clinton, the most pro-China president of modern times; and one of its close cronies was former president and pro-China stalwart George H.W. Bush, who got $80,000 in Global stock options for a single speech in Tokyo. It is no accident that Hutchison Whampoa Ltd. of Hong Kong, with its close ties to the Chinese Army, and with commercial control of both ends of the Panama Canal, has tried to buy Global Crossing. See Wes Vernon, "Global Crossing Tied to Clinton Defense Secretary," *NewsMax.com* (February 16, 2002), http://www.newsmax.com/archives/articles/2002/2/15/154416.shtml.

the *South China Morning Post* compared this attitude to that of the IBM executives who supplied punch-card technology to the Nazis during the Holocaust.[36]

The bottom line is that the American Internet population of about 203 million is fast reaching its saturation point, while China's 103 million users represent just a small fraction of its potential.[37] Any free speech and human rights concerns that Bill Gates might have had are swamped by these hard facts. Instead of Western corporations spreading democratic values by way of example, they are becoming "Sino-globalized." If such conduct can be excused by way of the bottom line— "business is business"—so can prostitution, arms sales, the drug trade, and human trafficking, not to mention the PRC's house specialty, organ sales, whose supply tends to correlate with the frequency of Chinese executions.

American arms dealers envy their European counterparts the contracts they are ready to make with China, assuming the EU arms embargo can be lifted. The consolation prize is that Taiwan will also have to step up its US arms purchases, but clearly the Soviets and now the Europeans are fishing in a bigger sea. So far American capitalists can enter this market only indirectly, through technological transfers that are tagged "civilian" but in fact are "dual purpose." The Taiwan government might be expected to complain about such sales, except that their capitalists are just as busy selling out Taiwan's national security.

Suffice it to say that neoliberal delusions of "peace through trade" have long since lost credibility. These myths persist only as camouflage for TNC interests. Ever since Tiananmen the democratic argument for engagement has had to borrow heavily on the collateral of future democratization, yet nothing obstructs that future so much as unqualified "engagement" policies: the complete disconnection of trade and human rights that was the prime goal of the unregistered lobbying firm Kissinger and Associates.

Are neoliberal investors oblivious to all this? The more astute ones surely know what democratic development would entail. First, it could spawn social legislation that would drive up the cost of labor. To some degree that drag on profits could be offset by a rise in domestic purchasing power. But this expanded market would probably not redound to a surge in imports from America, since Chinese nationalism would tilt the competitive playing field.[38] Foreign firms would then lose the inside track they have enjoyed with the CCP. This is just one more reason why TNCs prefer to keep democracy on permanent hold. The support they shower on the CCP makes good business sense, for the same reason that American capitalists on the board of I.G. Farben's US subsidiary found it expedient to fund the Nazis.[39]

---

36 Michael Logan, "Apartheid boycott offers lessons for US tech giants in China," *Asia Media* (February 21, 2006), http://www.asiamedia.ucla.edu/article.asp?parentid=39450.

37 Zeller, *op. cit.*

38 See Suisheng Zhao, "Nationalism's Double Edge," *The Wilson Quarterly* (Autumn 2005), http://www.wilsoncenter.org/index.cfm?fuseaction=wq.print&essay_id=146859&...

39 Three American board members were found guilty at the Nuremberg War Crimes Trial, though others such as Edsel B. Ford were never brought to trial. See Antony C. Sutton, *Wall Street and the Rise of Hitler* (Studies in Reformed Theology, 2000), Chapter 7.

It should not be surprising, therefore, that US engagement policy chugs along as usual. Neoliberals profess to believe that the market will align China with the Washington agenda for democracy and human rights, a goal that until 2000 was enshrined at least nominally in US tariff policy. The next year, with China's entry into the WTO, a purely economistic agenda was unveiled, driven by the dream of double-digit growth in a Chinese economy half-owned by US investors.[40] Short of that, US multinationals just want to avail themselves of low-cost production in a country that promises legions of non-unionized workers and a dearth of environmental protection.[41]

Given this capital injection, and the geopolitical indifference that money can buy in Washington, CCP strategists are confident of the party's staying power. This was reflected in the decision of President Hu to dust off the official good name of Hu Yaobang. As usual, the point of this action has been misunderstood in the West. Coming at a time when controls are being tightened on intellectuals, journalists, lawyers, and human rights activists, Hu's resurrection is anything but a backdoor admission that he was even partially right in his stand for concurrent political and economic development. Quite the contrary, this seeming exhumation is actually a political internment. President Hu is in effect proclaiming that the gamble of 1989 has been won. The Tiananmen era is history.

Neoliberals tacitly agree, since this position has enormous cash value. What is harder to explain is why many on the Left, who would be expected to contest this capitalist amnesia, have been reticent about the plight of China's working classes under the CCP/TNC bargain. Some go so far as to reduce the whole case against the CCP to a neoconservative plot,[42] on the apparent assumption that the enemy of one's enemy is by definition one's friend: If Bush and Cheney are rotten, Hu and Wen must be great guys. Unquestionably they are the better propagandists. Taking a lesson from Singapore's Lee Kuan Yew, today's CCP has learned to sugar-coat its global image, wrapping its militarism in "soft power" rhetoric and its domestic repression in double-digit economic growth.

Joshua Ramo's conception of the emerging "Beijing Consensus" takes this wrapping for the genuine article[43]—but then Ramo is an affiliate of Goldman Sachs. One would expect the Left to be more discerning, and certainly not to fall for the

---

40 The special target of this new agenda is China's state-owned banks. Currently foreign investors can own no more than 25 percent of a Chinese commercial bank. Likewise the prime target in Japan has been the Japanese postal service, which doubles as the country's major savings institution. See Edmund L. Andrews, *op. cit.*

41 Antonia Juhasz, "What Wal-Mart Wants from the WTO," *AlterNet* (December 31, 2005), http://www.alternet.org/story/29464.

42 See, for example, Gary Leupp, "Cheney, the Neocons, and China: The Solution to 'Enemy Deprivation Syndrome.'" *Dissident Voice* (April 20, 2006), http://www.dissidentvoice. org/Apr06/Leupp20.htm.

43 Joshua Cooper Ramo, *Beijing Consensus: Notes on the New Physics of Chinese Power* (London: Foreign Policy Center, 2004), pp. 6 and 13. Note that Ramo's conception of the Beijing Consensus departs from miracle-era "Asian values" in that he sees this new pattern as a prototype for the whole developing world. By contrast, the Asian exceptionalists saw their ideology as culturally unique.

Manichaean notion that to condemn the Washington Consensus requires categorical approval of the Beijing Consensus. Somehow it escapes notice that the two, despite their show of acrimony, are locked in a warm capitalistic embrace.[44] The one sells out democracy while the other sells out communism, yet they are united in their mutual willingness to sell out the working classes.

Fortunately there are exceptions to the Left's inattention to this mutuality. David Harvey, for example, charges in *The New Imperialism* that the end product of Sino-capitalism is class oppression. He would have us burn the infamous thing. Conversely, one of the most vocal proponents of the CCP/TNC partnership has been Henry Kissinger, who urges us to abandon any idea of reforming the Chinese junta. In his well-remunerated viewpoint this engine of maldevelopment is "inherent in the global economic and financial processes that the United States has been prominent in fostering."[45] In short, it is TINAesque. When many on the Left find themselves at odds with David Harvey and in perfect agreement with Henry Kissinger, it is time for some serious reflection on their stance concerning the Great Leap Backwards which is Sino-globalization.

The CCP Dilemma

For a quarter of a century the CCP governing class has stunted any kind of reform other than raw economic growth.[46] The result, in Jim Yardley's words, is "not only new wealth but a legacy of blackened rivers, grossly polluted skies and dwindling natural resources."[47] The distribution of that wealth, moreover, is so regressive that even the CCP's Chinese Academy of Social Sciences admits that the PRC has the world's biggest divide between urban rich and rural poor. Many African countries compare favorably with China's urban/rural income ratio of six to one.[48]

Nor does the new Sino-globalization have anything to do with the neoliberal shibboleth of "free enterprise." TNCs only wish that their CCP cronies, as their domestic guarantors, could wield even more political power. As things stand, provincial governments can impose protectionist fees that easily match the crony-capitalist intrusions of a Marcos or Suharto. China's entry into the WTO has hardly dented this fact, since local officials usually ignore national laws they find unprofitable.

---

44 In some sectors of the Left a more critical attitude is now emerging. See, for example, "Growth in Chinese Inequality Leads to Rise in Protest," *Socialist Worker*, 2066, 1 (September 2007), http://www.socialistworker.co.uk/print_art.php?id=12907.

45 Henry Kissinger, "China: Containment Won't Work," *Washington Post* (June 13, 2005), archived by the Global Policy Forum at http://www.globalpolicy.org/empire/analysis/2005/0613kissingerchina.htm.

46 See William H. Thornton, "Hu Goes There?: Sino-globalism and the ghost of Tiananmen," *ZNet* (April 25, 2006), http://www.zmag.org/content/print_article.cfm?itemID=10153&sectionID=103.

47 Jim Yardley, "Bad Air and Water, and a Bully Pulpit in China," *The New York Times* (September 25, 2004), http://www.nytimes.com/2004/09/25/international/asia/25fprofile.html.

48 Richard Spencer, "China rich-poor gap is world's worst," *Telegraph* (February 27, 2004), http://www.telegraph.co.uk/core/Content/displayPrintable.jhtml?xml=/news/2004/02/27/we...

US exporters soon discovered that little had changed after WTO regulations took effect. The actual cost of shipping an item from Shanghai to a central city could be double the national import tariff. An American automaker found, in fact, that the cost of sending a sedan from Shanghai to Ningxia Province was more than the cost of getting it from Detroit to Shanghai, as truckers had to pay huge bribes at every provincial border.[49] Local autocrats are all for capitalism, but strictly on their terms.

It is little wonder, therefore, that TNCs cheer for Beijing centrism. The TNC/CCP symbiosis that defines Sino-globalization is abetted on the Western side by the myth that China's "fourth generation" leaders are natural-born reformists as well as miracle makers. They are seen as the best hope for expanding democratization and closing the gap between urban vs. rural and coastal vs. interior economies. In fact, it is their brand of capitalist "reform" that in twenty years has taken China from one of the lowest income differentials in the world to the highest, with income in Shanghai eight to ten times that of other areas.[50]

The unrest this spawns will eventually erode one of the main sources of China's globalist appeal: its presumed political stability. President Hu Jintao and Premier Wen Jiabao face resistance not only from agricultural and industrial sectors,[51] but also from a bourgeoisie that seeks political power to match its financial status. Up against this economic behemoth, whose vanguard has been former President Jiang Zemin's "Shanghai clique," Hu and Wen turn all the more to global capital for support. Posing as "rule of law" activists, they do their best to court skittish foreign investors while suppressing local rivals, always under the rubric of anti-corruption investigations. This is the most sweeping political housecleaning China has seen since Tiananmen, involving the arrest or sidelining of leaders from Tianjin, Fujian, and Hunan, as well as top Shanghai officials such as Party Chief Chen Liangyu, who was detained along with another Politburo member. All are charged with corruption, but it so happens that nearly all of them are known for their loyalty to former President Jiang and their resistance to current President Hu.[52]

A neoliberalized Western press is pleased to take Hu's anti-corruption rhetoric at face value, finding "democratic" potential everywhere, even though the "reform" he touts is a strictly intra-party affair. There are intellectuals who denounce CCP dictates,[53] but so far they are voices in the political wilderness. The same holds for NGOs and citizen groups, which may be on the rise, but still lack political teeth.[54]

---

49 Hannah Beech, "The Emperor is Far Away," *Time Asia* (July 29, 2002), http://www.time.com/time/asia/magazine/printout/1,13675,501020805-332081,...

50 Richard Baum, "Where is China Going?," *UCLA Asia Institute* (December 13, 2002), http://internatinal. ucla.edu/asia/print.asp?parentid=2799.

51 David Harvey, *A Brief History of Neoliberalism* (Oxford: Oxford University Press, 2005), p. 149.

52 Joseph Kahn, "China's Corruption Inquiry Targets Beijing," *The New York Times* (October 27, 2006), http://www.nytimes.com/2006/10/27/world/asia/27china.html.

53 E.g., essays of Wang Hui. See Jeffrey N. Wasserstrom, "Reading China," *Boston Review* (Summer 2004), http://bostonreview.net/BR29.3/wasserstrom.html.

54 There is a growing flow of civic information and a new class of legal advocates for the common citizen. The question is whether these tools will serve People Power or prompt more intense repression, as happened in the late 1980s, even before Tiananmen. See Howard

Without democratic infrastructure in place, these reformists must approach their CCP overlords with a "by your leave" attitude that clips their political wings. And often they end up serving as pressure release mechanisms for the Beijing elite.

When Jiang's "third generationists" nearly sabotaged the new government's drive for national standards,[55] gullible Westerners read the conflict as one between regressive and progressive forces. Some even likened the Hu/Wen agenda to the fleeting reformism of Zhao Ziyang prior to the Tiananmen crackdown. That reading is laughable in view of the fact that the Hu team hails directly from the anti-Zhao camp.[56] In most respects the third and fourth generationists are birds of a feather. Reacting in horror to the Soviet collapse, Jiang Zemin and Li Peng were all the more determined to return Chinese development to the same economic track that Deng Xiaoping prescribed, and that Hu wholly endorses. The success of this model in GDP terms has caught the attention of the whole developing world. This success would have been voided, Robert Kaplan contends, if the Tiananmen demonstrations had led to democracy.[57] In effect he credits the "miracle" of the 1990s to the People's Liberation Army (PLA)!

In fact, as the late Gerald Segal argued, much of the PRC's celebrated growth has been bogus—or would have been so if global capital had not been there to keep it rolling. Even given that exogenous boost, some economists think China's growth rate is half that reported. Thomas Rawski concludes that after 1998 the economy was actually contracting. That may be overstated, but only because of extreme measures taken by the Beijing high command. China's former premier Zhu Rongzi confessed in a televised address that there would have been a collapse in 1998 had the government not supplied massive stimulus spending.

That is exactly the kind of Keynesian rescue operation that the IMF refused in the case of economies hit by the Asian Crash. Why does the neoliberal establishment remain mute in the case of China? And why is such depression medicine required in a time of record-breaking growth? How is it, moreover, that unemployment could have risen and energy-use fallen in the midst of a boom economy?[58] It is certainly odd that an economy growing at almost 10 percent for two decades would have created so few jobs. Through the 1990s there was just a one percent average employment increase per year. Only in the informal sector did employment actually increase.

W. French, "Chinese Turn to Civic Power as a New Tool," The New York Times (April 11, 2006), http://www.nytimes.com/2006/04/11/world/asia/11china.html.

55 Tian Jing and Wang Chu, "China power struggles: Resisting reforms," *Asia Times* (July 16, 2004), http://www.atimes.com/atimes/printN.html.

56 Thornton, "Hu Goes There?," *op. cit.*

57 Robert D. Kaplan, "Was Democracy Just a Moment?," *The Atlantic Online* (December 1997), http://www.theatlantic.com/issues/97dec/democ.html.

58 Arthur Waldron, "China's Economic Façade," *Washington Post* (March 21, 2002), http://www.taiwandc. org/wp-2002-01.htm. Rawski notes that energy consumption dropped by 12.8 percent between 1997 and 2000, though growth in energy efficiency is hardly a hallmark of Chinese production. See Thomas G. Rawski, "What's Happening to China's GDP Statistics?," a revised paper for *China Economic Review*, Vol. 12, No. 4 (December 2001), http://www.pitt.edu/~tgrawski/papers2001/gdp912f.pdf.

Somehow, against this drift, China will have to create 300 million new jobs over the next decade just to stave off a social explosion.[59] Faced with these disconcerting facts, the neoliberal press has been quick to spotlight recent news of a "labor shortage" in several leading industrial cities.[60] Wages have risen somewhat in these areas—and, after years of decline, the cost of goods from China is expected to rise. Factories want young laborers, and usually refuse to hire others. Reluctantly they are taking more workers in their thirties,[61] and there are indications that a dearth of young applicants could push industry westward into the interior.[62] These trends bear watching, but it would be delusional to suppose that they offer an instant-mix solution to the dilemma of a 300 million job deficit. To defuse this ticking social bomb, the government will have to take momentous action, yet any serious effort to close the urban/rural gap will reduce the rural desperation that has furnished the cities with a steady stream of impoverished workers. China's power elite is in trouble either way: if wages continue to rise, or if they do not.

The inescapable truth is that the Sino-globalist growth formula has largely bypassed two-thirds of China's population: those tied directly or indirectly to the land. Nor does the other third merit an unqualified "miracle" rating. To see how far off the mark that assessment is, it is only necessary to observe the marketing crisis at the country's shimmering new shopping malls. There are depressingly few customers to be seen here, and most of them are window shoppers who cannot possibly afford the inflated price tags of branded international products.[63] Little wonder there is a problem of branded fakes. Without them the malls would shut down.

The country's economic data is so inflated that the Asian Development Bank deducts at least two percent from official reports. Another three percent is generated by the one-shot economic stimulus of peasants leaving the land for urban jobs, with all the social problems that entails. Even that growth which is authentic is attended by ecological trauma of such a magnitude that it would deter FDI (foreign direct investment) if it were widely reported. Once all these factors are considered, the domestic side of China's economy turns out to be lackluster at best. There might even be a long-term recession in store if the economy were not being kept on FDI life support.[64]

59 Guy Ryder, "Whose Miracle in China?," *New Perspectives Quarterly*, Vol. 23, No. 1 (Winter 2006), http://www.digitalnpq.org/archieve/2006_winter/ryder.html.

60 David Barboza, "Labor Shortage in China May Lead to Trade Shift," *The New York Times* (April 3, 2006), http://www.nytimes.com/2006/04/03/business/03labor.html.

61 Keith Bradsher, "Wages Rise in China as Businesses Court the Young," *The New York Times* (August 29, 2007), http://www.nytimes.com/2007/08/29/business/worldbusiness/29labor.html.

62 Peter Ford, "To China's Migrants: Stay West, Young Man," *The Christian Science Monitor* (August 30, 2007), http://www.csmonitor.com/2007/0830/p04s01-woap.html.

63 Simon Montlake, "At China's Huge Malls, High Prices and Few Shoppers," *The Christian Science Monitor* (August 28, 2007), http://www.csmonitor.com/2007/0828/p01s01-woap.html.

64 Gerald Segal, "Does China Matter?," *Foreign Affairs*, Vol. 78, No. 5 (September/October 1999), pp. 25–26 (pp. 24–36).

Given this infusion, amounting to $60 billion in 2004,[65] there is no mystery as to how the Chinese economy keeps its "miracle" status afloat. It is global capital, in combination with legions of dirt cheap labor, that has turned the PRC into an export powerhouse with a massive trade surplus. By 2004 China was already the world's third biggest exporter, and the OECD predicts that by 2010 it will be the biggest.[66] The current annual trade surplus is approaching $150 billion. A currency adjustment might help restore balance, but the issue is complicated by the fact that most exports are actually from components underwritten by foreign investors.[67] The export explosion, moreover, rests not only on FDI but on a degree of labor suppression that Western capitalists could not dream of emulating.

How long can this last? By the mid-1990s there were signs of rising popular unrest, leading some to predict that Beijing would be increasingly besieged from within.[68] The challenge is not from democratic idealism but from grassroots revulsion against government corruption and indifference. For the CCP center to hold, Beijing will either have to radically reform or resort to measures so tough as to expose the myth of China's vaunted stability.

Hu's Balancing Act

Presently Beijing uses both a carrot and stick to reduce social unrest. Tax increases on farmers have negated most of the gains the rural sector made after the dissolution of agricultural collectives in the early 1980s. In the midst of a general crackdown on dissent (the stick), Premier Wen took the unprecedented step of abolishing the major agricultural tax (the carrot). Unfortunately this benign action was coupled with a new and even more devastating abuse: massive land appropriations by local officials trying to profit from the real estate boom.[69] Tax relief means nothing to a farmer robbed of his land.

In many cases farmers have been literally drowned out. Consider the human costs of China's mega-dams, starting with the prototype for all the rest: the Sanmenxia dam of the 1950s, which did to the Yellow River what the Three Gorges Dam is now doing to the Yangtze. Chinese statism sweeps aside the whole issue of environmental destruction, and cares little more about social displacement.[70] More than a million

---

65 Kurien, *op. cit.*

66 Larry Elliott, "China will soon be world's biggest exporter," *The Guardian* (September 17, 2005), http://www.guardian.co.uk/print/0,3858,5287985-108142,00.html.

67 Andrew Batson, "China's Trade Surplus Continues to Expand," *The Wall Street Journal* (August 10, 2006).

68 E.g, Arthur Waldron, "After Deng the Deluge," *Foreign Affairs* (September/October 1995), http://www.foreignaffairs.org/19950901fareviewessay5071/arthur-waldron/after-deng-the-d...

69 Joseph Kahn, "Painting the Peasants Into the Portrait of China's Economic Boom," *The New York Times* (August 7, 2006), http://www.nytimes.com/2006/08/07/books/07kahn.html

70 Andreas Lorenz and Wieland Wagner, "Cheap, Cheerful and Chinese?," *Spiegel Online* (November 17, 2005), http://service.spiegel.de/cache/international/spiegel/0,1518,druck-

people were uprooted by the Three Gorges project, which is now causing massive flooding, landslides, water pollution and estuary destruction.[71] These human and natural tragedies are inseparable. Naturally there was local protest, but no politically effective resistance. The last promising step in that direction was taken with the publication of Dai Qing's *Yangtze! Yangtze!* in the late 1980s. She was jailed after Tiananmen, and her book was banned.[72] In effect, eco-resistance was banned. It smolders out of sight, suggesting what might have transpired if a democratic mechanism had been available.

The Chinese minister of Public Security, Zhou Yongkang, admits that tens of thousands of "mass incidents" have arisen recently, with riots and protests up tenfold over the last ten years. The CCP is so desperate that it has begun to invoke Confucius in an effort to instill "moral standards."[73] What most concerns Beijing is that the epicenter of recent demonstrations has been shifting from the old industrial "rustbelt" of northeast China to thriving export zones. Mounting political instability could give the TNCs second thoughts about China, though it would take a great deal of it to send them packing. After all, the TNCs are not innocent bystanders in the exploitation that sparks these protests. The wage slavery and abysmal working conditions in their own factories is what makes China so attractive to them. Quite simply, they can get away with it here. With a sixth of rural Chinese unemployed, there should be plenty of fresh applicants when present workers quit or collapse. Any worker who complains, or even asks for raise, will not do so a second time.[74]

Late in 2005 the government was caught off guard at Dongzhou, a small village in Guangdong province, where paramilitary units opened fire on thousands of angry but peaceful protesters. State media were not fast enough in blocking coverage of the event, which was sparked when officials appropriated the land of local villagers for a coal-burning power plant, giving displaced families a mere pittance for their land,[75] and subjecting all residents to high pollution levels.[76] Up to thirty protesters

---

385446,00.html. While the official figure of the Three Gorges resettlement is 1.13 million, the World Bank puts it at 1.2 or more, with 60 percent of the displaced locals living below the poverty line as of January 1998. On the Chinese estimate see "Massive Resettlement out of Three Gorges Basically Ends," *People's Daily* (September 6, 2001), http://english. people. com.cn/english/200109/06/eng20010906_79488.html; and on the Bank's data see Martin Stein, "The Three Gorges: the unexamined toll of development-induced displacement," *FMR Review* (January 1, 1998), http://www.fmreview.org/text/FMR/01/02.htm.

71 Shai Oster, "Reservoir of Fear: In China, New Risks Emerge at Giant Three Gorges Dam," *The Wall Street Journal* (August 29, 2007), p. A1.

72 "Three Gorges Madness: An Interview with Dai Qing," *Multinational Monitor*, Vol. 18, No. 12 (December 1997), http://www.multinationalmonitor.org/hyper/mm1297.06.html.

73 "Who should own the good earth of China," *The Christian Science Monitor* (March 15, 2005), http://www.csmonitor.com/2006/0315/p08s01-comv.html.

74 "Three Gorges Madness," *op. cit.*

75 See William J. Dobson, "Quiet Riots," *The New Republic* (December 14, 2005), http://www.tnr.com/docprint.mhtml?i=w051212&s=dobson121405.

76 Families that agree to sing the government's song on the events of that day are now being promised over $6,000. See Howard W. French, "Chinese Pressing to Keep Village Silent

are said to have been killed,[77] making this one of the worst government atrocities since Tiananmen.

In all likelihood the decision to open fire was made locally, for Beijing is too well aware of the dangers of pulling this tiger's tail. However, it is equally aware of the danger of yielding to protesters' demands. Just over a month later another violent clash took place, this time in the village of Panlong, a short distance from the economic miracle cities of Shenzhen, Dongguan and Zhuhai.[78] The question is how much pressure the system can take before it explodes. With 8,700 acknowledged rural "incidents" in 1993, 32,000 in 1999, 58,000 in 2003, 74,000 in 2004, and 87,000 in 2005, the government is understandably on edge.[79]

Old Left factions within the National People's Congress have seized on this discord to challenge the wisdom of market-driven development. For the first time in more than a decade an actual ideological debate has erupted in the halls of power. Hu is playing on both sides of the fence, talking constantly of the need for "social equity," yet insisting all the while that China must "unshakably persist with economic reform."[80] The patent fact is that Deng Xiaoping's social compact—income growth in return for political stagnation—is not working.

It is no longer possible to hide the fact that most Chinese are losing on both sides.[81] Economic gains are poorly distributed, to put it mildly. This grim reality is exposed most graphically along the socioeconomic fault lines of development projects such as the Three Gorges Dam, which was another gift from Li Peng, the infamous "butcher of Tiananmen."[82] Locals uprooted here have yet to receive their promised compensation, and more than half now live in abject poverty. This is not even to consider their anguish from lost homes and broken communities.[83]

---

on Clash," *The New York Times* (December 17, 2005), http://www.nytimes.com/2005/12/17/international/asia/17chima.html.

77 Many feel the actual number is far above the official "government figure." See Audra Ang, "China Town Sealed After Protesters Slain," *Newsday.com* (December 10, 2005), http://www.newsday.com/news/nationworld/world/ats-ap_intl12dec09,0,2082641,print.story.

78 Howard W. French, "Police in China Battle Villagers in Land Protest," *The New York Times* (January 17, 2006), http://www.nytimes.com/2006/01/17/international/asia/17china.html.

79 Dobson, *op. cit.* ("Quiet Riots,")

80 Joseph Kahn, "A Sharp Debate Erupts in China Over Ideologies," *The New York Times* (March 12, 2006), http://www.nytimes.com/2006/03/12/international/asia/12china.html.

81 Dobson, *op. cit.*

82 In a recent essay, Li attempts to pin the full blame on his mentor Deng. See "China's Li blames Deng Xiaoping for Tiananmen," *The Age* (August 20, 2004), http://www.theage.com.au/2004/08/19/1092889274495.html?from=storylhs. Li's third major claim to fame was his decision to ignore opposition in Hong Kong to the country's biggest nuclear power plant at Daya Bay. See "Deng ordered Tiananmen crackdown, Li Peng says," *Taipei Times* (August 19, 2004), p. 5, http://www.taipeitimes.com/News/world/archives/2004/08/19/2003199330.

83 Yingling Liu, "Missing Voices on the Nu River Dam Project," *Worldwatch Institute* (November 29, 2005), http://www.worldwatch.org/features/chinawatch/stories/20051129-2.

Plans to harness the Nu River in Yunnan Province, involving some of China's last pristine areas, are meeting with unusual resistance,[84] yet no one seriously doubts the outcome. It was the concerted action of NGOs (almost unheard of just ten years before) that brought this issue to the fore, but that very success inspired a crackdown on NGOs. They were punished for their demand that the country's new "green laws" actually be enforced. Evacuations of local villages were being scheduled even before the required environmental impact studies had been carried out.[85] It is claimed that local residents will benefit from cheap electricity, but this is a hackneyed promise. Everyone knows that most of the power will be siphoned off by Eastern cities. In the case of the Manwan Dam, begun in 1986 and producing power since 1993, rates were set according to Eastern living costs, meaning that most locals could hardly afford them. The real beneficiaries have been power companies and local authorities,[86] whose status is roughly that of landed aristocrats of the imperial past.

Somehow neoliberals manage to remain oblivious to all this. What they conveniently read as a generational war for and against democratic reform is no more than a power struggle between CCP factions. In their conflict with urban entrepreneurs, Hu and Wen are forced to reach out to the rural masses for support, much as Thaksin did in Thailand. Meanwhile they are seeking a rapprochement with Jiang's urban power base. It is significant in that regard that Jiang's Politburo understudy, Zeng Qinghong, became the vice-president and made a functional peace with Hu. That accord marks the relative consolidation of the CCP order,[87] but what exactly does this regime stand for?

For it to stand at all requires a delicate balancing act. Hu speaks of a "new socialist countryside,"[88] yet must also placate foreign and domestic capital. Rural residents are promised free education, bigger subsidies, better health care and public works. What is left off the list is a farmer's right to any legal title to the land he plows. Without that most basic right the rural sector will be locked out of the country's celebrated affluence. This socio-economic double standard will kill the social harmony Hu has proclaimed as his core objective. The most he can hope for is enough rural pressure release to keep the system running. To do more would be a gift, in cost of labor terms, to China's Asian competitors.

Rival factions are of course waiting in the wings, but the new regime has no intention of repeating Deng's mistake of the 1980s: letting these upstarts onto the

---

84 "China Dam Project Tests New Environmental Policy," *Planet Ark: World Environment News* (October 25, 2005), http://www.planetark.com/avantgo/dailnewsstory. cfm?newsid=33139.

85 Jim Yardley, "Seeking a Public Voice on China's 'Angry River'," *The New York Times* (December 26, 2005), http://www.nytimes.com/2005/12/26/international/asia/26china. html?ei=5094.

86 Yingling Liu, *op. cit.*

87 Joseph Kahn, "China's Leader, Ex-Rival at Side, Solidifies Power," *The New York Times* (September 25, 2005), http://www.nytimes.com/2005/09/25/international/asia/25jintao. html.

88 Jim Yardley, "China Unveils Plan to Aid Farmers, but Avoids Land Issue," *The New York Times* (February 23, 2006), http://www.nytimes.com/2006/02/23/international/23rural. html.

national and international stage without their puppet strings attached. Since becoming president in 2002, Hu has worked relentlessly to restore his brand of central power. His regime is looking more repressive than any since the Mao era.[89] It is perhaps unfortunate that Jiang, a relative moderate, failed to retain power behind the scenes the way Deng did in his political afterlife. On September 19, 2004, Hu took command of the Army, Jiang's last political redoubt, making himself commander-in-chief as well as president and CCP general secretary. For good reason he kept Zeng off the military commission, the Party's most crucial committee.[90] With Jiang sequestered, and his Shanghai constituents orphaned, the Hu era was effectively signed and sealed.

89 Robert Marquand, "Hu Sets out Blueprint for China's Future," *The Christian Science Monitor* (October 6, 2005), http://www.csmonitor.com/2005/1006/p06s02-woap.htm; and Minxin Pei, "The Chinese Communist Party," *Foreign Policy* (September/October 2005), http://www.foreignpolicy.com/story/cms.php?story-id=3174&print=1.

90 "What price reform?," *The Economist* (September 23, 2004), http://economist.com/world/asia/PrinterFriendly.cfm?Story_ID=3222684.

Chapter 7

Sino-Globalization—Part 2:
Selling Chinese Maldevelopment

With Friends Like These

Much has been made of Hu's globalist tilt, and many have tried to see him as a budding Chinese Gorbachev.[1] He has graciously played along, extending the geoeconomic policies set in motion by Premier Zhu Rongji after the Asian Crash.[2] Zhu's crowning accomplishment was China's entry into the WTO, emblematic of full-fledged globalization. Hu's achievement is to have grafted that economic "miracle" to a politics that would have met Mao's full approval. What requires explanation is how this renewed hard-line gets at least tacit approval in the West.

China's emerging foreign policy marches to this same drummer, and should come as no surprise to those familiar with Hu's work in Tibet. Beijing's direction is suggested by the fact that it has extended economic, strategic or diplomatic lifelines to nearly every rogue state in the world.[3] Its close international friends have included Iran's Mahmoud Ahmadinejad, Zimbabwe's Robert Mugabe, Pakistan's Musharraf, Nepal's King Gyanendra and Uzbekistan's Islam Karimov.[4] China helped Mugabe pull off his rigged election of 2005,[5] and encouraged Karimov to stand his ground against international opprobrium after he ordered the Tiananmen-style slaughter at Andijan, killing hundreds of unarmed demonstrators.[6] Both China and Russia endorsed Karimov's version of this atrocity, and tripped over each other in their haste to sign new security treaties with him.[7] No Western power could match them

1 "Hu Done It," *The Economist* (September 23, 2004), http://economist.com/opinion/PrinterFriendly.cfm? Story_ID=3220315.

2 Willy Wo-Lap Lam, "The Chinese Leadership: Blazing New Trails in Reform," *World Economic Forum China Business Summit 2003 Report* (2003).

3 Parag Khanna, "Waving Goodbye to Hegemony," *The New York Times* (January 27, 2008), http://www.nytimes.com/2008/01/27/magazine/27world-t.html.

4 See Robert Skidelsky, "The Chinese Shadow," *The New York Review of Books*, Vol. 52, No. 18 (November 17, 2005), http://www.nybooks.com/articles/18437.

5 Joshua Kurlantzick, "The China Syndrome," *The American Prospect* (January 11, 2007), http: www. prospect.org/web/page.ww?section=root&name=ViewWebarticleId=12372.

6 Isabel Hilton, "Reaching Beyond the Myth of Mao," *Guardian* (June 4, 2005), http://www.guardian.co. uk/print/0,3858,5208236-103677,00.html.

7 Joshua E. Abrams, "The Trouble with Uzbekistan," *Nth Position* (January 2006), http://www. nthposition.com/thetroublewithuzbekistan.php.

in this ideological race to the bottom. The question is left open as to which of them will come out on top (the bottom in this case being the top) in Central Asia's new "great game."

There is no question, however, as to who takes the prize in Africa, where China's comparative advantage is on graphic display. The China National Petroleum Corporation (CNPC) specializes in working with pariah regimes that Western companies shy away from. Naively, the international community has tried to exert pressure on China to assist in a solution to the genocidal crisis in Darfur. In answer, Deputy Foreign Minister Zhou Wenzhong replied, "business is business." In Will Hutton's view this was "an awesome warning of the future if an unreconstructed China became yet more powerful."[8]

The self-appointed despots-for-life that China courts cannot hope to modernize their ramshackle authoritarianism without a great deal of technical assistance. That is where Beijing comes in. Already the PRC is exporting its state-of-the-art phone tapping and internet monitoring techniques to Mugabe, who in 2004 followed China's lead by making internet companies promise censorship assistance.[9] Belarus has likewise drawn on China's expertise to counter internet reform pressure,[10] while Iran has made good use of its special relationship with China in ignoring international consternation at its nuclear proliferation. This cozy arrangement was capped in October 2004 with the signing of a $100 billion, 25-year contract for natural gas between Tehran and Sinopec (China's third oil giant, along with CNPC and CNOOC—the China National Offshore Oil Corp.).[11]

The mystery is why China gets top geoeconomic billing from its foremost geopolitical rival, the United States. The simple answer is that TNCs are pulling the strings in Washington. But that begs the question as to why these corporations are so committed to this particular FDI magnet. What could it provide that its less Orwellian competitors on the Rim could not, especially after the Crash? The miracle years made Southeast Asian countries more technologically competitive, while the

---

8 Will Hutton, "New China, New Crisis," *Observer* (January 7, 2007), http://observer. guardian.co.uk/print/0,,329678151-102280,00.html.

9 "Caught in the Net: Zimbabwe," *Foreign Policy* (January/February 2006), http://www. foreignpolicy.com/story/cms.php?story_id=3344.

10 Kurlantzick, *op. cit.*

11 Michael Klare, "The Geopolitics of Natural Gas," *The Nation* (January 23, 2006), http://www.thenation.com/doc/20060123/klare. It is little wonder that China has resisted UN Security Council action against Iran's violations of "red line" provisions of the nuclear non-proliferation treaty of 1968. See Nazila Fathi and John O'Neil, "Ignoring Protests, Iran Resumes Nuclear Program," *The New York Times* (January 10, 2006), http://www.nytimes. com/2006/01/10/international/10cnd-iran.html. However, in December 2006 China did join other U.N. Security Council members in imposing light sanctions on Iran's trade in nuclear and missile-related materials. Given its dependence on Middle Eastern oil, even China recognizes that stability in the region is in its interest; and another mollifying factor is its close trade relations with Israel in military weapons and materials. See "A Quintet, Anyone?" *The Economist* (January 11, 2007), http://www.economist.com/world/asia/PrinterFriendly. cfm?story_id=8521894.

Crash and subsequent IMF restructuration made their labor much cheaper.[12] Most Southeast Asian countries have abundant natural resources, and are not saddled with such insurmountable environmental problems as China suffers. Why, then, do TNCs flock to China?

The euphemistic answer is that Southeast Asia lacks China's vaunted "stability." Less tactfully put, Southeast Asia has been too prone to the pressures of democratic reform. What China offers is an irresistible combination of commercial openness and despotic order. In his April 2006 visit to America, President Hu promised even greater investment openness. He knew this language would overshadow nonmaterial issues such as the pending show trial of *New York Times* reporter Zhao Yan, who as of Hu's visit had spent almost 20 months in prison without so much as a hearing.[13] It all boils down to the question of what counts most for today's Americans, elemental freedom and human rights in China or bargain prices at Wal-Mart.

The Zhao affair is all about civilizational clash, and the most troubling part of it is that for so many Americans it is not more troubling. Here, and on the whole issue of a free press, Beijing shoots itself in the foot. A combination of media censorship and rampant corruption allows pressing problems to fester out of sight. In Anhui Province, for example, forty companies sold fake baby powder resulting in thirteen known deaths and hundreds of chronic health problems. Only a few months after this came to light, new fakes were on the market. Worse still, officials in Henan sold blood to local hospitals with full awareness that it was HIV contaminated. The incident was blacked out from the media, while AIDS activists who protested the practice were arrested.[14]

Beijing is now making a show of combating corruption in the provinces, especially where land grabs are concerned. The Ministry of Land and Resources (MLR) estimates that 80 percent of these seizures involved local governments, and 20 percent were directly committed by them.[15] Meanwhile, in Henan and Shanxi provinces local officials were implicated in the kidnapping of hundreds of local residents, including children, for slave labor in coal mines and brick kilns.[16] The Hu regime feigns ignorance of all this, and adroitly uses the greed and corruption of local government as a lightening rod to deflect criticism from itself.

---

12 Consider the case of the Mattel toy company, which recently had to recall millions of toys due to a lead paint scandal in China. Mattel also owns plants in Indonesia and Thailand, where the labor costs are even cheaper and quality control is easier to manage. See "Seven Questions: China's Total Toy Recall," *Foreign Policy* (August 2007), http://www.foreignpolicy.com.

13 "Mr. Hu and Mr. Zhao," *The New York Times* Editorial (April 18, 2006), http://www.nytimes.com/2006/04/18/opinion/18tue1.html?

14 Martin Vander Weyer, "Just How Miraculous is China's Economic Miracle?," *Telegraph* (April 30, 2006), http://www.telegraph.co.uk/core/Content/displayPrintable.jhtml?xml=/arts/2006/04/30/bok...

15 Candy Zeng, "Beijing Vows Crackdown on Land Grabs," *Asia Times* (August 4, 2007), http://www.atimes.com/atimes/China_Business/IHOHCb02.htm.

16 Andrew Batson, "China Tightens Local Oversight," *The Wall Street Journal* (August 10, 2007), p. A4.

The Real 'Two China' Divide

Stamping out the problem will become harder as local magnates grow richer and forge their own global networks. For centuries the extra-legal income of Chinese officials dwarfed their actual salaries,[17] so today's bureaucrats have tradition on their side. Anti-corruption efforts are further undermined by the government's determination to control free speech and the media. This also explains why there is little effective environmental opposition here, despite the fact that public sentiment favors reform, NGOs are on the rise, and the media are cautiously sympathetic.[18] A case must reach crisis levels before it is even noticed. And even then the regime usually prosecutes the whistle-blowers rather than the criminals.

What kind of government casually accepts the fact that in many Chinese cities 80 percent of children suffer from lead poisoning?[19] Answer: the kind that solves the problem by arresting eco-dissidents. The lead poisoning issue went international in August 2007 when the Mattel toy company was forced to recall nearly two million made-in-China toys. Chinese officials seemed dismayed that other countries would become so agitated over a little lead in the toy paint. This scandal was just the latest in a series of similar recalls across a wide spectrum of consumer products: dog food, toothpaste, computer batteries, etc. The root of the crisis is not so much the technical factor of quality control as the philosophical issue of the value of human life. This includes the lives of Chinese workers who toil in unspeakable sweatshop conditions for eighty or more hours a week. There is a profound moral paradox in having three-quarters of the world's toys made in China under such torturous conditions.[20]

The West must also consider its complicity in one of the world's most horrendous environmental disasters. While the Chinese population has doubled in the last fifty years, its usable land has fallen by half, and is under ever increased pressure from land degradation as well as "development."[21] The Global Footprint Network (GFN) estimates that China's current growth pattern would require twice the available land to render it sustainable,[22] yet an estimated 1,500 square miles of land is buried every

---

17 Barrington Moore, *Social Origins of Dictatorship and Democracy: Lord and Peasant in the Making of the Modern World* (Boston: Beacon Press, 1966), p. 172.

18 *Ibid.*

19 Joshua Kurlantzick, "Purple Haze," *The New Republic* (August 30, 2004), http://www. tnr.com/docprint.mhtml?i=2004830&s=kurlantzick083004.

20 See Eric Clark, "Mattel's Real Toy Story: Slave Labor in Sweatshops," extract from Clark's *The Real Toy Story*, in *The Evening Standard* (August 16, 2007), http://www. thisislondon.co.uk/news/article-23408572-details/Mattel's+real+toy+story:+slav...

21 Gross land mismanagement has accelerated desertification and resulting dust storms, such as those that blanketed Seoul, Korea in April 2002, forcing schools to close and airports to cancel flights. See Lester R. Brown, "China is losing the war on advancing deserts," *The Herald Tribune* (August 13, 2003), http://www.iht.com/cgi-bin/generic.cgi?template=articlep rint.tmplh&ArticleId=106062.

22 "ROK 'requires a Land Area Six Times its Size' to Sustain its Growth," *Birds of Korea* (November 2003), http://www.birdskorea.org/rokfootprint.asp.

year by spreading deserts. Most of this desertification is in north central China, putting even Beijing at risk.[23]

Then there is the water crisis. With 22 percent of the world's population, China has only 8 percent of the world's fresh water.[24] As in India, China's economic takeoff rested on the agricultural spike that was made possible by millions of new wells across the land. Now, however, the water table is dropping fast,[25] threatening the very foundation of the boom economy. Moreover, at least 70 percent of China's lakes and rivers are polluted, leaving 360 million rural residents without safe drinking water. The government admits that over half the rural risings in 2005 were pollution related.[26]

That is not to say that cities have it so good. Urban water systems are awash in oil, trash, and feces. This alone could sabotage the country's development, as could air pollution and acid rain. Just living here is like smoking two packs of cigarettes per day.[27] Already 80 percent of Chinese cities have dangerously high levels of sulfur and nitrogen dioxide, according to a recent World Bank study.[28] The Chinese are literally inhaling the dark side of their growth formula.[29] It says much about the stultifying effect of the "Beijing Consensus" that few in government are willing to discuss these subjects even privately.

A rare exception is Yue Pan, Deputy Minister for the Environment, who predicts that in the not-so-distant future China will have more than 150 million environmental refugees.[30] Most of these eco-vagrants will be the same ex-farmers who were left behind by the capitalist transformation of the last quarter century. For them Deng's "reforms" amount to grand theft. They are witnessing, and increasingly protesting, the deconstruction of a socialized health care system that between 1952 and 1982 brought infant mortality down from 200 per thousand births to 34, while raising life

---

23 Joseph Kahn, "A Sea of Sand Is Threatening China's Heart," *The New York Times* (June 8, 2006), http://www.nytimes.com/2006/06/08/world/asia/08desert.html.

24 "China, India, and the 'State of the World,'" The Worldwatch Institute's *State of the World, 2006.*

25 Jeffrey Sachs, "War Climates," *TomPaine.com* (October 23, 2006), http://www.tompaine.com/print/War_climates.php.

26 Kathleen E. McLaughlin, "Chinese Villages, Poisoned by Toxins, Battle for Justice," *The Christian Science Monitor* (June 23, 2006), http://www.csmonitor.com/2006/0623/p01s03-woap.htm.

27 Kurlantzick, "Purple Haze," *op. cit.*

28 "Coal, China, and India: A Deadly Combination for Air Pollution?," *Worldwatch*, from Worldwatch Institute (December 14, 2005), http://www.worldwatch.org/features/vsow/2005/12/14.

29 As of 2003, only a quarter of the country's sewage was treated. It was already understood that, like other dams, the Three Gorges would undoubtedly trap pollutants, resulting in a vast toxic reservoir. See "Millions Face Water Shortage in North China, Officials Warn," *The New York Times* (June 6, 2003), http://www.nytimes.com/2003/06/06/international/asia/06WATE.html.

30 *Spiegel* Interview with Pan Yue, "The Chinese Miracle Will End Soon," *Der Spiegel* (March 7, 2005), http://service.spiegel.de/cache/international/Spiegel/0,1518,druck-345694,00.html.

expectancy from 35 to 68.[31] The rural clinics that spearheaded this miracle are now shutting their doors, as doctors and other health professionals flock to the cities. It is little wonder that infectuous diseases like SARS, hepatitis, and tuberculosis are turning rural China into a base camp for global epidemics of the future.

The sad irony is that China's urban growth economy depends upon the plight of the rural masses for its labor reservoir. Migrant workers are in effect illegal aliens in their own country. The *hukou* system of household registration has kept them out of the legal labor pool,[32] and any attempt to organize or strike has been treated as literal insurrection. For fractious workers this has meant beatings or jailings, while real dissidents face prolonged imprisonment and torture.[33]

Behind the urban/rural divide is a two-tiered property system that denies farmers legal title to, or even certain access to, the land they have tilled all their lives. In many cases their ancestors worked the same land in imperial times, yet these holdings can be confiscated and sold at the whim of local officials who are getting a fat cut of the profits. When farmers resist, paramilitary gangs are on hand to settle the matter.[34] More than 70 million farmers have had their land appropriated in the last decade, and 30 million more are on the waiting list. In one case, near the city of Yulin, local officials offering $60 per parcel of land faced resistance from a whole village, which seized control of the local Party office. Hundreds were injured in the ensuing crackdown.[35] The only remarkable thing about the Yulin incident is that it was widely reported.

It follows that the real "two China" divide is not between the PRC and Taiwan, but between the rich and poor in China proper. The Taiwan issue, like the Japanese reparations issue, is kept on hand for diversionary purposes whenever the genuine two China crisis starts to boil over. It has been a quarter of a century since rural families received any marked benefit from the country's capitalist turn. The land reforms of 1978, which dissolved Mao-era communes, did help the rural poor in raw income terms. But the bulk of that improvement was reaped by 1987. By leaving the

---

31 Bashir Mamdani, "Privatization and Health Care in China," *Indian Journal of Medical Ethics*, No. 1 (January/March 2006), http://www.ijme.in/141ss031.html.

32 It likewise denies them a broad range of rights and government services, and in the judicial context it effectively treats the life of a legal resident as having several times the value of a migrant. See Jim Yardley, "3 Deaths in China Reveal Disparity in Price of Lives," *The New York Times* (April 14, 2006), http://www.thenytimes.com/2006/04/14/world/asia/14china.html.

33 Mark Barenberg, "The Condition of the Working Class in China," *Dissent* (Summer 2004), http://www.dissentmagazine.org/menutest/articles/su04/china.htm.

34 Land rights activists are coming under literal assault for the crime of telling the truth. One of the most prominent ones, Fu Xiancai, will never walk again. He was savagely beaten after he ignored police warnings to stop talking to lawyers and foreign journalists. A police investigation concluded that he broke his own neck. See Jonathan Watts, "Chinese Police Decide Paralyzed Campaigner Broke His Own Neck," *Guardian* (July 28, 2006), http://www.guardian.co.uk/print/0,,329540179-108142,00.html.

35 Jim Yardley, "Farmers Being Moved Aside by China's Real Estate Boom," *The New York Times* (December 8, 2004), http://www.nytimes.com/2004/12/08/international/asia/08china.html.

countryside behind, post-Tiananmen globalization bypassed most Chinese. When that fact was advertised by husband and wife authors Chen Guidi and Wu Chuntao, their book was instantly banned by the Propaganda Department. Nonetheless it sold seven million copies in pirated editions, and even Wen Jiabao's chief advisor on rural affairs admitted in 2004 that he kept a copy at his bedside.[36]

What Chen and Wu dramatized was the well known fact that since 1989 the quality of rural life has been stagnant or worse. As of 2001 27 percent of rural Chinese still got by on less than $1 per day.[37] Health care needs trump education, marriage, and sometimes even food, with whole families thrown into destitution when breadwinners fall ill.[38] Increasingly the maladies of the elderly go untreated, while families with more than one sick member are having to draw straws as to which one will get even rudimentary health care. Millions must face this "Sophie's Choice" at some point, putting them among the 1.3 billion people in the world who have virtually no access to health care.

What makes this all the more onerous for 800 million rural Chinese is that they have been stripped of the socialist safety net that formerly saved them from utter destitution. This is the flip side of Deng's glorious revolution. The deal he struck was with elites who gladly accepted his dictum that "to get rich is glorious," no matter how many people might be trampled in the process. The strategic flaw in this selective enrichment scheme was its assumption that the "tramplees" would lie there and take it. Rising waves of protest in the countryside suggest otherwise.

Urban workers have usually been more tractable, but how much so is hard to verify, since statistics on labor issues are treated as state secrets.[39] Recently, in the city of Xiamen, this veil of secrecy was lifted as middle classes staged protests against heavy-handed government policies. Soon the Xiamen model was applied in Shanghai,[40] where working classes joined the protests. Beijing too well knows the significance of such broad-spectrum resistance. To avoid financial catastrophe China will have to completely overhaul its banking system, but doing that will leave SOEs (state owned enterprises) and the millions they employ derelict. The result will be massive proletarian outrage and possible insurrection.[41] This unrest, moreover, will not be hidden away in the countryside. If part of China's comparative advantage for Western investors has been its promise of stability, these fortune hunters could be in for a rude awakening.

---

36 Kahn, "Painting the Peasants Into the Portrait of China's Economic Boom," *op. cit.*

37 Pranab Bardhan, "Does Globalization Help or Hurt the World's Poor?," *Scientific American. com* (March 26, 2006), http://www.sciam.com/print_version.cfm?articleID=0004B7FD-C4E6-1421-84E683414B7...

38 Howard W. French, "Wealth Grows, but Health Care Withers in China," *The New York Times* (January 14, 2006), http://www.nytimes.com/2006/01/14/international/asia/14health. html.

39 Ryder, *op. cit.*

40 Maureen Fan, "Shanghai's Middle Class Launches Quiet, Meticulous Revolt," *The Washington Post* (January 26, 2008), p. A01.

41 C.T. Kurien, "Giants of the East," *Frontline*, Vol. 23, No. 26 (December 30, 2006 to January 12, 2007), http://www.hinduonnet.com/fline/stories/20070112000507400.htm.

Faith-based Globalism

Apart from overseas Chinese investors, who have cultural and linguistic ties with China, the major attraction for relocating here can only be political, or rather anti-political. China's cheap labor and economies of scale are a nice draw, but the clincher is an anti-liberal climate that makes Singapore's soft-authoritarianism look tame by comparison. China's cardinal advantage is twofold: its willingness to use draconian means to remove any obstacle to *fazhan* (development), and policies that would be impossible to implement in an even partially democratic society.[42]

While it may be that millions of Chinese escaped "absolute poverty" after Deng's reforms took effect, we have already noted that most of this uplift was due to agricultural growth that had flattened out by the mid-1980s. Most Chinese were then left in economic purgatory. Millions of manufacturing jobs have been lost since the mid-1990s, while nearly half of the labor force remains locked in subsistence agriculture.[43] Jeffrey Sachs extols Beijing's success at converting China's peasantry into a robust labor force on the coast.[44] The simple truth is that Chinese banks are too loaded down with bad loans to underwrite rural development,[45] and in any case CCP planners would be reluctant to fix a condition that is a prerequisite of the Chinese export boom. Reform must be limited to palliatives—just enough to ward off rebellion. As in pre-revolutionary France, where the monarchy maintained the illusion that it was on the side of the peasantry, the CCP elite has brilliantly cast itself as the protector of the rural masses against conniving local autocrats.

This inner circle has good reason to fear even pro forma democracy. One of its control tactics, borrowed from Singapore, is democratic inoculation: using ersatz democracy to guard against the real thing. In a white paper issued in October 2005 the government laid claim to an alternative "democracy" based on centrally determined goals.[46] This is very similar to the propaganda line hawked by the Party

---

42 In the mid-1990s, against the neoliberal grain, Gordon White posited a causal linkage between China's non-democratic government and its remarkable growth record. We entirely agree, but challenge White's equation of growth with development. See Gordon White, "Development and Democratization in China," in Adrian Leftwich (ed.), *Democracy and Development* (Cambridge, UK: Polity Press, 1996), p. 209 (pp. 209–29).

43 Yet those who escape this rural privatization may be even worse off, for factory workers—and especially illegal ones, fresh from the countryside—lack the most basic rudiments of human rights. In March 2004 the AFL-CIO filed a petition in Washington asking that US trade representatives take action on behalf of both Chinese workers and their American counterparts, who are being locked in mutually deleterious wage competition. The Bush administration summarily rejected the petition, calling it an exercise in "economic isolationism." See Barenberg, *op. cit.*

44 Jeffrey D. Sachs, "China since the late 1970s," draft for a conference paper accessed on January 8, 2007 at *UN Jobs*, http://unjobs.org/authors/jeffrey-d.-sachs.

45 See Pranab Bardhan, "China, India Superpower? Not so Fast!," *Yale Global* (October 25, 2005), http://yaleglobal.yale.edu/article.print?id=6407.

46 Matt Steinglass, "Whose Asian values?," *The Boston Globe* (November 20, 2005), http://www.boston. com/news/globe/ideas/articles/2005/11/20/whose_asian_values?mode...; and "China's Take on Political Democracy," *The Globalist* (November 14, 2005), http://www. theglobalist.com/DBWeb/printStoryId. aspx?StoryId=4899.

when it gained power in 1949.[47] A system that so completely subordinates society to the state, individuals to the mass, and law to the leader is hardly on the road to democracy, although Singapore does a better job than China of wrapping its "Asian values" in parliamentary garb.[48]

The Beijing elite well knows that its privileges could not survive much political development.[49] Taking a lesson in how not to reform from the Soviets,[50] China has forged a democracy-free developmental model that weds the statist control of Maoism to the economic engine of capitalism. This hybrid avoids the economic drag of democracy, environmental standards, and liberal bottlenecks such as unions and a free press. Shelving Marxism, the CCP reactivates the Confucian ideal of *datong*, or great harmony, which conditions Chinese to distrust the anomie of Western democratic processes.[51] The greater the messiness of the Sino-capitalist amalgam, the stronger the urge will be to enforce *datong* on the political side.

None of this bothers the purveyors of faith-based globalization. In their view the PRC is so deeply enmeshed in global commerce that fears of Chinese realpolitik are groundless.[52] This explains why so few have heeded Paul Kennedy's prescient warning of the late 1980s that the best military preparation for a budding Asian hegemon is precisely the growth-at-all-costs development model that China has implemented.[53] Neoliberal globalism takes this oversight one step further: if China's growth is what renders it harmless, the best defense against its burgeoning militarism is still more growth.

This is the geopolitical logic of unqualified capitalist "engagement," premised on the assumption—popularized in Thomas Friedman's "golden arches" maxim—that

---

47 Martin Hart-Landsberg and Paul Burkett, "Introduction: China and Socialism" *Monthly Review*, Vol. 56, No. 3 (July/August 2004), http://www.monthlyreview.org/0704intro.htm.

48 Likewise this voids the democratic claims of Singapore, where the emphasis also falls on the state over the society, the group over the individual, and the leader over the law. See Hans Antlöv and Tak-Wing Ngo, "Politics, Culture, and Democracy in Asia," in Hans Antlöv and Tak-Wing Ngo (eds), *The Cultural Construction of Politics in Asia* (Richmond, UK: Curzon Press, 2000), p. 9 (pp. 1–18).

49 See Minxin Pei, "The Dark Side of China's Rise," *Foreign Policy* (March/April 2006), http://www. foreignpolicy.com/story/cms.php?story_id=3373&print=1. The CCP cannot budge, therefore, in the face of reformist demands, such as those of Hong Kong's pro-democracy demonstration of December 4, 2005, when tens of thousands of protesters took to the streets. Although this was a smaller crowd than had demonstrated in July 2003 and July 2004, it was unique in that it was expressly aimed at political rather than economic reform. See "Many People, Few Votes," *The Economist* (December 8, 2005), http://www.economist. com/world/asia/displaystory.cfm?story_id=5280837.

50 See Richard Lourie, "And Now to Toast a Happy Eighty-Eighth!," *The Moscow Times* (November 7, 2005), http://www.themoscowtimes.com/stories/2005/11/07/006-html.

51 Shiping Hua, "A Perfect World," *The Wilson Quarterly* (Autumn 2005), http://www. wilsoncenter.org/index.cfm?fuseaction=wq.print&essay_id=146857&...

52 Christopher Findlay and Andrew Watson, "Economic Growth and Trade Dependency in China," in David S.G. Goodman and Gerald Segal (eds), *China Rising: Nationalism and Interdependence* (London: Routledge, 1997), p. 107 (pp. 107–33).

53 Paul Kennedy, *The Rise and Fall of the Great Powers: Economic Change and Military Conflict from 1500 to 2000* (London: Fontana Press, 1989), pp, 581–82.

bourgeois affluence precludes war. The basic idea is that the rich have too much to lose to make trouble. This guarantee, however, carries a limited warranty: it has full application only in the kind of plutocracy that Hu has flatly rejected. Under him the CCP yokes capitalism to nationalistic objectives that would have made Mussolini feel quite at home. It is a telling fact that the inner circle of Western globalists also feel at home with this merger. Some, such as Jeffrey Sachs, look to the current Chinese system as the very archetype of global development.[54] Somehow these Sino-apologists manage to ignore the darker sides of Chinese "development," such as rampant corruption, unenforceable contracts, politically dependent courts, pollution, land exhaustion, desertification, and an environmental Holocaust that by some estimates would entail a ten percent annual GDP decrease if a full account were given of its impact.[55]

Finally there is China's stupendous military buildup. After 17 years of double-digit military spending, China is recognized as a major security risk by one of its most astute observers, Japan.[56] It is no secret that China's real military budget is twice or even three times its official figure, and its mounting naval expenditures pose a risk to Japan's sea lanes as well as to Taiwan's existence as an independent nation.[57] The power of America's corporate lobby is well illustrated by the fact that these concerns, which are widely felt by the Pentagon, have hardly dented US engagement policy toward China. It is still an article of faith that the Chinese can be bought off with FDI, technological transfers, and the lure of export profits.

The attraction this viewpoint holds for transnational investors is easy to see,[58] but its geopolitical justification is another matter. More and more, China's quest for oil puts it in league with rogue states such as Iran and the Sudan, while its regional saber rattling competes with North Korea's. Its rapid increase in missiles aimed at Taiwan speaks for itself.[59] That alone should expose the lethal miscalculation of present US "engagement," but for slow learners an alarm bell was sounded by the East Asian Summit of December 2005 in Kuala Lumpur, where China was the belle

---

54 Jeffrey Sachs, interviewed by Jonathan Watts, "Be Here Now," *Guardian* (August 26, 2006), http://education.guardian.co.uk/print/0,,329562288-108229,00.htm.

55 Cao Changqing, "The West's Rosy Image of China is a Deception," *Asia Media—Media News Daily* (December 20, 2006), http://www.asiamedia.ucla.edu/print. asp?parentid=59840.

56 Norimitsu Onishi, "Chill Grows as Japan Calls China a Military Threat," *The New York Times* (December 22, 2005), http://www.nytimes.com/2005/12/22/international/asia/22cnd-japan.html.

57 Régis Arnaud, "La puissance militaire chinoise alarme Tokyo," *Le Figaro* (December 23, 2005), http://www.lefigaro.com/cgi/edition/genimprime?cle=20051223.FIGO221.

58 Some, such as multinational corporation consultant Dan Steinbock, are dissatisfied even with present "engagement" policies. Nothing less than full economic "integration" will satisfy Steinbock. See Dan Steinbock, "The Chinese Multinationals are Coming!," *The National Interest* (Fall 2005), http://www. inthenationalinterest.com/Articles/August%202005/August2005SteinbockPFV...

59 "Nudging China toward World Citizenship," *The Christian Science Monitor* (November 16, 2005), http://www.csmonitor.com/2005/1116/p08s01-comv.htm.

of the ball and the United States was conspicuously uninvited.[60] The summit served notice that whatever fears the region might have regarding the PRC, they are less pressing than those generated by current US unilateralism. Faced with a choice between the "Washington Consensus" and the emerging "Beijing Consensus," developing countries are choosing the less potent devil, especially since China has wisely adopted the rhetoric of soft power that the Bush administration jettisoned after 9/11.[61]

Sino-Globalization Comes to Washington

It says much about TNC priorities that Washington will express outrage over human rights violations in Burma (Myanmar) but not in Tibet. Its occasional finger-shaking over issues such as the Zhao affair are never backed up with the threat of sanctions.[62] The Chinese know it is all window dressing, for the TNCs call the shots. If Tiananmen was an embarrassment for neoliberal apologists, it was a dream come true for corporations setting up in China as foreign-invested enterprises (FIEs).[63] Far

---

60 Japan managed to get Australia, New Zealand and India invited to the December 2005 East Asia Summit, as a counterbalance to China, which in turn treated Japan with contempt. The cover story was that this diplomatic sneer was China's answer to Prime Minister Koizumi's recent visit to a Japanese war shrine. Clearly the bigger reason was Japan's close US ties and its attempt to foil China's dominance of the ASEAN region. See Rich Bowden, "Battle Looms Over Inaugural East Asia Summit," *Worldpress.org* (December 11, 2005), http://www.worldpress.org/print_article.cfm?article_id=2312&don't=yes. This growing rift had become apparent during Bush's 40-hour visit to China the previous month, punctuated as it was by a geopolitically pointed visit to Mongolia. See "Bush's Trip to China," *Worldpress. org* (downloaded December 23, 2005), http://www.worldpress.org/print_article.cfm?article_id=2304&don't =yes. That divide was further confirmed when the White House downgraded the upcoming state visit of President Hu to a mere "official visit." It is not clear at this point how effective Washington's new containment strategy will be, given its simultaneous engagement policies. The new coolness toward China is not appreciated by some US allies. Australia has protested Washington's containment efforts, including its recent diplomatic embrace of India. See Peter Kwong, "Hu's 'State Visit'," *The Nation* (May 1, 2006), http://www.thenation.com/doc/20060501/kwong.

61 Ashley J. Tellis, "A Grand Chessboard," *Foreign Policy* (January/February 2005), http://www. foreignpolicy.com/story/cms.php?story_id=2751&print=1. However, polls such as the Pew Global Attitudes Project show a sharp downturn in public trust toward China in Europe as well as America. Picking up on this drift, Daily Show host Jon Stewart joked about Chinese child laborers garnishing toys with lead paint for American children to eat. In short, human rights concerns are finally starting to register with Western publics, as opposed to Western governments and corporations. See Peter Ford, "Beyond Food and Toys, China Struggles with its Global Reputation," *The Christian Science Monitor* (September 12, 2007), http://www.csmonitor.com/2007/0912/p01s06-woap.html.

62 Finally, after three years of lobbying—including direct appeals to President Hu by President Bush and Secretary of State Condoleeza Rice—Zhao was released in September 2007.

63 How this ethical disaccord between neoliberal theory and TNC practice was resolved in favor of the latter is an implicit subtext in James Mann's study of Clinton's complete

from distressing the multinationals, China's rearguard politics was one of their main attractions. Capital inflows jumped from $11 billion in 1992 to $50 billion in 1999.[64] First the Asian Crash and then the Wall Street collapse tightened this Sino-globalist bond by eliminating other claims on surplus capital. The fact that US investors need China as much as it needs them has effectively turned American corporatists into unpaid Chinese lobbyists.

The PRC has been making great strides in formal lobbying as well, assisted by Washington insiders like Nancy Dorn.[65] Her most notable achievement was assisting the pro-China billionaire Li Ka-shing to secure control of both sides of the Panama Canal.[66] She was instrumental in convincing a suspicious Congress that this venture posed no threat to US security,[67] despite the fact that Li's company, Hutchison-Whampoa, is a partner of the China Ocean Shipping Company (COSCO), which happens to be the PLA's merchant marine branch. It should also be mentioned that Wang Jun, one of Li's partners in the China International Trust and Investment Corporation (CITIC), is China's main arms dealer to rogue states.[68] Through them he is almost certainly a big source of arms to global terrorists.

Dorn, however, is a small fish compared to China's biggest catch: the neoconservative superhawk and former China basher Richard Perle. He was retained by the bankrupt telecommunications giant Global Crossing to lubricate its purchase by Hutchison Whampoa.[69] Both the FBI and the Defense Department red-flagged

---

reversal on China. See Mann's *About Face: A History of America's Curious Relationship with China, from Nixon to Clinton* (New York: Alfred A. Knopf, 1999), Chapter 15. At the administrative level this reversal was consummated with the policy victory of Winston Lord (Clinton's assistant secretary of state for East Asia and the Pacific) over his more principled boss, Secretary of State Warren Christopher. See Mann, pp0. 276; and William H. Thornton, *Fire on the Rim: The Cultural Dynamics of East/West Power Politics* (Lanham, MD: Rowman & Littlefield, 2002), pp. 141–44.

64 Steinbock, *op. cit.*

65 In February 2002 Dorn became the Deputy Director of the OMB (Office of Management and Budget). Previously she had been Vice President Cheney's Assistant for Legislative Affairs, before which she was a key lobbyist for corporate clients. In that capacity she became a foreign agent for firms with very close ties to PLA intelligence. See "Decision Brief," *The Center for Security Policy*, No. 00-D67 (July 17, 2000), http://www.security-policy.org/papers/2000/00-D67.html.

66 A 1996 report by the US Ambassador to China, James Sasser, ties Li closely to the PLA's developing communications networks. Those ties are confirmed by Rand Corporation reports. See Charles R. Smith, "Global Double Crossing," *Newsmax.com* (February 27, 2003), http://www.newsmax.com/archieves/articles/2003/2/26/182009.shtml.

67 Another of Dorn's stellar lobbying achievements was getting the Republicans to back away from criticizing the Clinton administration for its failure to fulfill legally required sanctions against China's arms client, Pakistan, for its role in the proliferation of nuclear weapons and long-range missile technology. See "Decision Brief," *op. cit.*

68 Admiral Thomas H. Moorer, "Save Our Canal," *The New American*, Vol. 15, No. 16 (August 2, 1999), http://www.thenewamerican.com/tna/1999/08-02-99/vol5no16_canal.htm.

69 Jim Lobe, "Perle: 'Prince of Darkness' in the spotlight," *Asia Times* (March 25, 2003), http://www.atimes.com/atimes/China/EC25Ad04.html. Global Crossing was the fourth largest company to file for bankruptcy in history. It was slated to be sold in September 2003

this buyout on national security grounds, which put China in the market for an ex-hawk lobbyist with insider standing. What was most astonishing about Perle's new stance on China was that only three years earlier he had been a major signatory to the New American Century's call for unambiguous support of Taiwan against Chinese aggression. He had warned that Beijing's pursuit of regional hegemony points toward a new Cold War.

Flash forward to Perle as a non-registered lobbyist for Hutchison, and thus indirectly for the PLA, and you have a window on one of the major afflictions of American foreign policy: it is largely contrived by people whose primary concern is their future marketability in the lobby industry. Global Crossing, for example, gave former Clinton Secretary of Defense William Cohen a $500,000 "consulting" fee and put him on its board in the last year before the company folded. Clinton himself received $1 million for his library, while Global got an expedited $400 million defense contract.

Perle's reversal does not rate the label apostasy, as that would suggest a shift of real convictions. His motives were never anything but mercenary or careerist. The PRC has never lost when betting on the capitalist greed of American leaders. Indeed, China hardly needs paid lobbyists when it has a phalanx of TNCs to do its bidding. In the last decade, US corporations have invested $42 billion in China, from which General Motors presently rakes in 40 percent of its global profit.[70] At a 1999 ceremony hosted by Time Warner in honor of 50 years of Chinese communist rule, 300 of the world's leading capitalists came to pay homage. Time Warner chairman Gerald Levin introduced President Jiang Zemin as his "good friend," and described their relationship as "creating world harmony." Human rights were not mentioned, and at a later conference, when the issue of democracy did come up, Maurice Greenberg (chairman of the American International Group) brushed the matter aside, saying in effect that this question was irrelevant, since China's 1.3 billion people cannot eat democracy.[71]

The PRC's de facto agents include not only corporate CEOs but even former Secretaries of State, most notably Henry Kissinger. After leaving office, Kissinger became a media insider, first as a paid analyst of ABC News and then, in September 1989, as a member of CBS's board of directors. Thus he was ideally positioned

---

to a joint venture of Singapore Technologies Telemedia and Hutchison Whampoa. Although Hutchison pulled out of the deal, its relationship with the Singapore company is such that security concerns are still rife. At the time he was brokering this deal, Perle chaired an important civilian advisory group to the Pentagon. He resigned the chairmanship but remained as a member of the board. Like Enron, Global had duped its investors into believing it was solvent nearly to the end. There was the added problem of its anti-trust status, as it held a virtual monopoly in many areas of high-tech communications. To circumvent this obstacle, Anne Bingaman (former head of the Anti-trust Division of the Justice Department and wife of Senator Jeff Bingaman) was hired by Global, which paid her $2.5 million for six months of lobbying.

70 Hamish McDonald, "Hail to the Chief," *Yale Global*, from *The Sydney Morning Herald* (September 13, 2005), http:/yaleglobal.yale.edu/article.print?id=6259.

71 "China Fetes Capitalists, but the Air is Tense," *The New York Times* (September 29, 1999), http://www.nytimes.com/library/world/asia/092999china-fortune-500.html.

to amplify his startling support for Deng's handling of the Tiananmen crisis. It is no accident that his firm, Kissinger and Associates, has represented dozens of multinational corporations trying to invest in China. With partners like Lawrence Eagleburger, Brent Scowcroft, and L. Paul Bremmer,[72] Kissinger's operation works under cover of providing "strategic and advocacy services" rather than lobbying.[73] "Advocacy" connotes more of an inside operation than most lobbyists could ever dream of. This is corporate diplomacy at the moral level of insider trading, with national interests brokered like stocks on Wall Street.

The same applies to Kissinger's America-China Society, whose board includes Cyrus Vance (Secretary of State under Carter), William Rogers (Secretary of State under Nixon), Robert McFarlane (National Security Advisor under Reagan), Zbigniew Brzezinski (National Security Advisor under Carter), and Alexander Haig (Secretary of State under Reagan). It was Haig who played the key role in formulating the Chinese-American Joint Communiqué, whereby the United States committed itself to a one-China policy with limited and progressively declining arms sales to Taiwan. Haig left office early to begin cashing in on his vital contribution to the PRC.[74] What escapes mention is his contribution to US insecurity, since America almost certainly would end up supporting Taiwan in the event of an invasion.

Kissinger can avoid registering as a foreign agent for China because he does not directly accept fees from Beijing. What he sells is his ardent support for high tech transfers to China, unlimited "constructive engagement," and the (pre-WTO) promotion of China's MFN (most-favored-nation) trading status without regard to human rights.[75] In 1997, with most of the Pacific Rim reeling from the aftershocks of the Asian Crash, the Kissinger team was busy promoting China's well-timed membership in the WTO. Part of his reward would be his October 2001 appointment as advisor to CNOOC, where he joined the inveterate PRC water boy Simon Murray, a former managing director of Hutchison Whampoa. Such glaring conflicts of interest did not prevent Kissinger's sway over Bush II's China policy from exceeding Secretary of State Colin Powell's.[76]

This fact offers a window into two power structures that Kissinger conjoins. Late in the Cold War, China "engagement" became a subset of geopolitical realism, such that Kissinger's special relationship with the PRC won him appreciation within neoliberal ranks. He became the perfect corporate vehicle for downplaying, on

---

72 Eagleburger was Secretary of State under George Bush, Sr. Scowcroft, founder of the Scowcroft Group, was the National Security Advisor to both Presidents Ford and Bush, and from 1982 to 1989 was vice chairman of Kissinger and Associates. Bremmer, the managing director of Kissinger and Associates from 1989 to 2000, replaced General Jay Garner as Washington's chief administrator in Iraq.

73 "Kissinger Associates, Inc.," *Source Watch* (August 2005), Center for Media & Democracy, http://www.sourcewatch.org/index.php?title=Kissinger_Associates%2C_Inc.

74 Richard Bernstein and Ross H. Munro, *The Coming Conflict with China* (New York: Knopf, 1997), p. 121.

75 *Ibid.*, p. 107.

76 See Mike Schelstrate, "Henry Kissinger: Shadow Government Secretary of State," *Globalresearch.ca* (March 22, 2003), Center for Research on Globalization, http://www. globalresearch.ca/articles/SHE303A.html.

"realist" grounds, the impact of Tiananmen on US policy. So too he devoted himself in the 1990s to blocking any toughening of US China policy after the Soviet fall. It was now possible, without compromising realist objectives, to lay much greater stress on human rights and democratization in return for China's MFN status. Rather than counter that argument logically, neoliberals wheeled in Kissinger's ex cathedra testimony. His reasoning was reducible to three words: I say so.

After derailing efforts to factor Tiananmen into a long-term China policy, Kissinger worked assiduously to cancel MFN evaluations, thereby paving the way for China's WTO entry. Clintonesque liberals, in thrall to corporate globalism, joined in this effort to divorce commercial policy from human rights considerations. Though neoliberals did not officially abandon the humanistic concerns of earlier liberals, they relegated them to the future by clinging to the notion that Chinese affluence was a factory for democracy in the making.

Affluence versus Freedom

There are two reasons why CEOs can easily sell China to the American public, and more importantly to American stockholders, as democracy waiting to hatch. First, we usually see only the prosperous tip of the Chinese iceberg. That tip, moreover, has a soothing familiarity about it. We feel at home in Chinese gated communities with names like Palm Springs, Park Avenue and Napa Valley.[77] Second, we so closely associate prosperity with political progress that Chinese high-rises become symbols of political progress in the making. Peter Hitchens reminds us that a visit to East Berlin in the 1980s was far less deceptive than a visit to today's Shanghai. In the former, repression was served on a plate of blatant "backwardness, shortages and rationing. How reassuring it was that, a couple of miles to the West, society was both more virtuous and more rich. In Shanghai, Beijing or Guangzhou, the problem is the opposite …"[78]

The real specialty of the Chinese development model is in turning affluence against freedom. China's miracle economy bears stark testimony to what is possible when a giant reservoir of cheap and powerless labor is put at the disposal of global capital. Nevertheless there is still the question of how far Sino-globalization can be pushed before it is dragged down by the weight of its byproducts: graft, waste, and environmental spoilage, not to mention a class divide that is fast becoming a model for global "development."

Beggars used to be arrested in China's showcase cities. They were easy to prosecute because most had fled rural communities and were therefore in violation

---

77 Yilu Zhao, "Class Division Takes on a New Form," *The International Herald Tribune* (March 2, 2004), http://www.iht.com/cgi-bin/generic.cgi?template=articleprint. tmplh&ArticleId=132043.

78 Peter Hitchens, "The Danger of China: Peter Hitchens Says that the Miraculous New Chinese Economy is Not All That it Seems," *Spectator*, Vol. 300, Issue 9259 (January 21, 2006), http://www.spectator.co.uk/printer-friendly/14772/the-danger-of-china.thtml.

of the *hukou* registration system,[79] which has been aptly described as one of the most effective "apartheid" devices in the world.[80] Now there are simply too many violators to prosecute. Thus the rural/urban divide is reproduced inside cities. Inequality shot up 50 percent from 1980 to 1997, the years of China's capitalist takeoff, and is rising even faster today. While rural Chinese worry about basic subsistence needs, their country has become the third largest consumer of luxury goods.[81] The Asian Development Bank traces the advance of the country's Gini coefficient from 40.7 in 1993 to 47.3 in 2004. A Gini coefficient of 40 is considered a red flag for social explosion.[82]

CCP centrists stake everything on the ancient Mandate of Heaven: their right to rule by virtue of order and prosperity. But the Mandate also entails the right to rebel by reason of poverty and disorder.[83] To avert insurrection, Beijing must initiate reforms, but ever so carefully. It is edging close to a "can't win for losing" dilemma. Elizabeth Economy makes the point that Beijing can do nothing about the country's environmental crisis until it gets a grip on local government. But to do so it would have to call in reinforcements from NGOs, a free press, and the whole panoply of democratic horrors that would turn on Beijing itself.[84] Only the timely abetment of the TNCs has kept Beijing on the winning side of the Mandate. The Western "free market" has shamelessly favored China over the democratic competition. This has allowed the centrists to cover up the fact that nine percent of China's annual GDP—nearly all of its professed GDP growth—is presently lost to environmental degradation.[85] The bottom line is that the CCP has been bailed out by the TNCs.

Neoliberals dodge the moral dereliction of their China policy by taking it as axiomatic that capitalism will generate democracy as a natural by-product. In their view China's authoritarian development is transitory.[86] But after three decades of Dengism, that assumption is wearing thin. It is time to retire the a priori notion that China, because

---

79 Jim Yardley, "China is Paying a Price of Modernization: More Beggars," *The New York Times* (April 7, 2004), http://www.nytimes.com/2004/04/07/international/asia/07beggars.html.

80 Tim Luard, "China Rethinks Peasant 'Apartheid," *BBC News* (November 10, 2005), http://news.bbc. co.uk/go/pr/fr/-/2/hi/asia-pacific/4424944.stm.

81 Zijun Li, "Luxury Spending: China's Affluent Entering 'Enjoy Now' Phase of Consumption," *Worldwatch* (December 16, 2005), http://www.worldwatch.org/features/chinawatch/stories/20051216-1.

82 Paul Maidment, "China's Dangerous Rich," *Forbes.com* (August 8, 2007), http://www.forbes.com/2007/08/08/china-wealth-inequality-opinions-cx_pm_0808gini_prin...

83 See R. Taggart Murphy, "East Asia's Dollars," *New Left Review* 40 (July/August 2006), 60 (39–64).

84 Elizabeth C. Economy, "The Great Leap Backward?," *Foreign Affairs*, Vol. 86, No. 5 (September/October 2007), pp. 38–59.

85 Jennifer L. Turner and Lü Zhi, "Building a Green Civil Society in China," in the *Worldwatch Institute State of the World 2006: China and India* (January 2006), http://www.worldwatch.org/node/4000.

86 This assumption was recently called into question by Jehangir S. Pocha in an interview with Zheng Bijian, a close advisor to President Hu. Pocha stated that if present trends continue, China "will soon look like a fascist state." We of course agree, except that we do not share the residual optimism of Pocha's "if." See Zheng Bijian, interviewed by Jehangir S. Pocha, "Unlike Previous Powers, China's Rise will be Peaceful; Democracy will Come—in 25 years: An interview with Zhang Bijian, Chairman of the China Reform Forum," *NPQ: New*

it is capitalist, is also proto-democratic. The fact that all existing democracies are embedded in capitalist economies does not prove that capitalism requires democracy. Chinese capitalists have no incentive to press for democratic reform. Already China has the second largest economy in Asia, and as of 2005 it became the fourth largest in the world, having surpassed France, Britain, and Italy.[87]

Could this have happened without Tiananmen? How would things have gone if China had added the "fifth modernization" of democracy to Deng's development formula? Given the distrust that TNCs have shown for democratic development, it is clear that a democratic China could never have received the FDI boost it has enjoyed. Liberal idealists fail to see this because they were weaned on "third wave" democratic teleology. They refuse to believe that the unreformed Chinese system could emerge as a leading model of global development.[88] The slightest trace of reform on the part of the Chinese government is taken as proof that the long awaited democratic "wave" is finally breaking on China.[89] Typical in this regard is a Brookings Institution study that forecasts a sweeping anti-corruption movement issuing from special governance zone (SGZ) experiments.[90] Meanwhile all across rural China anti-corruption protesters armed with nothing more potent than placards and firecrackers confront lethal riot squads.[91] And the Xiamen model of urban protest is adding fuel to these flames. If there is any hope for Chinese democratization, it springs from this spreading resistance, not from TNC-directed SGZs.

The Making of a Chinese Century

In his *Planet of Slums*, Mike Davis scrutinizes the social and political demographics of a world which, for the first time in history, is mostly within city limits. And

---

Perspectives Quarterly (November 7, 2005), http://www.digitalnpq.org/articles/global/32/11-07/05/jehangir_s._pocha.

87 Keith Bradsher, "Chinese Economy Grows to 4th Largest in the World," *The New York Times* (January 25, 2006), http://www.nytimes.com/2006/01/25/business/worldbusiness/25cnd-yuan.htm. However, in per capita terms China remains a low-income country, ranking 100th in the world. See Zheng Bijian, "China's 'Peaceful Rise' to Great-Power Status," *Foreign Affairs*, Vol. 84, No. 5 (September/October 2005), p. 19 (pp. 18–24).

88 See Thornton, *Fire, op. cit.*, Chapter 6.

89 In fact, as Orville Schell stresses, China has its own history of democratic activism reaching from the final years of the Qing dynasty up through the Tiananmen demonstrations of 1989. See Orville Schell, "China's Hidden Democratic Legacy," *Foreign Affairs*, Vol. 83, No. 4 (July/August 2004), p. 117 (pp. 116–24).

90 It may be that every mighty oak began life as an acorn, but it should also be noted that not every acorn becomes a mighty oak. On the SGZ projection, see Shang-Jin Wei and Heather Mikiewicz, "A Global Crossing for Enronities": How Opaque Self-Dealing Damages Financial Markets around the World," *The Brookings Review*, Vol. 21, No. 2 (Spring 2003), pp. 28–31.

91 Howard W. French, "Visit to Chinese Anytown Shows a Dark Side of Progress," *The New York Times* (January 19, 2006), http://www.nytimes.com/2006/01/19/international/asia/19china.html.

in coming years nearly all population growth will be urban.[92] It is extremely unfortunate that the formative stage of this transformation has taken place under the aegis of neoliberal globalization, which has stunted the kind of urban planning and social security that could have humanized the process. Instead, the net effect of international programs has often been worse than no planning at all. Global institutions like the IMF and the World Bank have struck a decisive blow against the egalitarian potential of globalization. While the Third World has been saddled with crippling debt, authoritarian regimes have received the helping hand they needed to suppress domestic reform pressures.

There was no hiding the fact that the chief beneficiaries of this support system have been its most empowered members at home and abroad. Early apologists therefore turned to the artful argument of economic "trickle down." The only things that consistently trickled down were corruption and indifference. As newly uprooted rural masses poured into cities, the middle classes bought real estate and became the new slum lords of a burgeoning urban underclass. Classic liberal policies such as Kennedy's Alliance for Progress had counted on middle classes to become the vanguard for political reform. In fact they have become a vast bulwark against social democratization.

Nowhere is anti-democratic globalism more pronounced than in the PRC, where it helps to suppress the more than 200 million rural Chinese who have migrated to cities since the market reforms of the late 1970s. Another 250 to 300 million are expected to follow the same path in coming decades. Within ten years this paradigmatically rural country will have an urban majority,[93] and a cultural revolution to match. Already it is undergoing a capitalistic metamorphosis that would have been unimaginable to Mao or to Old Guard China watchers like John K. Fairbanks, whose liberal-left credulity made him miss the fact that Mao was anything but the agrarian democrat he imagined.[94] That delusion kept Fairbanks silent while 100 million Chinese perished under the Maoist reign of terror.

In their own way, neoliberal China watchers are no less credulous. They willfully ignore the horrors taking place behind the Great Wall of double-digit growth.[95] China's social chasm, however, has more to do with politics than economics. It could

---

92 Mike Davis, *Planet of Slums* (New York: Verso, 2006), pp. 1–2.

93 *Ibid.*, p. 12.

94 Fairbanks finally had his shock of awareness with the savage suppression of pro-democratic protesters at Tiananmen. He could only say that Chinese affairs were too complex for Westerners to understand. This is the same Fairbanks who once explained America's failure in Vietnam by the fact that it did not have academic experts on Vietnam as it did on China. Was this to suggest that Vietnam was easier to understand than China? On Fairbanks' reaction to Tiananmen, see Cao Changqing, *op. cit.*, and on his Vietnam comments see Morton A. Kaplan, "Intellectuals and Foreign Policy: From John King Fairbanks to Paul Wolfowitz," online in *The World and I* (February 1, 2004), http://goliath.ecnext.com/coms2/summary_0199-3877160_ITM.

95 But they are not alone. Many China watchers on the nominal Left are equally mute on human rights issues. There is some irony in the fact that the plight of China's working classes as well as its intellectuals is usually better covered by rightwing observers like Guy Sorman (*L'annee du Coqi Chinois et rebelles*) than the Left.

not exist if most Chinese had any real political voice. The natural question to ask is how such a seemingly dynamic economy could produce such rotten politics. But that is putting the cart before the horse. As Minxin Pei stresses, the Chinese system "can deliver robust growth year after year because it is so rotten."[96]

In the high tide of the Asian miracle, Japan was the undisputed "lead goose" of Asian development. But after the Asian Crash and Japan's "lost decade," the search was on for a new Asian model. China was the prime contender, capitalizing (quite literally) on its vast reservoir of cheap labor as well as the kind of political "stability" that only a police state could achieve. Then it happened: the collapse of the US New Economy poured doubts on the notion that the new century would be modeled on the Washington Consensus. This put China's rise in a new light. Now the question is not simply whether China can become Asia's new "lead goose," but whether it can challenge America on a global scale.

Even if the PRC slips from its geoeconomic pedestal, much as Japan did in the 1990s, the China development model may have a life of its own. As TNCs awaken to the coming eco-social meltdown in China, they will exit as fast as they fled other Rim countries at the time of the Asian Crash. The CPP/TNC symbiosis will then collapse, exposing the Chinese "miracle" as an archetype of maldevelopment. Unfortunately this revelation may not come before the Sino-globalist growth model has been embraced by much of the developing world. With or without PRC hegemony, therefore, this could turn out to be a Chinese century.

---

96 Minxin Pei, "Dangerous Denials," *Foreign Policy* (January/February 2005), http://www.foreignpolicy. com/story/cms.php?story_id=2753&print=1.

Chapter 8

The Price of Alignment:
India in the New Asian Drama

The Sino-Indian Factor

It has been widely accepted that China will be Asia's new "lead goose." There is, however, a major rival emerging in China's own backyard. India's new star status raises the question of how these two demographic titans will deal with one another. Can they respect each other's spheres of influence in a bifurcated Asia, or will they vie for supremacy on a pan-Asian scale? Clearly South Block (India's External Affairs Ministry) was alarmed by the pro-China axis that linked Pakistan, Nepal, and Bangladesh at the 13th Summit of SAARC (the South Asian Association for Regional Cooperation) in Dhaka and by China's attempt to sideline India at the December 2005 East Asia Summit in Kuala Lumpur.[1]

Needless to say, a certain degree of renewed Sino-Indian animosity would be in America's interest. Even if Andre Gunder Frank is right about the dawning of an Asian age, and even if Paul Kennedy is right about the relative eclipse of US economic power, Washington can still play a pivotal role in tipping the Asian balance one way or the other. The great enigma hanging over Indo-American relations after the Cold War has been Sino-American relations. Washington's vision of imminent Chinese democratization began as naiveté, but lives on as dogmatic denial. Not even Tiananmen could puncture this neoliberal balloon.

Indians have good reason to wonder why Americans have showered FDI and massive technological transfers on this archetype of undemocratic development;[2] yet, given the growing clout of its corporate sector, India is starting to "engage"

---

1 Mohan Malik, "China's Strategy of Containing India," *PINR—the Power and Interest News Report* (February 6, 2006), http://www.pinr.com/report.php?ac=view_report&report_id=434&language_id=1. ASEAN nations, with the exception of Malaysia, overruled China's attempt to exclude India's EAS participation. See Lijun Sheng, "China in Southeast Asia: The Limits of Power," *Japan Focus* (posted August 4, 2006), http://japanfocus.org/products/topdf/2184.

2 They are likewise dismayed by the munificent aid and technological assistance that has been showered on Pakistan, even when it was known that Pakistan was doing massive black market trade in nuclear weaponry. For thirty years India was treated as a pariah nation, yet in all those years they never produced anything comparable to Pakistan's A.Q. Khan scandal. See Ashton B. Carter, "America's New Strategic Partner?," *Foreign Affairs*, Vol. 85, No. 4 (July/August 2006), p. 40 (pp. 33–44).

China in a very similar way. By 2005 the PRC had replaced the United Arab Emirates as India's second largest trading partner, second only to the United States,[3] and 2006 has been declared the Sino-Indian friendship year. For Timothy Garton Ash these two powers are to Washington what Germany and America were to Britain in 1905.[4]

Business interests such as the FICCI (Federation of Indian Chambers of Commerce and Industry) hope to see the Sino-Indian relationship move toward the same "economics-driven-politics" that now locks America into full engagement with China.[5] In June 2006 a step was taken in this direction with the ratification of a China-India Free Trade Area (FTA) in the disputed border zone. And, in the same month, the corporations were delighted when India was invited to join China, Russia, Iran, and a host of Central Asian nations at a meeting of the Shanghai Cooperation Organization (SCO), where America was conspicuously excluded.[6] Clearly this was an attempt to fracture the encirclement of China that Washington is promoting. A sweeping China-India convergence would have enormous global repercussions, putting 2.3 billion people under one geoeconomic roof. But a greater concern is its geopolitical implications. When Chinese Premier Wen Jiabao paid a four day visit on India, Indian Prime Minister Manmohan Singh added a disconcerting note, suggesting that India should join with China to "reshape the world order."[7]

So far, however, there has been striking asymmetry in this rapprochement: while China primarily imports raw materials, it exports electronics, machinery and other manufactured goods.[8] Meanwhile it has worked diligently to prevent India from gaining a permanent seat on the UN Security Council, which would be a major step toward India's escape from the South Asian horizon of its geopolitics.[9] None of this comes as a surprise to South Block. No one has forgotten how the first India-China accord went up in smoke. After the Sino-Indian War of 1962, China made itself a key power broker and agent provocateur in South Asia by way of Pakistan. The idea was to block Soviet southward encroachment while pinning India down with a simmering conflict at its rear. America shared that goal on the anti-Soviet side, giving added impetus to an eventual thaw in US-China relations.

---

3 "China, India Move Closer in Trade," *Asia Times* (February 11, 2005), http://www.atimes.com/atimes/html.

4 Timothy Garton Ash, "Stagger on, Weary Titan," *The Guardian* (August 25, 2005), http://www.guardian. co.uk/comment/story/0,3604,1555724,00.html.

5 Swaran Singh, "China-India Economic Engagement: Building Mutual Confidence," *CSH (Centre de Sciences Humaines) Occasional Paper*, No. 10 (2005), from French Research Institute of India, New Delhi.

6 It is worth noting that China's willingness to include India in the Shanghai meeting reverses its determination to block India from joining the East Asia Summit of December 2005. Against China, Japan had called for the inclusion of both India and Australia. See Hiro Aida, "Japanese Asianism," *The Wall Street Journal* (July 14, 2006), http://online.wsj.com/article_print/SB115282281651006094.html.

7 Joseph S. Nye, "An India-China Axis?," *Project Syndicate* (2005), http://www.project-syndicate.org/print_commentary/nye20/English.

8 Malik, *op. cit.*

9 *Ibid.*

The weak link in this otherwise impeccable strategy was Pakistan's slippage into chronically failed statehood.[10] It took the combined efforts of China and America to keep their anti-Soviet buffer afloat, but the end of the Cold War removed any US incentive to continue the bailout. Instead, Washington began cultivating better relations with Pakistan's nemesis, India. Even without much US assistance, India's geoeconomic rise has been impressive enough to disturb China considerably. Beijing was no doubt relieved when 9/11 and the following "war on terrorism" pushed Pakistan back into Washington's good graces. In the zero-sum world of South Asian affairs this could be expected to torpedo the US-Indian reconciliation.[11] Delhi did indeed take it as a hard blow when Washington began praising Islamabad.[12]

However, with the Soviet factor removed, and with China moving front and center on the Asian stage, India could not afford cool relations with the "world's sole superpower." Its diplomatic opening toward China was but a mask for its underlying angst. There was no reason to doubt that when India showcased its thermonuclear capabilities in the late 1990s, the target was not Pakistan alone. And, for the same reason, America has looked to India as a vital part of its neo-containment strategy toward China.

While Washington tries to prevent the emergence of a peer competitor globally, Beijing seeks a multipolar global world combined with a unipolar Asia, with itself as the regional hegemon. India prefers multilateralism on *both* levels, but of course concurs with the US resolve to curb China's regional ambitions.[13] As one Indian strategist put it, Delhi envisions a tripolar world order by 2030, with China, India and America as the major powers. But then he added, "we don't want a China- or a US-dominated world, but if we had to choose, it would be easier for us to live with the latter."[14]

Washington certainly reciprocates those feelings, and makes Delhi a special exception to its nuclear nonproliferation dictum. In open violation of restrictions mandated by the Nuclear Nonproliferation Treaty,[15] India was able to sign a nuclear pact with Washington in July 2005. This allows for the sale of civilian nuclear fuel and technology to India.[16] A year later it test-fired its first long-range, nuclear-capable

---

10 The heinous nature of this failure was tragically exhibited in the October 2005 earthquake that claimed the lives of at least 17,000 schoolchildren when 10,000 Pakistani schools came crashing down, revealing the criminal negligence of the state in its choice of building materials and its indifference to basic safety standards. See David Montero, "The Pakistan Quake: Why 10,000 Schools Collapsed," *The Christian Science Monitor* (November 8, 2005), http://www.csmonitor.com/2005/1108/p01s03-wosc.htm.

11 Mohan Malik, "The China Factor in the India-Pakistan Conflict," *Parameters* (spring 2003), p. 36 (pp. 35–50).

12 Dennis Kux, "India's Fine Balance," *Foreign Affairs*, Vol. 81, No. 3 (May/June 2002), p. 97 (pp. 93–106).

13 Malik, "China's Strategy," *op. cit.*

14 Nye, *op. cit.*

15 See "A Cold War China Policy," *The New York Times* (November 19, 2005), http://www.nytimes.com/2005/11/19/opinion/19sat2.html.

16 These sales were discontinued in the mid-70s, when India was caught applying them to its secret weapons program. See "Still a Bad Deal," *The New York Times* (July 28, 2006), http://www.nytimes.com/2006/07/28/opinion/28fril.html.

missile, the Agni III.[17] The Western press all but ignored the event, whereas it went "ballistic" over North Korea's similar missile test of July 2006.

While India's nuclear capabilities are sure to impact the Asian balance of power, economic development could be even more decisive. Very much like US-Soviet competition during the Cold War, Sino-Indian power politics is capped by the possibility of mutually assured destruction. Nuclear parity shifts the contest to the economic sphere. The question is whether this will be a simple GDP competition, marked by another "race to the bottom" and an even greater spread between haves and have-nots. Or, with democracy on its side, will Indo-globalization take a more progressive path than Sino-globalization has?

"Democracy" in the New India

Much more is at stake here than economic expedience. A core issue is whether democracy will prove an asset or a liability for fast-track growth. As the world's most populous democracy, and its twelfth largest economy, India is where this issue will be decided. Could democracy be a vital feature of economic development, as Amartya Sen contends? If so, the PRC is setting itself up for a fall. It is confident, however, that Sen is wrong, given the fact that its political repression is bankrolled by TNCs that prefer police state protections to the turmoil and unpredictability of democracy. China's continued success will shatter the always dubious presumption (based on a tendentious reading of the experience of Korea and Taiwan) that commercial success leads automatically to democracy and human rights.[18]

A democratic counter-model is sorely needed. Though Japan is commonly dubbed Asia's most 'Western' state, thanks to its economic status, India has far better democratic credentials.[19] It is only necessary to compare its record to that of Pakistan to appreciate its democratic achievement,[20] and some expect that in coming years it will even surpass Japan economically. Despite India's well-justified Third World image outside its globalized sector (we need only mention its three hundred million

---

17 "India Test-Fires Nuclear-Capable Missile," *The New York Times* (July 9, 2006), http://www.nytimes.com/aponline/world/AP-India-Missile-Test.html.

18 The China model of democracy-free development is not only gaining converts in Asia, but throughout the global South. In Cuba, for example, Fidel Castro's brother Raul is a convert to the Sino-globalist commitment to capitalist development without freedom. See Carsten Volkery, "A Visit with Cuba's Persecuted," *Spiegel Online* (August 3, 2006), http://service.spiegel.de/cache/international/0,1518,430038,00.html.

19 Even Pankaj Mishra, a leading critic of Indian development, concedes that India is far better positioned democratically than post-communist or Latin American nations. See Pankaj Mishra, "The Myth of the New India," *The New York Times* (July 6, 2006), http://www.nytims.com/2006/07/06/opinion/06mishra.html.; and concerning Japan and India see C. Raja Mohan, "India and the Balance of Power," *Foreign Affairs*, Vol. 85, No. 4 (July/August 2006), pp. 24–25 (pp. 17–32).

20 General Pervez Musharraf, Pakistan's self-proclaimed President and the country's fourth military dictator, does not face the democratic obstacles that even Indira Gandhi yielded to in India. See William H. Thornton, *New World Empire: Civil Islam, Terrorism, and the Making of Neoglobalism* (Lanham, MD: Rowman & Littlefield, 2005), pp. 104–05.

illiterates),[21] its development model offers some uniquely attractive features. For example, its consumer-driven economy has helped it to escape global recessions.[22] The question is how much of this autonomy can survive its current globalist "reform." Will India succumb to the same democratic erosion that has attended globalization in other developing countries?

Amartya Sen holds out hope that a country can have both its democratic cake and its globalization. Against the raw economism that neoliberals share with their Chinese partners, giving the boot to democratic development, Sen insists that freedom is not only conducive to but constitutive of development.[23] GNP growth alone would thus be a road to maldevelopment. Realistically speaking, however, a country that did not show significant economic growth could not be taken seriously as a development model. Because today's India offers both developmental prerequisites, economic and political, it will be the prime test site for the alternative Asianism that Sen propounds.

Not only is India light years ahead of China in terms of personal freedom,[24] it even competes in economic terms, with an average growth of 6 percent a year from 1980 to 2002, and 7.5 percent from 2002 to 2006.[25] Unfortunately China and India both suffer from the undertow effect of mass deprivation. The World Bank estimates that almost 1.5 billion people in the two countries combined subsist on less than $2 per day.[26] To achieve high growth under these circumstances, elites in both nations have resolved to cater mainly to affluent classes, eschewing policies that would distribute wealth more equitably.

In India's case this growth strategy writes off the 300 million Indians in dire poverty, and puts at risk every postmaterial virtue that the India model has to offer. Sen has made much of the point that democracy, coupled with a free press, all but guarantees government responsibility. But that formula is hardly confirmed in the case of India, where many on both Left and Right are starting to question the developmental efficacy of democracy. The patent fact is that Indian democracy has been sleeping on the job. It has not lived up to its implicit promise of providing for the health and education of all Indians, and especially those in the country's 600,000 villages. Nor has it afforded the kind of basic protection to lower classes and minorities that even a minimalist "night watchman" state owes all citizens. Under

---

21 Arundhati Roy, *Power Politics* (Cambridge, Mass.: South End Press, 2001), p. 14.

22 Gurcharan Das, "The India Model," *Foreign Affairs*, Vol. 85, No. 4 (July/August 2006), pp. 2–3 (pp. 2–16).

23 Amartya Sen, *Development as Freedom* (New York: Alfred A. Knopf, 1999), p. 36.

24 There is some danger, however, that the China model could make inroads into democratic India. Within a week of the July 11, 2006 Bombay bombings, Indian authorities began imitating Chinese methods of blocking Internet Web sites they deemed inappropriate. See Eric Bellman and Peter Wonacott, "Indian Government Blocks Web Access," *The Washington Post* (July 19, 2006), p. D01.

25 Das, *op. cit.*, p. 2.

26 Pranab Bardhan, "China, India Superpower? Not so Fast!," *Yale Global* (October 25, 2005), http://yaleglobal.yale.edu/article.print?id=6407.

the spell of globalization, India is forfeiting the living economies that are its greatest wealth.[27]

First there was the Gujarat meltdown under the BJP, and now, under the resurrected Congress Party, an equally monstrous and utterly unnecessary economic disaster is unfolding. Despite the country's impressive aggregate growth, almost 380 million Indians presently subsist on less than a dollar a day.[28] Most are Adivasis (native tribal inhabitants) or Dalits (formerly known as untouchables). For these unfortunates the only real issue is their next meal. India is bisected by an invisible line between those who stand to profit from globalization and those who are getting fleeced. Vandana Shiva laments how every "living resource of the planet … is in the process of being privatized, commodified, and appropriated by corporations."[29] By no means is this rabid "incorporation" being achieved by way of the "free trade" policies that neoliberals harp on. Actual globalist policies are enforced by statist fiat.

That is just one more reason why India's agrarian majority has no stake in the state. How could they, asks Arundhati Roy, "when they don't even know what the state is?"[30] To them "India" is just a word they hear at election time. For the two hundred million Indians without clean drinking water,[31] democracy is just a legitimating mechanism for the country's privileged and semi-privileged classes. The latter are riding the wave of globalist upward mobility into a lifestyle of ersatz Westernization, epitomized by the call center. Here, on clocks set to US time, legions of globalized hirelings imitate the very accents of Americans calling in with problems ranging from computer crashes to lost credit cards.[32] The notion that this subculture of bogus identity is the hallmark of a "New India" is too ludicrous to warrant further comment.

Rural Crisis

What marks the New India, rather, is the slippage of a broad strata of the rural middle class into penury. Much of this downward mobility involves landed farmers who were respected members of their village communities until globalist restructuration broke on the countryside. With at least 100,000 farmer suicides between 1993 and 2003,[33] India is in a crisis that its leaders hardly register. The proximate reason for these deaths is a credit crunch and crashing produce prices, but the deeper cause is gross indifference on the part of the power elite.

---

27 See Vandana Shiva's concept of living economies and their relationship to Earth Democracy in her *Earth Democracy: Justice, Sustainability and Peace* (Cambridge, MA: South End Press, 2005), p. 5.

28 Mishra, *op. cit.*

29 Vandana Shiva, *India Divided: Diversity and Democracy under Attack* (New York: Seven Stories Press, 2005), p. 13.

30 Arundhati Roy, *The Cost of Living* (New York: The Modern Library, 1999), p. 116.

31 *Ibid.*

32 See Shashi Tharoor, "India Finds its Calling," *Foreign Policy* (March/April 2006), http://www. foreignpolicy.com/story/cms.php?story_id=3378&print=1.

33 Mishra, *op. cit.*

Even when this tragedy is mentioned in the major media, it is set within a paradigm of progress whereby agrarian suffering is cast as sad but inevitable collateral damage. Early in April, 2006, just as the Sensex Index crossed the 11,000 mark, and as hundreds of journalists covered India's Fashion Week, the annual suicide toll in Vidarbha (in eastern Maharashtra) rose above 400. Most papers and TV stations did not deign to mention this dark milestone.[34] It was too commonplace to count as real news during Fashion Week.

Such neglect is a gift to the recruitment efforts of Maoist Naxalites across rural India. They are fishing in the same impoverished sea as Hindu nationalists have been,[35] but with a bigger social net. The reason so little is known about this resistance movement is that the government and media have done a fine job of back-paging it, along with the rural plight that stokes it. That of course runs counter to Sen's confidence in a democratic press. It turns out that his thesis applies best where one establishment faction finds advantage in exposing the shortcomings of another faction. This informational artillery exchange may work for famines, as Sen well documents,[36] but it grinds to a halt when the interests of all major political players happen to coincide.

Consider, for example, the blanket exploitation of India's farmers, millions of whom are being backed into an economic corner. Outsiders are dismayed by reports of thousands of farmer suicides in an economy that purports to be booming. But the rural crisis should not be news at all, as it has been brewing for decades. Already in 1967, when the Naxalites made their debut, Prime Minister Indira Gandhi acknowledged that the movement was but the tip end of a horrendous "socioeconomic problem."[37] The fact that this problem has been left to fester ever since says much about the nature of Indian democracy.

The apathy of India's governing class has all but handed the Naxalites an invitation to expand their operations, recruiting villagers once known for political passivity. Now the movement is active in 14 states, from the coastal South to the Nepal border in the North.[38] What must be recognized is that the current violence on the Naxalite side is largely reactive. Consider the case of twelve Adivasis killed in January 2006 by police in the Jaipur district of Orissa. The local Adivasi population was being forced to evacuate its ancestral land in order to make room for industrial "development." Hundreds were fired on when they marched in peaceful protest.[39]

---

34 P. Sainath, "India Shining meets the Great Depression," *The Hindu* (April 2, 2006), http://www.indiatogether.org/cgi-bin/tools/pfriend.cgi.

35 Somini Sengupta, "Hindu Nationalists Are Enrolling, and Enlisting, India's Poor," *The New York Times* (May 13, 2002), http://www.nytimes.com/2002/05/13/international/asia/13HIND.html.

36 Sen, *op. cit.*, Chapter 7.

37 Ramachandra Guha, "People vs People," *Hindu Times* (June 4, 2006), http://www.hindustantimes.com/onlineCDA/PFVersion.jsp?article=http://10.18.141.122/n…

38 Jason Overdorf, "India's Maoists Step Up Rebellion," *Globe and Mail* (June 8, 2006), http://www.Theglobeandmail.com/servlet/story/RTGAM.20060608.wxnaxalites.08/BNStor…

39 "'Development' Aggression against the Indigenous in India," *Analytical Monthly Review* editorial (February 18, 2006), http://mrzine.monthlyreview.org/amr180206.html.

The victims' low status ensures that the event will soon be forgotten. Later, when some of them join the rebel cause, their actions will be reported as unprovoked acts of aggression.

At one point the epicenter of this resistance was Andhra Pradesh, but presently there is equal strife in the hills and valleys of Chhattisgarh, where state police fear to patrol. Either to avoid the appearance of another Kashmir, or simply to economize, the government has opted for a less formal counter-insurgency. As of June 2005 it unveiled a paramilitary program known as *Salwa Judum*, whose purpose is all too clear. With the encouragement of Raman Singh, Chhattisgarh's BJP Chief Minister, approximately 3,000 "special police" were issued arms and licensed to fight terror with terror. Unfortunately they got little or no training in how to distinguish armed foes from locals whose alleged support for the Naxalites was extorted. Quite predictably this "fire with fire" strategy has backfired, producing a cycle of violence verging on civil war. In the first year of *Salwa Judum* operations about a thousand innocent civilians were slain and another 40,000 displaced,[40] with tribals getting the worst of it.

The rebels, likewise, are drawing a non-negotiable line in the sand. One is either with them or against them, and the latter can be a death sentence. A case in point was the April 2006 abduction of 40 tribal villagers in Chhattisgarh, 13 of whom had their throats cut.[41] One sees less and less of the former Naxalite effort to support local struggles for social justice. Instead of reform, with its focus on incremental goals, the rebels now concentrate on violent revolution.[42] Establishment politicians grab this up as vindication of their own brutal tactics. Chhattisgarh Home Secretary B.K.S. Ray points to the extremist turn of the Naxalites as proof that they are nothing but "goonda" thugs or terrorists.[43] But the fact remains that the government had forty years to redress the underlying conditions that draw the local poor to this cause. Indeed, without the Naxalite rising this social injustice would still be invisible to the world, and even to many Indian urbanites.

Vandana Shiva stresses that rural indigents have not so much been "left behind" as robbed. What is pushing them to the brink of despair is much the same economic restructuration that is bankrupting small farmers throughout the developing world. The irony is that well-meaning economists like Jeffrey Sachs now offer this same globalist package as a blanket cure for global poverty.[44] Almost invariably such programs are run by urban elites who have far more in common with their counterparts half a world away than with the farmers at their back door.

This urban-rural divide, however, is hardly the original product of globalization. It is rooted in decades of Indian maldevelopment, whereby rural Indians got little more from independence than domestic colonialism. In Barrington Moore's view,

---

40 Overdorf, *op. cit.*

41 "Indian Maoists Slit Throats of 13 Hostages," *Reuters* (April 29, 2006), http://www.alernet.org/thenews/newsdesk/PEK5439.htm.

42 Overdorf, *op. cit.*

43 *Ibid.*

44 See Vandana Shiva, "Two Myths that Keep the World Poor," *Canadian Dimension* (November 29, 2005), from http://www.odemagazine.com/article.php?aID=4192.

the structural inertia of rural India precluded mass peasant rebellions like those of China.[45] The absence of that risk factor left urban elites secure enough that they felt free to quarantine the rural sector politically. For all practical purposes postcolonial India remained two nations, one urban and one rural.

In Gandhi's Footsteps

That is exactly the outcome that Gandhi tried so hard to avoid. His *Sarvodaya* (uplifting all) principle sought to integrate India by closing the gap between urban dynamism and rural stagnation. Mistaking Gandhi's defense of rural heterodoxy for anti-modernism, Moore missed the fact that Gandhi's village-centered ideology, much like Shiva's "earth democracy," not only offered a holistic vision of India's polity but a practical blueprint for genuine democratization. This was the only social strategy that had any hope of bringing the rural masses into the new democratic mainstream. Though Gandhi was no pastoral retreatist, his respect for the core values of rural life lay at the heart of his principle of *Swadeshi* (local self-sufficiency).[46]

Nehru's macro-modernism, by contrast, sacrificed those values in favor of the urban hubris that marked his vaunted Planning Commission.[47] This elite was only too pleased to take up where the British left off. It is almost comical that some neoliberal pundits charge Nehru with killing growth by keeping Gandhism at the heart of his program.[48] To the degree that it was diplomatically possible, Nehru did everything within his power to relegate Gandhism to the museum of ancient history. Blaming Gandhi for the Congress Party's bad governance is rather like blaming Jesus for the Inquisition or Marx for the Gulag Archipelago.

What Gandhi and Nehru did share, to their lasting credit, was a commitment to keep India free from the clutches of international powers. That resolve did not result in the complete economic dysfunction that neoliberals allege. One of the biggest contributors to India's "Hindu rate of growth" was the Planning Commission's bureaucratic ineptitude. Nor was that growth rate so negligible when it is born in mind that most of the country's agriculture production has remained invisible to standard economic analysis. As Shiva notes, household and local work hardly registers as productive activity, and seeds saved from previous harvests are not counted as a productive investment. Thus a large component of the nation's rural economy has

---

45 Barrington Moore, Jr., *Social Origins of Dictatorship and Democracy: Lord and Peasant in the making of the Modern World* (Boston: Beacon Press, 1966), p. 315.

46 Ela Gandhi, "Gandhi and Development," *Resurgence*, Issue 214 (September/October 2002), http://resurgence.gn.apc.org/issues/gandhi214.htm.

47 See Sudipta Kaviraj, "Dilemmas of Democratic Development in India," in Adrian Leftwich (ed.), *Democracy and Development: Theory and Practice* (Cambridge, UK: Polity Press, 1996), p. 117 (pp. 114–38).

48 Val MacQueen holds, for example, that for "70 years Mohandas Gandhi's myopic vision of backward-looking socialism ... was accepted as revealed wisdom by a string of Indian prime ministers, starting with his acolyte, Nehru." Val MacQueen, "The Most Optimistic Country in the World," *TCS (Technology, Commerce, Society) Daily* (June 28, 2006), http://www.tcsdaily.com/article.aspx?id=062806A.

been virtually erased from its official GDP. Worse still, policies that are designed to accelerate GDP growth often do grave injury to hidden economies of the rural sector, as when biotech firms push for agricultural monocultures at the expense of local diversity and sustainability.

Shiva reminds us that before the Green Revolution introduced its agricultural straitjacket, more than 200,000 kinds of rice were cultivated in India.[49] These had proven their survivability in the face of floods and draught, pestilence and every manner of disease. On top of that, these indigenous strains were cheap, not requiring special seeds and fertilizers available only from TNCs. Capital-intensive agribusinesses brought in "Golden rice" to combat vitamin A deficiency, while the dozens of natural greens that produced a surplus of Vitamin A were forced out of production, all in the name of progress.[50]

Prior to its globalist turn, India's economic growth was low but steady,[51] and came with no strings attached. It was obvious after the Asian Crash that the country's avoidance of export-driven growth had been prudent, if excessive. Its global alignment since the early 1990s has brought high growth (even comparable to China's, once Chinese statistical juggling and environmental rape is discounted) but has also widened the already vast chasm between haves and have-nots. This should come as no surprise. That is what globalization does.

Clearly India's greatest economic problem is distribution rather than growth. Those who are most at risk are never the ones reaping the profits. Four decades of macro-planning evaded the most rudimentary needs of the general population: a decent supply of food, clothing, housing, health care, sanitation, and primary education. In rural and urban areas alike, these public goods were distributed on the basis of political patronage, with women getting the worst deal of all. By the late 1980s one fifth of the urban population and a third of the rural population had fallen below the poverty line, defined in the strict sense of caloric intake.[52]

Even today half of all Indian children suffer malnutrition.[53] One might ask how this is possible in a booming economy, where growth rates have risen to 7 or 8 percent per year, and are expected to exceed 10 percent in the near future.[54] The real question, though, is "booming for whom?" Even non-business TV channels often

---

49 Vandana Shiva, *Stolen Harvest: The Hijacking of the Global Food Supply* (Cambridge, MA: South End Press, 2000), p. 84.

50 Bengal women commonly cultivate more than 150 such greens. See Vandana Shiva, "Globalization and Poverty," *Resurgence*, Issue 202 (October 2000), http://www.resurgence. org/resurgence/issues/shiva202. htm.

51 The Indian economy grew at an average annual rate of 1.7 per capita from 1950–51 to 1990–91, as compared to a 0 to 0.4 rate from 1880 to 1947. And in the period of the most intense government planning, from 1950 to 1964, there was a significant acceleration in industrial growth. See Jayati Ghosh, "Development Strategy in India: A Political Economy Perspective," in Sugata Bose and Ayesha Jalal (eds), *Nationalism, Democracy and Development: State and Politics in India* (Oxford: Oxford University Press, 1999), p. 166 (pp. 165–83).

52 *Ibid.*, p. 169.

53 Mishra, *op. cit.*

54 Girish Mishra, "Infatuation with Economic Growth," *Znet* (January 2, 2006), http://www.zmag.org/Content/print_article.cfm?itemID=9445&sectionID=10.

carry stock market ticker updates at the right hand corner of the screen, which for most viewers can only have a "let them eat cake" connotation. A large part of the millions applying for the National Rural Employment Guarantee Programme are landed farmers who would have been men of some status a decade ago. With this supplement they are trying desperately to hold onto their rural world. Less fortunate ones who give up entirely on rural life and flee to the cities may be jumping from the frying pan into the fire, for plant closings and rising urban unemployment have been the curious byproducts of India's New Economy. Cities such as Mumbai put on a shining global face by way of thousands of shanty-town demolitions.[55] Where are these outcasts to go, back to the countryside?

The fact is that—with the notable exception of the socialist-leaning state of Kerala—Indian democracy has been an appalling failure in terms of distributive justice. That exception, as Sen duly observes, is crucial to any assessment of where Indian development went wrong. Gunnar Myrdal got to the heart of India's developmental dilemma by noting that while few nations in the modern era have been launched on such high progressive hopes as this one was, the bottom line was that all the new leaders were drawn from the upper class. Most flatly equated their own good fortune with the nation's.[56] Vote or no vote, the great majority of Indians were as divorced from the policy concerns of the new regime as they had been from the Raj.[57]

Gandhi stood up for these invisible people, beseeching Indian leaders—as he expressed it in his memoirs—to "recall the face of the poorest and the weakest man whom you have seen and ask yourself if the step you contemplate is going to be of any use to him." This pre-Rawlsian injunction was too much for even the more scrupulous leaders of the fledgling democracy. Much as most American revolutionary leaders were arch-conservatives, and even Simon Bolivar was a political regressive except for his anti-Spanish animus, nearly all of India's independence leaders were wolves in sheep's clothing where village India was concerned.

In his sincere but misguided progressivism, Nehru thought it necessary to purge Gandhism from Indian modernism. This set the stage for a tragic sundering of the entire nation: not just between Hindus and Muslims, or city and country, but ultimately between haves and have-nots. As the Dalit Panther Manifesto put it in 1973, the "present legal system and state have turned all our dreams into

---

55 Sainath, *op. cit.*

56 Gunnar Myrdal, *Asian Drama: An Inquiry into the Poverty of Nations, Vol. I* (New York: Pantheon, 1968), p. 273.

57 On this much Myrdal and Sen can concur. Where they split is on the remedy. Having little of Sen's faith in social democracy, Myrdal could only hope for a better model of enlightenment elitism, closer to Nehru than Gandhi. If that was still possible in India, it was extremely unlikely in Pakistan, which Myrdal saw as its culturally handicapped. Like Sen, Myrdal underscored the non-economic determinants of development, but he was more prone to see these determinants as permanent barriers to development. And the case of Pakistan, as Mohammad Omar Farooq observes, seems to validate this judgment. See Mohammad Omar Farooq, "Development Experience of Bangladesh in Gunnar Myrdal's *Asian Drama* Perspective," presented on May 6, 2000 at the Bengal Studies Conference, http://www.globalwebpost.com/Farooqm/writings/q-academic/myrdal.html.

dust."[58] From this desolate vantage the only remaining road to emancipation would be through some form of revolution; but since India had never had an industrial revolution, it lacked the proletarian solidarity that urban-based popular resistance would require. Meanwhile caste prejudices dissolved any possible rural solidarity. Under these circumstances the full politicization of the countryside would almost certainly have moved the country in a reactionary direction.

Only Gandhi had the wherewithal—the cartographic skills, so to speak—to put the rural masses on India's political map in a non-reactionary manner. He well understood that simple rural empowerment could backfire. What he called for, therefore, was not just nonviolent revolution but also a multicultural Renaissance. That is why many are now re-discovering in Gandhi a way to bridge the ethno-religious divides that threaten India's political integrity. Some believe that this Gandhian heritage holds vital lessons for the West as well.[59] Rajeev Bhargava rightfully complains that Western scholars such as Will Kymlicha date the origins of multiculturalism from Canada's experiment of 1971, totally ignoring the Indian experience.[60] Moreover, under the spell of globalization, India's own leaders ignore Gandhi's contribution. The irony is that these self-described cosmopolitans are too parochial to grasp the global significance of Gandhian pluralism—this at a time when, as Bhargava notes, all societies are "becoming like India."[61]

Suffice it to say that Gandhi was far ahead of his time. Even Moore had to grant that Gandhi's theoretical stance was not regressive in the usual sense, as it was implicitly anticapitalist and patently anti-imperialist. Where everything that is not "modernist" (where "modern" connotes opposition to India's village world) is defined as backward, Gandhi could only be classified as "conservative." Even today 70 percent of the Indian population lives in the countryside, 110 million being farmers and another 500 million having their livelihoods tied to agriculture less directly.[62]

Millions of farmers are now cast as regressives because they have no place in the capitalist agribusiness that the WTO calls India's future. Gandhi opposed such macroism, both foreign and domestic, whereas Nehru officially opposed foreign-dominated development but in practice mimicked Soviet macroism. So it was that over 30 million people were displaced over a fifty year period as hundreds of village worlds were inundated by mega-dams.[63] The process continues unabated.

---

58 Quoted in Gail Omvedt, *Reinventing Revolution: New Social Movement, and the Socialist Tradition in India* (London: M.E. Sharpe, 1993), p. 47.

59 Several of these revaluations are contained in D.P. Chattopadhyaya (ed.), Vol. 10, Part 7 of *Political Ideas in Modern India* (New Delhi: Sage India, 2006). Concerning the Gandhian model of transculturalism see especially Rajeev Bhargava's contribution.

60 Rajeev Bhargava, "India's Model: Faith, Secularism and Democracy," *Open Democracy* (November 3, 2004), http://www.opendemocracy.net/articles/ViewPopUpAticle.jsp?id=1&articleID=2204.

61 *Ibid.*

62 Mishra, "Myth," *op. cit.*; and Scott Baldauf, "Soft spot in India's boom: the 60 percent tied to farms," *The Christian Science Monitor* (June 27, 2006), http://www.csmonitor.com/2006/0627/p01s04-wosc.html.

63 David Harvey, *The New Imperialism* (Oxford: Oxford University Press, 2003), p. 178. The real number, as Arundhati Roy notes, is probably around 70 million, but to err on the

Clearly more is involved here than a simple quest for hydraulic power. As Karl Wittfogel argued in his classic 1957 study of hydraulic oppression, the control of irrigation systems can be an all too potent political device. However, as Shiva points out, traditional irrigation systems in India were remarkably free of the centralized power politics that Marx and Wittfogel associated with hydraulic societies.[64] Far from being liberatory, Nehruvian centralism and now globalization have imposed the hydro-centralism that traditional India managed to avoid. Following in Gandhi's footsteps, Medha Patkar (founder of the Narmada Bachao, or Committee to Save the Narmada) has fought indefatigably to halt dam projects on the Narmada River. In the spring of 2006 she went on a long hunger strike to protest the displacement of another 35,000 farmers along the river.[65] What Narmada Bachao is ultimately contesting is the belated "hydraulization" of Indian culture and politics. Wittfogel's argument may not have applied to traditional India, but it perfectly fits the ravages of current Indo-globalization.

Indo-Globalization and the BJP/Congress Pact

This village-be-dammed policy is tantamount to class war, but by no means are its victims limited to the countryside. Lower class urban communities can also have a "village" character, and they are equally at risk, especially when their inhabitants happen to be Muslim. The host of "Chota Pakistans" that dot India's cities are now under full assault. Such Muslim ghettos once blended easily with their Hindu counterparts, sharing festivals and public celebrations, but increasingly they are sequestered and pushed into abject poverty. Bullied by Hindu police, and denied basic municipal benefits such as running water, these urban "villagers" are cast as dirty people who deserve their lot.

Theirs is simply the most glaring case of Muslim disempowerment. The average Muslim income is 11 percent below the national average, and that gap widens when government services such as education are added to the scales. Part of the problem is that Muslims are so poorly represented in politics and public administration, including the police and armed forces, that their legal rights are all but nullified.[66] The BJP has turned this bigotry into a basic operating principle, but that only amplifies an injustice that the Congress Party has quietly condoned for decades.[67]

---

ultra-conservative side, she more than halves that number, settling on the figure of 33 million displacements in the last 50 years. See Roy, *Cost*, p. 17.

64 Vandana Shiva, *Water Wars: Privatization, Pollution and Profit* (Cambridge, MA: South End Press, 2002), pp. 122–23.

65 Scott Baldauf, "Gandhi Evoked for All Manner of Causes," *The Christian Science Monitor* (April 6, 2006), http://www.csmonitor.com/2006/0406/p07s02-wosc.html.

66 Dionne Bunsha, "Living through Horror," *The Hindu* (July 20, 2006), http://www.thehindu.com/thehindu/br/2006/06/20/stories/2006062000541500.htm.

67 There are, however, huge differences in the two parties' degrees of discrimination. In May 2006, for example, the BJP staged marches in Delhi to protest the Congress Party's attempt to increase the number of Muslims in the armed forces, and more generally to contest

In 1995, when the Hindu nationalist Shiv Sena Party gained power in the state of Maharashtra, it promptly renamed Bombay as Mumbai, symbolically expelling the transculturalism that the word Bombay signified. But the vortex of anti-Muslim hostility would be the state of Gujarat, where the radical Hindu BJP holds complete sway. After the infamous riots of 2002, Muslim ghettos sprang up as a desperate defensive measure, their inhabitants being afraid to return to their native villages. Gujarat is simply the most exposed crag of a national crisis. Reputable sources report that the country's new anti-poverty program—promising up to 100 days of employment per year to the rural poor—is in practice excluding many of those who need it most, such as the Muslims who already face discrimination from every side.[68]

This systematic suppression of Muslims has a functional purpose beyond its religious motives. As poverty deepens across rural India, the Hindu majority, which could easily join the Naxalite cause in full revolution, is adroitly diverted. The hostility of the Hindu-underclass is sated at the expense of helpless Muslims.[69] For all its public aversion to the BJP, the Congress Party elite is in fact a beneficiary of the BJP's Hindutva (Hindu fascist) politics. The Congress is made to look benign by comparison, while in fact its neoliberal program of dispossession through privatization, which is the real source of the new sectarian warfare, proceeds apace.

Like the British before, the Congress elite has defined progress as profits flowing to a privileged class. When the end of the Cold War deprived this elite of its Soviet prop, the way might have been paved for a "Senian moment," when domestic as well as foreign colonialism could at last be expelled. To avert that dread outcome India's power elite once more looked outside itself for a prepackaged development model, this time on the capitalist side. As it had in China and Southeast Asia, globalization came to the rescue of the Old Guard.

Again the rural masses found themselves political exiles, and this time their very livelihoods were under siege. Agro-industry has little need of them, but the urban New Economy has even less. Out of 400 million workers nationwide, only 1.3 million have any place in the new info tech and business services. Other developing countries have created labor-intensive industries that can absorb surplus labor,[70] but India, modeling itself on the American New Economy of the 1990s, has opted for high-tech development. Rural refugees and urban indigents are left in the lurch. Having slammed the developmental door on most of its citizens, India's ruling classes cannot risk the repercussions of genuine democratic politics. The more they globalize, the more they will have to dismantle the nation's democratic foundations. Thus India is already gravitating toward the illiberal devices of Sino-globalization.

In the absence of any democratic recourse, the Naxalite upsurge is not surprising, yet it is an aberration in terms of Indian social history. For decades theorists of rebellion and revolution have taken a dismissive attitude toward Indian social

---

the present government's "soft" approach to terrorism. See Scot Baldauf, "Gandhi Evoked for All Manner of Causes," *op. cit.*

68 Anuj Chopra, "Hindu, Muslim Ghettos Arise in Gujarat," *The Christian Science Monitor* (July 5, 2006), http://www.csmonitor.com/2006/0705/p0702-wosc.htm.

69 *Ibid.*

70 Mishra, "Myth," *op. cit.*

resistance in the nonviolent tradition of Gandhi. Given their chronic desperation, the apparent passivity of India's rural masses seemed to confirm Marx's disparaging verdict on them. With certain rare exceptions, such as the Telangana rebellions of the late 1940s,[71] the story has been one of acquiescence in the face of monumental poverty and exploitation. Although Barrington Moore recognized the revolutionary potential of the Indian peasantry, their actual conduct earned them a place in his classic study of peasant resistance only as a negative case. Not surprisingly he blamed much of this passivity on Gandhi.

Without defending Gandhi, subaltern scholars have challenged Moore's negativity on the question of rural rebellion. Michael Adas counters such revisionism by noting the paucity of full rebellions in India.[72] His argument made sense at the time of his writing, in the late 1980s, but has been negated by the recent Naxalite explosion. Another side of his thesis, however, has even greater application today. Adas astutely concluded that the relative absence of violent protest is best understood not in terms of rural idiocy (Marx) or Gandhian passivity (Moore), but as evidence of a system of ongoing negotiation that reduced the pressure for rebellion or revolution.[73]

The current breakdown of this mediatory system goes far to explain the kind of resistance we are now seeing. The increasing potency of the Naxalite movement bears testimony to globalization's impact on the rural heart of India by way of agribusiness, dam financing and the WTO-directed forfeiture of trade protections, especially where agricultural products are concerned. Adding insult to injury, the corporate take-over of rural India is proceeding under the ironic guise of "eliminating poverty." In Arundhati Roy's words, this subterfuge is "a mutant variety of colonialism, remote controlled and digitally operated."[74]

"ReOrienting" India

That remoteness removes the last shred of ethical restraint from the macroism that Nehru implanted at the expense of Gandhism. This virtual war on "small things" (to borrow Roy's terminology) has enjoyed the full approval of world opinion on both Right and Left. Only now is a theoretical foundation taking shape that could put Gandhism in a positive light; for the modernism that declared Gandhism defunct is steeped in the same orientalist bias that Andre Gunder Frank traces from Marx to Huntington.[75] Frank's determination to "ReOrient" social thought affords theoretical space for the retrieval of non-Western visions of the good society, free at last from the modernist prism that treats not only Gandhism but most of Indian culture as an

---

71 See Michael Adas, "South Asian Resistance in Comparative Perspective," in Douglas Haynes and Gyan Prakash (eds), *Contesting Power: Resistance and Everyday Social Reactions in South Asia* (Berkeley, CA: University of California Press, 1991), p. 292 (pp. 290–305).

72 *Ibid.*, p. 296.

73 *Ibid.*, p. 302.

74 Roy, *Power Politics, op. cit.*, p. 14.

75 Andre Gunder Frank, *ReOrient: Global Economy in the Asian Age* (Berkeley, CA: University of California Press, 1998), pp. 15 and 19.

obstacle to development. Nehru's approach to modernization has amounted to an orientalist war on India itself.

Sen notes how that same prismatic distortion led to a gross misinterpretation of his mentor Rabindranath Tagore. Like Gandhi, Tagore was either dismissed as un-modern or lauded for his primitivism. Either way he is pressed into a convenient orientialist stereotype. Gandhi and Tagore were either vilified or valorized for the wrong reasons, the one being regarded as a charka-obsessed traditionalist, while the other was taken for a classic Asian mystic or wizard.[76]

The same procrustean logic that mistook these alter-modernists for anti-modernists wrote off India as a whole. Urban elites in both India and the West treated rural India as a cultural backwater that was best swept away, or sunk behind Nehruvian mega-dams. But Nehru was right on one point: there was no way to reconcile Gandhi with ordinary development. Any return to Gandhism, which is to say Indian pluralism, must be premised on some form of postdevelopment. So too, Sen's "development-as-freedom" thesis will be a hard sell in the Third World without a democratic case-in-point. India will be either the proving ground or the disproving ground for neo-Gandhism and Senism alike.

There is no question that India is now making its mark on the world, but which India is this? Pankaj Mishra points out how middle-class India likes to cast itself as the one and only voice of the future, with all other Indias declared moribund.[77] It is this bourgeois monolith that has given India the bomb and is fast indenturing it to the global market. Like the agro-industrial monocultures that Shiva deplores, the nation is being streamlined. At first glance this growth engine may seem impressive, but India's astonishing cultural variegation, like its 2000 strains of indigenous rice, has no place in current Indo-globalization. Agrarian biodiversity is simply the canary in India's developmental mine shaft. The biggest loser of all will be democratic pluralism, which is fast giving way to the political equivalent of TNC rice.

Oddly this transformation poses no problem for the radical Right. BJP Hindutva has no trouble reaching an accommodation with global capitalism, just as CPP elites in Beijing have had no trouble striking a symbiotic accord with capitalist elites in the West. In this sense Sino-globalism and Indo-globalism are on the same track. The difference is that India still possesses the formal apparatus of democracy. Once before, when Indira Gandhi overlooked this fact, the Indian equivalent of People Power came out of hibernation and struck down the tyranny she clearly had in mind.

Again, in May 2004, a unexpected popular recoil against Hindutva and fascist globalism threw the BJP out and restored the Congress Party. The fact that the anti-Hindutva side of that popular reaction has been honored does not mean that its antiglobalist side has been put to rest. Tragically it has been pushed into the

---

76 Amartya Sen, *The Argumentative Indian: Writings on Indian History, Culture and Identity* (New York: Farrar, Straus and Giroux, 2005), Chapter 5.

77 Pankaj Mishra, "A New Sort of Superpower," *New Statesman* (January 30, 2006), http://www. newstatesman.com/200601300015. From this vantage, Indian history is something to escape, which is exactly how Fukuyama saw history in general. Unlike Fukuyama, however, India's anti-historicists of the Right see democracy as an invitation to disorder and mismanagement.

waiting arms of Naxalite resistance. The unintended effect of the Naxalite upsurge could be a more egalitarian democratic politics. Only this threat, it seems, can relieve the social pressures that are pushing India toward a civil war that could make the Hindu/Muslim conflict seem almost tame. This is hardly the route to democratic development that Gandhi would have chosen, but is there any other?

Force alone will never suffice. Sen and Mishra, the pluralist heirs of Gandhi, look to the richness of India's multifarious traditions as the ultimate safeguard against the ravages of globalist integration.[78] To achieve Indo-globalization by sacrificing the best of India's traditions would be a very hollow accomplishment. There is still hope, however, that India can join the world on its own terms. In that case Indo-globalization would bear little resemblance to Sino-globalization, and developing countries would finally have an authentic democratic role model.

---

[78] Concerning the cultural side of this pluralism, see especially Amartya Sen, *The Argumentative Indian: Writings on Indian History, Culture, and Identity* (New York: Farrar, Straus and Giroux, 2005), and Pankaj Mishra, *An End to Suffering: The Buddha in the World* (New York: Farrar, Straus and Giroux, 2004).

Chapter 9

The Japan Model Goes Global: A New Reverse Course

Sanpo II: The Tyranny of Managed Consent

The statist ideology that came to be known as "Asian values" had its trial run in postwar Japan. Any attempt to cast this illiberal growth model as "normal" for Japan will run aground on the nation's labor history. Activistic unions staged more than 250 strikes per year in the 1920s. Even the military dictatorship that took over in 1938—disbanding all unions and funneling workers into *Sanpo*, the all-embracing Industrial Patriotic Society—could not extinguish the spirit of social democracy that drove unionization. Its robust survival was demonstrated by the tidal wave of re-unionization that swept Japan after its surrender in September 1945. Within four months twelve hundred independent unions had enlisted nine hundred thousand members, and by the end of the 1940s that number had swelled to 6.7 million, or 56 percent of the workforce.[1] Any political process that did not reflect this liberal-left voting bloc could hardly be called democratic.

For a fleeting moment Japan did have its "Tokyo Spring," the liberal democratic interlude that showed how different Japanese development could have been. The 1947 "reverse course" erased all that, restoring much of the same power structure that had taken the nation to war. This reactionary turn was in line with America's geopolitical agenda, and could be described as the indigenization of US policy; but even more so it was spawned by a Japanese elite that was more threatened by "Tokyo Spring" reformism than by US hegemony. This resurgent ruling class successfully enlisted America in its private war on democratization.

Shigeru Yoshida (who became prime minister in May 1946 and again in October 1948, remaining in office until December 1954) traced the tragic blunder of the war to the failure of Japan's prewar leadership to march in step with prevailing international power relations. Yoshida's grand strategy was to couple conservative elitism with Washington-directed internationalism. By focusing all its energy on economics and very little on defense, Japan could turn the terms of defeat into victory. The advent of the Liberal Democratic Party (LDP) in 1955 put the old warlords in control of a new model of authoritarianism: the tyranny of managed consent. By the late 1950s some Americans already thought the postwar econo-state of Japan was getting too good a deal, and the Eisenhower administration

---

1 Patrick Smith, *Japan: A Reinterpretation* (New York: Pantheon Books, 1997), p. 23.

was starting to regret the inclusion of Article 9 (which de-militarized Japan) in the 1947 Constitution.[2]

In fact, as Francis Fukuyama observes, the legitimacy of America's vanguard role in the Far East rested largely on Article 9. Japan's interests were also well served, since its neighbors would never have flocked behind the Japanese "lead goose" if its wings had not been clipped militarily.[3] Thus Washington and Tokyo struck a win/win alliance with the Yoshida Deal. This "1955 system" not only turned Japan into a permanent military garrison on Russia's eastern flank, but provided a blueprint for another kind of containment: the supplanting of liberal Left reformism by "Asian values" economism. This dual containment, whereby "stability" became a codeword for US-sponsored repression, would be duplicated throughout the Asia Pacific in coming decades. The apolitics of the Japan model—with oppositional democracy suspended and national security outsourced to the United States—remained in place throughout the recovery era and the subsequent "miracle" years.[4]

Stability on these terms was of course unpopular in many quarters, and would be fiercely contested. The elites' first impulse was to get tough. The infamous Nobusuke Kishi, grandfather of the recent prime minister Shinzo Abe, was brought in by high-placed members of his family as conservatism's pit bull.[5] He had the perfect resume in terms of both nationalist zeal and sheer ruthlessness. During the war he had directed the abduction and mass transport of Chinese forced laborers to Japan. A large percentage of them would die en route, and over one in six who survived the transit would perish in the slave labor camps that awaited them.[6]

For this, and for his "Albert Speer" role as Commerce and Industry Minister in Tojo's war cabinet, Kishi spent three years in prison awaiting trial as a class A war criminal. Yet, by order of US intelligence, he was summarily released and planted into the thick of postwar politics. Part of his task was to marshal the support of Old Guard elites for the LDP agenda. Within this recycled "Tojo club" he passed for a man of reason, if only because in 1944 he had finally resigned from Tojo's cabinet over his insistence that Japan should sue for peace if American forces reached Saipan.[7]

---

2 Michael J. Green, "Japan is Back: Why Tokyo's New Assertiveness is Good for Washington," *Foreign Affairs*, Vol. 86, No. 2 (March/April 2007), p. 143 (pp. 142–47).

3 Francis Fukuyama, "Abe's Nationalism Continues a Troubling Trend," *Taipei Times* (March 28, 2007), p. 9.

4 The Yoshida Deal, culminating in the security treaty of 1951, essentially made Japan an American military outpost, while the Ikeda deal of 1960 saved the Yoshida Deal from hostile critics on both the Right and Left by buying off their constituencies with the promise of fast-track economic growth. See Ian Buruma, "The Japanese Malaise," *The New York Review of Books*, Vol. 48, No. 11 (July 5, 2001), p. 39 (pp. 39–41).

5 Yoshida's daughter was married to Kishi's cousin, and his brother, Eisaku Sato was the Secretary-General of Yoshida's cabinet. See "Bonus to be Wisely Spent," *Time* (January 25, 1960), http://www.time.com/time/magazine/article/0,9171,939094,o00.html.

6 William Underwood, "Chinese Forced Labor, the Japanese Government and the Prospects for Redress," *ZNet* (July 7, 2005), http://www.zmag.org/content/print_article.cfm?itemID=8245&sectionID=1.

7 "A vigorous Visitor with an Urgent Message," *Time* (June 24, 1957), http://www.time.com/time/magazine/article/0,9171,824999,00.html.

Compared to Kishi, Yoshida could pass for a moderate.[8] Kishi's attempt to run the country the old fashioned way made him a lightning rod for mounting opposition after his election in 1958. By the spring of 1960 hundreds of thousands of protesters were demonstrating against his pet project, the revised US-Japan Security Treaty. To get it ratified, the Diet had to meet late at night with no opposition members present, an action that helped solidify resistance across class lines. When violent mine strikes erupted that summer, they were joined by thousands of Security Treaty protesters. It took 15,000 police to crush these demonstrations, which targeted the same Mitsui Corp. coal mine that 15 years before had played host to thousands of Kishi's slave laborers, including allied POWs.[9]

Continued unrest forced Kishi's resignation. That would be the last significant barrier to the "1955 system." From then on the undertow effect of economic growth would doom all real resistance.[10] Henceforth the Japan model could operate more on the side of carrot than stick, since by 1960 the Japanese were the best fed, best housed and best clothed populace in Asia.[11] This de facto political bribe was effective so long as the economy was booming, and the boom would last so long as Japan was an essential piece on the Cold War chessboard. It is no accident that the 1955 system started to unravel as the Cold War waned. Without this geopolitical buttress, the Japan model was on borrowed time. Prolonged recession would shred the economic carrot that kept the system running.

That unraveling has been the nightmare of all export-driven "miracle" regimes on the Pacific Rim. Japan's brand of repression has been different only in that it has been less centered, not bearing the stamp of any single dictator. Thus LDPism was better camouflaged than most authoritarianisms. Ironically it was Kishi's ouster, which seemed to be a victory for the liberal Left, that entrenched the power of the Right by concealing its total triumph. Although the Japan model was mimicked throughout the Rim, this degree of manufactured consent was an act other Asian nations could not follow. Japan would have no political equivalent to Chiang Kai-shek, Marcos, Park Chung Hee, Lee Kuan Yew, Suharto or Mahathir, not to mention Mao or Deng.

To snuff out liberal opposition, LDPism had no need of dictators. It could buy the votes it needed through a combination of high growth and sweeping job security. Ordinary workers and middle class salarymen were seduced by a system that by every non-political measure was moving Japan into the First World. Hereafter popular resistance was out of the question. Japan's democratic façade would meet no serious challenge so long as the Cold War lasted. *Sanpo* was effectively reborn under a democratic cloak.

---

8 Kishi wanted an all-out war on the Left by a recycled hard Right, and saw Yoshida as an obstacle in that path. The irony is that to defeat Yoshida he first had to enter an alliance with the Socialists. See "Bonus to be Wisely Spent," *op. cit.*

9 Underwood, *op. cit.*

10 Yoshikazu Sakamoto, "Coming to Grips with Japan's History and Role in the World," *History News Network: HNN Article Archive 2005* (week of November 21, 2005), http://www.hnn.us/articles/18400.html.

11 "Bonus to be Wisely Spent," *op. cit.*

A New Reverse Course

By the late 1980s the idea of "Japan as number one" had started to wash over from economic into geopolitical discourse. Increasingly there was talk of Japan's ability to say 'no' to its US guardian. Deputy Finance Minister Eisuke Sakakibara spoke for much of the nation's elite when he proclaimed that Japan had "surpassed capitalism"[12]—meaning Western liberal capitalism. The Japan model took false consciousness to such heights that class divisions lost their political edge and labor/management disputes became tea parties. Not even Huxley or Orwell could have imagined a more compliant working class, or a country happier to be kept on another's geopolitical tether. When Japanese talked of saying "no" to America, what they actually wanted was a more cushy Yoshida Deal, as opposed to no Deal. They wanted to have it both ways: global primacy without much military spending.

At that very moment, however, Japan began the slide that would suspend all talk of economic preeminence. This timing was no accident, for Japan was becoming geopolitically expendable. In 1991, when it grudgingly and belatedly donated $13 billion to the Gulf War coalition, Japan found it could not buy international respect. Having contributed no manpower to the cause, it was seen as little more than a camp follower.[13] Nor would the world forget that Tokyo's original offer of assistance was a piddling $10 million.[14]

Japan's economic slump can be traced to the G-7 Plaza Accord of 1985, where the Bank of Japan was pressured to shift its monetary policy dramatically, raising the yen's value against the US dollar. The idea was to force Tokyo to reduce its reliance on exports while expanding domestic demand.[15] Interest rate cuts and currency appreciation would theoretically encourage purchases of US goods. By 1987 the Bank of Japan's rate had dropped to 2.5, where it remained until May 1989. But things did not go as planned. Taking advantage of easy credit, export industries hiked capital spending.[16] This compounded the dilemma of overproduction that haunted all Asian "miracle" economies, but Japan most of all. Meanwhile low interest inflated stock and property prices, which were expected to stimulate domestic consumption. What it mainly stimulated was inflation, property speculation and a stupendous market bubble. Too late the Bank of Japan tried to cool the market,[17] raising rates from 2.5 to 6 percent in 1990. Soon the banking sector found itself inundated with non-performing loans, and was all but forced to seek more lucrative investments in Southeast Asia.[18]

---

12 Green, "Japan is Back," *op. cit.*

13 Bennett Richardson, "Japan Redefines 'Self-Defense,'" *The Christian Science Monitor* (February 6, 2004), http://www.csmonitor.com/2004/0206/p06s01-woap.htm.

14 Tomohito Shinoda, "Ozawa Ichiro as an Actor in Japan's Foreign Policy Making," *IUJ (International University of Japan) Research Institute Working Paper—Asia Pacific Series*, No. 17 (1999), http://www.iuj.ac.jp/research/wpap017.cfm.

15 William Engdahl, *A Century of War: Anglo-American Oil Politics and the New World Order* (London and Ann Arbor: Pluto Press, 2004, revised edition), p. 226.

16 Rob Hoveman, "Japan Sinking Fast," *Socialist Review*, Issue 227 (February 1999), http://pubs.socialist reviewindex.uk/sr227/hoveman.htm.

17 Engdahl, *A Century of War, op. cit.*, p. 226–27.

18 Hoveman, *op. cit.*

The ensuing slump and deflation suspended Japan's geopolitical aspirations, paving the way for China's emergence as the region's economic and military debutante. And what did America get for its effort to curb Japanese excesses? Briefly the strategy did seem to work. In the late 1980s Japan began to open itself up to higher imports and lower trade surpluses. But these gains quickly disappeared once the bubble broke. Trade surpluses returned with a vengeance in the 1990s.[19] The unequivocal winner in this post-Cold War reshuffling would be China, and that would mean a geopolitical as well as geoeconomic sea change.

Japan, however, was still the world's second richest country and its largest exporter of capital. It continued to play a huge role in global development,[20] and its role in Asia would actually be greater as a result of its domestic woes. This is because its post-bubble banking crisis (some estimates put the bad loans held by Japanese banks as high as $1 trillion) prompted investment in Asia's "tiger" and "tiger cub" economies, where labor costs were low and currencies had the advantage of being pegged to the US dollar. More and more Japanese exports also went to Rim neighbors.

This set Japan up for another fall. The Asian Crisis of 1997–98 threatened to turn prolonged stagnation into full-fledged depression.[21] Meanwhile Japan's integration into an increasingly neoliberal global order produced much social trauma, as evidenced by a rising suicide rate. Nonetheless the general economic malaise has been exaggerated. If the economy had suffered as much as is commonly reported, there would have been more pressure for sweeping political change. The largely cosmetic reforms that were ushered in by Junichiro Koizumi could not have sufficed.

It must be asked why, in stark contrast to China, Japan has tended to underscore its problems and understate its economic might. Likewise it must be asked why Western observers would fall for this subterfuge. The answer to the first question is that Japan's glittering image as "number one" was becoming a liability. Without any Cold War rationale, American tolerance for Japan's export engine was bound to wear thin. As for the second question, neoliberalism's claim to being the only sure path to prosperity inclined the mainstream media to accept Japan's self-inflicted demotion in global standing. The highly regulated and centrally-planned Japan model—which accomplished many of the things that overt fascism had vainly attempted—gave the lie to the incontestable superiority of so-called free markets.[22]

The real issue no longer seemed to be which was a better growth engine, neoliberalism or "Asian values" economism. The salient question had become which Asian economism would take the lead. There is no denying that compared to China's boom, or to Japan's own "miracle" years, the 1990s were lackluster for Japan. The root of the problem, however, was more political than economic. The diffuse power structure that had served Japan so well in masking its authoritarian elitism now prevented it from executing a concerted strategy for economic reform.

---

19 "Japan—International Trade," from *the Encyclopedia of the Nations* (downloaded June 2, 2007).

20 Robert Locke, "Japan, Refutation of Neoliberalism," *Post-Autistic Economic Review*, Issue No. 23 (March 21, 2005), http://www.paecon.net/PAEReview/issue23/Locke23.htm.

21 Hoveman, *op. cit.*

22 Locke, "Japan, Refutation of Neoliberalism," *op. cit.*

Koizumi's predecessor, Yoshiro Mori, epitomized the country's bureaucratic morass, and Koizumi did not depart from him nearly so much as his hair style would suggest. Aside from his "cool biz" look, Koizumi was little more than a paper *henjin* (maverick). The real thing, Ichiro Ozawa, had been expelled from the party long before. Likewise, when Koizumi chose Makiko Tanaka (daughter of the ex-prime minister Kakuei Tanaka) as his foreign affairs minister, it was not so much to chart a new foreign policy as to tap the popular appeal of her acerbic style. Like her boss, she seemed refreshing after the humdrum 1990s. But she lacked experience in world affairs, and will be remembered primarily for her penchant for breaking appointments with top foreign diplomats, including the US Deputy Secretary of State Richard L. Armitage, who at that moment was carrying an urgent message on security strategy from President Bush.[23] While Koizumi himself was less abrasive than Tanaka, he was also less iconoclastic. He rose out of Mori's LDP faction, and stayed within its orbit. For him the word "reform" meant little more than a neoliberal shedding of government social responsibilities.

Ian Buruma suspected from the first that Koizumi was not so much primed to be a Japanese Gorbachev as a Berlusconi.[24] Hope for more egalitarian reform would have to come from outside the LDP network. By 1998, deepening economic crisis had inspired a merger of previously independent parties under the DPJ (Democratic Party of Japan) label. But it was not until 2003, when the DPJ incorporated Ichiro Ozawa's center-right Liberal Party, that it gained enough seats to pose a real threat to the LDP establishment. While this might give Japanese voters a two-party choice,[25] it also diluted DPJ progressivism. The contest would now be between the LDP Right and another Right—that of Ozawa's more ardent remilitarization. Only after his efforts to reunite with the LDP were spurned did Ozawa merge with the DPJ.

This dismal choice was still an improvement over the 1955 system, and the LDP was determined to roll back the clock. It turned to a man who had what it took to look radical without threatening the system nearly so much as Ozawa did. Koizumi convinced the public that he was at odds with the LDP establishment when in fact he was its chosen savior. Though he took office in April 2001 on the promise to break Japan's political deadlock, his real mission was to prevent the kind of substantive reform that had been in the air in the early 1990s. In education, for example, the idea had been to boost Japan's competition within the New World Order by stressing creativity and individualism. After the lost decade, however, more and more parents and politicians blamed "individualism" for an ongoing decline in test scores. To them "creativity" simply meant a lack of discipline.[26] The irony is that to bury

23 Calvin Sims, "Japan Finds Diplomacy Can Turn a But Unruly," *The New York Times* (May 23, 2001), http://www.nytimes.com/2001/05/23/world/23JAPA..html.

24 Ian Buruma, "The Japanese Berlusconi?," *The New York Review of Books*, Vol. 48, No. 12 (July 19, 2001), p. 42 (pp. 42–44).

25 Norimitsu Onishi, "Japan's Voters Have Actual Choice Tomorrow at the Polls," *The New York Times* (November 8, 2003), http://www.nytimes.com/2003/11/08/international/asia/08JPAP.html.

26 Norimitsu Onishi, "Japan's Conservatives Push Prewar 'Virtues' in Schools," *The New York Times* (June 11, 2006), http://www.nytimes.com/2006/06/11/world/asia/11tokyo.html.

substantive creativity the LDP establishment turned to a man who epitomized the creative "look."

In foreign as well as domestic affairs, Koizumi was part of a new reverse course. This Elvis-loving prime minister was walking a political tightrope as the Yoshida Deal entered its sixth decade. To do Washington's bidding he of course would have to affirm Japan's US alliance. It was Washington's paradoxical wish that Tokyo prove its fealty by breaking free of the abject military dependence that had been imposed in 1946 by Article 9. Although Japan had begun rearming in the early 1950s, its Self Defense Forces (SDF) had been too tightly fettered by Article 9 and the Yoshida Deal to allow much geopolitical maneuvering or real political discourse, those being two sides of the same "abnormal" coin. Dissident voices were muzzled on both sides of the political spectrum: left pacifists as well as nationalist reactionaries. Far from being a manifestation of native Japanese values, this bracketing of democratic discourse was a bargain struck between elites on both sides of the Pacific.

The "abnormalization" of Japanese foreign policy had its flip side in an equally truncated domestic politics. Until the 1990s the LDP system had kept its end of the Yoshida bargain: affluence in return for silence. That silence was finally broken when the post-miracle malaise combined with a major scandal to suspend the LDP's thirty-eight year grip on power. Meanwhile the Gulf War put a spotlight on the dysfunctional side of the whole econo-state concept. The Japan Renewal Party temporarily took the helm in the early 1990s, but cracks soon began to form in its ruling coalition. The 1955 system was back on track by 1996, after the Japan Socialist Party showed its true colors by cutting a deal with the LDP.

The only lasting benefit from this oppositional interlude was the electoral reforms of 1994, but neither they nor Koizumi's later revisionism would do much to remedy the political inertia that has been the bedrock of the Japan model. Indeed, it is arguable that Koizumi's success in renovating the political décor of the LDP constituted a democratic setback by giving one-party rule a new lease on life. His landslide victory in the snap election of September 2005 gave him a mandate to refreeze the system, putting the DPJ out to pasture. As Brad Glosserman wryly put it, Japan was going boldly backwards.[27]

The Japan That Still Says Yes

Two opposite forces propelled Japan's foreign relations under Koizumi. After the very unmiraculous 1990s, more and more Japanese shifted their focus to the simple enjoyment of life. Many began to look back on the feudal past as a time of enviable stability in contrast to a capitalism where "all that is solid melts into air." This reversion could take two antithetical forms: the apotheosis of *nihonjinron* (the innate superiority of all things Japanese), much like the ethos celebrated in *The Last Samurai*, or a more pastoral, flower-child-like retreatism.

---

27 Robert Marquand, "Koizumi's Revolution Gains Momentum," *The Christian Science Monitor* (September 29, 2005), http://www.csmonitor.com/2005/0929/p01s02-woap.html.

In the latter case, the reigning cultural icon would no longer be the salaryman, but rather the "freeter," a youth who is content to take odd jobs to sustain an easy lifestyle.[28] Where international commitments are concerned, the "freeter" attitude discourages international commitments. This collides, however, with rising defense imperatives in East Asia. While the Chinese threat looms larger in the long run, North Korea takes center stage in terms of sheer bluster. Either one, however, is enough to give policy-minded Japanese second thoughts about Article 9.

Koizumi had little choice but to return nationalism to mainstream Japanese politics. His inflammatory visits to the Yasukuni war shrine, which did so much to antagonize China and South Korea, were mere window dressing. A more substantive *nihonism* was broached in December 2001 when the Japanese navy trailed a suspicious "fishing" vessel bearing Chinese markings out of Japanese territory and deep into Chinese waters. When the boat opened fire, Japanese naval vessels returned fire and sank it, killing all its crew. This was the first time Japan had sunk a foreign ship since World War II, and Japan watchers took note of the fact that such an action would have been unthinkable ten years before.[29]

This "Chinese" boat turned out to be a North Korean spy ship, and the next year North Korea gave Japan a much greater jolt by announcing its intention to develop nuclear weapons. Early in 2003 Tokyo reciprocated by threatening a preemptive strike, and added that it might also develop its own nuclear weapons.[30] The then Deputy Chief Cabinet Secretary Shinzo Abe put himself on the short list for Koizumi's successor by announcing that it would not be unconstitutional for Japan to use tactical nuclear weapons if need be. Just two years before Japan's No. 2 defense chief had been fired for simply mentioning nuclear weapons.[31] Since the 2001 incident, the Japanese navy has fired on other North Korean ships, and has confronted Chinese naval vessels in a conflict over oil reserves in the East China Sea.[32] Only the far Right would have advocated such behavior in the past. The shifting public attitude is suggested by the curious spectator cult that arose as 10,000 Japanese a day went to ogle at the salvaged North Korean spy ship.[33]

Notwithstanding these rumblings, most analysts still view China and Russia as the big players in Asia's emerging "great game," giving Japan little more than honorable mention. Japan did gain some regional standing in zero-sum terms when a newly elected President Bush took a relatively tough stance toward China, but 9/11 changed that in a flash. And Russia was never put under much scrutiny. Early in his administration Bush lavished praise on Putin and refused to be distracted by local

---

28 Norimitsu Onishi, "This 21st-Century Japan, More Contented Than Driven," *The New York Times* (February 4, 2004), http://www.nytimes.com/2004/02/04/international/asia/04LETT.html.

29 Eugene A. Matthews, "Japan's New Nationalism," *Foreign Affairs*, Vol. 82, No. 6 (November/December 2003), p. 74 (pp. 74–90).

30 *Ibid.*, p. 75.

31 Robert Marquand, "Pacifist Japan Beefs up Military," *The Christian Science Monitor* (August 15, 2003), http://www.csmonitor.com/2003/0815/p06s02-woap.html.

32 "Japan's Leap to be a 'Normal' Nation," *The Christian Science Monitor* (September 13, 2005), p. 8.

33 Marquand, "Pacifist Japan Beefs up Military," *op. cit.*

events such as the Chechen Holocaust. The same president who famously screamed "evil" whenever he encountered global friction was in this case determined to "see no evil." This ghastly indifference was reinforced by the President's ever-expanding "war on terrorism," which ironically moved him closer to many of the world's worst state terrorists.

Had Russia and the US continued their romance, Japan could have been pushed even further off the geopolitical map.[34] But Putin's growing animosity, plus the geopolitical bonding of China and Russia within the Shanghai Cooperation Organization (SCO), forced a tacit reassessment in Washington. For once America and Europe were moving in the same direction. Even France came on board this time, as Chirac's pro-Russia tilt was replaced in 2007 with the unabashed pro-Americanism of Nicolas Sarkozy. These tectonic shifts put Japan closer to the epicenter of Asian power politics.

Along with Russia's rogue-state assertiveness, China's rise challenges Japan as nothing has since World War II. Beijing used Koizumi's visits to the Yasukini Shrine as an excuse for rejecting Tokyo's repeated invitations for high level talks. But the real issue was geoeconomic competition. Deng-era terms of endearment no longer applied. Japan had been giving Official Development Assistance (O.D.A.) to China since its opening in 1979, a time when China was a net oil exporter. Buying from China was a way of reducing Middle East energy dependence. Now, however, China has become a major oil importer and Japan has been reducing its O.D.A.[35]

During Japan's miracle years and before China's rise, it was easy for radical nationalists like Shintaro Ishihara—the testy author of *The Japan that Can Say No* (1989) and later the governor of Tokyo (reelected in 2007)—to broadcast a double-barreled strategy for Japanese supremacy. Ishihara stood ready to confront Washington and Beijing alike in the name of a Japan that dared to stand alone. But after the deflated '90s, and under the shadow of a fully awakened Chinese dragon, few Japanese could muster such hubris. Ishihara, however, has not budged an inch. He sees the overheated Chinese economy as a disaster waiting to happen, and still considers Japan the real sleeping dragon. His case for Japanese re-militarization is based as much on America's relative decline as on China's putative clout. In his view the US is not the reliable guardian it once was.[36]

Either way—whether because China is a greater danger or because America is a lesser protector—the case for Japan's "normalization" is now front and center. For this task the next prime minister, Shinzo Abe, came ill prepared, having had little foreign affairs experience. What swung the public behind him was his tough rhetoric concerning North Korea's ballistic missile tests early in 2006.[37] He followed

---

34 Howard W. French," Setting Sun? Japan Anxiously Looks Ahead," *The New York Times* (August 11, 2002), http://www.nytimes.com/2002/08/11weekinreview/11FREN.html.

35 Adam Wolfe, "The Potential Deterioration of Sino-Japanese Relations," *PINR: The Power and Interest News Report* (December 6, 2006), http://www.pinr.com.

36 Shintaro Ishihara, "Japanese Passivity," *Foreign Policy* (September/October 2005), http://www.foreignpolicy.com/story/cms.php?story_id=3164&print=1.

37 Chris Hogg, "Japan's Political 'Blue Blood,'" *BBC News* (September 26, 2006), http://news.bbc.co.uk. go/pr/fr/-/2/hi/asia-pacific/5362392.stm.

in Koizumi's footsteps—not to mention his grandfather's—by raising the Japan Defense Agency to ministry status and announcing plans to revamp its whole concept of security. Japanese and US interests are so tightly intertwined that both sides see Article 9 as redundant and obstructive. The key point is that a remilitarized Japan will still say "yes" to America.

It has little choice, given its regional situation. Abe's staff made it clear that Japan was ready to play "a huge great game" in resource competition with China and Russia; and in January 2007, while visiting Europe, Abe drove home the point that under him Japan would be a steadfast partner on NATO's Eastern flank. So too he sought closer security ties with democratic India and Australia. Accordingly he spoke of an "arc of freedom and prosperity" extending from Japan through India and into Europe.[38]

Abe recognized that the global competition is dividing between camps of development with and without freedom. The question was which side Japan would take. For years Abe himself had supported nationalist propagandists who pushed for revising textbooks to deemphasize Japan's wartime horrors,[39] and later he drew fierce criticism from South Korea by questioning the degree of coercion that was used in recruiting "comfort women" for Japan's wartime brothels.[40] Given his grandfather's record, he had a stake in this national amnesia, which is akin to European Holocaust denial. But none of that concerned Washington, since Abe had no problem reconciling radical nationalism with a sweeping affirmation of America's strategic vision.

Koizumi set the stage for this Yoshida II hybrid with the December 2003 creation of the US-Japanese Security Consultative Committee. Its "2 plus 2" meetings (involving US secretaries of state and defense and their Japanese counterparts) have moved the security alliance beyond Cold War asymmetry, whereby Japan served as a passive "shield" for America's Asian "spear." A common liberal argument for keeping Article 9 is that it helps Japan resist pressure to join America's infamous "coalitions of the willing."[41] However, by sending Japanese support forces to Iraq, Koizumi had already broken that taboo. Japan was now more of a spear carrier. All that remained was to give its participation some real teeth. That would mean a Japan that can and will say "yes," but as a full-fledged spear thrower.

------

38 "Abe Blows Japan's Trumpet, Cautiously," *The Economist* (May 3, 2007), http:// economist.com/world/asia/PrinterFriendly.cfm?story_id=9116791. Clearly this ran against the grain of elitist Japan's perennial resistance to Western norms. It hardly needs to be said that Abe's personal concern for freedom was purely instrumental. By family tradition his position on any issue was for hire. Like his grandfather he stood in a long line of "Choshu men," who have a reputation for doing anything for profit. It was the Choshu clan that first fired on foreign ships passing through the Shimonoseki Strait at the entrance of the Inland Sea. But seeing the military might of these invaders, Choshu leaders "reversed course" and fraternized with them unabashedly. See "Bonus to be Wisely Spent," *op. cit.*

39 Norimitsu Onishi, "Japan's Likely Next Premier in Hawkish Stand," *The New York Times* (September 2, 2006), http://www.nytimes.com/2006/09/02/world/asia/02japan.html.

40 "Abe: Japan Won't Apologize Again for WW2 Sex Slaves," *Chinadaily* (March 5, 2007), http://www.chinadaily.com/world/2007-03/05/content_819776.htm.

41 Joseph S. Nye, "The Rise of Liberal Japan," *The Chosun Ilbo* (updated June 15, 2007), http://english.chosum.com/cgi-bin/printNews?id=200706150010.

Nihonism Goes Global

The payoff for this transformation could be enormous. First, Japan's offer of $5 billion and 2,000 peacekeeping troops in support of the Iraq occupation bought it cover for a currency policy that was sure to dent US exports. The tactic worked: the Bush administration fell silent on the whole issue.[42] Second, part of Japan's geopolitical normalization is the likely lifting of its self-imposed ban on arms sales. That restriction—invoked by Prime Minister Takeo Miki in 1976—[43]made Japan's arms production extremely costly in per unit terms. However, this and other normalization measures carry the risk of unnerving Asian neighbors. Such "2 plus 2" logic can therefore equal "5," by de-stabilizing rather than balancing the Rim. And in the case of arms sales, there is a further domestic risk: since this military-industrial upgrade requires no constitutional revision, it could be slipped through without much democratic input.

Beneath the surface of "2 plus 2" parity, Japan is fully aware that it cannot afford to say "no" on any issue that Washington deems vital to its interests. A repressed need to say "no" to *something* may account for Japan's opprobrious practice of whaling. Essentially this is an emotional escape mechanism that lets Japan say "no" without major repercussions. So long as the international community is not prepared to spill geopolitical capital over whales, Japan can have its whale meat and its "normality" also.

Nonetheless there is a hidden price to pay for this atavistic indulgence, and for the sake of the whales one hopes Japan's elite will get the point. As a *New York Times* editorial put it, the protection of whales is "one small, bright spot of global consensus ..."[44] Stepping outside that ethical boundary will label Japan a pariah nation at heart. If it is utterly untrustworthy on this rare common ground of international decency, its reliability on other issues will be thrown into doubt. The moral high ground that Japan seeks by supporting the Kyoto Protocol (as of 2002) and by encircling China and Russia with a professed arc of democracy is sacrificed with every whale it kills.[45]

The most pressing issue of normalization, however, is undoubtedly the repeal or substantial rewrite of Article 9. The critical question is whether this will be accomplished through democratic or semi-authoritarian means. Under Abe serious

---

42 Alexandra Starr, "Beware a more Muscular Japan," *The Christian Science Monitor* (October 30, 2003), http://www.csmonitor.com/2003/1030/p09s02-coop.html.

43 Dan Blumenthal and Chris Griffin, "Japan: A Liberal, Nationalist Defense Transformation," *AEI: American Enterprise Institute* (November 17, 2005), http://www.aei. org/include/pub_print.asp?pubID =23464.

44 "Japan's Whaling Obsession," *The New York Times* (April 1, 2007), http://www. nytimes.com/2007/04/01/opinion/01sun2.html.

45 The truth is that few Japanese even like whale meat. Its everyday consumption in the early postwar era was strictly due to its low cost. The practice came to be associated with the pre-miracle era when the label "made-in-Japan" was synonymous with cheap, mediocre exports. As the nation's economy burgeoned, its whale-eating habit declined, and died away almost completely after the 1960s. The government's reembrace of this ersatz tradition is a moral outrage that reveals as much about Japan's political climate as the Gulf War did about its geopolitical "abnormality."

debate on the matter has been discouraged,[46] which was probably unnecessary, since some polls showed a large majority of Japanese in favor of revising Article 9.[47] Abe's reactionary tilt fits a pattern: the rising current of Japanese thought—capsulated in Masahiko Fujiwara's bestselling novel of 2005, *The Dignity of a State*—that denies the value of Western-style democracy for Japan and Asia in general. Fujiwara wants to restore Japan's ebbing social capital by way of *samurai* "deep emotion" and a de-emphasis on Western reason.

This militant *nihonism* is obviously not the way of the "freeter," and will not get rave reviews from neighboring Asian countries. They too well remember Japan's last attempt to de-Westernize the region, by way of conquest.[48] Yet in Japan, as Fukuyama observes, there is a thriving market for right-wing fantasies about Japan's "liberation" of Asia. Watanabe Soichi, a collaborator of Shintaro Ishihara, draws large audiences to hear him relate how grateful Japan's wartime neighbors were for being included in the Greater East Asia Co-Prosperity Sphere. Manchurians, he declares, wept when the Japanese pulled out.[49]

While the new LDP brought *nihonism* in from the cold, Western media took little interest. They remained as oblivious to this unsavory side of Koizumi's administration as they had been to the dark side of Yeltsin's. They cheered his weakening of traditional factions within the party, overlooking the fact that for decades those intra-LDP divisions were the closest thing Japan had to effective political opposition.[50] It remains to be seen if Koizumi's successors can match his democratic machinations. Just as Grandfather Kishi went too far in exposing his real agenda, Abe consistently mangled his image politics. Managed consent requires a better cover. In 2004 Koizumi had faced a major pension scandal, but was able to extricate himself by posing as an anti-establishment revolutionary.[51] In 2007, in the throes of yet another pension scandal, Abe came across as a business-as-usual LDPer.[52]

---

46 The West is so glad to see Article 9 up for revision that it has underreported the manner in which this is being pursued. At Abe's behest, the Japanese parliament passed a bill mandating a referendum on the issue, but it also took steps to manage the outcome. It banned political advertising on TV and radio for two weeks prior to the vote, silenced school teachers on the issue, and required no minimum turnout, so that passivity would work in favor of the amendment. See Bruce Ackerman and Norikazu Kawagishi, "Japan's Revolution is Far Too Quiet," *Foreign Policy* (May 2007), http://www. foreignpolicy.com/story/cms. php?story_id=3844&print=1.

47 Blumenthal and Griffin, *op. cit.* However, it should be noted that different polls on the subject report widely divergent results, depending on the wording of the questions.

48 Harold James, "The Return of 'Asian' Values," *Project Syndicate* (May 2007), http://www.project-syndicate.org/commentary/james13.

49 Francis Fukuyama, "The Trouble with Japanese Nationalism," *Project Syndicate* (March 2007), http://www.project-syndicate.org/print_commentary/fukuyama2/English.

50 See Shin'ichi Kitaoka, "Japan's Dysfunctional Democracy," *Asia Program Special Report* from Woodrow Wilson International Center for Scholars, No. 117 (January 2004), pp. 6–8.

51 "Japan's Politics," *The Economist* (June 14, 2007), http://www.economist.com/agenda/PrinterFriendly. cfm?story_id=9340418.

52 This followed in the wake of a lurid agricultural scandal that led to the suicide of Japan's Farm Minister. He did his boss no favor by leaving behind a suicide note saying "*Banzai* [long

In just three weeks in May and June 2007 Abe's ratings fell 17 percent, to a disconcerting 32.9. This was fast approaching the critical 30 percent line where a normally diffident Japanese press tends to go on the offensive.[53] In an effort to ensure LDP consensus on postal reform, Koizumi had expelled dissenting politicians from the party. Abe let them back in, thus advertising himself as a faithful LDP functionary.[54] Even the US trade representative Susan Schwab, a neoliberal who would be expected to applaud the privatization of Japan Post, openly lambasted the projects' lack of transparency.[55] This shady operation was conceived and executed by Koizumi, yet Abe took the heat. The good news was that his political bungling re-opened the door for opposition politics. After the LDP lost the upper house in the July 2007 elections, Abe was at risk of being remembered as the prime minister who won the game for the opposing team.

This brought the country close to the point Richard Katz had predicted in a 2003 *Foreign Affairs* article. Katz sounded a long overdue death knell for the LDP. In his view Japan's protracted economic debility was first and foremost a crisis of governance.[56] He could be optimistic about the country's economic prospect only because he saw no hope for continued LDP hegemony: "Just as the Soviet Communist Party could not be the vehicle of reform, even with Mikhail Gorbachev at its head, neither can the LDP."[57] But Koizumi faired much better than Katz expected. By tying *nihonism* to the new forces of globalization, he unleashed a new Japan model on the 21st century.

It would be bad news for Japan and the whole region if this model were to void Katz's prediction by giving the presently constituted LDP a new lease on life. There are other possibilities, however. The Democrats' triumph in the elections for the Upper House thrust Ichiro Ozawa back into the limelight after years in the political wilderness. His resurgent power is such that Abe's stated reason for resigning was that Ozawa refused to meet him. Once again, as in 1993, Ozawa is pulling strings behind the scene to end the LDP system.

How this could affect relations with the US remains to be seen. For PR purposes Ozawa made a great show of renouncing Japan's anti-terrorism law, which was imposed as a diplomatic sop for the Americans. Ozawa's obvious intention was to

---

life] to Prime Minister Abe." See "Minister Says 'Banzai' to Japan, Abe in Suicide Note," *The Hindu* (May 31, 2007), http://www.hindu.com/thehindu/holnus/003200705310341.htm.

53 A Jiji Press poll taken in mid-June 2007 put support for Abe's government at 28.8. See "Support for Japan's Abe Plunges Below 30 Percent," *The Nation* (June 15, 2007), http://nationalmultimedia.com/option/print.php?newsid=30036957.

54 Jason Miks, "Despite Some Foreign Policy Success, Japan's Abe Faces Problems at Home," *World Politics Review* (June 14, 2007), http://www.worldpoliticsreview.com/article.aspx?id=849.

55 "US Calls for More Transparency in Japan's Postal Privatisation," *The Financial Express*, No. DA 1589 (June 8, 2007), http://www.financialexpress-bd.com/index3.asp?cnd=6/8/2007&section_id=22&newsid =6...

56 Richard Katz, "Japan's Phoenix Economy," *Foreign Affairs*, Vol. 82, No. 1 (January/February 2003), p.116 (pp. 114–28).

57 *Ibid.*, p. 118.

cast the LDP as Washington's puppet party.[58] But at a time when China and Russia are laying claim to geopolitical primacy at Japan's doorstep, it is doubtful that the DPJ will want to distance itself from the US. Abe's resignation lent hope to those seeking a democratic transformation, though (with Fujiwara in mind) the key question is what direction this will take. The lesson of Kishi's fall should not be forgotten: what looked like a democratic milestone turned out to be a triumph of the Right. Likewise, the choice of LDP stalwart Yasuo Fukuda as prime minister looks like an improvement over Abe, but in the face of Japan's reactionary turn, Fukuda's very moderation indicates that he will do little or nothing to buck the trend.

The mounting storm clouds are well exemplified by the new wave of textbook revisions that has inflamed Chinese and Koreans and now is roiling Okinawans. Near the end of World War II, as America launched its invasion of Okinawa, Japanese soldiers forced the island's natives from shelters and effectively used them as human shields. Moreover, they convinced them that suicide would be preferable to the fate awaiting them under the Americans. Thousands killed themselves, and many killed their own mothers and siblings as delusive acts of mercy. For decades these horrid facts were at least fleetingly mentioned in Japanese school books, but now, in the name of a new patriotism, they are being airbrushed out of history.[59]

Meanwhile, on similar patriotic grounds, Japan's Defense Agency is being upgraded to full ministry status. With Japan reasserting itself militarily and geopolitically, it matters more than ever what kind of country this is. As did other Rim nations after the Asian Crash, Japan is reviving its economy at the expense of political reform. All that remains, in order to complete a Marxian passage from tragedy to farce, is for the new Japan model to be declared a democratic success story. What it actually represents is a new reverse course.

This applies to foreign as well as domestic affairs. In place of Abe's Eurasian "arc of freedom," Yasuo Fukuda is reviving the coldly pragmatic "Fukuda Doctrine" set forth by his father Takeo Fukuda (prime minister from December 1976 to December 1978).[60] Whatever position Japan may take with regard to China's Asian hegemony,[61] the Fududa Doctrine will pose no ideological challenge to Sino-globalization. Both growth principles are recipes for development without freedom.

---

58 Wieland Wagner, "Japan's New Strongman: Opposition Leader Ozawa Eyes Power in Tokyo," *Spiegel Online* (September 17, 2007), http://www.spiegel.de/international/world/0,1518,506152.00.html.

59 Normititsu Onishi, "Okinawans Protest Japan's Plan to Revise Bitter Chapter of World War II," *The New York Times* (October 7, 2007), http://www.nytimes.com/2007/10/07/world/asia/07okinawa.html.

60 "The Return of the Fukuda Doctrine," *The Economist* (December 13, 2007), http://www.economist.com/world/asia/PrinterFriendly.cfm?story_id=10286958.

61 It is hardly a secret that Japan's plan to install a missile defense shield and to equip its warships with similar anti-ballistic capabilities is not inspired by North Korea alone.

Chapter 10

After the New World Order: The Rise of Second Way Globalization

Second Way Redux

In his infamous Munich speech of February 10, 2007, Russian President Vladimir Putin effectively took Russia out of the New World Order. If this was not quite a declaration of renewed Cold War,[1] it at least made official the cold peace that Putin had crafted out of Russia's post-Soviet wreckage. The end of the old Cold War could no longer be viewed as the full or even partial eclipse of Second World ways and means. There was to be no instant-mix global harmony. It finally had to be recognized that Putin's increasingly bellicose nationalism was a world class problem.

If geopolitics had never been entirely expelled from the First World's "end of history" teleology (NATO's eastward expansion testified to that), the chosen mechanism for post-Cold War relations had been commercial engagement. Now, after Munich, a balance would have to be struck between geoeconomic and geopolitical priorities. Once more power politics was front and center. This was much to the relief of Europe's less secure regions, such as the Baltics,[2] which abut Russia and well know that trade deals are no substitute for tangible security measures. The Mars/Venus dichotomy that Robert Kagan drew between America and Europe had also divided Europe's newcomers from its Old Guard. The Munich speech gave "Old Europe" a badly needed refresher course on geopolitical realities, pushing the two Europes together while moving both closer to America. NATO, accordingly, got a new lease on life.

True as the world harmony myth might have been in terms of Russia's openness to global capital, no such transition was possible where governance was concerned. Soviet communism had been as much a means of social order as a mode of production, and its premise was the elimination of competing values and institutions. Russia and much of the ex-Soviet sphere had accomplished that feat so well that they now faced the dark choice between anarchy and hyper-statism. As in China, the erasure of competing social structures ensured that, with or without "communism," some form of authoritarianism would be necessary for the foreseeable future.

---

1 While insisting that there was "no confrontational bias" on Russia's part, and "no talk of any kind of a new Cold War," Foreign Minister Sergei Lavrov adumbrated Russia's intentions to counter Washington's global power with its own. See "Lavrov Criticizes U.S. Unilateralism," *The Moscow Times* (March 19, 2007), p. 3.

2 See "A Cool Peace," *The Economist* (March 1, 2007), http://www.economist.com/world/europe/PrinterFriendly.cfm?story_id=8775610.

Boris Yeltsin, accordingly, did his best to impose a new Kremlinism even as he rammed through capitalist privatization. As in post-Tiananmen China, the West chose to register only the economic side of this coin. Yeltsin's authoritarian halfway house fell so far short of Russia's authoritarian need that the public would thereafter welcome any leader who could restore social stability and a modicum of economic hope. The argument can be made, paradoxically, that some of the most geopolitically ominous policies to come out of Russia under Yeltsin—such as the invasion of Chechnya and the almost indiscriminate arms sales to China—were the result of inadequate Kremlinization.[3] Putin came prepared to finish the job, removing any ambiguity as to Russia's neo-authoritarian drift.

The looming chaos that invited Putinism in Russia haunted most of the former Soviet empire, and was greater where ethnic conflict was a factor. In Yugoslavia, for example, the collapse of "communist" cohesion released centrifugal forces that Tito himself would have found daunting. When it became clear that national unity would redound to Serbian supremacy, Slovenian and Croatian declarations of independence were sure to follow. These in turn pushed Bosnian Muslims in the same direction, since life under a rump Yugoslavia dominated by Serbs was unthinkable. The mere mention of the names Slobodan Milosovic, Radovan Karadzic, and Ratko Mladic reminds us what little choice there was.

Even Milosevic, however, paled in comparison with some of his authoritarian counterparts in Central Asia. In Turkmenistan, for instance, the ex-Soviet puppet Saparmurat Niyazov (aka Turkmenbashi, or leader of all Turkmen) cast himself as a virtual God. By official edict his book, the *Ruhnama* (book of the soul) had to be regarded on a par with the Koran. A grand Mufti who disagreed was still in prison when Niyazov died in December 2006. So were countless others who publicly questioned any part of the official creed. We can never know how many, like the Radio Liberty journalist Ogulsapar Muradov, were tortured to death in prison.

Niyazov's chosen successor, Berdymukhamedov, the former commander-in-chief of the armed forces, is not going to make human rights reform a top priority. Nonetheless opinion polls will confirm that almost everyone is "happy" here, and of course there is no hunger in Turkmenistan, for to say otherwise would be suicidal. Meanwhile foreign nations will court any leader who gives them a ticket to Turkmenistan's massive gas reserves.[4]

Suffice it to say that the Second Way—the domestic and foreign policy orientation of the erstwhile Second World—more than survived the Soviet fall. Outrage against this fact (along with munificent financial assistance from the West via oil-fueled NGOs) helped to inspire the series of "democratic" insurgencies that began with the Serbian revolt of 2000 and culminated in a spate of "color revolutions": Georgia's Rose Revolution of 2003, Ukraine's Orange Revolution of 2004, and Kyrgyzstan's Tulip Revolution of 2005. Together these uprisings raised hopes of a renewed democratic "Third Wave."

---

3 See Stephen J. Blank, "The Dynamics of Russian Weapon Sales to China," Strategic Studies Institute of the US Army War College (March 4, 1997).

4 "Turkmenistan still in Shadow," *Guardian Weekly* (downloaded March 18, 2007), http://www.guardian. co.uk/guardianweekly/stroy/0,,2029219,00.html.

The region's autocrats had less to fear than they imagined. Much as Russia's Yeltsin was forced to turn on his own parliament to secure his reforms, so too Ukraine's President Yushchenko found it necessary to dissolve parliament when anti-reform opposition grew too powerful. The country's "blue flag" anti-reformists, unlike Russia's pro-democratic opposition, command a sizable and growing following in free elections. The paradox is that to suppress these anti-democrats is itself an anti-democratic action.[5] The ex-Soviet world cannot seem to escape this authoritarian Catch-22.

Beijing, however, is taking no chances. For it the Kyrgyz rising was one revolution too many, and too close. President Hu Jintao issued a report titled "Fighting the People's War without Gunsmoke," which outlined the Party's strategy for preventing similar insurrections within Chinese borders. Bulletin boards would be closed or tightly regulated and websites forced to register. But the main thrust of Hu's *neijin waisong* (tight inside with lax looking outside) formula has been aimed at NGOs, which Beijing regards (not without some justification) as Washington's "black hands." All prominent NGO activities would be frozen, while high profile groups like the Empowerment and Rights Institute (supported by America's National Endowment for Democracy) have been subjected to police investigations and raids.[6] China packaged this crackdown as anti-terrorism, the same label Russia would apply to its unrelenting state terrorism in Chechnya. In both cases the Western press took the bait, giving minimal attention to either horror story.

It is now painfully obvious that the Cold War victory of the West was not nearly so definitive as neoliberal pundits once imagined. It turns out that the First World had been heavily dependent on the Second for its moral and political bearings. Minus its bipolar sparring partner, America no longer felt much need for the soft power tactics that once put a good face on First World hegemony. Post-Cold War globalization became so relentless in its quest for cheap labor that not even the state terrorism of Tiananmen could hamper the process. Raw capitalist economism now stood unrivaled on the global stage.

Nevertheless, even in the glory days of the American New Economy, more astute neoliberals recognized the need for a "Third Way" repair kit to reduce class tensions at home and restore soft power abroad. Unfortunately this was a case of too little too late. Whereas the Cold War non-aligned movement had afforded a Third Way for the Third World, Clinton and Blair offered at best a Third Way for the First World. Their neoliberal development formula was fast losing credibility in the global South. By hollowing out democracy and converting "development" into an engine for profits over people, First World intransigence paved the way for Second World resurgence.

---

5 See Anne Applebaum, "A Tale of Two Cities," *Slate* (April 17, 2007), http://www.slate. com/toolbar.apx?action=print&id 2164333.

6 Yongding (pseudonym), "China's Color-Coded Crackdown," *Yale Global Online* (October 18, 2005), http://yaleglobal.yale.edu/article.print?id=6376.

Global Race to the Bottom

For a quarter of a century neoliberalism has been in the business of keeping up appearances, assuring us constantly that a new era of global cooperation and prosperity is right around the corner. The World Bank trumpets the "spectacular" record of Third World growth, hardly mentioning that the Bank's data are focused mainly on the export-driven gains of China, East Asia and neoliberalized India, *sans* Africa.[7] Nor is it mentioned that the trade imbalances of these export engines are globally unsustainable, to say nothing of their social and ecological ravages.[8] Chinese exports, which will exceed $1 trillion in 2007, depend on a rigged currency and Western markets willing and able to buy 25 percent more per year with little reciprocity, and no MFN (most favored nation) reform requirements. Meanwhile a major banking crisis looms, while corruption, inequality and pollution soar at an even faster rate than the country's vaunted GDP.

The pressing question is when this second "Asian miracle" will collapse, or politically explode. Inside China and India national averages mask grating economic disparities. Three fourths of rural Chinese have seen their already meager incomes fall after the PRC joined the WTO in 2001.[9] Each year in China millions flee the famished countryside for industrial jobs that often pay as little as a few cents per hour. Of the nation's 760 million workforce, 200 million are migrant peasants willing to accept work on almost any terms. Less fortunate migrants remain unemployed, creating the vast army of surplus workers that is now estimated at 175 million in China and 100 million in India.[10] India's growth— 6 percent annually over the last ten years, and 8 percent for the last three—is even more skewed than China's, in that it aims to create a "knowledge superpower" without delay, skipping the slow process of industrial development that might provide jobs for uprooted agricultural workers.

In both cases it is the misery of the countryside that props up national competitiveness by keeping urban wages "down on the farm," so to speak. Increasingly India looks to China rather than the West as its developmental icon, and dreams of joining the two systems (India's high tech and China's basic manufacturing) in a

---

7 Concerning the World Bank's report, see Ashley Seager, "World Poverty is in Retreat: Africa Left behind in Economic Progress," *The Guardian* (November 17, 2004), http://www.guardian.co.uk/print/0,3858, 5064579-103676,00.html.

8 Will Hutton, "Does the Future Really Belong to China?," *Prospect Magazine*, Issue 130 (January 2007, http://www.prospect-magazine.co.uk/printarticle.php?id=8174.

9 Joshua Kurlantzick, "Fragile China," *Democracy: A Journal of Ideas*, Issue No. 3 (winter 2007), http://www.democracyjournal.org/article.php?ID=6503.

10 Gabor Steingart, "Putting Profits Before Human Lives," *Spiegel Online* (October 18, 2006), http://www.spiegel.de/international/0,1518,druck-442552,00.html. Even the World Bank must admit that the spreading income gap between skilled and unskilled workers is fueling inequality within and between countries. See François Bourguignon, "Prognosis on Globalization: The Poor will get Richer," *NPQ (New Perspectives Quarterly)*, Vol. 23, No. 4 (Fall 2006), http://www.digitalnpq.org/articles/economic/141/12-21-2006/françois_ bourguignon.

single "Chindia" economic sphere.[11] The China model also joins two of the most revolutionary forces of modern times: the "creative destruction" of Schumpeterian capitalism and the "permanent revolution" of Maoist statism. This Sino-globalist merger is even more socially disruptive than the neoliberal restructuration of Third World countries in the 1980s and 1990s.

What neoliberalism shares with Asian statism is the kind of radical economism that Keynesian economics had presumably expunged. In fact it was merely suspended, even in the First World. That is why some features of Marxism are more relevant today than ever. Cutthroat economism now wears the label of globalization, which is the real culprit behind many problems that go by other names. In India, for example, much ethnic and sectarian violence has its source in the "jobless growth" of globalist restructuring. This dubious "development" is marked by a decline in employment elasticity (the employment increase that accompanies each unit of GDP increase). While the public sector has been downsizing, private sector investment has been so capital intensive and regionally imbalanced that employment elasticity in agriculture has fallen nearly to zero. Meanwhile the rural cost of living has soared. The result is massive distress migration, both rural-to-urban and rural-to-rural. The latter is especially conducive to violence, as limited jobs go to migrants who tend to be more tractable and willing to work for far less,[12] stirring volcanic resentment among displaced locals.

In cities and the countryside alike this process fosters an unmitigated "race to the bottom" among unskilled and semi-skilled laborers. With intermediate rungs of the social ladder knocked out, the notion that globalization offers most workers a ticket into middle class affluence is a sheer myth. Developing countries throughout the world must drastically cut wages, job security, and benefits, thereby blocking upward mobility for the working classes. That of course is the very opposite of what neoliberal "trickle down" theory promised. The World Bank therefore shifts the focus of its optimism to the distant future, predicting that by 2030 the number of people subsisting on $1 per day will drop by half, from 1.1 billion to 550 million.[13]

Globalization on these terms has well served the 20 percent of the world's population that holds 85 percent of global wealth.[14] In America and Japan it serves the middle classes less and less. Clyde Prestowitz paints a grim picture of the coming "Chindian" turn of globalization as high tech services go East, allowing Chindia to excel at both high and low end productions. It is now clear that "trickle down" will have to be put on indefinite hold, cutting off the exit door for the 1.4 billion people, or half the world's workers, who earn less than $2 a day. Meanwhile, according to

---

11 "The Myth of Chindia," *The Economist* (November 22, 2006), http://www.economist. com/daily/columns/asiaview/PrinterFriendly.cfm?story_id=8311987.

12 Swati Narayan, "Unemployment and Migration," *India Together* (March 2004), http:// www. indiatogether.org/2004/mar/eco-migration.htm.

13 Bourguignon, *op. cit.*

14 Asoka Bandarage, "Beyond Globalization and Ethno-religious Fundamentalism," *Development*, Vol. 47, No. 1 (2004), p. 35 (pp. 35 41); and Clyde Prestowitz, "Chindia Changes the Game," *Comparative Advantage* (December 8, 2005), http://www.econstart.org/ blog/?p=32.

Oxfam International, the aid provided by rich nations is half what it was in 1960.[15] Even inside developed countries there has been a frontal assault on welfare benefits. This is happening at a time when working class incomes are stagnant at best, and real job security is a thing of the past.[16]

In all these respects the lower classes of the global North and South have begun to share a common predicament. The trick is getting them to see it. This startling convergence gained recognition at the activist level during the 1999 Seattle protests, after which globalist institutions scrambled to improve their public relations on both sides of the South/North divide. This tacit admission that the system needed a major overhaul was absent just two years before, at the time of the Asian Crash. Apart from a few voices in the wilderness, the blame for this very unnatural disaster was laid squarely on the Asians themselves, with most of the punishment laid on workers who had nothing to do with the bad decisions that triggered the Crash.

Only gradually was it admitted by a small number of global technocrats that systemic reform was imperative—e.g., the free flow of short-term financial capital must be curtailed, and displaced workers must be given prompt and sustained assistance.[17] This minority opinion gained credibility as it dawned on the power elite that their hegemony was in jeopardy if they did not show some "Third Way" concern for underprivileged classes. By the time of the Cancún WTO meeting of 2003 there was broad agreement that affluent countries must stop subsidizing their farm products and elemental manufactures such as textiles and clothing. Unless First World markets are opened to agricultural imports from developing nations,[18] globalization will remain just another name for economic imperialism.

Despite his dependence on First World funding, former UN Secretary General Kofi Annan joined the ranks of the alterglobalists at Cancún. As he put it, "We are told that free trade brings opportunity for all people, not just a few. ... Sadly, the reality of the international trading system today doesn't match the rhetoric. ... Instead of fair competition, there are subsidies by rich countries that tilt the playing field against the poor."[19] In another speech Annan went even further, voicing doubts not only about First Way TINAism (the conceit that "There Is No Alternative" to neoliberal globalization) but about the whole globalist order, including Third Way TINA-lite: "In just a few short years, the prevailing atmosphere has shifted from

---

15 Elizabeth Becker, "Number of Hungry Rising, U.N. Says," *The New York Times* (December 8, 2004), http://www.nytimes.com/2004/12/08/international/08hunger.html.

16 Steve Early, "Democracy Matters," *Labor Forum: A Journal of Ideas, Analysis and Debate* (Spring 2004), http://qcpages.qu.edu/newlaborforum/html/131article4.html.

17 Pranab Bardhan, "Protesters Greet Yet Another WTO Meeting," *Yale Global* (September 8, 2003), http://yaleglobal.yale.edu/article.print?id=2390.

18 John Audley, "The Cancún circus: A worn-out act by rich nations," *The International Herald Tribune* (September 18, 2003), http://www.iht.com/cgi-bin/generic.cgi?template=arti cleprint.tmplh&ArticleId= 110274.

19 Kofi Annan quoted in Kevin Sullivan, "Annan Decries Trade Policies," *The Washington Post* (September 11, 2003), p. A15.

belief in the near inevitability of globalization to deep uncertainty about the very survival of our tenuous global order."[20]

The "globalization" that Annan denounced is the triumphal mode that held sway throughout the 1990s under the auspices of the so-called Washington Consensus. This ideology swore fealty to democracy, yet neutered democratic values by surrendering them to the dictates of the market. The flagship of this First Way restructuration was the US New Economy, which seemed all but invincible before the tech crash of 2000. Even China's stupendous rise seemed secondary by comparison, and its ideological implications were hardly considered. Globalists clung to the glib assumption that China, through the osmosis of trade relations, would be transformed into a docile American clone, as would Europe, India or any other player in the global system. It was all part of the neoliberal teleology that emerged as the globalist reversal of the Cold War domino theory.[21] Capitalism was on the offensive, and from now on would take its marching orders from Washington.

Despite mounting ethnic and nationalist strife in much of the world, and the cultural retrenchment of Islamism, neoliberal globalists saw no serious obstacles in their path until September 11, 2001. Only then did they realize that the world was not going to surrender to them by dent of commerce alone. It would need a little help from the Pentagon. The shotgun marriage of neoliberalism and neoconservatism— or, more broadly, power economics and power politics—gave rise to the neoglobalist militancy that took America into Iraq and declared a borderless "war on terror" that was in fact an endless war on Islamism.[22] These actions have done much to unravel the putative victory of the First Way after the Cold War.

The chief beneficiary of 9/11 was definitely not Al Qaeda. Curious as it may seem, the real victor could well be the PRC. China's star is rising over the whole developing world and much of the developed world as well. With $1 trillion in foreign exchange reserves, Beijing is a power to be reckoned with both economically and geopolitically. In October 2003, when President Bush visited Australia, he was pilloried in the streets and even shouted down by Senators while addressing the parliament. Yet when China's President Hu Jintao visited a few days later, he got an unprecedented red carpet in both spheres. No doubt some of this contrast was Iraq-related, but that is just the tip of the globalist iceberg. Hu's visit not only laid the foundation for a free-trade deal, but signaled what the polls had already detected: China's former ill repute was fast shifting to America.[23]

---

20 Kofi Annan quoted in John G. Ruggie, "TINA and Global Responsibility," *The Globalist: For Global Citizens, by Global Citizens* (September 6, 2004), http://www.theglobalist.com/DBWeb/printStoryId.aspx? StoryId=4054.

21 William H. Thornton, *Fire on the Rim: The Cultural Dynamics of East/West Power Politics* (Lanham, MD: Rowman & Littlefield, 2002), p. 134.

22 William H. Thornton, *New World Empire: Civil Islam, Terrorism, and the Making of Neoglobalism* (Lanham, MD: Rowman & Littlefield, 2005), p. 48, and *passim*. By late 2006 even Tony Blair had tacitly admitted this error by dropping the term "war on terror" from all official communications.

23 Joshua Kurlantzick, "China's Charm Offensive," *Commentary* (October 2006), p. 35 (pp. 35–39).

This reversal is all the more astonishing in view of the Second Way development model that China epitomizes, marked as it is by a dearth of even marginal concern for democracy, human rights, or environmental sustainability. China's economic "miracle" is used to legitimize a degree of repression that neoliberal pundits could not have imagined in a country with double digit growth. While Hu's regime has cracked down on dissent more than at any time since Tiananmen, China has made trade relations with rogue states its comparative advantage. Under its "go global" policy, unconditional soft credit has been extended to disreputable governments all across Asia, Latin America, and especially Africa.

Often Beijing will take a net loss economically in order to win geopolitically. Chinese companies capitalize on government largesse and cheap labor (often including prison labor) in order to outbid foreign firms on construction projects. Forging regime alliances is frequently more important to China than making profits.[24] And this is a two-way street: African dictators who play along get China's diplomatic cover and copious military assistance.[25] China's every success amounts to a victory for the Second Way, and so far most of its ventures have been successful in terms of its zero-sum contest with Washington.

Into Africa: The Second Way Goes on Safari

Africa is no longer the sideshow that it was during the Cold War. It is now at the heart of a mounting trade war that pits a relatively reformed First Way against an utterly amoral Second Way. The key to China's prime mover status in African affairs is its perfect match with the authoritarian style of most African regimes. Consider the case of South Africa, reputedly the most liberal of African states. The bottom line is that South Africa is China's biggest trade partner in Africa,[26] and it also happens to hold the rotating presidency of the UN Security Council.

President Thabo Mbeki resists putting UN reform pressure on any regime, such as Burma's, that China wants left alone. This helps to explain Mbeki's support of President Robert Mugabe of Zimbabwe, a brutal dictator that only China could court at this point.[27] Beijing has not only shielded this despot from UN sanctions,[28] but

---

24 Louisa Lombard, "Africa's China Card," *Foreign Policy* (April 2006), http://www. foreignpolicy.com/story/cms.php?story_id=3419&print=1.

25 Craig Timberg, "In Africa, China Trade Brings Growth, Unease," *The Washington Post* (June 13, 2006), p. A14.

26 Tangpua Siamchinthang, "China's Influence on Myanmar: Casting the Shadow of Darkness, Not Peace," *Wordpress.org* (March 1, 2007), http://www.worldpress.org/print_article.cfm?article_id=2819&dont=yes.

27 See Joshua Kurlantzick, "How African Leaders Appease Robert Mugabe," *The New Republic Online* (March 21, 2007), http://www.tnr.com/doc.mhtml?i=w70319&s= kurlantzick032107. Only after Mugabe's ruthless crackdown of March 2007 drew intense international attention did Mbeki issue a very mild rebuke. See Michael Wines, "In Zimbabwe, Mugabe Critics Face Beatings," *The New York Times* (April 8, 2007), http://www.nytimes. com/2007/04/08/world/africa/08zimbabwe.html.

28 Joseph Khan, "China, Shy Giant, Shows Stings of Shedding its False Modesty," *The New York Times* (December 9, 2006), http://www.nytimes.com/2006/12/09/world/asia/09china.html.

has backed his sham reelection of 2005. Along with trucks of campaign T-shirts, technical assistance was provided for blocking opposition radio broadcasts and internet communications.[29] Furnishings for the presidential mansion were thrown in as a goodwill gesture. One can well understand why Mugabe would encourage a Chinese culture cult among his entourage.[30]

In the Sudan, likewise, China has used the leverage of a $2 billion oil deal to undermine international sanctions on behalf of Sudan's internal refugees. Human Rights Watch and other NGOs inform us that Chinese investment is financing Sudanese arms imports and exacerbating the genocidal crisis in Darfur.[31] When Washington imposed anti-terrorist sanctions against Sudan in 1997,[32] China seized the chance to replace departing Western oil companies with its own; and more recently it has impeded US and British efforts to impose UN sanctions. To avoid a Chinese veto, the Security Council had to choose between a much compromised proposal and no action whatsoever. A watered-down version was finally passed by a vote of 11 to 0, with China, Russia, Pakistan and Algeria abstaining.[33]

Surprisingly, some progress seemed to be taking place on the issue by April 2007, though not through ordinary governmental channels. Oddly, this reversal began with the indefatigable efforts of a literature professor named Eric Reeves, who single-handedly pressed NGOs and private citizens to join him in branding China's 2008 Olympics the "Genocide Games," on the model of Hitler's infamous Berlin games of 1936.[34] The torch then passed to the actress Mia Farrow and (however grudgingly) the director Steven Spielberg, who was an official artistic advisor for the upcoming Olympics. Farrow warned Spielberg that if he did not press China to stop obstructing action on Darfur he could "go down in history as the Leni Riefenstahl of the Beijing Games."[35]

A few days later Spielberg dispatched a letter to President Hu Jintao, and shortly afterward a senior Chinese official, Zhai Jun, was in route to Sudan to push the Sudanese government to accept a UN peacekeeping force to protect refugees and aid agencies that had been forced to withdraw.[36] Already as many as 450,000 people had died after a government backed militia, the Janjaweed, began their atrocities in 2003.[37] Millions more could perish if action is not taken soon. Moral persuasion

---

29 Kurlantzick, "China's Charm Offensive," *op. cit.*

30 Ben Schiller, "The China Model of Development," *Open Democracy* (December 20, 2005), http://www.openDemocracy.net.

31 Kurlantzick, "How African Leaders," *op. cit.*

32 See "Background Note: Sudan," *Bureau of African Affairs* (March 2007), http://www. state.gov/r/pa/ei/bgn/5424.htmlrelations.

33 Paul McLeary, "A Different Kind of Great Game," *Foreign Policy* (March 2007), http://www. foreignpolicy.com/story/cms.php?story_id=3744&print=1.

34 See Kevin Cullen, "Genocide Games," *Boston.com* (March 25, 2007), http://www. boston.com/news/globe/ideas/articles/2007/03/25/genocide_game?mode=PF.

35 Helene Cooper, "Darfur Collides with Olympics, and China Yields," *The New York Times* (April 13, 2007), http://www.nytimes.com/2007/04/13/washington/13diplo.html.

36 *Ibid.*

37 Edward Cody, "China Given Credit for Darfur Role," *The Washington Post* (January 13, 2007), p. A13.

could never work with the Chinese, but as Reeves and Farrow have proved, there are other ways to motivate a mercantile dragon.

Unfortunately such tactics can only work where an intense and sustained international spotlight is available, as in Darfur. That is not the case in Nigeria, where gross social injustice has generated a huge amount of anti-government resistance but little international attention. With almost no outside support, rebel fighters have shut down a fifth of the country's oil production. The US has reacted with characteristic ambivalence, first providing limited military assistance to the government, but then yielding to the decision of Congress to halt further aid due to the Nigerian military's record of corruption and human rights violations. It is well known that military personnel are themselves deeply involved in the selling of stolen oil. Again China is stepping in to fill the void. It will sell arms to any state, and especially to those with the right resources for export.[38] Already the PRC is a heavy supplier of Nigerian arms and military equipment, including dozens of fast boats for fighting insurgents in the Niger Delta. Meanwhile China is investing $2.3 billion in a local oil firm owned by a former Nigerian defense minister.[39]

There can be no doubt that this Sino-globalist option is a strong factor in President Olusegun Obasanjo's willingness to jeopardize close relations with the United States and the European Union by subverting free elections and democratic processes in general. Granted, Nigeria's peacekeeping assistance in Somalia and Darfur (not to mention Nigerian oil) has made Washington and London reluctant to take a firm stand on Obasanjo's dictatorial turn.[40] Without his China card, however, he could not afford to slam the door so tightly on democratic reform.

All this belies Beijing's highly advertised principle of noninterference in other nations' domestic affairs. Second Way globalization is still in its infancy, but is already making it difficult for the IMF and the World Bank (however belatedly) to attach "good governance" conditions to their loans. In March 2002 the IMF issued a report slamming the Angolan government for its almost perfect record of unaccountability and corruption. The United States and Britain then withdrew from an upcoming donors' conference, leaving the Angolans to stew over their limited options.[41] They had little choice but to capitulate, such that in 2004 they were close to sealing a conditional loan with the IMF.

Suddenly, however, they dropped this negotiation in favor of an unconditional loan from China's Exim Bank.[42] With an annual oil revenue of $10.6 billion in 2005, double that of 2004, Angola's corporate class has every reason to adore the People's Republic, but this can hardly be said of ordinary Angolans. In a country that ranks 160 out of

---

38 Esther Pan, "China, Africa, and Oil," *Council on Foreign Relations* (January 26, 2007), http://www.cfr.org/publications/9557/#4.

39 Dino Mahtani, "Nigeria Turns to China for Defense Aid," *Financial Times* (February 27, 2006), http://www.ft.com/cms/s/ef8dbc30-a7c6-11da-85bc-0000779e2340,dwp_uuid= 9c33700c-4...

40 "Nigeria's Imperiled Elections," *The New York Times* (April 11, 2007), http://www.nytimes.com/2007/04/11/opinion/11wed3.html.

41 James Traub," China's African Adventure," *The New York Times* (November 19, 2006), http://www.nytimes.com/2006/11/19/magazine/19china.html.

42 Schiller, *op. cit.*

177 on the UN's Human Development Index, and rests content with an average life expectancy of 38,[43] unconditional loans serve only to freeze the status quo.

The same reactionary turn was seen recently in the Central African Republic (CAR) after François Bozizé seized power in a violent coup. To its credit, the African Union dropped CAR from its membership list, signaling to the developed world that this rogue government should not be assisted in any way. Within a few weeks Beijing extended CAR a $2.5 million interest-free loan and invited Bozizé for an official visit. Soon new buildings were springing up, telecommunications equipment was arriving, and more millions in interest-free loans and grants were pouring in to solidify Bozizé's presidency.[44]

These cases are windows on a fast emerging global pattern. Wherever there is a conflict between profit and principle, China is likely to appear, intervening aggressively in the name of "noninterference." Having grown 700 percent in the 1990s,[45] China's Africa trade has since quadrupled, rocketing from $10.6 billion in 2000 to $40 billion in 2006.[46] But more is involved here than fast bucks, and the neocolonial onus cannot be pinned on China alone. Both the IMF and the PRC have geopolitical closet agendas, the one First Way and the other Second. The problem is that antiglobalists have been so focused on combating the inroads of First Way globalization that they have given a virtual free pass to the Second Way. Only now is China's foreign policy, which in many ways is the mirror image of its domestic repression,[47] getting its due from progressive circles. Human rights groups are finally starting to spotlight Beijing's role in sustaining tyranny and genocide.

So far, however, these efforts are trumped by China's commercial clout. As part of its "year of Africa," Beijing sponsored 1700 delegates from 50 African nations at its November 2006 Africa summit. Pushing aside all non-economic development issues, President Hu announced his offer to double aid to the region and to extend $5 billion in unconditional loans and credits. Thus the Cold War struggle between First World capitalism and Second World communism has given way to a contest between rival capitalisms. Being far less burdened with moral baggage, China's state capitalism is winning the new "great game" in Africa.[48]

This is China's second full-scale excursion into African affairs. In the 1960s and 1970s it advanced a Cold War agenda that included construction projects all across the continent: roads, railways, hospitals, stadiums, etc. This public relations program atrophied in the 1980s as China concentrated on its domestic agenda of "socialism with Chinese characteristics."[49] But now, given its mounting economic

43 Traub, *op. cit.*

44 Louisa Lombard, *op. cit.*

45 Esther Pan, *op. cit.*

46 Craig Timberg, *op. cit.*

47 Jean-Jacques Mével, "Pékin, Capitale de l'Afrique Pour Trois Jours," *Le Figaro.fr* (November 3, 2006), http://www.lefigaro.fr/international/20061103.FIG000000148_pekin_capital_de_l_afrique_pour_trois_jours.htm.

48 Paul McLeary, "A Different Kind of Great Game," *Foreign Policy* (February 2007), http://www.foreignpolicy.com/story/cms.php?story_id=3744.

49 Paul Mooney, "China's African Safari," *Yale Global Online* (Janurary 3, 2005), http://yaleglobal.yale.edu/article.print?id=5106.

might, China's return to Africa is much more forceful than its original foray. The only political condition that China attaches to its trade is that Taiwan must be de-recognized. A measure of its success is the fact that only seven African nations—one fourth of the total—presently have formal relations with Taiwan.[50]

This honeymoon may not last long, however. Familiarity with China's ways and means is already breeding wariness and even contempt in some places. The corporate social responsibility that was forced on US firms in the 1970s and 1980s has become one of their best selling points. Proletarian issues like working conditions now redound to their favor, while Chinese trade patterns send an even more effective message to producers: the flood of Chinese textile imports into countries like South Africa and Nigeria is giving local entrepreneurs second thoughts about putting too many eggs in the Chinese basket.[51]

These misgivings went public during President Hu's Africa tour of early February 2007. Staged as a postscript to China's Africa Summit, the tour became bumpier the further south it went, and in Zambia Hu hit a brick wall of opposition. Michael Sata, the runner-up in the country's September 2006 presidential elections, had gained popularity among the urban poor with his pledge to kick the Chinese out and (as the coup de grâce) to recognize Taiwan.[52] In the last decade over 30,000 Chinese had poured into Zambia, where low pay and abysmal working conditions give Chinese-run operations the look of penal colonies. Chinese mining operations in Zambia and the Congo make heavy use of child labor, and often assign children the most dangerous jobs of all, such as hauling out ore and rock from small hand-dug shafts in hillsides. After rains these mini-tunnels are highly prone to collapse, claiming the lives of dozens of miners every month.[53] Chinese nationals were the target of riots that broke out in Lusaka in October 3, 2006,[54] and fears of renewed protests forced Hu to cancel his planned visit to Zambia's copper belt.

In Gabon, similarly, a Chinese energy company was forced to shut down due to its reckless environmental practices.[55] But so far such resistance is still the exception to China's more general red carpet reception. Anti-Chinese sentiments have had little or no impact on policy, for the simple reason that most African rulers share the slash-and-burn "development" mentality of their Chinese partners. First Way economism, moreover, is more than ready to join in the neocolonical party. A case in point is Rwanda, where the neoliberal exemplar Jeffrey Sachs has set up a "Millennium Village" as a laboratory for his anti-poverty theories. Once Russia was his laboratory, and it still is suffering the consequences. True to form, Sachs has little but praise for China's domestic growth model. He joins neoliberals like Bill Clinton and Bill Gates in lauding the GDPism of Rwanda's President Paul Kagame, whom

---

50 *Ibid.*

51 See Paul McLeary, *op. cit.*

52 Scott Baldauf, "Chinese Leader's almost Triumphal Trip to Africa," *The Christian Science Monitor* (February 9, 2007), http://www.csmonitor.com/2007/0209/p01s04-woaf.html.

53 "Zambia & Congo: China's African Takeover," aired on Britain's *Channel 4 News* on April 7, 2007, 7:35PM.

54 Siamchinthang, *op. cit.* ("China's Influence on Myanmar,")

55 McLeary, *op. cit.* ("A Different Kind of Great Game,")

Bush praises as a "man of action" who "gets things done."[56] Such action heroes were once called fascists, but now—so long as they bow to global capital—they get state visits. Bush has welcomed Kagame to the White House three times.[57]

NGOs such as Amnesty International and Freedom House confirm that Kagame does indeed get things done—things like murder and mounting repression. He has camouflaged all this, however, by adroitly playing his anti-genocide card. His cover story is that too much democracy would reignite genocide and upset the economic stability that foreign investors demand.[58] In this regard there is no ethical disparity between First and Second Way capitalists. Neither is averse to the authoritarian drift of organizations like the Southern African Development Community (SADC). Its shift from economic to military cooperation wears a rule-of-law veneer, but in places like Zimbabwe it stands ready to define democratic opposition as illegal insurrection.[59]

Democratic reform in Africa will have to issue from the kind of grassroots resistance that we see in the copper fields of Zambia, not from the top-down remedies that neoliberal cronies like Jeffrey Sachs concoct. Such "adopt a dictator" development schemes were used throughout the Cold War, and always with the same dismal results. It is time to face the fact that sustainable economic development requires concurrent economic and political development.

The SCO as Second World Prototype

Much as the United States has claimed semi-official hegemony over Latin America with its Monroe Doctrine, China has been laying de facto claim to a broad swath of underdeveloped Asia. This could be called hegemony-by-default, for the French and American defeats in Indochina left a "great-power" vacuum in the whole region. When the Chinese attempted to fill this void militarily in 1979—ostensibly in response to Vietnam's invasion of Cambodia, but in fact as a geopolitical probe—a newly unified Vietnam repelled them with surprising ease. In that very year, however, China began the economic transformation that would shift the entire Asian balance of power, especially in less developed areas such as the Mekong River Basin.

With biodiversity comparable to the Amazon's, the Mekong region is oddly ignored by the international community. Chinese engineers are hard at work erecting giant dams, blowing up rapids, and clearing irreplaceable forests. Other major players in this ecological and cultural apocalypse are the Asian Development Bank (ADB), the Mekong River Commission, and the region's own Second Way regimes: Laos, Cambodia, Vietnam and Burma, plus an increasingly authoritarian

---

56 Stephen Kinzer, "Big Gamble in Rwanda," *The New York Review of Books*, Vol. 54, No. 5 (March 29, 2007).

57 *Ibid.*

58 *Ibid.*

59 James Kirchick, "Would South Africa Send Troops to Help Mugabe?," *The New Republic Online* (April 10, 2007), http://www.tnr.com/doc.mhtml?i=070409+s=kirchick0 41007.

Thailand.[60] The impact all this will have on the 60 million inhabitants of the Basin can only be imagined. Their voices will not be heard, but amphetamine traffickers will be well served.

In the Middle East, also, China is challenging the First Way competition. It helps that Washington is closely identified with Israeli hard-liners while the PRC is on good terms with every country in the region. Nonetheless China would not risk confrontation with America in this oil zone without Russian backing.[61] These two contrarians have joined hands in resisting the imposition of strong UN sanctions to contain Iran's nuclear threat.[62] Their common cause, combined with Europe's general revulsion against America's Iraq war, marks the beginning of the end of US unipolarity.

It is in Eurasia, however, that the raw essence of Second Way globalization is on full display. As of 2005 it was still not clear which direction this region would tilt ideologically and geopolitically. Recent popular revolts in Ukraine and Georgia were reputed to have been heavily influenced by the West.[63] To counter this suspicion, Viktor Yushchenko, President of Ukraine, stresses that the nation's democracy and freedom movement is in fact a revival of its own democratic tradition, which reaches back to its first constitution of 1710. This would mean that his country's de facto "return to Europe" is in fact a return to itself.

In any case, the US push for NATO membership for both nations underscores the geopolitical issues at stake. The March 2005 Tulip Revolution suggested that Kyrgyzstan might also be leaning toward the West, but reforms stalled as the new president, Kurmanbek Bakiev, quickly pledged to continue former President Akayev's close relations with Beijing.[64] So too the December 2005 "re-election"

---

60 Denis D. Gray, "Asia's 'Last Frontier' Poised for Irrevocable Change," *New Frontiers*, Vol. 10, No. 3 (May/June 2004).

61 "A quintet, anyone?" *The Economist* (January 11, 2007), http://www.economist.com/world/asia/PrinterFriendly.cfm?story_id=8521894.

62 See Nazila Fathi and John O'Neil, "Ignoring Protests, Iran Resumes Nuclear Program," *The New York Times* (January 10, 2006), http://www.nytimes.com/2006/01/10/international/10cnd-iran.html. However, in December 2006 China joined other U.N. Security Council members in imposing moderate sanctions on Iran's trafficking of nuclear and missile-related materials. China recognizes that stability in the region is in its interest, and another mollifying factor is its close military trade relations with Israel. See "A quintet, anyone?," *op. cit.*; and in March 2007 Russia likewise called a halt to its nuclear fuel shipments to Iran, in accord with UN sanctions. Iran, however, claims that Moscow, far from acting on principle, is simply trying to bargain for a better fuel deal. See "Russia Moves Away from Iran and Cuts Nuclear Fuel Shipments," *Pravda* (March 13, 2007), http://english.pravda.ru/print/russia/politics/88251-russia_bushehr-0; and meanwhile China continues to supply Iran with conventional arms. See John Garver, "Close, But Not Too Close," *Asia Times* (April 16, 2007), http://www.atimes.com/atimes/printN.html.

63 See Viktor Yushchenko, "Ukraine has to be Realistic," *The Moscow Times* (March 16, 2007), p. 8.

64 Bagila Bukharbayeva, "Kyrgyzstan Faces Unrest 2 Years On," *The Moscow Times* (March 23, 2007), p. 4. Rule by Akayev's family was simply replaced with rule by Bakiev's. Street protests in November 2006 briefly led to a new constitution, clipping Bakiev's wings, but within a month he had managed to regain his lost powers. See "Wilting Tulips,"

of Nursultan Nazarbayev in Kazakhstan (he got 95 percent of the vote in what an OSCE report flagged as a rigged election)[65] gave China a new lease on its strategic relations in the region.[66]

The most crucial Second Way shift, however, came with the Andijan massacre of May 2005 in Uzbekistan. President Islam Karimov found himself branded by the West as the region's chief pariah. When the European Bank for Reconstruction and Development (EBRD) withdrew its support, Uzbek officials turned to Russia, signing a strategic partnership that boded well for Moscow's re-entry into Central Asia. Not to be outdone, the Chinese rushed to offer a similar agreement. By jointly declaring Andijan "an internal affair of Uzbekistan,"[67] the two Second way titans effectively turned back the geopolitical clock to the "domino" days before Mao split the Second World by breaking with the Soviets.

This newfound togetherness forms the axis of the Shanghai Cooperation Organization (SCO), which links Russia and China with like-minded authoritarians in Central Asia.[68] Initially promoted by Beijing as an "anti-terrorist" organization,[69] the SCO has expanded the definition of terrorism to include almost any de-stabilizing action, such as a peaceful pro-democracy march or the dissemination of information that could discomfit a dictatorial regime. Needless to say, this definition has long obtained in China itself, where independent religious organizations, or even exercise clubs like the Falun Gong, are considered subversive.

Apart from Tibetan Buddhists, the Muslim Uighurs of Xinjiang have been the main victims of China's war on religious affiliation. The government's "strike hard" policy has subjected Uighurs to secret trials and summary sentences for "separatism," with the death penalty often being imposed for simple religious expression.[70] This so closely parallels Karimov's anti-Islamism that the two regimes were almost sure

---

The Economist (April 12, 2007), http://www.economist.com/world/asia/PrinterFriendly. cfm?story_id=9013602.

65 "The Land that Time Forgot," *Sunday Herald* (Scotland, March 19, 2007), http://www. sundayherald. com/arts/display.var.1217740.0.the_land_that_time_forgot.php.

66 Zamir Chargynov, "Revolution, Repression and Re-election in 2005: China's Response to Political Developments in Central Asia," *China and Eurasia Forum Quarterly*, Vol. 4 No. 1 (2006), pp. 31–36.

67 Craig Murray, "Karimov Looks to China and Russia for Support" (May 28, 2005), http://www. craigmurray.co.uk/archives/2005/05/karimov_looks_t.html.

68 In addition to the SCO, Russia's Central Asian presence is also being felt in the Eurasian Economic Commonwealth (EEC) and the Collective Security Treaty Organization (CSTO). The latter, which is more security oriented, overlaps with the SCO in providing a counterbalance to NATO. The difference, however, is that Russia dominates the EEC and CSTO. See Sergei Blagov, "The Geopolitical Balance in Central Asia Tilts toward Russia," *Eurasianet* (June 7, 2005), http://www.eurasianet.org/departments/insight/articles/ eav070605a_pr.shtml.

69 René Wadlow, "The Shanghai Cooperation Organization: A Balance of Opportunity," *World Affairs*, Vol. 10, No. 2 (Summer 2006), p. 58 (pp. 56 59).

70 Human Rights Watch, "Overview: Human Rights Issues in China," *Human Rights Watch* (January 18, 2006), http://hrw.org/english/docs/2006/01/18/china12270_txt.htm.

to join hands at some point. And like Karimov, China has tried to dupe the West into believing its noxious measures are part of a seamless "war on terrorism."[71]

Russia joined the SCO as part of its "look East" policy. Like China it seeks in the SCO a firewall against American encroachment as well as Islamic jihad. The latter is kept front and center for public relations purposes, but clearly the organization's more important function is its budding role as a "NATO of the East." Being an emerging energy superpower, and the world's second biggest arms exporter, Russia is no diplomatic lightweight. But to tap this potential it has needed multilateral channels that the West refused to offer. Thus Russia turned East. All that is lacking for the return of geopolitical bipolarity is a firm strategic alliance between Russia and China.[72] If Iran, Pakistan, and Afghanistan can be brought in,[73] the groundwork will have been laid for a resurgent Second World.[74]

Granted, Russia's commitment to the SCO is tenuous. Russian officials have steadfastly opposed China's attempts to establish a military presence in Central Asia. They may even prefer American bases to Chinese ones.[75] Moscow is certainly aware that Beijing will be the prime beneficiary as the SCO matures, just as it will gain more than India in the emerging "Chindia" alliance. The union of these geopolitical atavisms in a possible "Ruchindia" will only heighten China's power. But Russia's weak domestic economy relative to China's will prevent it from challenging this arrangement any time soon. For now it will continue providing oil, gas, and other raw materials in exchange for Chinese manufactured goods. That is the assumption behind the much discussed "BRIC" thesis, set forth by financial pundits at Goldman Sachs. Presently the economies of Brazil, Russia, India and China (hence "BRIC") weigh in at about 15 percent of current G6 worth, but Goldman Sachs futurology puts them at 50 percent by 2025 and over 100 percent within four decades.[76]

---

71 "In the Name of Counter-Terrorism: Human Rights Abuses Worldwide," *Human Rights Watch Briefing Paper* (March 25, 2003), http://hrw.org/un/chr59/counter-terrorism-bck4.htm.

72 Paul Dibb, "The Bear is Back," *The American Interest Online*, Vol. 2, No. 2 (November/December 2006), http://www.the-american-interest.com/ai2/article.cfm?Id=187&MId=6.

73 See Qudssia Akhlaque, "Pakistan, Russia Agree to Expand Relations," *Dawn*, Shawwal 24, 1427 (November 17, 2006), http://www.dawn.com/2006/11/17/top10.htm.

74 Despite the intense international opprobrium leveled against Iran's nuclear buildup, it was invited to join India, Pakistan, and Mongolia as observers at the 5th SCO summit in 2006. This was hardly a surprise, as China has $100 billion in long-term oil and gas contracts with Iran, while Russia has contracts worth billions to build Iranian nuclear reactors. See John Chan, "Shanghai Summit: China and Russia Strengthen Bloc to Counter the US in Asia," *The World Socialist Web Site* (June 23, 2006), http://www.wsws.org/articles/jun2006/shan-j23_prn.shtml.

75 Stephen Blank, "China Joins the Great Central Asian Base Race," *Eurasianet.org* (November 16, 2005), http://www.eurasianet.org/departments/insight/articles/eav111605_pr.shtml.

76 Dominic Wilson and Roopa Purushothaman, "Brazil, Russia, India and China in 2050," *Private Sector Development (PSD) Blog—World Bank Group* (January 11, 2006), http://psdblog.worldbank.org/psdblog/2006/01/brazil_russia_i.html.

Obviously the "BRIC" formula locks Russia and Brazil into the permanent role of commodity vendors for their "Chindia" superiors. It is unlikely that Russia will accept that role for more than ten years or so.[77] Meanwhile, though, it has much to gain from the SCO compact. Gazprom, Russia's chief energy firm, is well along toward becoming the biggest oil and gas pump in the world, with the SCO serving as its body guard and veritable wholesale broker. A ten-year SCO alliance should be enough to dislodge the First World's grip on globalization.

This is happening faster than anyone could have expected. In the last four years oil prices have trebled, accelerating the shift from the global petro-dominance of the original "seven sisters" (compressed in the 1990s into four: ExxonMobil and Chevron on the American side and BP and Royal Dutch Shell on the European side) to seven new challengers: Saudi Arabia's Aramco, Russia's Gazprom, China's CNPC, Iran's NIOC, Venezuela's PDVSA, Brazil's Petrobras and Malaysia's Petronas. All of these are outside the OECD (Organization for Economic Co-operation and Development), and hence outside the flagging dominion of Washington-directed globalization.

These predominantly state-owned upstarts are already the rule makers of the energy world, dwarfing their Western rivals in oil and gas production as well as reserves. It is the greater breadth of the old firms, which also sell gasoline, diesel and petrochemicals, that keeps their revenues higher. The newcomers already have the upper hand in geoeconomic terms,[78] and are proving very adept at translating that advantage into geopolitical clout. The strategic stakes were underscored in 2005 with the first Russian and Chinese joint military exercises in forty years.[79] By then Russia was the world's major supplier of arms to the Third World, with contracts at around $7 billion.[80] Although it keeps its ethical image polished by not selling arms to any country under UN sanctions, its Security Council veto allows it to have the last word on where sanctions can be applied.

The stark fact is that neither the UN nor any other global institution is in a position to block the export of the Second Way. The New World Order that Fukuyama saw as the end and pinnacle of history is now just another historical artifact. The new Second Way gives the memory of post-Cold War triumphalism a darkly comic aspect, much as the phrase "war to end all wars" had become a bad joke by the 1940s. Historians will debate whether a better outcome was ever possible. The patent fact is that the new Second Way is here to stay, and will be harder to contain than the non-capitalist Second Way of years past.

Those on the Left who celebrate America's relative decline should take a closer look at what is replacing it. Instead of globalization under the management of a highly

---

77 Yevgeny Rendersky, "Intelligence Brief: Russia in the S.C.O.," *PINR* (November 3, 2005), http://www.pinr.com/report.php?ac=view_printable&report_id=391&language_id=1.

78 Carola Hoyos, "The New Seven Sisters: Oil and Gas Giants Dwarf Western Rivals," *Financial Times* (March 11, 2007), http://www.ft.com/cms/s/471ae1b8-d001-11db-94cb-000b53410621,dwp_uuid= 0bda728c-...

79 Marcel de Hass, "Russia-China Security Cooperation," *PINR* (November 27, 2006), http://www.pinr. com/report.php?ac=view_printable&report_id=588&language_id=1.

80 Richard Weitz, "Russian Arms Trade with Developing World Continues to Grow," *World Politics Watch* (November 30, 2006), http://worldpoliticswatch.com/article. aspx?id=376.

defective yet democratically reformable First Way, Second Way globalization is unabashedly authoritarian. Regimes that cannot rise to the challenge of fair elections or elemental human rights are now in possession of nuclear arsenals, and that is not to mention the weaponry at the disposal of non-governmental terrorists. Their power is multiplied by the fact that they are outside the "rational" domain of mutually assured destruction. Moreover, at a time when environmental degradation eclipses even the threat of war and global terrorism, the Second Way ignores ecological imperatives.

That is not, however, an argument for the unreformed First Way of the Clinton and Bush years. While promising higher living standards for all, First Way globalization gave us a planet of slums.[81] Poverty on such a scale redounds to anarchy. In the absence of any better solution to this global meltdown, the Second Way has the edge over the liberal competition, at least in the short run. It promises a government capable of keeping a lid on the social chaos that capitalism generates. Senian "development as freedom" will not work here, as it presupposes a level of social and moral capital that globalization fast erodes. The grim choice, it seems, is between sheer anarchy or Second Way development without freedom.

---

81 See Mike Davis, *Planet of Slums* (New York: Verso, 2006).

Conclusion

The Crisis of Asian Globalization:
Toward a Senism of the Left

The Re-Politicization of Development

One of the central pillars of Cold War international relations was the solicitude shown by the world's most "liberal" capitalism for the most illiberal capitalism of the time, that of the Asian tigers. There is no sufficient economic explanation for this American support system. Being primarily a product of power politics, it lasted so long as the Pacific Rim was needed as a vital geopolitical buffer. The Soviet fall cleared the way for full-thrust economic globalization on Washington's terms.

It was not immediately apparent how onerous those terms would be. At first, post-Cold War foreign investment and financial speculation stoked what looked like a new super-miracle on the Rim. Few took serious notice of how the lending binge of the mid-1990s recklessly expanded foreign debt relative to reserves. When the bubble finally broke in 1997, massive capital exodus sent the region into a ruinous plunge. The IMF took its time responding, and finally applied a "rescue" formula that quite predictably (after many hard lessons, such as the Mexican Tequila Crisis of 1994–95) turned the Asian Crash into the Asian Crisis, effectively converting a recession into a depression. To add insult to injury, the globalist fire sale that followed was broadly self-described as economic therapy rather than the socioeconomic pillage that it was.

This protracted Crisis put globalization on trial, but more specifically it put politics back into development discourse. Not since the glory days of Third Worldism had politics held the developmental spotlight.[1] The direction this restoration took owed much to Amartya Sen, who not only re-politicized development discourse, but did so from within the inner sanctum of the world system. Though Senism is not ordinarily associated with radical critique, its egalitarian focus is loaded with oppositional portent. It follows from Sen's axiom of "concurrence," as we term it,[2] that democratization is central at all stages of development. In his view the Asian Crisis confirmed the high cost of undemocratic governance. While Asian exceptionalists hold that liberal democracy is not needed on the Rim, and indeed would be a hindrance, Sen foregrounds the instrumental as well as intrinsic value of

---

1 Forrest D. Colburn, "Good-bye to the 'Third World,'"*Dissent* (Spring 2006), http://www.dissentmagazine .org/article/?article=446&print=1.

2 See Songok Han Thornton, "Postmaterial Development: The Search for a New Asian Model," *Development and Society*, Vol. 33, No. 1 (June 2004), p. 32 (pp. 25–38).

the freedom factor in all real development.[3] His outlook, moreover, is deeply rooted in Asian axiology. In lieu of the statist economism that monopolized the term "Asian values" during the "miracle" years, Sen proposes an "Eastern strategy" that draws on the deeper and more humane traditions of Asia.

From this vantage it is obvious that development reaches far beyond the GDPism that dominates the standard discourse of growth. What has passed for development in much of Asia is mere profit-taking, and when the social and ecological costs of that taking are weighed in the balance, the result is often a net loss. Sen's focus on human capabilities points toward more sustainable development, but also collides with current power structures in the East and West alike. In short, despite Sen's reluctance to face the fact, his work is inherently oppositional, especially on the Eastern side. His critique of Singaporean "Asian values" has been incisive, yet he stops short where neoliberalism is concerned. Thus his work has been far better at dealing critically with the "Asian miracle" than with the inroads of neoliberal globalization after the Asian Crash.

In fact, both "Asian values" and neoliberalism lost credibility in the post-miracle years. By the mid-1990s the specter of cultural anarchy haunted much of the developing world, with the conspicuous exception of the Rim. By eliminating that exception, the Crash and subsequent Crisis put the socioeconomic efficacy of the whole capitalist system on trial. Stricken countries reacted to the Crash according to their very different cultural and political contours. One thing they shared, however, was the undertow effect of Washington-directed globalization.

At this of all times their autonomous modes of development and social security were gutted. Structural adjustment conditions attached to international loans all but precluded Keynesian recovery procedures, while IMF and World Bank recovery schemes bailed out the financiers who had been most responsible for the Crash. The moral hazard this entailed was not the worst of it. These programs also constituted a bailout of pre-Crash power structures that had lost their economic foundations. In a complete inversion of reality, this reactionary "recovery" operation was hailed by neoliberal pundits, such as the swaggering globalist Thomas Friedman of the *New York Times*, as a factory for democratization.

Many believe the Asian "miracle," now fully globalized, is back on track, relegating the Asian Crisis to history. But for broad sectors of the working classes the social and cultural meltdown of the Crisis never ended. The elemental security that workers once knew is still melting away, though this hardly registers on the radar screen of our mainstream media. We are assured that the Rim has more than recovered from its little setback of 1997. Even where that is patently not the case—where, for example, thousands of children still dig in garbage pits for their daily bread—the problem is attributed to insufficient neoliberal restructuration. Stellar "reform" cases such as Korea and Thailand are contrasted with relative laggards such as Indonesia and the Philippines.

This dichotomy holds up only insofar as lower class privation in those flagship states has gone unreported. Even in Japan—long famous for its relative egalitarianism—the divisive impact of neoliberal restructuration is only now

---

3 Amartya Sen, *Development as Freedom* (New York: Alfred A. Knopf, 1999), p. 37.

becoming a hot political issue.[4] The norm throughout Asia, however, is an almost exclusive focus on the profits that are once more rolling in for those who really count in globalized economies. For them post-Crash Asia is better than ever, as the working classes have been put in line, and democracy put on ice.

As more and more Asian leaders join the transnational capitalist class (TCC), the typical Asian state is transformed into a globalist instrumentality.[5] Those citizens who do not enjoy TCC status, and have yet to reap any benefit from the "Asian miracle," are effectively rendered stateless. For these invisible people the pro forma voting rituals that pass for Asian democracy are almost meaningless. Senism attempts to rectify that, but very timidly. It is, we hold, a necessary but insufficient first step toward the repatriation of this "other Asia." Sen gives democracy some symbolic teeth, but no real fangs.

Crucially, however, he regards democracy as a prerequisite rather than consequence of development. This "concurrence model" integrates economic and political goals at all stages of development. That is a start, but there is still the danger that democratization could end up legitimizing the extant power elite. How can we be sure that the outcome will not be another case of democratic minimalism? Developmental "concurrence," we suggest, must be coupled with the kind of active resistance that Sen's own politics eschews. It is well to march to Sen's drummer, including his post-Western view of democratization, so long as we register the fact that he has paid scant attention to the TNCs that monopolize today's global economy.[6] Nor can we fail to note his neglect (until quite recently) of vital issues of environmental and cultural sustainability. In short, the Senian model is very much an unfinished product, and at some point must be liberated from Sen's own politics.

It is this more radical Senism that should be applied to the question of Asian maldevelopment. In many Rim countries a crossroads was reached with the capitalist "setback" of 1997. For all its social trauma, the Crash did have a silver lining: the enormous emancipatory potential of "unguided" political reformism. Globalization worked against that potential by seizing control of the post-Crash "reform" process. Equating development with pure economism, it snuffed out the grassroots democracy that the Crash had unleashed. The signature feature of globalist "reform" was what it did not include. While new deals were struck with domestic power elites, the broader issues of political development were jettisoned.

Globalization should be put on trial for two developmental crimes: first, for funding many of the region's most oppressive regimes during the miracle years, and second, for thwarting the democratic resistance that the Crash unleashed. Walden Bello was right to dub the Crash and its aftermath the "Stalingrad" of prevailing globalization. Never was there a greater need for an international community of conscience rather than capital. Sending in the IMF was like sending the fox to save the chickens.

---

4 "The Rising Sun Leaves Some Japanese in the Shade," *The Economist* (June 15, 2006), http://www. economist.com/world/asia/PrinterFriendly.cfm?story_id=7066297.

5 See Rémy Herrera, "The Neoliberal 'Rebirth' of Development Economics," *Monthly Review*, Vol. 58, No. 1 (May 2006), http://www.monthlyreview.org/0506herrera.htm.

6 *Ibid.*

The carpetbagger mentality that the IMF exhibited in that dark hour sent a strong cautionary message to Asians about Washington-directed globalization. The most vocal remonstrance came from Malaysia's Mahathir, who upbraided the IMF and financial speculators such as George Soros. At first Thailand was the model of globalist cooperation, but eventually it too recoiled from IMF dictates. Under Thaksin it pointedly paid back its rescue loans early, symbolically declaring its economic independence. The last Rim nation to pay off its emergency loans was Indonesia. By deciding to pay back its $7.8 billion outstanding debt four years before the 2010 due date, Jakarta will save $200 million in interest. But, like Thailand, its primary purpose is to free itself from Washington's neoliberal grip.[7]

This same geoeconomic rebound is a factor in the growing tendency to exclude Washington from regional meetings such as the East Asian Summit of December 2005 in Kuala Lumpur. One should not assume, however, that this blow to US hegemony signals a categorical retreat from globalization, for new modes of globalist maldevelopment are waiting in the wings. The Senian model is at best a weak player in this new Asian drama.

Korean Social Democratization: A Good Idea While it Lasted

Consider the case of South Korea, where all the ingredients for Senian success seemed to be in place by the early 1990s. This serves warning that democracy cannot rest content with material goals alone. To do so will over time (in this case a very short time) hollow democracy out to the point that even material growth is at risk from government corruption and unaccountability. What looms large here is the challenge of sustaining, not just launching, democratic development. For one brief moment Korea nearly met our "concurrence" criteria of economic and political simultaneity for sustainable development. What went wrong?

Long before the Crash, Korean development had slipped into a shallow consumerist ethos that tipped the balance of concurrence toward pure economism. The formal apparatus of democracy continued to function, but served mainly as a legitimating device for a new set of power elites. With the generals out of the Blue House, the competition now centered on the question of which civilians would take their place, and in whose interest.

In large part this was a question of funding, and after the Crash the major source of funds would be recovery loans from the IMF. Domestic corporatists were pleased to play along, not only because the IMF was bailing them out, but equally because it mandated anti-labor policies which they were delighted to implement. Now, as they blended into TCC ranks, Korean corporatists began a sweeping rollback of the gains that the working classes had made in the later "miracle" years. To call this a "full recovery" requires a social conscience somewhere between Hayek and Ayn Rand.

The impact of globalization on Korean democratization cannot be brought into focus until we get past two common misperceptions: 1) that the Korean democratic

---

7 "Indonesia IMF Payback is End of Key Chapter for Asia," *Turkish Daily News* (June 15, 2006), http://www.turkishdailynews.com/tr/article/php?enewsid=46222.

breakthrough of the late 1980s was the simple product of the economic "miracle," and 2) that the "miracle" itself was the product of a faithfully applied Japan model. Much as classic modernization theory applied a one-size-fits-all model of development to the Third World, the Pacific Rim possessed its own one-size model whereby NICs were expected to fly in line with the Japanese "lead goose." To casual observers it seemed that Korea, first among the geese, was doing exactly that. Nothing could be farther from the truth. At every stage Korea's capitalist development was conditioned by its unique political culture, including a strike-prone oppositionalism that could not be farther removed from the authoritarianism of Singapore-school "Asian values." This working class recalcitrance all but compelled the overt repression that distinguished Korea's Parkian development model from Japan's more subtle mechanisms of control.

So too, Korean democratization was marked by a grassroots dynamism that was nowhere to be seen in "miracle" era Japan. Sen's generic principle of democratic development neglects this sui generis factor, especially where political resistance is concerned. Although Sen is less prone than most European Third Wayers to reduce democracy to parliamentary terms, his approach still misses the subversive element that sparked Korea's democratic takeoff. That oppositionalism had survived years of real repression, only to wither away in the early 1990s as public interest shifted from street demonstrations to sports events and the latest bargains in department stores.

This apolitical turn set the stage for the more pronounced de-radicalization of a presumed "reform" administration after the Crash. The very word "reform" was restructured as the country surrendered to the strictures of IMFism. There were street protests, of course, but they had more of a pressure-release than a subversive quality. Their major effect was to divert public wrath from Korea's nascent TCC establishment to the foreign devil, the IMF, which was conveniently immune to democratic resistance. Not having to stand for elections, it did what it does best: measuring progress on the scale of profits over people.

Tellingly, the thrust of Kim Dae Jung's "reform" was toward even stronger ties between government and corporate enterprise.[8] Companies that had long dreamed of shedding the excess baggage of workers' employment entitlements would now get their wish, with full government approval, while their extravagant borrowing habits—with debt ratios often reaching 350 percent—were tacitly pardoned.[9] Fueled by corruption and cronyism, total external debt had mushroomed in the 1990s. But those same defects had prevailed throughout the "miracle" years when the Asian system was praised as the rising star of global capitalism. It was financial liberalization,

---

8 "Declaration of Present Situation in Korea," *Civil Society*, Vol., 35, No. 45 (October–December 2001), provided by CCEJ News (Citizen's Coalition for Economic Justice), http://www.domos.or.kr/eng/ngos. html.

9 See "WSSD [World Summit on Sustainable Development] Stand for the 'World Summit on $hameful Deals'?," *The Green Korea Report* (October 28, 2002), http://www.greenkorea.org/English/gkreport/gkreport11.htm.

rather, that precipitated the Korean Crash by reducing the relative power of the Blue House, the one brake that had always constrained Korean corporatism.[10]

Thus the social democratization that Korea initiated in the late 1980s was all but extinguished by the commercialism that followed. Corporations emerged as the real victors in Korea's "democratic" revolution. The Crash of 1997 simply entrenched this cultural transformation. Here there would be no flood of grassroots political reform, as in Indonesia and Thailand. Korea's political inertia of the late 1990s was closer to that of the Philippines, but for very different reasons.

Inertia as Usual: The Fall of Philippine People Power

Having barely participated in the "Asian miracle," the Philippines did not have so far to fall in 1997. Its before-and-after transformation was blunted, moreover, by the fact that it had "been there before." Full-thrust globalization had been a big factor in the restoration of "booty capitalism" in the post-Marcos years,[11] albeit with greater international access to the booty. Hence globalist "reform" had a decade-long head start here. Corazon Aquino's rising dependence on US-directed globalization, still in its late Cold War infancy, pushed her away from "people power" and into the waiting arms of old power structures.[12] This outraged the Left, making peace with the National Democratic Front (NDF) impossible.

The administration had little choice but to re-embrace the military, which did not hesitate to turn its newfound powers against human rights activists and NGOs as well as NDF insurgents.[13] Aquino was too busy trying to satisfy Washington's agenda for economic liberalization to give much thought to the promises she had made her supporters. The consternation many felt toward her US tilt gave nationalist elites a new base of mass support. Thus she found herself at the crossroads of nationalist versus internationalist interests. More successful Asian "miracle" economies could avoid this fateful choice until the Asian Crash forced it on them, but Aquino got to that juncture a decade before, and ended up a more obliging US puppet than Marcos ever was.

The combined force of populist and Old Guard nationalism brought promises of change in the 1992 elections. It was not long, however, before Fidel Ramos also forgot his campaign pledges and pushed for trade liberalization. The pattern established here, at a time when other Asian NICs were still resisting globalist restructuring

---

10 The Japanese system, by contrast, had depended upon the less statist mechanism of MITI to accomplish this function. See Chalmers Johnson, *MITI and the Japanese Miracle: The Growth of Industrial Policy, 1925–1975* (Stanford, CA: Stanford University Press, 1982) concerning MITI; and concerning the Korean Blue House see Gregory Henderson, *Korea: The Politics of the Vortex* (Cambridge, Massachusetts: Harvard University Press, 1968).

11 Alasdair Bowie and Danny Unger, *The Politics of Open Economies: Indonesia, Malaysia, the Philippines and Thailand* (Cambridge: Cambridge University Press, 1997), p. 100.

12 W. Scott Thompson, *The Philippines in Crisis: Development and Security in the Aquino Era, 1986–92* (New York: St. Martin's Press, 1992), pp. 52–3.

13 Gerald Clark, *The Politics of NGOs in South-East Asia: Participation and Protest in the Philippines* (London: Routledge, 1998), p. 82.

with all their economic might, would be replicated throughout the region after the Crash. No Asian NIC accepted neoliberal principles willingly. The Philippines took this turn earlier than its more affluent neighbors because it saw no way around it. The paradox is that its two-decade economic slump made it the lead goose in terms of globalization, which is to say neocolonization.

Taking this globalist "reform" path pushed the Philippine small-farm sector even deeper into recession or outright destitution. This laid the foundation for another generation of militant resistance. When the rural insurgency happened to be Muslim, it could easily be tagged terrorism, but its real source was still government corruption and ineptitude. The Crash did nothing to correct that. Having suffered far less capital exodus than the top Asian "tigers" would, the Philippine power structure was unfortunately not exploded by the Crash.

Neocolonial Indonesia

Indonesia would be more fortunate in that respect, but ingrained habits have proven much harder to remove than a dictator. As in Singapore, economic dynamism had long been used by Suharto's Golkar regime as its stamp of legitimacy. Nonetheless the country's reformist tradition was so deeply rooted that extreme measures were necessary to keep it in line. These bore testimony not to the Golkar Party's hegemonic strength, but to its weakness. Real hegemony, as Antonio Gramsci understood it, would not require such flagrant domination.

To attract foreign investment it was necessary for Jakarta to create the illusion of national stability, which required that repressive mechanisms be kept out of view. With the ghost of Marcos' ouster in the Philippines haunting all Rim regimes in the late 1980s and early 1990s, the image had to be projected that the government could offer investors a reasonable degree of systemic reliability. Marcos had gone too far in flaunting his cronyism and nepotism. Golkar cronyism was of course no secret, but Suharto employed a phalanx of Western-trained technocrats to paper over the arbitrary nature of his rule.

Unlike Thailand, where the problem was chronic indecision, Indonesia's power structure was strong on decisive action but weak on the predictability that investors demanded.[14] It was this chronic uncertainty that finally, a full decade after the fall of Marcos, convinced the international community that Suharto also must go. Since international support had sustained Suharto's New Order after its bloody rise to power, the removal of that exogenous crutch doomed the regime's inner circle, if not the Golkar Party as such. Not even the technocrats could save Suharto at that point.

Political reform would obviously have to issue from within Indonesia itself. Its major source was the country's unique tradition of civil Islam. Suharto had done everything within his power to repress Islamism (political Islam) or, failing that, to co-opt it. For decades reform energies had simmered within the Muslim community. The Crash of 1997 broke the hegemony that had locked those energies outside

---

14 Andrew MacIntyre, "Political Institutions and the Economic Crisis in Thailand and Indonesia," in T.J. Pemple (ed.), *The Politics of the Asian Financial Crisis* (Ithaca: Cornell University Press, 1999), p. 144 (pp. 143–62).

the political process. Here, far more than in Korea or the Philippines, the Crash constituted an unprecedented political opportunity.

US engagement could have brought these hopes to full fruition, but, as in the Philippines long before, neoliberal globalization threw its weight on the opposite side of the scales. This reactionary pressure was redoubled after 9/11, with the "war on terrorism" used as an excuse to restore military as well as economic assistance to the Jakarta regime. The most resistant anti-Jakarta zone, Aceh, held out until the tsunami of December 2004 took it out of action. After that the most active resistance has been from West Papua, where a virtual civil war continues. Unfortunately the natural resources of this area ensure that Washington and the international community will all the more side with Jakarta's militarists.

Nowhere is globalization more nakedly exposed as a neocolonial force. The recent death of the country's leading dissident writer, Pramoedya Ananta Toer, seems emblematic of the demise of the resistance he pushed for all his life, much of which was spent in the Indonesian equivalent of the Soviet Gulag. While academic "postmodernists" drone on about cultural difference, there is little interest shown in the actual fighting fronts of difference, such as Aceh and West Papua. This is especially the case after 9/11, when Islamist resistance can so easily be cast as terrorism. Under this guise the newly "reformed" Jakarta is emerging as an even more potent colonial force than the New Order was under Suharto.

Reactionary Globalization

Like Russia's Putin, Thailand's Thaksin contested one side of globalization: the inadequate spoils allocated to his domestic cronies. Under the flag of a new nationalism these domestic elites set a ghastly precedent for the whole developing world by turning the legitimating device of democracy against democratic freedom. The result, in Thaksin's case, was a virulent new strain of the East Asian security state. This was the antithesis of the hopes raised by post-Crash reformism, as capsulated in the new Thai constitution. The contest of two Asianisms, Sen's radical democratism and Thailand's corporate statism, harbingers the mounting global struggle between development with or without freedom. Sadly, the neoliberal politics of globalization favors the latter. This de-liberalization is carried out in the name of security imperatives, but the ones calling the shots are precisely those who stand to profit by greater insecurity, which inspires public surrender to authoritarianism.

Those who thought Thaksinocracy was history just because the tycoon himself was ousted, should have rememberd the reformist expectations that attended the exits of Marcos and Suharto. What distinguished Thaksin's political machine from theirs was his greater globalist connectivity. Contrary to neoliberal preachment, that is not a politically liberatory bond. Its true face was revealed years before in the globalist tilt that Aquino gave the Philippine model. And it is on even more graphic display in post-Tiananmen China, which Thaksin certainly took note of in constructing his model of de-liberalized globalism. Unbeknownst to most power brokers in Washington, these regional hybrids have already supplanted neoliberalism as the cutting edge of Asian power economics.

Thaksin and other post-Crash authoritarians are mindful of the fact that even the worst abuses of the Chinese Communist Party (CCP) have met no serious criticism from neoliberal quarters. Indeed, the arch-globalist Jeffrey Sachs now sings the praises of the unreformed Chinese system as a model for Third World development. Breaking with the democratic teleology that neoliberals have clung to since the late 1980s, Sachs joins Hu Jintao in spurning charity and human rights in favor of unqualified national and personal self-interest. Pollution, exploitation, and a complete dearth of democracy are accepted as price tags of progress: "It's ugly, but—in terms of incomes—it works," Sachs gushes.[15]

He especially recommends the China model for Latin America, which he takes as a foil for comparison with East Asian dynamism. The chasm between the two outcomes, he believes, is due to Asia's embrace of globalization.[16] In fact it has more to do with Asian statism, on the one hand, and the early surrender of most Latin nations to neoliberal restructuration, on the other. Ironically Sachs himself helped to frame the terms of that surrender, just as he is now framing the terms of an even more invasive and illiberal globalization. In his capacity as special advisor to the former UN Secretary General Kofi Annan he recommended Sino-globalism as the model for African development as well.[17]

The American public shows no more concern than Sachs does about the spreading influence of the China model. When it comes to a choice between human rights and "everyday low prices" at Wal-Mart, Hu Jintao knows how little he has to fear from ordinary Americans. The only question is whether the center will hold in China itself. Much depends on investor confidence. There may still be hope for a Chinese century *if* the CCP can weather its domestic storms. But that is a big "if." Overseas Chinese investors may feel enough affinity toward Mother China to cut it some slack, but Western investors will not. Just as China has been able to turn Western technology against the West, other developing regions will turn the Sino-globalist model against the PRC.

The good news for China's power elite is that the country's rural crisis, which has been the mainspring of its economic advantage, will be there for the foreseeable future to safeguard low wages and protect against capital flight. The bad news is that the basic elements of the Chinese development model are already taking flight. They are no more country-specific than Fordism was for Americans. The difference is that Fordism soon bonded with democratic politics to produce the New Deal and the liberal model of "free world" development, whereas Sino-globalism can only produce a socioeconomic race to the bottom. Wherever it reaches, the China model will spell the end of democratic development, streamlining capitalism by stripping it of its liberal baggage. Fukuyama's "end of history" thesis is thus turned on its head. Joshua Kurlantzick stresses how China's increasingly contentious foreign policy,

---

15 Jeffrey Sachs, interviewed by Jonathan Watts, "Be Here Now," *The Guardian* (August 26, 2006), http://education.guardian.co.uk/print/0,,329562288-108229,00.htm.

16 Jeffrey Sachs, "Lessons for Brazil from China's Success," transcript posted on November 5, 2003.

17 "UN Sees China as Model for African Development," *Forbes.com* (August 16, 2006), http://www.forbes.com/business/feeds/afx/2006/08/15/afx2952489.html.

combined with this seemingly unbeatable growth model, suggests to authoritarian regimes from Vietnam to Cuba that they have no reason to budge in the face of democratic reform pressure.[18]

The rise of China was not due to its own actions alone. Ironically, the China model could never have thrived without assistance from Washington on a scale reminiscent of the Marshall Plan. Much as capital once poured into the Philippines after Marcos ousted his political opponents and declared martial law in 1972, global capital found the "stability" of post-Tiananmen China irresistible. It is time for Americans to make up their minds as to what kind of China policy they want. The choice is not between containment or engagement, but rather what kind of engagement, corporate or democratic? The myth that these are one and the same has too long voided the Senian question. Facing that question would be a moral imperative even if it concerned only China, but now the entire global South confronts the Senian choice of development with or without democratic input. The TNC establishment would have us believe that the only choice is between stagnation and a corporate-dominated growth that ensures union-free factories and subsistence wages.

In fact, even in terms of economic efficiency, Sino-globalization would be a loser in any fair contest of development models. Its social and ecological unsustainability will finally catch up with it, and its ruthless tactics could also backfire politically. That is what happened when Mali's military dictator imitated Tiananmen, killing hundreds of protesters in March 1991. This copy-cat crime spawned one of Africa's most promising democratic transitions.[19] One reason there was no such political rebound in China after Tiananmen is that the Washington Consensus, cheered on by Henry Kissinger, came to the aid of the Beijing Consensus. This could be the greatest blunder of recent American foreign policy.

It is odd that Sen, in setting forth his dichotomy between development with or without freedom, neglects to mention that freedom has its worst enemy in the geocorporatism that propels Washington-based globalization and abets Sino-globalization. There is no place for substantive democracy where politics is scripted by either of these illiberal capitalisms. It is a question of which subsumes which. If the American public cannot get its democratic priorities straight, taking back the political sphere from Washington's K Street lobbyists, the China model will continue to enjoy the full faith and confidence of US power brokers.

That alone may not guarantee Beijing's global primacy, for there are too many developing countries waiting in line to turn the China model against China. Beijing knows it cannot put all its eggs in the economic basket. To fulfill its great power ambitions it must move quickly to translate its budding economic clout into military and geopolitical might. While most of its saber rattling has been directed at Taiwan, it has quietly expanded its sphere of power into the soft underbelly of Southeast Asia: Burma and the underdeveloped Mekong region. Western sanctions against Burma (Myanmar) have given China a virtual free pass as the Burmese junta's major

---

18 Joshua Kurlantzick, "The China Syndrome," *The American Prospect* (January 11, 2007), http: www. prospect.org/web/page.ww?section=root&name=ViewWebarticleId=12372.

19 Robert Pringle, "Miracle in Mali," *The Wilson Quarterly* (Spring 2006), http://www. wilsoncenter.org/index.cfm?fuseaction=wq.print&essay_id=178661&stoplayo...

protector and trading partner. This puppet state is now a staging ground for Sino-globalist expansion throughout the region.

The Senian Moment

Sino-globalization is simply the latest and most virulent strain of the prevailing Asian growth model. Sen's *Development as Freedom* (1999) is a frontal assault on the Singapore-school tenet that political repression is necessary for Asian economic growth.[20] The region's power elites have long dismissed liberal concerns such as human rights and environmental protection as luxuries to be deferred until *after* development reaches a point they deem adequate. That point is of course forever postponed. The 1997 Asian Crash put this delaying tactic under suspicion even among hard-line technocrats who felt no intrinsic affection for democracy. The long-term efficacy of authoritarianism could no longer be taken for granted.

This was the Senian moment, the start of a paradigm shift that sent Western capitalists rushing to construct a fire wall between their own ("liberal") and Eastern ("crony") capitalism. That orientalist gambit lost its fire power, however, in the wake of the Enron scandal and a multitude of similar revelations concerning *Western* cronyism.[21] This paved the way for a full antiglobalist critique, equally applicable to the East and West. Although Sen has denied his place in the pantheon of antiglobalism, he has contributed as much as anyone to the movement's intellectual foundations. His refusal to endorse this critical discourse marks the point where Senism takes leave of Sen's own politics.

The same "resistance to resistance" can be seen in Sen's long neglect of environmentalism.[22] There is a deep affinity between Senism and the eco-egalitarianism of Arundhati Roy, or even the more radical Vandana Shiva. Sen of all people should not have missed the complementarity of environmentalism and democratization, which African activists like Ken Saro-Wiwa and Wangari Maathai have dramatically demonstrated (the price, in Saro-Wiwa's case, was his Shell-condoned execution).[23] Only after Suharto's expulsion did ordinary Indonesians start to learn the details about the ecological pillage of the New Order. Clearly environmental consciousness requires democratic openness, and it is doubtful that democracy can be sustained in an ecological disaster zone.

While cracking the door for revisionist Asian values, the Crash also invited the revival of an earlier Asian modernism. It is often forgotten that the "Asian model"

---

20 Sen, *op. cit.*, p. 15.

21 See Seth Mydans, "In a Contest of Cultures, East Embraces West," *The New York Times* (March 12, 2003), http://www.nytimes.com/2003/03/12/international/asia/12LETRhtml?pagewanted=print& position...

22 See Akash Kapur, "A Third Way for the Third World," *The Atlantic Monthly* (December 1999), p. 284 (pp. 124–29), http://theatlantic.com/issues/99dec/9912kapur.htm.

23 "Ken Saro Wiwa and 8 Ogoni People Executed: Blood on Shell's Hands," *Greenpeace* (November 10, 1995), http://archive.greenpeace.org/comms/ken/murder.html.

of the 1960s and early 1970s found room for equity along with growth.[24] This accords with the thrust of the Economic and Social Council (ECOSOC) meeting of 1972, which endorsed balanced growth and the reduction of inequality as prime developmental concerns. That egalitarian factor would be aborted by Singapore-school Asianism and neoliberalism alike. No wonder the two got along so well for so long. For all its trauma, the Crash had the salutary effect of putting equality and other progressive concerns back on the developmental map.

Being universal in nature, these concerns run against the grain of Asian exceptionalism. We should bear in mind that before the Asian "miracle" many Latin American and African countries had been on an economic par with future Asian dragons. South Korea and Ghana, for example, had been at roughly the same level of development in the early 1960s.[25] The subsequent Asian "miracle," however, explained itself in sui generis terms that not only discredited "dependency" theory but camouflaged the enormous economic advantage that accrued from America's geopolitical commitment to the Pacific Rim.

Faith in global capitalism had eroded during the stagflated 1970s, and Latin America's "lost decade" of the 1980s dealt it another blow. With the whole world system on trial, the East Asian contrast was more than welcome in the West. So long as the Cold War lasted, Western capitalists were inclined to tolerate and even applaud "Asian values."[26] The official lesson in the Asian/Latin American contrast was that capitalism could fail only when infected by Left policies. Asian governments might radically depart from the precepts of liberal capitalism, but all was considered well on the Eastern front so long as the Asian tigers were solidly on the Right. Ironically their quasi-exceptional success story revived confidence in capitalism as the universal path to development.

Nonetheless there was a problem connecting the global to the local, as Eastern and Western capitalism were in many ways incommensurable. It was the task of Western-trained technocrats to close this gap. In Indonesia they worked closely with the Army to anchor Suharto's New Order and hence to repress democracy, though they called the process anti-communism.[27] Here and in most Rim NICs, Singapore's soft authoritarianism (which was only soft for those who submitted to its dictates)[28]

---

24 Jack Donnelly, "Repression and Development: the Political Contingency of Human Rights Trade-Offs," in David P. Forsythe (ed.), *Human Rights and Development* (London: Macmillan, 1989), p. 307 (pp. 305–28).

25 Samuel P. Huntington, "Foreword: Cultures Count," in Lawrence E. Harrison and Samuel P. Huntington (eds), *Culture Matters: How Values Shape Human Progress* (New York: Basic Books, 2000), p. xiii (pp. xiii–xvi).

26 William H. Thornton, *Fire on the Rim: The Cultural Dynamics of East/West Power Politics* (Lanham, MD: Rowman & Littlefield, 2002), p. 12.

27 Dewi Fortuna Anwar, *Indonesia in ASEAN: Foreign Policy and Regionalism* (New York and Singapore: St. Martin's Press and Institute of Southeast Asian Studies, 1994), p. 279.

28 Real resistance was never easy in Singapore. An old joke was that communists in Malaysia could hide in the jungle, but in Singapore they could only take cover in the Botanic Gardens. See Chia Thye Poh, "Singapore," in Chee Soon Juan (ed.), *To be Free* (Clayton, Australia: Monash Asia, 1998), p. 245 (pp. 241–86).

became the salient model of development. It is now largely forgotten that in the late 1950s and early 1960s Singapore had been remarkably open and democratic.[29] By smothering this tradition, Lee Kuan Yew's cohorts gave Singapore its image as a stable commercial hub,[30] the jewel in the crown of Asian globalization.

Current globalist theory, by contrast, has sidestepped democracy in favor of the "free market" as the alpha and omega of development.[31] The Crash brought Asia to a fateful crossroads between these two priorities—the market vs. democracy. Sen's development-as-freedom model is essentially a map of the road not taken. Once economism is accepted as the prime mover of all development, it is a short step to the acceptance of political repression as a price worth paying for economic progress. China's renewed hardline is the harbinger of a developmental paradigm shift whereby globalization has exactly the opposite effect of what Huntington and Fukuyama predicted in the late 1980s. Massive infusions of global capital are putting some of the worst regimes in Asia out of reach of domestic reform. Thus globalization turns out to be a rescue operation for endangered authoritarians. Deng Xiaoping's genius was to see that potential early enough to save the most dreadful and decrepit Asianism of them all: the Chinese Communist Party, to which he gave new life by way of capitalist resuscitation.

Two of the most central claims of neoliberal globalism are hereby exploded: the notion that globalization is fundamentally pro-democratic and anti-nationalistic. By no means is China the only locus of this dark truth. The "black-van" side of Japanese political culture has been the LDP's ever-present shadow, and most Asian governments have their equivalent of Yakuza (Japanese mafia) politics. Both major parties in Taiwan accuse each other of such ties, and both are telling the truth. If Senism is the sunny side of Asia's internal politics, this is its sinister side, and it hardly needs to be said which of the two is closer to the halls of power.

The brazen oppression of Asia's newly globalized regimes is startling even to seasoned realists. Neoglobalists such as Thaksin and Hu Jintao have not simply recycled the old Asian statism. Pre-Crash miracle-mania went far toward reducing development to economic growth, which in turn was used to justify political stagnation.[32] Yet through it all a rule-of-law veneer was usually applied, if only

---

29 Cho-Oon Khong, "Singapore: Political Legitimacy Through Managing Conformity," in Muthiah Alagappa (ed.), *Political Legitimacy in Southeast Asia: The Quest for Moral Authority* (Stanford: Stanford University Press, 1995), p. 109 (pp. 108–35).

30 Sometimes they went too far even for their own good. The result was such a dearth of interest in politics among Singaporean youth that it became hard to recruit fresh talent for the People's Action Party (PAP). Prime Minister Goh Chok Tong was forced to raise salaries to attract even marginally qualified government functionaries. See Trish Saywell, "Singapore: the Young and the Restless," *The Far Eastern Economic Review* (December 21, 2000), http://www.feer.com/_0012_21/p024region.html.

31 Jan Aart Scholte, "The Globalization of World Politics," in John Baylis and Steve Smith (eds), *The Globalization of World Politics: An Introduction to International Relations* (Oxford: Oxford University Press, second edition, 2001), p. 14 (pp. 13–32).

32 Surin Pitsuwan, "The Asian Crisis, Good Governance and the *Tsunami* of Globalization," in Charles Sampford, Suzanne Condlln, Margaret Palmer and Tom Round

to placate Western allies. Now, under the tutelage of Sino-globalization, nothing matters except the economic bottom line, which doubles as the official party line.

Conclusion: Toward a Senism of the Left

The Crash led many to demand more and better politics,[33] but no ASEAN country was willing to forfeit even a fraction of its GDP growth for non-material goals. If Rim governments could not deliver a full and speedy economic recovery, the public would soon give up on the democratic side of reform. The departures of Suharto and Mahathir left a regional leadership vacuum that any human rights or democratic activist would have to welcome. But a prolonged economic slump invited a reversion to old voting habits, or worse.

Washington had good reason for keeping its silence concerning the reactionary tilt of globalized regimes such as India's BJP and Thailand's TRT—now reborn as the PPP. Right populists, after all, were considered more pliable than Left ones. Thaksin became the archetype of "glocal" (global/local) authoritarianism. The paramount fact from Washington's perspective was that capitalism was safe on his watch. Propelled by a resurgent economy, in growth terms second only to China, Thailand's corporate poster boy was instantly recognized by global power brokers as a formidable agent of de-radicalization.

The White House took Thaksin and India's Vajpayee as members in good standing on the "us" side of Bush II's us/them global divide. Like Bush they voided the pluralist meaning of democracy while milking its populist appeal. Thai democracy was welcomed precisely because it was a sham. Real democracy was dangerously unpredictable. Over the last quarter century the bond between Thai politicians and criminal gangs had tightened, while vote-buying became so rampant that many voters saw it as a legal entitlement.[34] If this is the best that Asian democracy can offer, authoritarianism will win by default. At least it makes the trains run on time, and keeps the unions in line, or in China's case nonexistent.

The Crash, in sum, brought development theory to a stark crossroads: either democratization would have to be upgraded to a first priority issue, on a par with economic growth, or downgraded in the manner of Hindutva, Singaporean Asianism, Thaksinomics, or Sino-globalism. Thailand epitomized the "glocal" turning of the tide so far as reform is concerned. Thai "democracy" had long operated in a gray zone of decentralized patronage, whereby public office was a purchasable commodity and effective leadership was all but impossible. It turned out that most Thais did not

---

(eds), *Asia Pacific Governance: from Crisis to Reform* (Aldershot, UK: Ashgate, 2002), p. 26 (pp. 25–30).

33 See Allen Hicken, "The Politics of Economic Reform in Thailand: Crisis and Compromise," *William Davidson Institute Working Paper*, No. 638 from The William Davidson Institute (January 2004), p. 24 (pp. 1–30).

34 James Ockey, "The Rise of Local Power in Thailand: Provincial Crime, Elections and the Bureaucracy," in Ruth McVey (ed.), *Money and Power in Provincial Thailand* (Copenhagen, Denmark: NIAS Publishing, Nordic Institute of Asian Studies and Singapore: Institute of Southeast Asian Studies, 2000), pp. 85–86 (pp. 74–96).

much care, so long as the economy stayed on track; and it soon became apparent that Thaksinocracy epitomized a pan-Asian trend.

This second phase of post-Crash politics is comparable to Japan's "reverse course" of the late 1940s, which likewise had Washington's tacit blessing. Both paved the way for a rearguard acceptance of growth at all costs. The 2006 coup that ousted Thaksin had less to do with moral revulsion at his corruption than with the fact that he did not push the new Asian developmentalism far enough. Like an Asian Juan Perón, he diverted too much revenue to the purchase of rural and working class support. Urban entrepreneurs wanted a less compromised economism of the Right. The bland acceptance by ASEAN neighbors first of "democratic" Thaksinocracy and then of a patently anti-democratic post-Thaksinocracy says much about the drift of Asian globalization. This should hardly come as a surprise after ASEAN extended membership to the brutal Burmese junta in 1997.

Repression was systematized after General Than Shwe took command of the Burmese military government in 1992. Since 1996, when total war was declared on minorities such as the Karen and Shan, 2,700 villages have been destroyed and over a million people uprooted. The last hope for reconciliation died in 2004 with the arrest of the relative "reformist" prime minister Khin Nyunt.[35] In 2007 the world watched in horror as this same brutality was turned on Burma's most intrepid champions of democracy—its Buddhist monks. Protests that began that summer in reaction to huge price hikes for subsidized fuel morphed into a full-fledged democracy movement when thousands of monks joined the demonstrations. Troops accustomed to the slaughter of helpless minorities did not balk at shooting unarmed monks. Thousands were rounded up in late night raids on temples, despite the valiant effort of local citizens to protect them.

Even crusty ASEAN leaders were shaken by this display of Tiananmen-style repression. It was tacitly conceded that the ASEAN policy of unqualified engagement toward Burma—motivated in part by wariness toward China's increasing grip on the region—had been a dismal failure. They had little or no diplomatic leverage to show for their concessions to Than Shwe's regime in the face of Western censure and sanctions. This craven approach epitomizes the so-called "Asian values" mode of ASEAN policy.

In recent years, in subtle but deliberate contrast to China's utter amorality, ASEAN had been edging toward a policy more geared to democracy and human rights. The case of Burma would answer the question of whether ASEAN's new rhetoric had any teeth. Likewise, Japan's highly advertised promotion of an "arc of freedom and prosperity" would be put to the test here.[36] Burma was the point where authoritarian and democratic Asianisms collided categorically, and at the ASEAN Summit of November 2007 the Burmese junta went on trial. In short, the politics of "Asian values" went on trial with it, and in short order the definitive verdict came back: innocent of all charges. Until then the project of post-Crash reform had

---

35 Michael Green and Derek Mitchell, "Asia's Forgotten Crisis: A New Approach to Burma," *Foreign Affairs* (November/December 2007), http://www.foreignaffairs.org/20071110faessay86610/michael-green-derek-mitchell/asia-s-forgotten-crisis.html.

36 *Ibid.*

smoldered out of harm's way. Now, once and for all, it was smothered, so far as the region's actual governments were concerned. Constitutional reform-from-above was defunct. Any substantive change would have to issue from grassroots sources, and would have to be powered by more radical ends and means. Democracy was not going to unfold by itself.

Neither, however, could it unfold through political reform alone. The genius of Senism lies in its implicit thesis of political and economic concurrence. The Crash brought Senism out of its academic closet. It had become much harder for globalists to dodge the issue of political reform by way of a presumed democratic teleology. If the liberal democratic road to development was to be taken at all, it would have to be taken more assertively. More would be needed for political reform than the minimal device of elections and ballots. It is little wonder that Sen's "democracy as freedom" thesis earned him global credibility and a Nobel Prize at this time, for *pro forma* democracy had patently flunked the test in "miracle" era Asia. Even some classic modernists finally wavered in their belief that economic growth is the last word on development. It was time, they thought, to give substantive democracy a chance.

Senism was no longer a fringe model, but would it be anything more than a passing fad? To be sure, Sen's democratic axiom cuts both ways: if economic growth is not sustainable without political development, so too democratization is unsustainable without a solid and well distributed economic foundation. Sen may be at heart an egalitarian—as his praise of Kerala, India's most socialistic state, amply proves—but he is still a mainstream economist. If democracy is one engine of his development model, its twin engine is still economic growth. Having almost sputtered out in the post-Marcos Philippines, that second engine went entirely dead in Indonesia after the Crash, leading in both cases to a lack of Senian concurrence.

Likewise, Thailand's democratic reformism died of economic inertia, giving rise to Thaksinocracy. The irony is that the Crash at once activated and deactivated this political reformation. The economic downturn that spawned democracy could also kill it. Just as it had in postwar Japan, US foreign policy played the role of axman. America's distrust of grassroots democratization was never more fully exposed. What US-led globalization has fostered is the kind of procedural democracy that can be bought and sold, Thai-style. And since the highest "democratic" bidder is sure to be the most globally connected one, it is not hard to see how neocolonial globalism operates, turning the very word "reform" into a geocorporate wish list.

Clearly Sen has overrated the formal apparatus of democracy as a guarantor of real and sustainable development. Dictators have less to fear from universal suffrage than from the social and cultural resistance that globalization voids. This takes us into the thick of the new Asian drama, where incommensurable Asianisms are facing off in a climactic developmental value war. The Left-Senian model we adumbrate is fighting on two fronts: with neoliberal globalization on the one hand and Asian authoritarianism on the other, though often the two work in tandem.

Despite their profound contextual differences, Thai globalism and Sino-globalism are alike in their anti-Senism. Both are globalized nationalisms with an abiding commitment to development without Senian attributes. The question is how far the rest of Asia and the whole developing world will follow them. India may be the crucial "swing state," as C. Raja Mohan calls it,[37] but at present it is clearly swinging in China's direction. The difference between Indo- and Sino-globalism will blur over time unless India can reclaim the twin pillars of its distinctly Asian democracy: its Gandhian commitment to the underprivileged masses and its Nehruvian determination to preserve nonaligned independence.[38] Current globalization nullifies the former and seriously weakens the latter.

It hardly needs to be said which side of the Asian values debate gets the support of the World Bank, IMF and WTO. This conflict will be familiar to those who remember the political schism within Western countries during and after the Great Depression, as depicted by Karl Polanyi in *The Great Transformation* (1944). Our sense of déjà vu is no accident, for the Asian Crisis—which in fact has never ended, but in many respects is expanding beyond the Rim to all of Asia—is the Asian equivalent of the Depression so far as the working classes are concerned. Once again the issue is more political than economic, for the real problem is not so much underdevelopment (where the solution could be economic growth alone) as politically guided maldevelopment (requiring social democratic rather than neoliberal restructuration).

For several decades "Asian values" have been defined by a power elite that would seem never to have heard of social or ecological accounting, much less accountability. If the "other Asia" that Senism addresses was never a prominent feature on the Cold War map, globalization is making it all the more obscure. What is needed is a new political cartography. Simply to have "democracy" or not is beside the point. It is easy to set up a pro forma "democracy" that keeps socially significant choices off the ballot.

The post-Senism we advance takes democracy to the antiglobalist barricades, which may be the only place where an effective "vote" can be cast. Under the throes of current globalization, democracy has two basic choices: to be oppositional or to be cosmetic. The latter serves the interests of present power structures, while the former moves Senism to the Left. It is unfortunate that today's Left so often sidelines democracy as a first priority issue. This allows the Right to seize the moral high ground of "freedom," which in its hands becomes a formula for economic serfdom. Having so egregiously ignored the democratic movements in Eastern Europe that precipitated the fall of the Soviet empire,[39] the Left now equally ignores the democratic and human rights imperative in China and much of Asia.

It is hoped that this study can encourage a fecund exchange between Senism and the Left, with the latter taking a Senian turn and the former a Left turn, even without Sen's approval. Let us close, though, on a point of total agreement with Sen: the recognition that simple economic growth is not development, and certainly it is not

---

37 C. Raja Mohan, "India and the Balance of Power," *Foreign Affairs*, Vol. 85, No. 4 (July/August 2006), pp. 24–25 (17–32).

38 See William H. Thornton and Songok Han Thornton, "The Price of Alignment: India in the New Asian Drama," *Journal of Developing Societies*, Vol. 22, No. 4 (December 2006), pp. 401–20.

39 See Andrei Codrescu, "Liberalism, not Interventionism, will Work in Iran," *The Villager*, Vol. 76, No. 32 (January 3–9, 2007), http://www.thevillager.com/villager_192/talkingpoint.html.

Asian development. To freeze development in this reactionary mode (which by the way was imported from the West) would spell the end of the democratic hopes that the Crash engendered. This would kill the nascent Asian Renaissance in every non-material sense, and finally in the material sense as well.

Perhaps the worst case scenario at this point is the possibility that Asians, for lack of an effective political map, will not even know they are approaching an epic developmental crossroads. They could pass right through it without realizing that once upon a time they had a choice. Senism holds up a warning sign that there is grave danger ahead, and in this respect Asian development is no exception. The whole global South is fast approaching this same crossroads of development with or without freedom. Rhetoric aside, the Washington Consensus leads us to the same illiberal destination that the Beijing Consensus does. What is needed, we argue, is a real Third Way, which is to say a Senism of the Left.

Index

For Product Safety Concerns and Information please contact our EU
representative GPSR@taylorandfrancis.com Taylor & Francis Verlag GmbH,
Kaufingerstraße 24, 80331 München, Germany

Batch number: 08153780

Printed by Printforce, the Netherlands